Reactive Programming with Kotlin

By Alex Sullivan

Reactive Programming with Kotlin

By Alex Sullivan

Copyright ©2020 Razeware LLC.

Notice of Rights

All rights reserved. No part of this book or corresponding materials (such as text, images, or source code) may be reproduced or distributed by any means without prior written permission of the copyright owner.

Notice of Liability

This book and all corresponding materials (such as source code) are provided on an "as is" basis, without warranty of any kind, express of implied, including but not limited to the warranties of merchantability, fitness for a particular purpose, and noninfringement. In no event shall the authors or copyright holders be liable for any claim, damages or other liability, whether in action of contract, tort or otherwise, arising from, out of or in connection with the software or the use of other dealing in the software.

Trademarks

All trademarks and registered trademarks appearing in this book are the property of their own respective owners.

ISBN: 978-1-950325-25-2

About the Author

Alex Sullivan is the author of this book. Alex is a freelance mobile architect in Boston, where he enjoys reactive programming, experimenting with different programming languages, and tinkering with fun approaches to building mobile applications. In his spare time, Alex enjoys traveling and relaxing with his partner, binging unhealthy amounts of Netflix and reading. Alex hopes to one day find a cat he's not allergic to and rant about bracket placement to him or her.

About the Editors

Victoria Gonda is a tech editor for this book. Victoria is a software developer with a passion for accessible and quality apps. When she's not traveling to speak at conferences, she works remotely from Chicago. Her interest in tech started while studying computer science and dance production in college. In her spare time, you can find Victoria relaxing with a book, her partner, and her pets. You can connect with her on Twitter at @TTGonda.

Alex Curran is a technical editor of this book. He is a mobile-focused Principle Engineer at a finance startup, with a keen interest in development best practices and encouraging collaboration between iOS, Android, and backend developers. In his spare time, he cooks, reads avidly, and makes natural soaps by hand. You can find him anywhere at @amlcurran.

Amanjeet Singh is a tech editor for this book. Amanjeet is an Android Engineer based out of India and an open source enthusiast. As a developer he always tries to build apps with optimized performance and good architectures which can be used on a large scale. In spare time, you can find Amanjeet traveling, eating and watching movies. You can find him on twitter at @droid_singh.

Dedications

"To my wonderful partner Pallavi, without whom I would have never been able to start this undertaking. Your support and encouragement mean the world to me."

— *Alex Sullivan*

Matei Suica is the final pass editor for this book. Matei is a software developer that dreams about changing the world with his work. From his small office in Romania, Matei is always trying to work on Apps that will help millions. When the laptop lid closes, he likes to read and go to the gym. You can find him on Twitter: @mateisuica

About the Artist

Vicki Wenderlich is the designer and artist of the cover of this book. She is Ray's wife and business partner. She is a digital artist who creates illustrations, game art and a lot of other art or design work for the tutorials and books on raywenderlich.com. When she's not making art, she loves hiking, a good glass of wine and attempting to create the perfect cheese plate.

Acknowledgments

We'd also like to thank the *RxSwift: Reactive Programming with Swift* authors, whose work served as the basis for parts of this book:

- **Scott Gardner** has been developing iOS apps since 2010, Swift since the day it was announced, and RxSwift since before version 1. He's authored several video courses, tutorials, and articles on iOS app development, presented at numerous conferences, meetups, and online events, and this is his second book. Say hello to Scott on Twitter at @scotteg.
- **Junior Bontognali** has been developing on iOS since the first iPhone and joined the RxSwift team in the early development stage. Based in Switzerland, when he's not eating cheese or chocolate, he's doing some cool stuff in the mobile space, without denying to work on other technologies. Other than that he organizes tech events, speaks and blogs. Say hello to Junior on Twitter at @bontoJR.
- **Florent Pillet** has been developing for mobile platforms since the last century and moved to iOS on day 1. He adopted reactive programming before Swift was announced and has been using RxSwift in production since 2015. A freelance developer, Florent also uses Rx on Android and likes working on tools for developers like the popular NSLogger when he's not contracting for clients worldwide. Say hello to Florent on Twitter at @fpillet.
- **Marin Todorov** is one of the founding members of the raywenderlich.com team and has worked on seven of the team's books. Besides crafting code, Marin also enjoys blogging, teaching, and speaking at conferences. He happily open-sources code. You can find out more about Marin at www.underplot.com.

Table of Contents

Book License 17
Before You Begin 19
What You Need 21
Book Source Code & Forums 23
About the Cover 25
Section I: Getting Started with RxJava 27
Chapter 1: Hello, RxJava! 29
Defining RxJava and RxKotlin 29
Introducing asynchronous programming 31
Learning the foundations of RxJava 39
App architecture 47
RxAndroid and RxBinding 48
Installing RxJava 49
Community 50
Key points 51
Where to go from here? 51
Chapter 2: Observables 53
Getting started 53
What is an observable? 54
Lifecycle of an observable 55
Creating observables 56
Subscribing to observables 58
Disposing and terminating 62
The create operator 64
Creating observable factories 67
Using other observable types 69

Challenges	72
Key points	73

Chapter 3: Subjects 75
Getting started	76
What are subjects?	77
Working with publish subjects	78
Working with behavior subjects	81
Working with replay subjects	84
Working with async subjects	87
Working with the RxRelay library	88
Challenge	90
Key points	92
Where to go from here?	92

Chapter 4: Observables & Subjects in Practice 93
Getting started	94
Using a BehaviorSubject in a ViewModel	95
Adding photos	96
Communicating with other views via subjects	101
Creating a custom observable	105
Review: Single, Maybe, Completable	107
Using Single in the app	110
Key points	113
Where to go from here?	113

Section II: Operators & Best Practices 115

Chapter 5: Filtering Operators 117
Getting started	117
Ignoring operators	117
Skipping operators	122
Taking operators	127
Distinct operators	130

  Challenge... 133
  Key points 135
  Where to go from here?...................................... 135
Chapter 6: Filtering Operators in Practice 137
  Improving the Combinestagram project 138
  Challenge... 150
  Key points 151
  Where to go from here?...................................... 151
Chapter 7: Transforming Operators....................... 153
  Getting started 153
  Transforming elements....................................... 154
  Transforming inner observables.............................. 156
  Observing events... 163
  Challenge... 167
  Key points 169
  Where to go from here?...................................... 169
Chapter 8: Transforming Operators in Practice............ 171
  Getting started with GitFeed................................ 172
  Fetching data from the web 173
  Transforming the response 175
  Processing the response 176
  Persisting objects to disk 178
  Adding a last-modified header 179
  Challenge... 184
  Key points 186
  Where to go from here?...................................... 187
Chapter 9: Combining Operators 189
  Getting started 189
  Prefixing and concatenating................................. 190
  Merging 195

    Combining elements 198
    Triggers 202
    Switches 206
    Combining elements within a sequence 207
    Challenge: The zip case 210
    Key points 211
    Where to go from here? 211

Chapter 10: Combining Operators in Practice 213
    Getting started 214
    Preparing the EONET API class 214
    Add events into the mix 217
    Combining events and categories 220
    Downloading in parallel 223
    Wiring up the days seek bar 229
    Challenge: Adding a progress bar 232
    Key points 233
    Where to go from here? 233

Chapter 11: Time-Based Operators 235
    Getting started 236
    Buffering operators 236
    Time-shifting operators 248
    Timer operators 251
    Challenge 255
    Key points 256

Section III: Intermediate RxJava 257

Chapter 12: Error Handling in Practice 259
    Getting started 259
    Managing errors 262
    Handling errors with catch 263
    Catching errors 266

Retrying on error	268
Errors as objects	274
Challenges	279
Key points	281
Where to go from here?	281

Chapter 13: Intro to Schedulers 283
What is a scheduler?	284
Setting up the project	285
Switching schedulers	287
Pitfalls	293
Best practices and built-in schedulers	297
Key points	301
Where to go from here?	302

Chapter 14: Flowables & Backpressure 303
Backpresssure	303
Buffering danger!	305
Natural backpressure	307
Introduction to Flowables	307
Backpressure strategies	309
Flowables, Observables, Processors and Subjects — Oh, My!	314
Key points	319
Where to go from here?	319

Chapter 15: Testing RxJava Code 321
Getting started	321
Introduction to TestObserver	324
Using a TestScheduler	326
Injecting schedulers	330
Using Trampoline schedulers	331
Using subjects with mocked data	332
Testing ColorViewModel	335

Key points 339
Where to go from here? 339

Chapter 16: Creating Custom Reactive Extensions 341
Getting started 341
Extending a framework class 343
Wiring the extension up 345
Wrapping the locations API 347
The lift and compose functions 353
Testing your custom reactive extension 356
Key points 358
Where to go from here? 359

Section IV: RxJava Community Cookbook 361

Chapter 17: RxBindings 363
Getting started 364
Extending ValueAnimator to be reactive 365
Using RxBindings with Android widgets 367
Dangerzone! 369
Working around the issue 370
Fetching colors from an API 375
Displaying an information dialog 377
Challenges 382
Key points 384
Where to go from here? 384

Chapter 18: Retrofit 385
Getting started 385
Recap of Retrofit 386
Including Rx adapters 388
Creating a JSON object 389
Updating the JSON 393
Retrieving JSON 398

Key points 402
  Where to go from here? 402

Chapter 19: RxPreferences 403
  Getting started 404
  Using SharedPreferences 406
  Listening for preference updates........................... 407
  Using RxPreferences 410
  Subscribing to preference changes........................ 411
  Dealing with old versions of RxJava....................... 413
  Saving custom objects... 414
  Key points 419
  Where to go from here? 420

Chapter 20: RxPermissions 421
  Getting started 422
  Requesting the location permission....................... 423
  Using RxPermissions 426
  Requesting another permission 428
  Reading from external storage 430
  Writing the weather to external storage 431
  Reacting to orientation changes 433
  Key points 436
  Where to go from here? 436

Section V: Putting It All Together 437

Chapter 21: RxJava & Jetpack.. 439
  Getting started 440
  RxJava and Room.. 442
  Reacting to database changes............................... 446
  Updating individual items 447
  Starting the app with cached data......................... 449
  Paging data in.. 450

Key points 457
　　　Where to go from here? 457
Chapter 22: Building a Complete RxJava App 459
　　　Introducing QuickTodo 459
　　　Architecting the application 460
　　　Task model 462
　　　Task data access object 463
　　　Task repository 465
　　　Replacing callbacks with observables 475
　　　Editing tasks 478
　　　Challenges 488
　　　Where to go from here? 490
Conclusion 491

Book License

By purchasing *Reactive Programming with Kotlin*, you have the following license:

- You are allowed to use and/or modify the source code in *Reactive Programming with Kotlin* in as many apps as you want, with no attribution required.

- You are allowed to use and/or modify all art, images and designs that are included in *Reactive Programming with Kotlin* in as many apps as you want, but must include this attribution line somewhere inside your app: "Artwork/images/designs: from *Reactive Programming with Kotlin*, available at www.raywenderlich.com".

- The source code included in *Reactive Programming with Kotlin* is for your personal use only. You are NOT allowed to distribute or sell the source code in *Reactive Programming with Kotlin* without prior authorization.

- This book is for your personal use only. You are NOT allowed to sell this book without prior authorization, or distribute it to friends, coworkers or students; they would need to purchase their own copies.

All materials provided with this book are provided on an "as is" basis, without warranty of any kind, express or implied, including but not limited to the warranties of merchantability, fitness for a particular purpose and noninfringement. In no event shall the authors or copyright holders be liable for any claim, damages or other liability, whether in an action or contract, tort or otherwise, arising from, out of or in connection with the software or the use or other dealings in the software.

All trademarks and registered trademarks appearing in this guide are the properties of their respective owners.

Before You Begin

This section tells you a few things you need to know before you get started, such as what you'll need for hardware and software, where to find the project files for this book, and more.

What You Need

To follow along with the tutorials in this book, you'll need the following:

- **A PC running Windows 10 or a recent Linux such as Ubuntu 20.04 LTS, or a Mac running the latest point release of macOS Catalina or later**: You'll need one of these to be able to install the latest versions of IntelliJ IDEA and Android Studio.

- **IntelliJ IDEA Community 2020.1 or later**: IntelliJ IDEA is the IDE upon which Android Studio is based, and it's used in the book to look at pure Kotlin projects that demonstrate techniques in RxJava. You can download the latest version of IntelliJ IDEA Community for free here: https://www.jetbrains.com/idea/

- **JDK 8 or later**: You'll need a Java Development Kit installed for use with IntelliJ IDEA projects (Android Studio will use its own version of the JDK). You can download the Oracle JDK from here: https://www.oracle.com/technetwork/java/javase/downloads/index.html

- **Android Studio 4.0 or later**: Android Studio is the main development tool for Android. You can download the latest version of Android Studio for free here: https://developer.android.com/studio

- **An intermediate level** knowledge of Kotlin and Android development. This book is about learning RxJava specifically; to understand the rest of the project code and how the accompanying demo projects work you will need at least an intermediate understanding of Kotlin and the Android SDK.

All the Android sample projects in this book will work just fine in an Android emulator bundled with Android Studio, or you can also use a physical Android device.

Book Source Code & Forums

Where to download the materials for this book

The materials for this book can be cloned or downloaded from the GitHub book materials repository:

- https://github.com/raywenderlich/rxa-materials/tree/editions/2.0

You can download the entire set of materials for the book from that page.

Forums

We've also set up an official forum for the book at https://forums.raywenderlich.com/t/about-the-reactive-programming-with-kotlin-category. This is a great place to ask questions about the book or to submit any errors you may find.

About the Cover

Reactive Programming with Kotlin

The common starling, pictured on the cover of this book, seems just that: common. It isn't particularly large — roughly only 8 inches long. It isn't particularly musical and is considered noisy in flocks and communal roosts. It's also not particularly beautiful, with dark glossy feathers and a subtle metallic sheen.

And, yet, this simple bird continues to hold our attention, even being referenced in literature as early as Shakespeare. Why?

First, it has a talent for mimicry and, like the reactive sensibilities explored in this book, is highly responsive to its environment. It has up to 20 distinct imitations of other birds, and it is even known to mimic ringing phones and car alarms.

And, most impressively, a flock of starlings in flight is a gorgeous display of reactivity in motion. You've probably seen it, yourself: thousands of birds creating fluid shapes — called murmurations — in the air, never pausing, each bird responding to the next.

While we can't know how these birds evolved to this level of cooperation and responsiveness, we hope to draw some inspiration from them in this book as we guide you through developing your own reactive programming.

You can learn more about these birds, here: https://en.wikipedia.org/wiki/Common_starling.

See them in flight, here: https://video.nationalgeographic.com/video/short-film-showcase/00000158-457d-d0be-a1dc-4f7f8e650000.

Section I: Getting Started with RxJava

In this part of the book, you're going to learn about the basics of RxJava. You are going to have a look at what kinds of asynchronous programming problems RxJava addresses, and what kind of solutions it offers.

Further, you will learn about the few basic classes that allow you to create and observe event sequences, which are the foundation of the Rx framework.

You are going to start slow by learning about the basics and a little bit of theory. Please don't skip these chapters! This will allow you to make good progress in the following sections when things get more complex.

Chapter 1: Hello, RxJava!

By Alex Sullivan & Marin Todorov

This book aims to introduce you, the reader, to the RxJava, RxKotlin and RxAndroid libraries and to writing reactive Android apps with Kotlin.

Defining RxJava and RxKotlin

You may be asking yourself "Wait, why am I reading about Rx**Java** when I'm using Kotlin to build Android apps?" Great question! RxJava has been around since 2013, well before developers began to accept Kotlin as a mainstream programming language, and is part of a long list of **Rx**-based libraries written for different platforms and systems. Since Kotlin has such excellent interoperability with Java, it wouldn't make sense to completely rewrite RxJava for Kotlin — you can just use the existing RxJava library instead!

However, just because RxJava doesn't need to be completely rewritten to work in Kotlin doesn't mean that it couldn't benefit from all of the great features in the Kotlin programming language.

That's where **RxKotlin** comes into play. **RxKotlin** is a library that expands RxJava by adding a ton of utilities and extension methods that make working with RxJava much more pleasant in Kotlin. That being said, since RxJava is a complete library on its own you absolutely do not need RxKotlin to use the RxJava library in a Kotlin-based Android app.

But what exactly *is* RxJava? Here's a good definition:

> **RxJava** *is a library for composing asynchronous and event-based code by using observable sequences and functional style operators, allowing for parameterized execution via schedulers.*

Sound complicated? Don't worry if it does. Writing reactive programs, understanding the many concepts behind them and navigating a lot of the relevant, commonly used lingo might be intimidating — especially if you try to take it all in at once, or when no one has introduced it to you in a structured way.

That's the goal of this book: to gradually introduce you to the various RxJava APIs and Rx concepts by explaining how to use each of the APIs, and then covering their practical usage in Android apps.

You'll start with the basic features of RxJava, and then gradually work through intermediate and advanced topics. Taking the time to exercise new concepts extensively as you progress will make it easier to master RxJava by the end of the book. Rx is too broad of a topic to cover completely in a single book; instead, we aim to give you a solid understanding of the library so that you can continue developing Rx skills on your own.

We still haven't quite established what RxJava *is* though, have we? Start with a simple, understandable definition and progress to a better, more expressive one as we waltz through the topic of reactive programming later in this chapter.

> **RxJava**, *in its essence, simplifies developing asynchronous programs by allowing your code to react to new data and process it in a sequential, isolated manner. In other words, RxJava lets you observe sequences of asynchronous events in an app and respond to each event accordingly. Examples are taps by a user on the screen and listening for the results of asynchronous network calls.*

As an Android app developer, this should be much more clear and tell you more about what RxJava is, compared to the first definition you read earlier in this chapter.

Even if you're still fuzzy on the details, it should be clear that RxJava helps you write asynchronous code. And you know that developing good, deterministic, asynchronous code is *hard*, so any help is quite welcome!

Introducing asynchronous programming

If you tried to explain asynchronous programming in a simple, down-to-earth language, you might come up with something along the lines of the following:

An Android app, at any moment, might be doing any of the following things and more:

- Reacting to button taps
- Animating a view across the screen
- Downloading a large photo from the internet
- Saving bits of data to disk
- Playing audio

All of these things seemingly happen at the same time. Whenever the keyboard animates out of the screen, the audio in your app doesn't pause until the animation has finished, right?

All the different bits of your program don't block each other's execution. Android offers you several different APIs that allow you to perform different pieces of work on different threads and perform them across the different cores of the device's CPU.

Writing code that truly runs in parallel, however, is rather complex, especially when different bits of code need to work with the same pieces of data. It's hard to determine which piece of code updates the data first or which code has read the latest value.

Using Android asynchronous APIs

Google has provided several different APIs that help you write asynchronous code. You've probably used a few of them before, and chances are they left you feeling a bit frustrated or maybe even *scared*.

You've probably used at least one of the following:

- **AsyncTask**: To do some work on the background and then update elements in your UI with the result of that background work. You have to make sure to properly handle canceling a running AsyncTask when your Activity or Fragment shuts down since you could otherwise get a NullPointerException when the AsyncTask tries to update UI elements that don't exist anymore.

- **IntentService**: To start a fire-and-forget background job using an Intent. You typically use an IntentService if you want to do some work that doesn't need to touch the UI at all — saving an object to a database, for example.

- **Thread**: To start background work in a purely Java way without interacting with any Android APIs. Threads come with the downside of being expensive and not bound to any sort of ThreadPool.

- **Future**: To clearly chain work which will complete at some undetermined point in the future. Futures are considerably clearer to use than AsyncTasks, but run into some of the same problems around null pointers when a Fragment or Activity has been destroyed.

The above isn't an exhaustive list — there's also Handler, JobScheduler, WorkManager, HandlerThread and **Kotlin coroutines**.

Comparing Coroutines and RxJava

Now that Kotlin coroutines have started to become popular in the Android development world, you may be asking yourself if it's still worthwhile to learn about RxJava.

Many comparisons have been made between using RxJava and using coroutines for Android development. Each review will give you a different answer about which tool you should use.

In reality, RxJava and coroutines work at different levels of abstractions. Coroutines offer a more lightweight approach to threading and allow you to write asynchronous code in a synchronous manner. Rx, on the other hand, is used primarily to create the event-driven architecture mentioned above, and to allow you to write reactive applications. So, while they both offer an answer for doing asynchronous work off the main thread, they're really different tools that are both useful depending on the context.

If you're simply looking for an easy way to replace `AsyncTask`, then coroutines may make more sense than pulling RxJava into your application. However, if you do want to move towards a reactive, event-driven architecture, then RxJava is your best bet!

Understanding asynchronous programming challenges

Since most of your typical classes would do something asynchronously, and all UI components are inherently asynchronous, it's impossible to make assumptions about what order the **entirety** of your app code will get executed.

After all, your app's code runs differently depending on various external factors, such as user input, network activity, or other OS events. Each time the user fires up your app, the code may run in a completely different order depending on those external factors. (Well, except for the case when you have an army of robots testing your app, then you can expect all events to happen with precise, kill-bot synchronization.)

We're definitely not saying that writing good asynchronous code is impossible. After all, there's a litany of tools — like the ones listed above — that Android developers have been using to write asynchronous apps since well before RxJava hit the scene.

The issue is that complex asynchronous code becomes very difficult to write in part because of the variety of APIs that you as an Android developer will end up using:

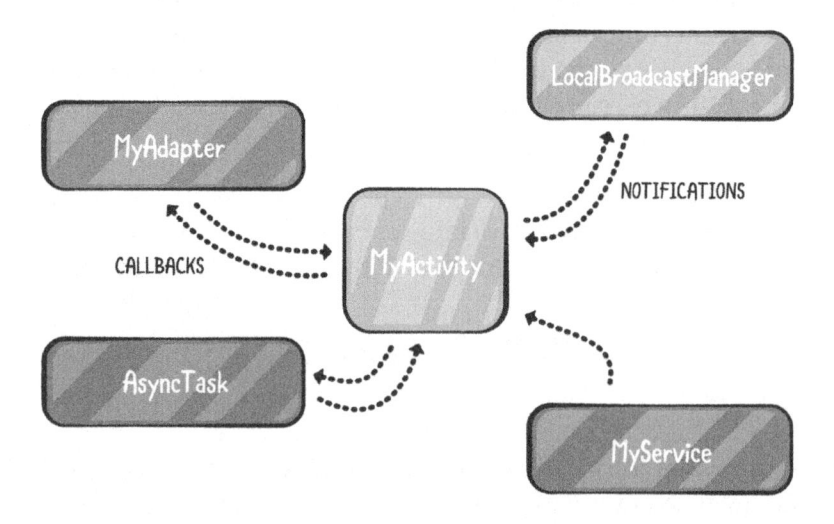

You may be using an `AsyncTask` to update your UI, an `IntentService` to save something to a database, a `WorkManager` task to sync your app to a server, and other various asynchronous APIs. Since there is no universal language across all the asynchronous APIs, reading and understanding the code, and reasoning about its execution, becomes difficult.

To wrap up this section and put the discussion into a bit more context, you'll compare two pieces of code: one synchronous and one asynchronous.

Synchronous code

Performing an operation for each element of a list is something you've done plenty of times. It's a very simple yet solid building block of app logic because it guarantees two things: It executes **synchronously**, and the collection is **immutable** from the outside world while you iterate over it.

Take a moment to think about what this implies. When you iterate over a collection, you don't need to check that all elements are still there, and you don't need to rewind back in case another thread inserts an element at the start of the collection. You assume you always iterate over the collection in *its entirety* at the beginning of the loop.

If you want to play a bit more with these aspects of the `for` loop, try this in an app or IntelliJ IDEA project:

```
var list = listOf(1, 2, 3)
for (number in list) {
  println(number)
  list = listOf(4, 5, 6)
}
print(list)
```

Is `list` mutable inside the `for` body? Does the collection that the loop iterates over ever change? What's the sequence of execution of all commands? Can you modify `number` if you need to? You may be surprised by what you see if you run this code:

```
1
2
3
[4, 5, 6]
```

Asynchronous code

Consider similar code, but assume each iteration happens as a reaction to a click on a button. As the user repeatedly clicks on the button, the app prints out the next element in a list:

```
var list = listOf(1, 2, 3)
var currentIndex = 0
button.setOnClickListener {
  println(list[currentIndex])

  if (currentIndex != list.lastIndex) {
    currentIndex++
  }
}
```

Think about this code in the same context as you did for the previous one. As the user clicks the button, will that print all of the list's elements? You really can't say. Another piece of asynchronous code might remove the last element, *before* it's been printed.

Or another piece of code might insert a new element at the start of the collection *after* you've moved on.

Also, you assume only that the click listener will ever change `currentIndex`, but another piece of code might modify `currentIndex` as well — perhaps some clever code you added at some point after crafting the above function.

You've likely realized that some of the core issues with writing asynchronous code are: a) the order in which pieces of work are performed and b) shared mutable data.

These are some of RxJava's strong suits!

Next, you need a good primer on the language that will help you start understanding how RxJava works, what problems it solves, and ultimately let you move past this gentle introduction and into writing your first Rx code in the next chapter.

Constructing an asynchronous programming glossary

Some of the language in RxJava is so tightly bound to asynchronous, reactive and/or functional programming that it will be easier if you first understand the following foundational terms.

In general, RxJava tries to address the following aspects of app development:

1. State, and specifically, shared mutable state

State is somewhat difficult to define. To understand state, consider the following practical example.

When you start your laptop it runs just fine, but after you use it for a few days or even weeks, it might start behaving weirdly or abruptly hang and refuse to speak to you. The hardware and software remains the same, but what's changed is the state. As soon as you restart, the same combination of hardware and software will work just fine once more.

The data in memory, the data stored on disk, all the artifacts of reacting to user input, all traces that remain after fetching data from cloud services — the sum of these and more is the state of your laptop.

Managing the state of your Android apps, especially when shared between multiple asynchronous components, is one of the issues you'll learn how to handle in this book.

2. Imperative programming

Imperative programming is a programming paradigm that uses statements to change the program's state. Much like you would use imperative language while playing with your dog — "Fetch! Lay down! Play dead!" — you use imperative code to tell the app exactly *when* and *how* to do things.

Imperative code is similar to the code that your computer understands. All the CPU does is follow lengthy sequences of simple instructions. The issue is that it gets challenging for humans to write imperative code for complex, asynchronous apps — especially when shared, mutable state is involved.

For example, take this code, found in onCreate() of an Android Activity:

```
override fun onCreate(savedInstanceState: Bundle?) {
  super.onCreate(savedInstanceState)

  setupUI()
  bindClickListeners()
  createAdapter()
  listenForChanges()
}
```

There's no telling what these methods do. Do they update properties of the Activity itself? More disturbingly, are they called in the right order? Maybe somebody inadvertently swapped the order of these method calls and committed the change to source control. Now the app might behave differently due to the swapped calls.

3. Side effects

Now that you know more about mutable state and imperative programming, you can pin down most issues with those two things to **side effects**.

Side effects are any change to the state outside of the current scope. For example, consider the piece of code in the example above. bindClickListeners() probably attaches some kind of event handlers to some widgets. This causes a side effect, as it changes the state of the view: the app behaves one way *before* executing bindClickListeners(), and differently *after* that.

Side effects are also defined at the level of individual functions in your code. If a function modifies any state other than the local variables defined inside the function, then the function has introduced a side effect.

Any time you modify data stored on disk or update the text of a TextView on screen, you cause side effects.

Side effects are not bad in themselves. After all, causing side effects is the ultimate goal of *any* program! You need to change the state of the world somehow after your program has finished executing.

Running for a while and doing nothing makes for a pretty useless app.

The issue with producing side effects is doing it in a controlled way. You need to be able to determine which pieces of code cause side effects, and which simply process and output data.

RxJava tries to address the issues (or problems) listed above by utilizing the remaining two concepts.

4. Declarative code

In imperative programming, you change state at will. An alternative style of programming to imperative is **functional programming**. In functional code, you don't cause any side effects.

Since we don't live in a perfect world, the balance lies somewhere in the middle of these two extremes. RxJava combines some of the best aspects of imperative code and functional code.

In addition to not causing side effects, functional code tends to be **declarative**. Code is declarative when it focuses on the *what* that you want to do, instead of the *how* that encompasses the imperative way of programming. Declarative code lets you define pieces of behavior, and RxJava will run these behaviors any time there's a relevant event and then provide the behaviors an immutable, isolated data input to work with.

By programming declaratively, you can work with asynchronous code, but make the same assumptions as in a simple `for` loop: that you're working with immutable data and you can execute code in a sequential, deterministic way.

5. Reactive systems

"Reactive systems" is a rather abstract term and covers web or mobile apps that exhibit most or all of the following qualities:

- **Responsive**: Always keep the UI up to date, representing the latest app state.
- **Resilient**: Each behavior is defined in isolation and provides for flexible error recovery.
- **Elastic**: The code handles varied workload, often implementing features such as lazy pull-driven data collections, event throttling, and resource sharing.
- **Message driven**: Components use message-based communication for improved reusability and isolation, decoupling the lifecycle and implementation of classes.

In short, reactive systems *react* to user and other events in a flexible and coherent fashion.

The terms and concepts defined above are just the start of your RxJava vocabulary. You'll see more terms as you progress through the book. Now that you have a start on understanding the problems RxJava helps solve and how it approaches these issues, it's time to talk about the building blocks of Rx and how they play together.

Learning the foundations of RxJava

Reactive programming isn't a new concept; it's been around for a fairly long time, but its core concepts have made a noticeable comeback over the last decade.

In that period, web applications have became more involved and are facing the issue of managing complex asynchronous UIs. On the server side, reactive systems (as described above) have become a necessity.

A team at Microsoft took on the challenge of solving the problems of asynchronous, scalable, real-time application development that we've discussed in this chapter. They worked on a library, independently from the core teams in the company, and sometime around 2009, offered a new client and server-side framework called Reactive Extensions for .NET (Rx).

It was an installable add-on for .NET 3.5 and later became a built-in core library in .NET 4.0. It's been an open-source component since 2012. Open sourcing the code permitted other languages and platforms to reimplement the same functionality, which turned Rx into a cross-platform standard.

Today you have RxJS, RxSwift, Rx.NET, RxScala, RxJava, and more. All these libraries strive to implement the same behavior and same expressive APIs. Ultimately, a developer creating an Android app with RxJava can freely discuss app logic with another programmer using RxJS on the web or RxSwift on iOS.

Like the original Rx, RxJava works with all the concepts you've covered so far: It tackles mutable state, it allows you to compose event sequences and improves on architectural concepts such as code isolation, reusability and decouplings.

Let's revisit that definition:

> **RxJava** *finds the sweet spot between traditionally imperative Java/Kotlin code and purist functional code. It allows you to react to events by using immutable code definitions to asynchronously process pieces of input in a deterministic, composable way.*

You can read more about the family of Rx implementations at http://reactivex.io. This is the central repository of documentation about Rx's operators and core classes. It's also probably the first place you'll notice the Rx logo, the electric eel:

> **Note**: I personally thought for some time that it was a piece of seaweed, but research shows that it is, in fact, an electric eel. (The Rx project used to be called Volta.)

In this book, you are going to cover both the cornerstone concepts of developing with RxJava as well as real-world examples of how to use them in your apps.

The three building blocks of Rx code are **observables**, **operators** and **schedulers**. The sections below cover each of these in detail.

Observables

The `Observable<T>` class provides the foundation of Rx code: the ability to asynchronously produce a sequence of events that can "carry" an immutable snapshot of data T. In the simplest words, it allows classes to subscribe for values emitted by another class over time.

The `Observable<T>` class allows one or more observers to react to any events in real time and update the app UI, or otherwise process and utilize new and incoming data.

The `ObservableSource<T>` interface (which the `Observable<T>` class implements) is extremely simple. An `Observable` can emit (and observers can receive) only three types of events:

- **A next event**: An event which "carries" the latest (or *next*) data value. This is the way observers "receive" values.

- **A complete event**: This event terminates the event sequence with success. It means the `Observable` completed its life-cycle successfully and won't emit any other events.

- **An error event**: The `Observable` terminates with an error and will not emit other events.

When talking about asynchronous events emitted over time, you can visualize an observable sequence of integers on a timeline, like so:

Observable<Int>

| 4 | 8 | 15 | 16 | 23 | 42 |
time 0:01   0:05   0:10   0:15   0:20   0:25

The blue boxes are the next events being emitted by the `Observable`. The vertical bar on the right represents the complete event. An error event would be represented by an x on the timeline.

This simple contract of three possible events an `Observable` can emit is anything and everything in Rx. Because it is so universal, you can use it to create even the most complex app logic.

Because the observable contract does not make any assumptions about the nature of the `Observable` or the `Observer`, using event sequences is the ultimate decoupling practice.

You don't ever need to use callbacks to allow your classes to talk to each other.

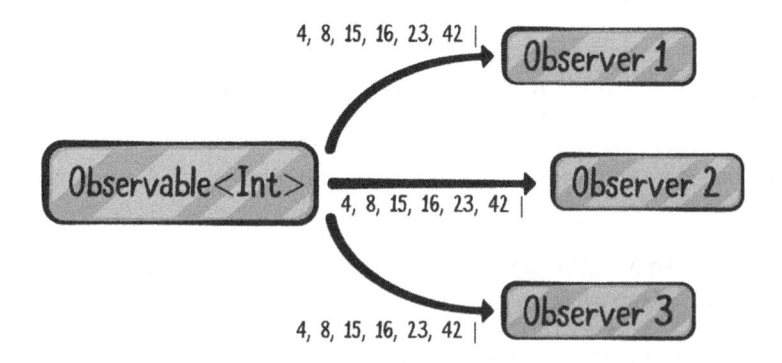

To get an idea about some real-life situations, you'll look at two different kinds of observable sequences: **finite** and **infinite**.

Finite observable sequences

Some observable sequences emit zero, one or more values, and, at a later point, either terminate successfully or terminate with an error.

In an Android app, consider code that downloads a file from the internet:

- First, you start the download and start observing for incoming data.

- Then you repeatedly receive chunks of data as parts of the file come in.

- In the event the network connection goes down, the download will stop and the connection will time-out with an error.

- Alternatively, if the code downloads all the file's data, it will complete with success.

This workflow accurately describes the lifecycle of a typical observable. Take a look at the related code below:

```
API.download(file = "http://www...")
  .subscribeBy(
    onNext = {
      // append data to a file
```

```
    },
    onComplete = {
        // use downloaded file
    },
    onError = {
        // display error to user
    }
)
```

`API.download()` returns an `Observable<String>` instance, which emits `String` values as chunks of data come over the network. Calling `subscribeBy` tells the observable that you'd like to subscribe for events that you're going to provide lambdas for.

You subscribe to `next` events by providing the `onNext` lambda. In the downloading example, you append the data to a temporary file stored on disk.

You subscribe to an `error` event by providing the `onError` lambda. In the lambda, you can display a `Throwable.message` in an alert box or do something else.

Finally, to handle a `complete` event, you provide the `onComplete` lambda, where you can do something like start a new Activity to display the downloaded file or anything else your app logic dictates.

Infinite observable sequences

Unlike file downloads or similar activities, which are supposed to terminate either naturally or forcefully, there are other sequences which are simply infinite. Often, UI events are such infinite observable sequences.

For example, consider the code you need to react to a `Switch` being toggled in your app:

- You add an `OnCheckedChangedListener` to the switch you want to listen to.

- You then need to provide a lambda callback to the `OnCheckedChangeListener`. It looks at the `isChecked` value and updates the app state accordingly.

This sequence of switch checked changes does not have a natural end. As long as there is a switch on the screen, there is a possible sequence of switch checked changes. Further, since the sequence is virtually infinite, you always have an initial value at the time you start observing it — namely, whether the switch is on or off.

Observable<Boolean>

It may happen that the user never toggles the switch, but that doesn't mean the sequence of events is terminated. It just means that there were no events emitted.

In RxJava, you could write code like this to react to the switch changing:

```
switch.checkedChanges()
  .subscribeBy(
    onNext = { isOn ->
      if (isOn) {
        // toggle a setting on
      } else {
        // toggle a setting off
      }
    }
  )
```

checkedChanges() is a soon-to-be-discovered extension method on CompoundButton that produces an Observable<Boolean>. (This is very easy to code yourself; you'll learn how in upcoming chapters).

You subscribe to the Observable returned from checkedChanges() and update the app settings according to the current state of the switch. Note that you skip the onError and onComplete parameters to subscribeBy, since these events will not be emitted from that observable — a switch is either on or it's not.

Operators

`ObservableSource<T>` and the implementation of the `Observable` class include plenty of methods that abstract discrete pieces of asynchronous work, which can be composed together to implement more complex logic.

Because they are highly decoupled and composable, these methods are most often referred to as **operators**. Since these operators mostly take in asynchronous input and only produce output without causing side effects, they can easily fit together, much like puzzle pieces, and work to build a bigger picture.

For example, take the mathematical expression (5 + 6) * 10 - 2.

In a clear, deterministic way, you can apply the operators *, ( ), + and – in their predefined order to the pieces of data that are their input, take their output and keep processing the expression until it's resolved.

In a somewhat similar manner, you can apply Rx operators to the pieces of input emitted by an `Observable` to deterministically process inputs and outputs until the expression has been resolved to a final value, which you can then use to cause side effects.

Here's the previous example about observing switch changes, adjusted to use some common Rx operators:

```
switch.checkedChanges()
    .filter { it == true }
    .map { "We've been toggled on!" }
    .subscribeBy(
      onNext = { message ->
        updateTextView(message)
      }
    )
```

Each time `checkedChanges()` produces either a `true` or `false` value, Rx will apply the `filter` and `map` operators to that emitted piece of data.

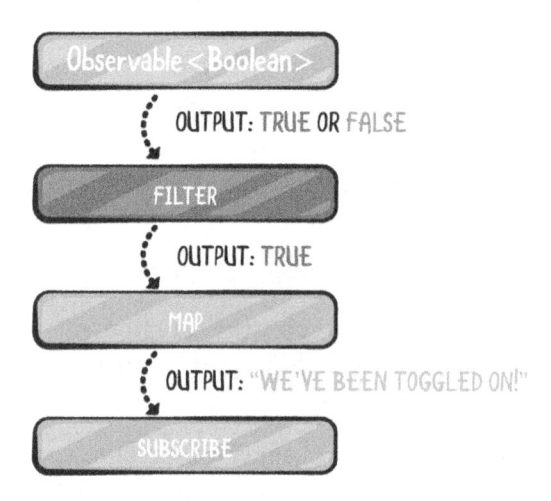

```
        Observable<Boolean>
                │
                OUTPUT: TRUE OR FALSE
                ▼
             FILTER
                │
                OUTPUT: TRUE
                ▼
              MAP
                │
                OUTPUT: "WE'VE BEEN TOGGLED ON!"
                ▼
           SUBSCRIBE
```

First, `filter` will only let through values that are `true`. If the switch has been toggled off the subscription code will not be executed because `filter` will restrict those values.

In case of `true` values, the `map` operator will take the `Boolean` type input and convert it to a `String` output — the text `"We've been toggled on!"`.

Finally, with `subscribeBy` you subscribe for the resulting `next` event, this time carrying a `String` value, and you call a method to update some text view with that text onscreen.

The operators are also highly **composable** — they always take in data as input and output their result, so you can easily chain them in many different ways, achieving much more than what a single operator can do on its own!

As you work through the book, you will learn about more complex operators that abstract even more-involved pieces of asynchronous work.

Schedulers

Schedulers are similar to the `ThreadPools` that you see in normal Java and Kotlin code. If you're not familiar with `ThreadPools`, you can think of them as a collection of `Threads` that are all joined together and available to use.

RxJava comes with a number of predefined schedulers, which cover 99% of use cases. Hopefully, this means you will never have to go about creating your own scheduler.

In fact, most of the examples in the first half of this book are quite simple and generally deal with observing data and updating the UI, so you won't look into schedulers at all until you've covered the basics.

That being said, schedulers are very powerful.

For example, you can specify that you'd like to observe for next events on the `IO` scheduler, which makes your Rx code run on a background thread pool — you may want to use this scheduler if you're downloading files from the network or saving something to a database.

`TrampolineScheduler` will run your code concurrently. The `ComputationScheduler` will allow you to schedule your subscriptions on a separate set of `Threads` that are reserved for heavy lifting computation tasks.

Thanks to RxJava, you can schedule the different pieces of work of the same subscription on different schedulers to achieve the best performance. Even if they sound very interesting and quite handy, don't bother too much with schedulers for now. You'll return to them later in the book.

App architecture

It's worth mentioning that RxJava doesn't alter your app's architecture in any way; it mostly deals with events, asynchronous data sequences and a universal communication contract.

You can create apps with Rx by implementing a normal Model-View-Controller (MVC) architecture. You can also choose to implement a Model-View-Presenter (MVP) architecture or Model-View-ViewModel (MVVM) if that's what you prefer.

In case you'd like to go that way, RxJava is also very useful for implementing your own unidirectional data-flow architecture.

It's important to note that you definitely do *not* have to start a project from scratch to make it a reactive app; you can iteratively refactor pieces of an exiting project or simply use RxJava when appending new features to your app.

The MVVM architecture was originally developed by Microsoft specifically for event-driven software created on platforms which offers data bindings. RxJava and MVVM definitely do play nicely together, and towards the end of this book you'll look into that pattern and how to implement it with RxJava.

The reason MVVM and RxJava go great together is that a ViewModel allows you to expose `Observable<T>` properties, which you can bind directly to UI widgets in your Activity, or translate them into `LiveData` objects from **Android Jetpack** and then subscribe to those instead. This makes binding model data to the UI very simple to represent, and to code. You'll see how to integrate the use of RxJava with `LiveData` later in the book.

RxAndroid and RxBinding

RxJava is the implementation of the common Rx API. Therefore, it doesn't know anything about any Android-specific classes.

There are two companion libraries that can be used to fill in a few of the gaps between Android and RxJava.

The first is a tiny library called **RxAndroid**. RxAndroid has one specific purpose: to provide a bridge between Android's `Looper` class and RxJava's schedulers. Chances are, you'll use this library simply to receive the results of an `Observable` on the UI thread so that you can update your views.

The second library is a broader library called **RxBinding**. RxBinding provides a large number of utility methods to turn callback-styled view listeners into observables. You actually already saw an example of this library being used, the `checkedChanges()` method used earlier on a `Switch`:

```
switch.checkedChanges()
  .subscribeBy(
    onNext = { boolean ->
      println("Switch is on: $boolean")
    }
  )
```

`checkedChanges()` is an extension method provided by the RxBinding library to turn a normal `CompoundButton` like `Switch` into a stream of on or off states.

RxBinding provides similar bindings for many of the Android view classes, such as listening for clicks on a `Button` and changes to the text in an `EditText`.

Installing RxJava

RxJava is available for free at https://github.com/ReactiveX/RxJava.

RxJava is distributed under the Apache-2.0 license, which, in short, allows you to include the library in free or commercial software, on an as-is basis. As with all other Apache-2.0 licensed software, the copyright notice should be included in all apps you distribute.

Including RxJava in a Gradle-based project, such as an Android app, takes two lines — add the following to the `dependencies` block in your module's `build.gradle` file:

```
implementation "io.reactivex.rxjava3:rxjava:3.0.2"
implementation "io.reactivex.rxjava3:rxkotlin:3.0.0"
```

The first `implementation` line is for RxJava. The second is for including the RxKotlin extensions. You can omit the RxJava import if you include RxKotlin, but since the RxKotlin library may not include the latest RxJava library, it's good practice to include both. You'll generally want to include the latest versions of both libraries.

> **Note**: You may have noticed that the dependency for RxJava actually says `rxjava3` in it. There's three major versions of RxJava: RxJava1, RxJava2, and RxJava3. RxJava2 added a lot of useful new tricks and types to the library, while RxJava3 added Java8 support. This book will be using RxJava3. You can find some of the differences between the versions in the **What's different in 2.0** article: https://github.com/ReactiveX/RxJava/wiki/What's-different-in-2.0, and the **What's different in 3.0** article: https://github.com/ReactiveX/RxJava/wiki/What's-different-in-3.0.

Community

The RxJava project is alive and buzzing with activity, not only because Rx is inspiring programmers to create cool software with it, but also due to the positive nature of the community that formed around this project.

The RxJava community is very friendly, open minded, and enthusiastic about discussing patterns, common techniques, or just helping each other.

You can find channels dedicated to talking about RxJava in both the Android United Slack and the official Kotlin Slack.

The first can be found, here: http://android-united.community/. If you request an invite, it should be approved quickly.

The official Kotlin Slack can be found here: https://kotlinlang.slack.com/.

Search for **rx** in both Slacks and you should find what you're looking for!

Both Slacks are friendly and inviting. The members are always available to troubleshoot some particularly tricky Rx code, or to discuss the latest and greatest in the world of RxJava and RxKotlin.

Key points

- **RxJava** is a library that provides an Rx framework for Java-based projects such as Android apps.
- RxJava can be used even when using the Kotlin language for app development.
- The **RxKotlin** library adds some Kotlin related utilities and extensions on top of RxJava.
- RxJava and all Rx frameworks provide for a way to program using **asynchronous**, **event-based** code.
- RxJava helps you build **reactive systems** in a **declarative** style.
- The main elements you'll use in RxJava are **observables**, **operators**, and **schedulers**.
- The **RxAndroid** and **RxBinding** libraries assist you in using RxJava on Android.

Where to go from here?

This chapter introduced you to many of the problems that RxJava addresses. You learned about the complexities of asynchronous programming, sharing mutable state, causing side effects and more.

You haven't written any RxJava yet, but you now understand why RxJava is a good idea and you're aware of the types of problems it solves. This should give you a good start as you work through the rest of the book.

And there is plenty to work through! You'll start by creating very simple observables and work your way up to complete real-world Android apps using the MVVM architecture.

Move right on to Chapter 2, "Observables"!

Chapter 2: Observables

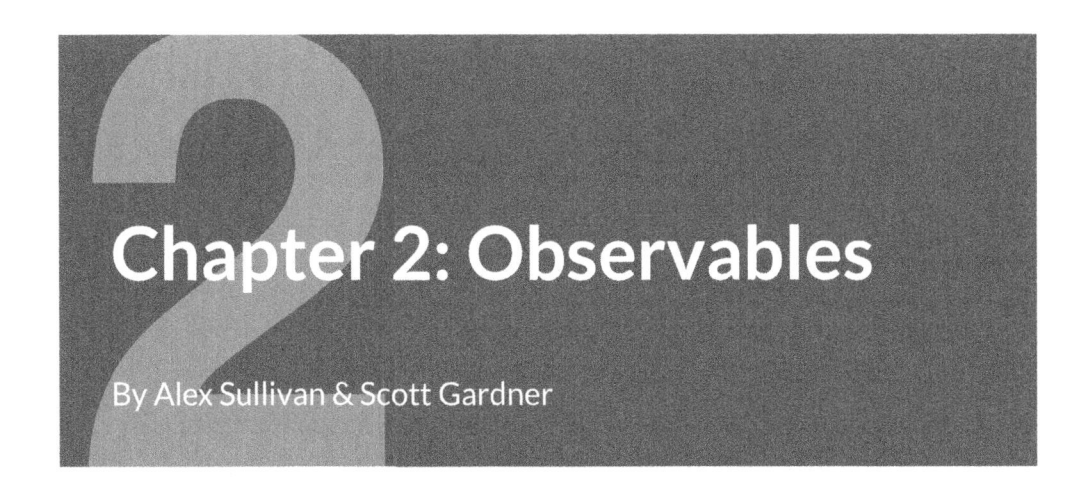

By Alex Sullivan & Scott Gardner

Now that you're all setup with RxJava, it's time to jump in and start building some observables!

In this chapter, you're going to go over a few different examples of creating and subscribing to observables. Things are going to be pretty theoretical for now, but rest assured that the skills you pick up in this chapter will come in very handy as you start working through real-world projects.

Getting started

You'll work through these theoretical examples of observables using a normal IntelliJ IDEA project. You'll move on to Android Studio projects once you switch to working on real-world Android applications.

Use the **File ▸ Open** command in IntelliJ IDEA to open the root folder of the starter project. Accept the defaults in any pop-ups that occur, and the project will then be opened. You'll primarily be working in the **main.kt** file in the **src/main/kotlin** folder of the project. For now, there's just an empty `main()` function. You'll fill it out as you progress through the chapter.

Before you start diving into some RxJava code, take a look at the **SupportCode.kt** file. It contains the following helper function `exampleOf(description: String, action: () -> Unit)`:

```
fun exampleOf(description: String, action: () -> Unit) {
  println("\n--- Example of: $description ---")
  action()
}
```

You'll use this function to encapsulate different examples as you work your way through this chapter. You'll see how to use this function shortly.

But, before you get too deep into that, now would probably be a good time to answer the question: What *is* an observable?

Observables are the heart of Rx. You're going to spend some time discussing what observables are, how to create them and how to use them.

What is an observable?

You'll see "observable," "observable sequence," and "stream" used interchangeably in Rx. And, really, they're all the same thing. In RxJava, everything is a sequence…

EVERYTHING IS A SEQUENCE

…or something that *works* with a sequence. And an `Observable` is just a sequence with special powers. One of them, in fact the most important one, is that it is *asynchronous*. Observables produce events, the process of which the library refers to as *emitting*, over a period of time. Events can contain values, such as numbers or instances of a custom type, or they can be recognized user gestures, such as taps.

One of the best ways to conceptualize this is by using marble diagrams, which are values plotted on a timeline.

The left-to-right arrow represents time, and the numbered circles represent elements of a sequence. The observable will emit element 1, some time will pass, and then it will emit 2 and 3. How much time, you ask? It could be at *any* point throughout the life of the observable — which brings you to the lifecycle of an observable.

Lifecycle of an observable

In the previous marble diagram, the observable emitted three elements. When an observable emits an element, it does so in what's known as a **next** event.

Here's another marble diagram, this time including a vertical bar that represents the end of the road for this observable:

This observable emits three tap events, and then it ends. This is called a **complete** event, as the sequence has now **terminated**. For example, perhaps the taps were on a view that had been dismissed. The important thing is that the observable has terminated, and it can no longer emit anything. This is normal termination.

However, sometimes things can go wrong:

An error has occurred in this marble diagram; it's represented by the red X. The observable emitted an **error** event containing the error. This is no different than when an observable terminates normally with a **complete** event. If an observable emits an **error** event, it is also terminated and can no longer emit anything else.

Here's a quick recap:

- An observable emits **next** events that contain elements. It can continue to do this until it either:
- ...emits a **complete** event, which terminates it.
- ...emits an **error** event, which terminates it.
- Once an observable is terminated, it can no longer emit events.

Now that you understand what an observable is and what it does, you'll create some observables to see them in action.

Creating observables

Switch back from the current file to **main.kt** and add the code below to the `main()` function. You'll also need to include the import `io.reactivex.rxjava3.core.Observable`:

```
exampleOf("just") {
   val observable: Observable<Int> = Observable.just(1)
}
```

In the code above, you used the `just` static method to create an observable with **just** one item: the *Integer* 1.

In Rx, methods that operate on observables are referred to as **operators** — so you just utilized the `just` operator.

`just` is aptly named, since all it does is create an observable sequence containing *just* the provided elements. `just` can take more than one item as well — try updating the previous line to take in a few more items:

```
val observable = Observable.just(1,2,3)
```

This time, you didn't explicitly specify the type. You *might* think that because you gave it several integers, the type is Observable<List<Int>>. However, if you hover over the `Observable.just(1,2,3)` expression and click **View ▸ Expression Type** you'll see that the type is actually Observable<Int>.

`just` has ten overloaded methods that take a variable number of arguments, each of which are eventually emitted by the observable. If you want to create an observable of type Observable<List<Int>>, then you can pass a List<Int> into the `just` operator. Replace the observable you previously defined with the following:

```
val observable = Observable.just(listOf(1))
```

Now, hover over the `Observable.just(listOf(1))` expression and click **View ▸ Expression Type** again. You'll see that the type is now Observable<List<Int>>. That means that this new observable will emit one item — and that single item will be a list of Int values. It can be a little tough to wrap your mind around an observable that emits lists, but with time it will become second nature.

Another operator you can use to create observables is `fromIterable`. Add this code to the bottom of the `main()` function:

```
exampleOf("fromIterable") {
  val observable: Observable<Int> =
    Observable.fromIterable(listOf(1, 2, 3))
}
```

The `fromIterable` operator creates an observable of individual objects from a regular list of elements. That is, it takes all of the items in the provided list and emits those elements as if you had instead written `Observable.just(1, 2, 3)`.

Hover over the `Observable.fromIterable(listOf(1, 2, 3))` expression and click **View ▸ Expression Type** again. You'll see that the type of this observable is Observable<Int> rather than Observable<List<Int>>.

`fromIterable` can be handy if you have a list of objects you want to convert into an observable sequence.

The IntelliJ IDEA console is probably looking pretty bare at the moment if you've run this code. That's because you haven't printed anything except the example header. Time to change that by **subscribing** to observables.

Subscribing to observables

As an Android developer, you may be familiar with `LocalBroadcastManager`; it broadcasts notifications to observers, which are different than RxJava `Observables`. Here's an example of of a broadcast receiver that listens for a `custom-event` Intent:

```
LocalBroadcastManager.getInstance(this)
    .registerReceiver(object : BroadcastReceiver() {
  override fun onReceive(context: Context?, intent: Intent?) {
    println("We got an intent!")
  }
}, IntentFilter("custom-event"))
```

Subscribing to an RxJava observable is similar; you call observing an observable **subscribing** to it. So instead of `registerReceiver()`, you use `subscribe()`. Unlike `LocalBroadcastManager`, where developers typically use only the `getInstance()` singleton instance, each observable in Rx is different.

More importantly, an observable won't send events until it has a subscriber. Remember that an observable is really a sequence definition; subscribing to an observable is more like calling `next()` on an `Iterator` in the Kotlin Standard Library:

```
val sequence = 0 until 3
val iterator = sequence.iterator()
while (iterator.hasNext()) {
  println(iterator.next())
}

/* Prints:
0
1
2
*/
```

Subscribing to observables is more streamlined than this, though. You can also add handlers for each event type an observable can emit. Recall that an observable emits `next`, `error`, and `complete` events. A `next` event passes the emitted element to the handler, and an `error` event contains a throwable instance.

To see this in action, add this new example to the IntelliJ project (insert the code somewhere *after* the closing curly bracket of the previous example):

```
exampleOf("subscribe") {
  val observable = Observable.just(1, 2, 3)
}
```

This is similar to the previous example, except, this time, you're simply using the `just` operator. Now add this code at the bottom of this example's lambda, to subscribe to the observable:

```
observable.subscribe { println(it) }
```

Cmd-click on the `subscribe` operator, and you'll see that it takes a `Consumer` of type `Int` as a parameter. `Consumer` is a simple interface that has one method, `accept()`, which takes a value and returns nothing. You'll also see that `subscribe` returns a `Disposable`. You'll cover disposables shortly.

Run your `main()` function. The result of this subscription is that each event emitted by the `observable` prints out:

```
--- Example of: subscribe ---
1
2
3
```

> **Note**: The console should automatically appear whenever you run the project, but you can manually show it by clicking the **Run** tab in the bottom left of the IntelliJ IDEA window after you run the `main()` function. You can also select **View ▸ Tool Windows ▸ Run**. This is where the `println` statements display their output.

You've seen how to create observables of one element and of many elements. But what about an observable of zero elements? The `empty` operator creates an empty observable sequence with zero elements; it will only emit a `complete` event.

Add this new example to the project:

```
exampleOf("empty") {
  val observable = Observable.empty<Unit>()
}
```

An observable must be defined as a specific type if it can't be inferred. So, since `empty` has nothing from which to infer the type, the type must be defined explicitly. In this case, `Unit` is as good as anything else. Add this code to the example to subscribe to it, importing `io.reactivex.rxjava3.kotlin.subscribeBy` to resolve the compile errors:

```
observable.subscribeBy(
  // 1
  onNext = { println(it) },
  // 2
  onComplete = { println("Completed") }
)
```

You're using a new `subscribeBy` method here instead of the `subscribe` method you used previously. `subscribeBy` is a handy extension method defined in the `RxKotlin` library, which we'll touch on later in the book. Unlike the `subscribe` method you used previously, `subscribeBy` lets you explicitly state what event you want to handle — `onNext`, `onComplete`, or `onError`. If you were to only supply the `onNext` field of `subscribeBy`, you'd be recreating the `subscribe` functionality you used above.

Taking each numbered comment in turn:

1. Explicitly handle the **next** event by printing the carried value, just like before.

2. A `complete` event doesn't carry any value, so just print "Completed" instead.

Run this new example. In the console, you'll see that `empty` only emits the `completed` event which makes the code print "Completed":

```
--- Example of: empty ---
Completed
```

But what use is an *empty* observable? Well, they're handy when you want to return an observable that immediately terminates or intentionally has zero values. As opposed to the `empty` operator, the `never` operator creates an observable that doesn't emit anything and *never* terminates. It can be used to represent an infinite duration. Add this example to the project:

```
exampleOf("never") {
  val observable = Observable.never<Any>()

  observable.subscribeBy(
      onNext = { println(it) },
      onComplete = { println("Completed") }
  )
}
```

Nothing is printed, except for the example header. Not even "Completed". How do you know if this is even working? Hang on to that inquisitive spirit until the **Challenges** section of this chapter.

So far, you've been working mostly with observables of explicit variables, but it's also possible to generate an observable from a range of values.

Add this example to the project:

```
exampleOf("range") {
  // 1
  val observable: Observable<Int> = Observable.range(1, 10)

  observable.subscribe {
    // 2
    val n = it.toDouble()
    val fibonacci = ((Math.pow(1.61803, n) -
            Math.pow(0.61803, n)) /2.23606).roundToInt()
    println(fibonacci)
  }
}
```

Taking it section by section:

1. Create an observable using the `range` operator, which takes a `start` integer value and a `count` of sequential integers to generate.

2. Calculate and print the *nth* Fibonacci number for each emitted element.

> **Note**: The *Fibonacci sequence* is generated by adding each of the previous two numbers in the sequence, starting with 0 and 1: 0, 1, 1, 2, 3, 5, 8, ...

There's actually a better place than in the `subscribe` method, to put code that transforms the emitted element. You'll learn about that in Chapter 7, "Transforming Operators."

Except for the `never()` example, up to this point, you've been working with observables that automatically emit a `completed` event and naturally terminate. This permitted you to focus on the mechanics of creating and subscribing to observables, but that swept an important aspect of subscribing to observables under the rug.

It's time to do some housekeeping and deal with that aspect before moving on.

Disposing and terminating

Remember that an observable doesn't do anything until it receives a subscription. It's the subscription that triggers an observable to begin emitting events, up until it emits an `error` or `completed` event and is terminated. You can manually cause an observable to terminate by canceling a subscription to it.

Add this new example to the project:

```
exampleOf("dispose") {
  // 1
  val mostPopular: Observable<String> =
          Observable.just("A", "B", "C")
  // 2
  val subscription = mostPopular.subscribe {
    // 3
    println(it)
  }
}
```

Quite simply:

1. Create an observable of strings.

2. Subscribe to the observable, this time saving the returned `Disposable` as a local constant called `subscription`.

3. Print each emitted `event` in the handler.

To explicitly cancel a subscription, call `dispose()` on it. After you cancel the subscription, or **dispose** of it, the observable in the current example will stop emitting events.

Add this code to the bottom of the example:

```
subscription.dispose()
```

Managing each subscription individually would be tedious, so RxJava includes a `CompositeDisposable` type. A `CompositeDisposable` holds disposables — typically added using the `add()` method — and will call `dispose()` on all of them when you call `dispose()` on the `CompositeDisposable` itself. Add this new example to the project. You'll need to import `io.reactivex.rxjava3.disposables.CompositeDisposable`:

```
exampleOf("CompositeDisposable") {
  // 1
  val subscriptions = CompositeDisposable()
  // 2
  val disposable = Observable.just("A", "B", "C")
      .subscribe {
        // 3
        println(it)
      }
  // 4
  subscriptions.add(disposable)
  // 5
  subscriptions.dispose()
}
```

Here's how this disposable code works:

1. Create a `CompositeDisposable`.

2. Create an observable and disposable.

3. Subscribe to the observable and print out the emitted item.

4. Add the `Disposable` return value from `subscribe` to the `subscriptions` `CompositeDisposable`.

5. Dispose of the disposables.

This is the pattern you'll use most frequently: creating and subscribing to an observable and immediately adding the subscription to a `CompositeDisposable`.

Why bother with disposables at all? If you forget to call `dispose()` on a `Disposable` when you're done with the subscription, or in some other way cause the observable to terminate at some point, you will *probably* leak memory.

If you forget to utilize the `Disposable` returned by calling `subscribe` on an `Observable`, **Android Studio** will make it very clear that something is not right in an Android project!

```
71
72          Observable.just( item1: "A",  item2: "B",  item3: "C")
73              .subscribe { it: String!
74                  println(it)
  The result of subscribe is not used more... (⌘F1)
77
78
```

Imagine leaking an huge view hierarchy just because you forgot to unsubscribe from a long running observable that you don't even need anymore!

The create operator

In the previous examples, you've created observables with specific `next` event elements. Another way to specify all events that an observable will emit to subscribers is by using the `create` operator.

Add this new example to the project:

```
exampleOf("create") {

  val disposables = CompositeDisposable()

  Observable.create<String> { emitter ->

  }
}
```

The `create` operator takes a single parameter named `source`. Its job is to provide the implementation of calling `subscribe` on the observable. In other words, it defines all the events that will be emitted to subscribers.

Command-click on create to see it's definition:

```
 * @param <T> the element type
 * @param source the emitter that is called when an {@code Observer} subscribes to the returned {@code Observable}
 * @return the new {@code Observable} instance
 * @throws NullPointerException if {@code source} is {@code null}
 * @see ObservableOnSubscribe
 * @see ObservableEmitter
 * @see Cancellable
 */
@CheckReturnValue
@NonNull
@SchedulerSupport(SchedulerSupport.NONE)
public static <T> Observable<T> create(@NonNull ObservableOnSubscribe<T> source) {
    Objects.requireNonNull(source, s: "source is null");
    return RxJavaPlugins.onAssembly(new ObservableCreate<>(source));
}
```

The source parameter is an ObservableOnSubscribe<T>. ObservableOnSubscribe is a SAM (Single Abstract Method) interface that exposes one method — subscribe. That subscribe method takes in an Emitter<T>, which has a few methods that you'll use to build up the actual Observable. Specifically, it has onNext, onComplete, and onError methods that you can invoke.

Change the implementation of create to the following:

```
Observable.create<String> { emitter ->
    // 1
    emitter.onNext("1")

    // 2
    emitter.onComplete()

    // 3
    emitter.onNext("?")
}
```

Here's the play by play:

1. Emit the string 1 via the onNext method.

2. Emit a completed event.

3. Emit another string ? via the onNext method again.

Do you think the second onNext element (?) could ever be emitted to subscribers? Why or why not?

To see if you guessed correctly, subscribe to the observable by adding the following code on the next line after the `create` implementation:

```
.subscribeBy(
    onNext = { println(it) },
    onComplete = { println("Completed") },
    onError = { println(it) }
)
```

You've subscribed to the observable, now run the code. The result is that the first next event element and "Completed" print out. The second next event doesn't print because the observable emitted a `completed` event and terminated before it.

```
--- Example of: create ---
1
Completed
```

Add the following line of code between the `emitter.onNext` and `emitter.onComplete` calls:

```
emitter.onError(RuntimeException("Error"))
```

Run the code after you've made those changes. The observable emits the error and then is terminated.

```
--- Example of: create ---
1
Error
```

What would happen if you emitted neither a `completed` nor an `error` event? Comment out the `onComplete` and `onError` lines of code to find out.

Here's the complete implementation:

```
exampleOf("create") {
  Observable.create<String> { emitter ->
    // 1
    emitter.onNext("1")
//    emitter.onError(RuntimeException("Error"))
    // 2
//    emitter.onComplete()

    // 3
    emitter.onNext("?")
  }.subscribeBy(
      onNext = { println(it) },
      onComplete = { println("Completed") },
      onError = { println("Error") }
  )
}
```

Run those changes. Congratulations, you've just leaked memory! :] The observable will never finish, and since you never disposed of the Disposable returned by Observable.create the sequence will never be canceled.

```
--- Example of: create ---
1
?
```

Feel free to uncomment the line adding the complete event or dispose of the returned Disposable if you can't stand leaving the code in a leaky state.

Creating observable factories

Rather than creating an observable that waits around for subscribers, it's possible to create observable factories that vend a new observable to each subscriber.

Add this new example to the project:

```
exampleOf("defer") {

  val disposables = CompositeDisposable()
  // 1
  var flip = false
  // 2
  val factory: Observable<Int> = Observable.defer {
    // 3
    flip = !flip
```

```
    // 4
    if (flip) {
      Observable.just(1, 2, 3)
    } else {
      Observable.just(4, 5, 6)
    }
  }
}
```

Here's the explanation:

1. Create a `Boolean` flag to flip which observable to return.

2. Create an observable of `Int` factory using the `defer` operator.

3. Invert `flip`, which will be used each time `factory` is subscribed to.

4. Return different observables based on whether `flip` is `true` or `false`.

Externally, an observable factory is indistinguishable from a regular observable. Add this code to the bottom of the example to subscribe to `factory` four times:

```
for (i in 0..3) {
  disposables.add(
      factory.subscribe {
        println(it)
      }
  )
}

disposables.dispose()
```

Run this code. Each time you subscribe to `factory`, you get the opposite observable. You get 123, then 456, and the pattern repeats each time a new subscription is created:

```
--- Example of: defer ---
1
2
3
4
5
6
1
2
3
4
5
6
```

Using other observable types

In addition to the normal `Observable` type, there are a few other types of observables with a narrower set of behaviors than regular observables. Their use is optional; you can use a regular observable anywhere you might use one of these specialized observables. Their purpose is to provide a way to more clearly convey your intent to readers of your code or consumers of your API. The context implied by using them can help make your code more intuitive.

There are three special types of observables in RxJava: `Single`, `Maybe` and `Completable`. Without knowing anything more about them yet, can you guess how each one is specialized?

- `Singles` will emit either a `success(value)` or `error` event. `success(value)` is actually a combination of the `next` and `completed` events. This is useful for one-time processes that will either succeed and yield a value or fail, such as downloading data or loading it from disk.

- A `Completable` will only emit a `completed` or `error` event. It doesn't emit any value. You could use a `Completable` when you only care that an operation completed successfully or failed, such as a file write.

- And `Maybe` is a mash-up of a `Single` and `Completable`. It can either emit a `success(value)`, `completed`, or `error`. If you need to implement an operation that could either succeed or fail, and optionally return a value on success, then `Maybe` is your ticket.

You'll have an opportunity to work more with these special observable types in Chapter 4, "Observables & Subjects in Practice," and beyond. For now, you'll run through a basic example of using a `Single` to load some text from a text file named **Copyright.txt**, because who doesn't love some legalese once in a while?

This file is in the **src** folder of the project.

Add this example to `main()`, importing `io.reactivex.rxjava3.core.Single` when you do:

```
exampleOf("Single") {
  // 1
  val subscriptions = CompositeDisposable()
  // 2
  fun loadText(filename: String): Single<String> {
    // 3
    return Single.create create@{ emitter ->

    }
  }
}
```

Here's what you do in this code:

1. Create a composite disposable to use later.

2. Implement a function to load text from a file on disk that returns a `Single`.

3. Create and return a `Single`.

Add this code inside the `create` lambda to complete the implementation:

```
// 1
val file = File(filename)
// 2
```

```
if (!file.exists()) {
  emitter.onError(FileNotFoundException("Can't find $filename"))
  return@create
}
// 3
val contents = file.readText(Charsets.UTF_8)
// 4
emitter.onSuccess(contents)
```

From the top:

1. Create a new `File` from the filename.

2. If the file doesn't exist, emit a `FileNotFoundException` via the `onError` method and return from the `create` method.

3. Get the data from the file.

4. Emit the contents of the file.

Now you can put this function to work. Add this code to the example:

```
// 1
val observer = loadText("Copyright.txt")
    // 2
    .subscribeBy(
        // 3
        onSuccess = { println(it) },
        onError = { println("Error, $it") }
    )

subscriptions.add(observer)
```

Here, you:

1. Call `loadText()`, passing the root name of the text file.

2. Subscribe to the `Single` it returns.

3. Pass `onSuccess` and `onError` lambdas to the `subscribeBy` method, either printing the contents of the file or printing the error.

Run the example, and you should see the text from the file printed to the console, the same as the copyright comment at the top of the project:

```
--- Example of: Single ---
Copyright (c) 2014-2020 Razeware LLC
...
```

Try changing the filename to something else, and you should get the file not found exception printed instead.

Challenges

Practice makes *permanent*. By completing challenges in this book, you'll practice what you've learned in each chapter and pick up a few more tidbits of knowledge about working with observables. A starter project as well as a finished version are provided for each challenge. Enjoy!

Challenge: Perform side effects

In the `never` operator example earlier, nothing printed out. That was before you were adding your subscriptions to composite disposables, but if you *had* added it to one, you could've used a handy operator to print a message when the disposable was disposed.

Operators that begin with `doOn`, such as the `doOnDispose` operator, allows you to insert **side effects**; that is, you add handlers that take some action but that won't affect the observable. For `doOnDispose`, that is whenever the disposable is disposed of.

There's a few other handy `doOn` methods that you can use. There's a `doOnNext` method, a `doOnComplete` method, a `doOnError` method and a `doOnSubscribe` method that you can also use to perform some side effect at the right moment.

To complete this challenge, insert the `doOnSubscribe` operator in the `never` example. Feel free to include any of the other handlers if you'd like; they work just like `doOnSubscribe`'s handler does.

And while you're at it, create a composite disposable and add the subscription to it.

Don't forget you can always peek into the finished challenge project for "inspiration."

Key points

- Everything is a **sequence** in RxJava, and the primary sequence type is `Observable`.
- Observables start emitting when they are **subscribed** to.
- You must **dispose** of subscriptions when done with them, and you'll often use a `CompositeDisposable` to do so.
- `Single`, `Completable` and `Maybe` are specialized observable types that are handy in certain situations.

Chapter 3: Subjects

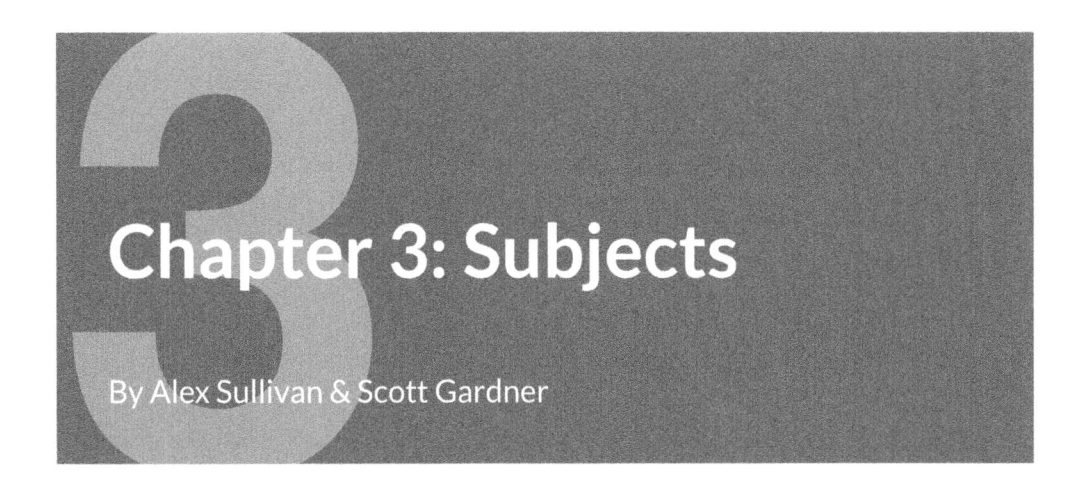

By Alex Sullivan & Scott Gardner

You've gotten a handle on what an Observable is, how to create one, how to subscribe to it, and how to dispose of things when you're done. Observables are a fundamental part of RxJava, but a common need when developing apps is to manually add new values onto an Observable at runtime that will then be emitted to subscribers. What you want is something that can act as both an Observable and as an **observer**. And that something is called a **subject**.

In this chapter, you're going to learn about the different types of subjects in RxJava, see how to work with each one and why you might choose one over another based on some common use cases.

Getting started

Open the starter project for this chapter in IntelliJ IDEA and add the following code to the **Main.kt** file:

```
exampleOf("PublishSubject") {
  val publishSubject = PublishSubject.create<Int>()
}
```

Here, you create a `PublishSubject` using a static method `create`. The class is aptly named, because, like a newspaper publisher, it will receive information and then turn around and publish it to subscribers, possibly after modifying that information in some way first. The subject here is of type `Int`, so it can only receive and publish integers. After being instantiated, it's ready to receive data.

Add the following code to the example:

```
publishSubject.onNext(0)
```

This sends a new integer into the subject. The console doesn't print out anything yet because there are no observers. Create one by adding the following code to the example:

```
val subscriptionOne = publishSubject.subscribe { int ->
  println(int)
}
```

You created a subscription to `publishSubject` just like in the last chapter, printing next events. You're using the default RxJava `subscribe` method rather than the fancier `subscribeBy` since you only care about the next event for now. But, when you run, still nothing shows up in IntelliJ IDEA's output console. Isn't this fun? You're going to learn about the different subjects shortly.

What's happening here is that a `PublishSubject` only emits to *current* subscribers. So if you weren't subscribed when something was added to it previously, you don't get it when you do subscribe. Think of the tree-falling analogy. If a tree falls and no one's there to hear it, does that make your illegal logging business a success? :]

To fix things, add this code to the end of the example:

```
publishSubject.onNext(1)
```

Notice that, because you defined the publish subject to be of type Int, only integers may be sent into it.

Now, because publishSubject *has* a subscriber, it will emit that integer:

```
--- Example of: PublishSubject ---
1
```

In a similar fashion to the subscribe parameters, onNext is how you add a new next event *into* a subject, passing the element as the parameter:

```
publishSubject.onNext(2)
```

Now the 2 is printed as well:

```
--- Example of: PublishSubject ---
1
2
```

With that gentle intro, now it's time to learn all about subjects.

What are subjects?

Subjects act as both an Observable and an observer. You saw earlier how they can receive events and also be subscribed to. The subject received next events, and each time it received an event, it turned around and emitted it to its subscriber.

There are four subject types in RxJava:

- PublishSubject: Starts empty and only emits new elements to subscribers.
- BehaviorSubject: Starts with an optional initial value and replays it or the latest element to new subscribers.
- ReplaySubject: Initialized with a buffer size and will maintain a buffer of elements up to that size and replay it to new subscribers.
- AsyncSubject: Starts empty and only emits the last item it receives before it's completed to subscribers.

Taking on each of these in turn, you're going to learn a lot more about subjects and how to work with them next.

Working with publish subjects

Publish subjects come in handy when you simply want subscribers to be notified of new events from the point at which they subscribed, until they either unsubscribe, or the subject has terminated with a `complete` or `error` event.

In the following marble diagram, the top line is the publish subject and the second and third lines are subscribers. The upward-pointing arrows indicate subscriptions, and the downward-pointing arrows represent emitted events.

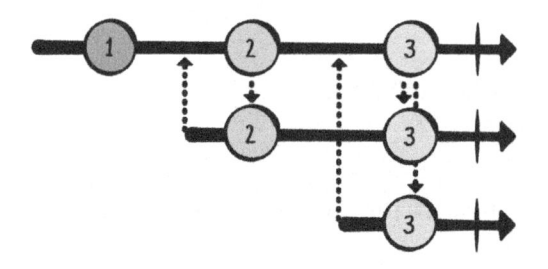

The first subscriber subscribes after 1, so it doesn't receive that event. It does get 2 and 3, though. And because the second subscriber doesn't join in on the fun until after 2, it only gets 3.

Returning to the project, add this code to the bottom of the same example:

```
val subscriptionTwo = publishSubject
  .subscribe { int ->
    printWithLabel("2)", int)
  }
```

`printWithLabel` is a simple helper function that — you guessed it — prints a label and a corresponding value. In the example above, `"2)"` is the label.

As expected, `subscriptionTwo` doesn't print anything out yet because it subscribed after the 1 and 2 were emitted. Now, enter this code:

```
publishSubject.onNext(3)
```

The 3 is printed twice, once for `subscriptionOne` and once for `subscriptionTwo`.

```
1
2
3
2) 3
```

Add this code to terminate `subscriptionOne` and then add another `.next` event onto the subject:

```
subscriptionOne.dispose()

publishSubject.onNext(4)
```

The value 4 is only printed for subscription 2), because `subscriptionOne` was disposed.

```
1
2
3
2) 3
2) 4
```

When a publish subject receives a `completed` or `error` event, also known as a **terminal** event, it will emit that terminal event to new subscribers and it will no longer emit `next` events. However, it will *re-emit* its terminal event to future subscribers. Add this code to the example:

```
// 1
publishSubject.onComplete()

// 2
publishSubject.onNext(5)

// 3
subscriptionTwo.dispose()

// 4
val subscriptionThree = publishSubject.subscribeBy(
    onNext = { printWithLabel("3)", it) },
    onComplete = { printWithLabel("3)", "Complete") }
)

publishSubject.onNext(6)
```

Here's what you do with the code above:

1. Send the `complete` event through the subject via the `onComplete` method. This effectively terminates the subject's observable sequence.
2. Send another element 5 into the subject. This won't be emitted and printed, though, because the subject has already terminated.
3. Don't forget to dispose of subscriptions when you're done!
4. Create a new subscription to the subject, using the `subscribeBy` method to listen for the `onComplete` event.

Maybe the new subscriber `subscriptionThree` will kickstart the subject back into action? Nope, but you do still get the `complete` event:

```
...
3) Complete
```

Actually, *every* subject type, once terminated, will re-emit its stop event to future subscribers. So it's a good idea to include handlers for stop events in your code, not just to be notified when it terminates, but also in case it is already terminated when you subscribe to it.

You might use a publish subject when you're modeling time-sensitive data, such as in an online bidding app. It wouldn't make sense to alert the user who joined at 10:01 am that at 9:59 a.m. there was only one minute left in the auction. That is, of course, unless you like one-star reviews to your bidding app.

Sometimes, you want to let new subscribers know what the latest element value is, even though that element was emitted before the subscription. For that, you've got some options.

Working with behavior subjects

Behavior subjects work similarly to publish subjects, except they will *replay* the latest next event to new subscribers. Check out this marble diagram:

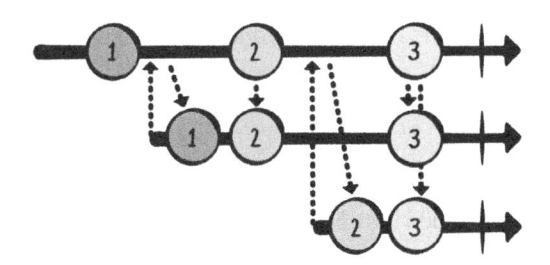

The first line from the top is the subject. The first subscriber on the second line down subscribes after 1 but before 2, so it gets 1 immediately upon subscription, and then 2 and 3 as they're emitted by the subject. Similarly, the second subscriber subscribes after 2 but before 3, so it gets 2 immediately and then 3 when it's emitted.

Add this new example to your project:

```
// 1
exampleOf("BehaviorSubject") {
  // 2
  val subscriptions = CompositeDisposable()
  // 3
  val behaviorSubject =
      BehaviorSubject.createDefault("Initial value")
}
```

Here's the play-by-play:

1. Start a new BehaviorSubject example.

2. Create a `CompositeDisposable`, which you'll use later on.

3. Create a new `BehaviorSubject` using the static factory method `createDefault`, which takes an initial value to be immediately emitted.

> **Note**: `BehaviorSubject` can also be initialized *without* an initial value. You can use the `create` static factory method to make one without an initial value.

Now, add the following code to the example:

```
val subscriptionOne = behaviorSubject.subscribeBy(
  onNext = { printWithLabel("1)", it) },
  onError = { printWithLabel("1)", it) }
)
```

This creates a subscription to the subject, but the subscription was created *after* the subject was. No other elements have been added to the subject, so it replays the initial value to the subscriber.

```
--- Example of: BehaviorSubject ---
1) Initial value
```

Now, insert the following code right *before* the previous subscription code, but *after* the definition of the subject:

```
behaviorSubject.onNext("X")
```

The X is printed, because now *it's* the latest element when the subscription is made:

```
--- Example of: BehaviorSubject ---
1) X
```

Add the following code to the end of the example — but, first, look it over and see if you can determine what will be printed:

```
// 1
behaviorSubject.onError(RuntimeException("Error!"))
// 2
subscriptions.add(behaviorSubject.subscribeBy(
  onNext = { printWithLabel("2)", it) },
  onError = { printWithLabel("2)", it) }
))
```

Taking it section-by-section:

1. Add a `RuntimeException` error event into the subject.

2. Create a new subscription to the subject.

Did you figure out that the error event will be printed twice, once for each subscription? If so, right on!

```
1) X
1) java.lang.RuntimeException: Error!
2) java.lang.RuntimeException: Error!
```

Another benefit of using a `BehaviorSubject` is it allows you to access whatever its latest value is imperatively. Add the code below to create another example:

```
exampleOf("BehaviorSubject State") {

  val subscriptions = CompositeDisposable()
  val behaviorSubject = BehaviorSubject.createDefault(0)

  println(behaviorSubject.value)
}
```

After running the example, you should see the following:

```
--- Example of: BehaviorSubject State ---
0
```

BehaviorSubjects allow you to reference their last emitted value — notice the `behaviorSubject.value` call in the last line of the example.

Add the following to the example:

```
// 1
subscriptions.add(behaviorSubject.subscribeBy {
  printWithLabel("1)", it)
})

// 2
behaviorSubject.onNext(1)
// 3
println(behaviorSubject.value)
// 4
subscriptions.dispose()
```

Let's break the above down section by section:

1. Subscribe to the BehaviorSubject and add its disposable to a CompositeDisposable so you can dispose of it later.

2. Call onNext sending another value into the subject.

3. Print whatever the current value of the subject is.

4. Dispose the subscriptions.

Using the `value` in a BehaviorSubject can help you bridge the gap between the Rx world and the non-Rx world!

Behavior subjects are useful when you want to pre-populate a view with the most recent data. For example, you could bind controls in a user profile screen to a behavior subject, so that the latest values can be used to pre-populate the display while the app fetches fresh data.

But what if you wanted to show more than the latest value? For example, on a search screen, you may want to show the most recent five search terms used. This is where replay subjects come in.

Working with replay subjects

Replay subjects will temporarily cache — or **buffer** — the latest elements they emit, up to a specified size of your choosing. They will then replay that buffer to new subscribers.

The following marble diagram depicts a replay subject with a buffer size of 2. The first subscriber (middle line) is already subscribed to the replay subject (top line) so it gets elements as they're emitted. The second subscriber (bottom line) subscribes after 2, so it gets 1 and 2 replayed to it.

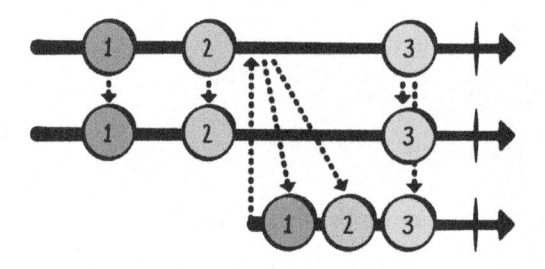

Keep in mind that, when using a replay subject, this buffer is held in memory. You can definitely shoot yourself in the foot, here, if you set a large buffer size for a replay subject of some type whose instances each take up a lot of memory — like images. Another thing to watch out for is creating a replay subject of a **list** of items. Each emitted element will be a list, so the buffer size will buffer that many lists. It would be easy to create memory pressure here if you're not careful.

Add this new example to your file:

```
exampleOf("ReplaySubject") {

  val subscriptions = CompositeDisposable()
  // 1
  val replaySubject = ReplaySubject.createWithSize<String>(2)
  // 2
  replaySubject.onNext("1")

  replaySubject.onNext("2")

  replaySubject.onNext("3")
  // 3
  subscriptions.add(replaySubject.subscribeBy(
     onNext = { printWithLabel("1)", it) },
     onError = { printWithLabel("1)", it)}
  ))

  subscriptions.add(replaySubject.subscribeBy(
     onNext = { printWithLabel("2)", it) },
     onError = { printWithLabel("2)", it)}
  ))
}
```

From the top:

1. You create a new replay subject with a buffer size of 2. Replay subjects are initialized using the static method `createWithSize`.

2. Add three elements onto the subject.

3. Create two subscriptions to the subject.

The latest two elements are replayed to both subscribers. 1 never gets emitted, because 2 and 3 were added onto the replay subject with a buffer size of 2 before anything subscribed to it:

```
--- Example of: ReplaySubject ---
1) 2
1) 3
2) 2
2) 3
```

Now, add the following code to the example:

```
replaySubject.onNext("4")

subscriptions.add(replaySubject.subscribeBy(
  onNext = { printWithLabel("3)", it) },
  onError = { printWithLabel("3)", it)}
))
```

With this code, you add another element into the subject, and then create a new subscription to it. The first two subscriptions will receive that element as normal because they were already subscribed when the new element was added to the subject, while the new third subscriber will get the last two buffered elements replayed to it:

```
...
1) 4
2) 4
3) 3
3) 4
```

You're getting pretty good at this stuff by now, so there should be no surprises, here. What would happen if you threw a wrench into the works here? Add this line of code right after adding 4 onto the subject, before creating the third subscription:

```
replaySubject.onError(RuntimeException("Error!"))
```

This *may* surprise you. And if so, that's OK. Life's full of surprises:

```
1) 4
2) 4
1) java.lang.RuntimeException: Error!
2) java.lang.RuntimeException: Error!
3) 3
3) 4
3) java.lang.RuntimeException: Error!
```

What's going on here? The replay subject is terminated with an error, which it will re-emit to new subscribers as you've already seen subjects do. But the buffer is also still hanging around, so it gets replayed to new subscribers as well, before the stop event is re-emitted.

Working with async subjects

The last type of subject in the RxJava arsenal is the `AsyncSubject`. **Async** subjects are a bit stranger and definitely a bit rarer than the other types of subjects you've encountered, but they're still valuable. Here's the lowdown.

An `AsyncSubject` will only ever emit the *last* value it received before it's `complete`. So if you pass several values into an `AsyncSubject` and then call `onComplete` on it, subscribers will only see the last value you passed into the subject and then a `complete` event. If the subject receives an `error` event, subscribers will see nothing!

The following marble diagram demonstrates the above. The first line is the `AsyncSubject` — it gets a 1 value, a 2 value, and a 3 value, and then `completes` (denoted by the vertical bar after the 3 value).

The other two lines are subscribers, and they only receive the last value, the 3 value, before also getting a `complete` event.

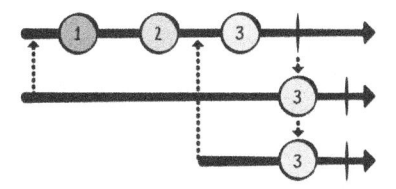

Add the following example in your project:

```
exampleOf("AsyncSubject") {
  val subscriptions = CompositeDisposable()
  // 1
  val asyncSubject = AsyncSubject.create<Int>()
  // 2
  subscriptions.add(asyncSubject.subscribeBy(
     onNext = { printWithLabel("1)", it) },
     onComplete = { printWithLabel("1)", "Complete") }
  ))
  // 3
   asyncSubject.onNext(0)
   asyncSubject.onNext(1)
   asyncSubject.onNext(2)
   // 4
   asyncSubject.onComplete()

   subscriptions.dispose()
}
```

Taking things step by step, again:

1. Build an `AsyncSubject` that will handle `Ints`.
2. Subscribe to the subject, printing out both `next` events and `complete` events.
3. Send three values into the subject: 0, 1, and 2.
4. `complete` the subject.

What kind of output would you expect to get? Run the project and you should see the following:

```
--- Example of: AsyncSubject ---
1) 2
1) Complete
```

Since 2 was the last element sent into the subject before it completed, the subscriber only sees 2 before it receives the `complete` event.

`AsyncSubjects` definitely take a back seat to some of the other subjects you've seen in this chapter, but they can be super useful in the right scenario! For example, imagine you have a game summary screen that you want to update with the final values of some game. An `AsyncSubject` would be perfect to listen for score changes, since the only score you care about is the last one before the game finishes and the subject completes!

Working with the RxRelay library

Subjects are fantastic — but, sometimes, they don't *quite* get it right. You'll often want to represent an infinite stream that will *never* terminate. That means it will never send a `complete` event or an `error` event. For example, say you have a `subject` that pipes through the current user of your app, so you can update a profile page when a new user logs in. As long as your app is alive, that stream should be active!

If you use a normal subject, someone could inadvertently call `onComplete` or `onError`, thus terminating the stream. That means that when Dave logs out of your app and Susy logs in, she'll see all of Dave's profile information. Sounds like trouble waiting to happen!

Enter the **RxRelay** library. RxRelay mimics all of the subjects you've come to know and love, but without the option of calling `onComplete` or `onError`.

Add the following to your project and don't worry about the compiler error:

```
exampleOf("RxRelay") {
  val subscriptions = CompositeDisposable()

  val publishRelay = PublishRelay.create<Int>()

  subscriptions.add(publishRelay.subscribeBy(
    onNext = { printWithLabel("1)", it) }
  ))

  publishRelay.accept(1)
  publishRelay.accept(2)
  publishRelay.accept(3)
}
```

In the above example, you're using a `PublishRelay` instead of a `PublishSubject`. Most things about the relay are the same — just like in a `PublishSubject`, a subscriber will only receive elements *after* they subscribe. But by using a `PublishRelay` you guarantee no one else in the codebase will call `onComplete` or `onError` in the stream.

Including the RxRelay library is easy — just add the following to your `build.gradle` file, then run Gradle sync:

```
implementation 'com.jakewharton.rxrelay3:rxrelay:3.0.0'
```

You can now run the example and see the result:

```
--- Example of: RxRelay ---
1) 1
1) 2
1) 3
```

RxRelay comes with a replacement relay for `PublishSubject`, `BehaviorSubject`, and `ReplaySubject`. There's no relay version of `AsyncSubject` since it depends on the subject receiving a `complete` event — so it wouldn't make sense in Relay land!

Challenge

Challenge: Create a blackjack card dealer using a publish subject

Put your new super subject skills to the test by completing this challenge. There are start and end versions for each challenge in the chapter downloads.

In case you're not familiar with it, blackjack is a card game where the goal is to get 21 or as close as possible without going over, which is called getting "busted."

The starter project for this challenge implements a publish subject to model a hand of cards. To do so, the type of the subject is a list of pairs of String and Int to store the suit and the card value.

```
val dealtHand = PublishSubject.create<List<Pair<String, Int>>>()
```

Aces are high, so an Ace of Spades has a value of 11 compared to a Queen of Hearts which has a value of 10.

In the SupportCode.kt file for this challenge, there is a cards list of pairs of String and Int to represent a standard deck of 52 cards.

```
val cards = mutableListOf(
    Pair("", 11), Pair("", 2),Pair("", 3), ...)
```

There's also a couple of functions here. cardString() will take a list of card pairs and extract just the strings representing the cards.

```
fun cardString(hand: List<Pair<String, Int>>): String {
    return hand.joinToString("") { it.first }
}
```

And points() tallies up the points for the passed in list of card pairs.

Remember that you can't go over 21 points or else you're *busted*, so there's also an error sealed class to model that.

```
sealed class HandError: Throwable() {
    class Busted: HandError()
}
```

And there's an extension function on IntRange to get a random Int in a range:

```
fun IntRange.random() =
    Random().nextInt(endInclusive - start) + start
```

OK, back in the main function, you have two tasks.

The first is to add code below the comment "Add code to update dealtHand here" that will evaluate the result returned from calling points(), passing the hand list. If the result is greater than 21, add the error HandError.Busted() onto dealtHand. Otherwise, add the hand onto dealtHand as a next event.

Your second task is to subscribe to the dealtHand right below the comment indicating to do that. Handle both the next and error events. For next events, you can just print out the result from calling the cardString() and points() functions from the support code. And for an error event, just print out the error.

All right that's it. Good luck on this challenge!

Key points

- Subjects are Observables that are also observers.

- You can send events over subjects by using `onNext`, `onError` and `onComplete`.

- **PublishSubject** is used when you only want to receive events that occur after you've subscribed.

- **BehaviorSubject** will relay the latest event that has occurred when you subscribe, including an optional initial value.

- **ReplaySubject** will buffer a configurable number of events that get replayed to new subscribers. You must watch out for buffering too much data in a replay subject.

- **AsyncSubject** only sends subscribers the most recent `next` event upon a `complete` event occurring.

- The **RxRelay** library can be used with relays in place of subjects, to prevent accidental `complete` and `error` events to be sent.

Where to go from here?

You've now learned about Observables and observers, and seen how to combine them into a single type called a subject.

Now it's time to put all you've learned into practice in an Android app. You'll start to do so in the next chapter!

Chapter 4: Observables & Subjects in Practice

By Alex Sullivan & Marin Todorov

By this point in the book, you understand how observables and different types of subjects work, and you've learned how to create and experiment with them in an IntelliJ project.

It could be a bit challenging, however, to see the practical use of observables in everyday development situations, such as binding your UI to a data model, showing a new activity or fragment and getting output out of it.

It's OK to be a little unsure how to apply these newly acquired skills to the real world. In this book, you'll work through theoretical chapters such as Chapter 2, "Observables," and Chapter 3, "Subjects," as well as practical step-by-step chapters — just like this one!

In the "...in Practice" chapters, you'll work on a complete app. The starter Android Studio project will include all the non-Rx and other setup code. Your task will be to add the other features using your newly-acquired reactive skills.

That doesn't mean to say you won't learn few new things along the way — *au contraire*!

In this chapter, you'll use RxJava and your new observable superpowers to create an app that lets users create nice photo collages — the reactive way.

Getting started

Open the starter project for this chapter, **Combinestagram**, in Android Studio 4.0 or newer. It takes a couple of tries to roll your tongue just right to say the name, doesn't it? It's probably not the most marketable name, but it will do.

Add the dependencies for **RxJava**, **RxKotlin** and **RxAndroid** in the **app/build.gradle** file:

```
implementation "io.reactivex.rxjava3:rxkotlin:3.0.0"
implementation "io.reactivex.rxjava3:rxandroid:3.0.0"
implementation "io.reactivex.rxjava3:rxjava:3.0.2"
```

Since RxJava 3.0 uses Java 8 features, you'll also need to let gradle know that you intend to use those features. Add the following in the android block of the same file:

```
compileOptions {
  sourceCompatibility JavaVersion.VERSION_1_8
  targetCompatibility JavaVersion.VERSION_1_8
}
```

Sync the gradle file, build and run the app, and you'll see the beginnings of the project you'll bring to life:

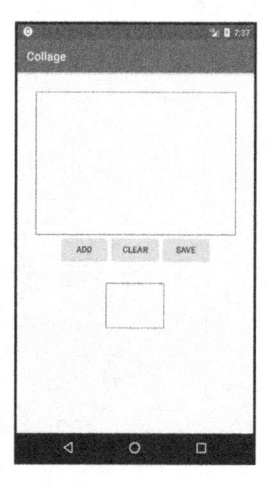

In this screen, the user can see their collage as the app builds it. They can add new photos to the collage, clear out the contents of the collage or save it to their phone.

Feel free to take a peek into the utility **X.kt** file where a list of `Bitmap`s is converted into a collage.

You'll also notice a few other classes in the project. There's a **PhotosBottomDialogFragment** to select photos for the collage and a **SharedViewModel**, which is a `ViewModel` that that the **MainActivity** and **PhotosBottomDialogFragment** will share.

In this chapter, you are going to focus on putting your new skills to practice. Time to get started!

Using a BehaviorSubject in a ViewModel

Start by adding a `BehaviorSubject`, a `CompositeDisposable`, and a `MutableLiveData` to the **SharedViewModel** class:

```
// 1
private val disposables = CompositeDisposable()
// 2
private val imagesSubject: BehaviorSubject<MutableList<Photo>>
    = BehaviorSubject.createDefault(mutableListOf())
// 3
private val selectedPhotos = MutableLiveData<List<Photo>>()
```

1. The `CompositeDisposable` for the subscriptions.

2. The `imagesSubject` will emit `MutableList<Photo>` values.

3. Finally, you'll use the `selectedPhotos` variable, that is a `LiveData` object, to stream a list of photos to the **MainActivity**.

> **Note**: It may seem a little strange to use `LiveData` and RxJava in the same project, since they're both streaming libraries that implement the **Observer** pattern. However, they actually both have unique strengths and weaknesses that you can utilize to build better apps. You'll see more details about this in Chapter 22, "Building a Complete RxJava App".

Take a look at the `Photo` data class. It contains a `Drawable` resource ID. You'll use that later on to actually build the collage.

Next up, add the following code to the **SharedViewModel** class:

```
init {
  imagesSubject.subscribe { photos ->
    selectedPhotos.value = photos
  }.addTo(disposables)
}

fun getSelectedPhotos(): LiveData<List<Photo>> {
  return selectedPhotos
}
```

You're subscribing to the `imagesSubject` stream and updating the `selectedPhotos` value with the items emitted by the subject. Since you're a responsible RxJava user, you're adding the `Disposable` returned by the `subscribe()` method to the `CompositeDisposable` you created earlier.

Speaking of being responsible RxJava users, add the following code below the `init` block:

```
override fun onCleared() {
  disposables.dispose()
  super.onCleared()
}
```

`ViewModels` `onCleared()` method is a great place to dispose of any disposables you may have lying around. Since a `ViewModel` is only cleared when the `Activity` that created it finishes, you won't prematurely finish your `Observables` and `Subjects`, and you won't leak any memory.

Adding photos

It's time to start adding some photos to the collage. Add the following code to the **SharedViewModel**:

```
fun addPhoto(photo: Photo) {
  imagesSubject.value?.add(photo)
  imagesSubject.onNext(imagesSubject.value!!)
}
```

`addPhoto()` takes a `Photo` object and adds it to the current list of photos in the collage.

Since you're using a `BehaviorSubject`, you can easily extract the current list of photos from it and add this new photo to that list. You then emit that list again to notify any observers of the newly updated list of photos.

Navigate to **MainActivity** and replace the `println()` call in `actionAdd()` with the following:

```
viewModel.addPhoto(PhotoStore.photos[0])
```

For now, you're always using the first photo from the static list of photos that comes shipped with the app. Don't worry, you'll update that later on.

It's time to hook everything up and see a collage! Add the following to the bottom of the `onCreate()` method of **MainActivity**, importing `androidx.lifecycle.Observer` when prompted:

```
// 1
viewModel.getSelectedPhotos().observe(this, Observer { photos ->
  photos?.let {
    // 2
    if (photos.isNotEmpty()) {
      val bitmaps = photos.map {
        BitmapFactory.decodeResource(resources, it.drawable)
      }
      // 3
      val newBitmap = combineImages(bitmaps)
      // 4
      collageImage.setImageDrawable(
        BitmapDrawable(resources, newBitmap))
    }
  }
})
```

The code may seem complicated, but it's actually very simple:

1. You're observing the `selectedPhotos` live data, which emits lists of `Photo` objects.

2. Then, if there are any photos, you're mapping each `Photo` object to a `Bitmap` using the `BitmapFactory.decodeResource()` method.

3. Next up, you're combining that list of bitmaps using the `combineImages()` method.

4. Finally, you're setting the `collageImage` image view with the combined bitmap.

Run the app. When you tap the **Add** button you should see images in the central collage image view. Tab the button again to add more images.

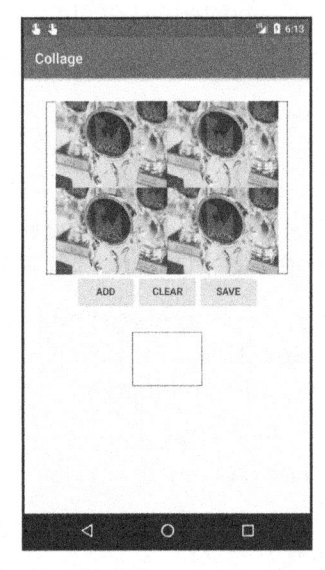

Looking good! Now try to tap the **Clear** button.

You haven't hooked up the **Clear** action yet, so nothing should happen. If something does happen, then that's magical, and you've discovered a new way of building apps without writing any code!

Add the following function to the **SharedViewModel** class:

```
fun clearPhotos() {
  imagesSubject.value?.clear()
  imagesSubject.onNext(imagesSubject.value!!)
}
```

clearPhotos() works very similarly to addPhotos(), except instead of adding a new photo into the existing list you're clearing out that list and emitting the now empty list.

Now, navigate back to the MainActivity class and replace the println() statement in the actionClear() method with the following:

```
viewModel.clearPhotos()
```

Last but not least, add this `else` statement to the `if` statement in the selected photos observing code in the `onCreate()`:

```
if (photos.isNotEmpty()) {
  // ...
} else {
  collageImage.setImageResource(android.R.color.transparent)
}
```

Now if the `photos` list has no photo objects in it, you're clearing out the image in the `collageImage` image view.

Run the app again. This time you should be able to clear photos.

Recapping reactive programming

Reactive programming can be hard to follow at times, so here's a recap of what's happening in the app so far:

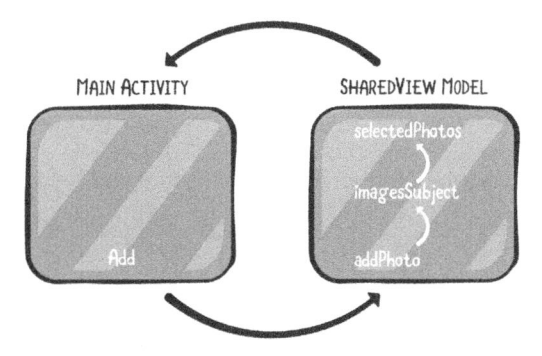

1. Whenever the user taps the **Add** button, the `MainActivity` class is calling the `addPhoto()` method in `SharedViewModel` with a single static photo.

2. The **SharedViewModel** class then updates a list of photos that is stored in `imagesSubject`, and it calls `onNext()` with the updated list of photos.

3. Since the view model is subscribed to `imagesSubject`, it receives the `onNext()` notification and forwards the new list of photos through to the `selectedPhotos` live data.

4. Since the `MainActivity` class is subscribing to the `selectedPhotos` live data, it's notified of the new list of photos. It then creates the combined bitmap of photos and sets it on the `collageImage` image view. If the list of photos is empty, it instead clears that image view.

At this stage of the app, this may seem like overkill. However, as you continue to improve the **Combinestagram** app, you'll see that this reactive stream-based approach has many advantages!

Driving a complex UI

As you play with the current app, you'll notice the UI could be a bit smarter to improve the user experience. For example:

- You could disable the **Clear** button if there aren't any photos selected just yet or in the event the user has just cleared the selection.

- Similarly, there's no need for the **Save** button to be enabled if there aren't any photos selected.

- You could also disable the save functionality for an odd number of photos, as that would leave an empty spot in the collage.

- It would be nice to limit the amount of photos in a single collage to six, since more photos simply look a bit weird.

- Finally, it would be nice if the activity title reflected the current selection.

Let's set out now to add these improvements to **Combinestagram**.

Open up **MainActivity.kt** and add an `updateUi()` method below `onCreate()`:

```
private fun updateUi(photos: List<Photo>) {
  saveButton.isEnabled =
      photos.isNotEmpty() && (photos.size % 2 == 0)
  clearButton.isEnabled = photos.isNotEmpty()
  addButton.isEnabled = photos.size < 6
  title = if (photos.isNotEmpty()) {
    resources.getQuantityString(R.plurals.photos_format,
      photos.size, photos.size)
  } else {
    getString(R.string.collage)
  }
}
```

In the above code, you update the complete UI according to the ruleset we've talked about. All the logic is in a single place and easy to read through.

Now add a call to `updateUi()` to the bottom of the `Observer` lambda observing for `selectedPhotos`:

```
if (photos.isNotEmpty()) {
  // ...
} else {
  // ...
}
updateUi(photos)
```

Run the app again, and you will see all the rules kick in as you play with the UI:

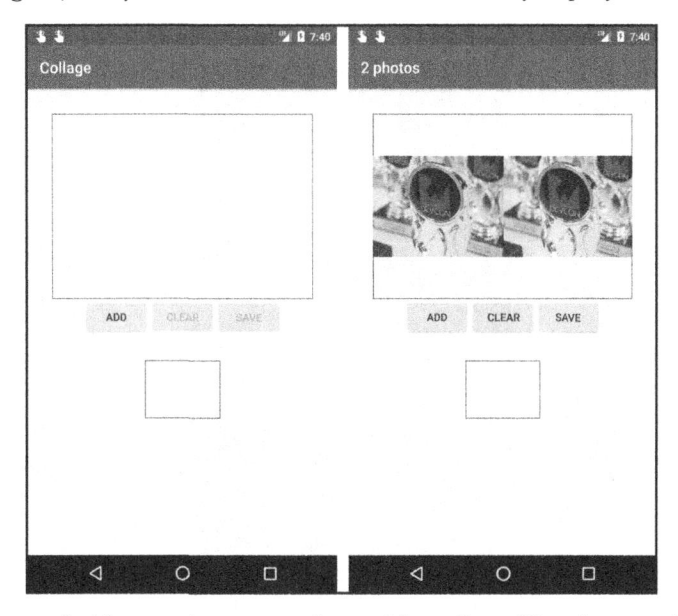

By now, you're probably starting to see the real benefits of Rx when applied to your Android apps. If you look through all the code you've written in this chapter, you'll see there are only a few simple lines that drive the whole UI!

Communicating with other views via subjects

Combinestagram is *almost* perfect. But users may want to actually pick from multiple photos instead of just one hardcoded one. Maybe.

Instead of serving up one static image, you'll instead display a bottom dialog fragment wherein the user can select from a list of photos.

First off, delete the `addPhoto()` method in **SharedViewModel**.

Next up, replace the contents of `actionAdd()` in **MainActivity** with the following:

```
val addPhotoBottomDialogFragment =
  PhotosBottomDialogFragment.newInstance()
addPhotoBottomDialogFragment
  .show(supportFragmentManager, "PhotosBottomDialogFragment")
```

The above code simply shows the **PhotosBottomDialogFragment** dialog when the user taps the **Add** button. Try it out now, by running the app. You should see the following after tapping the **Add** button:

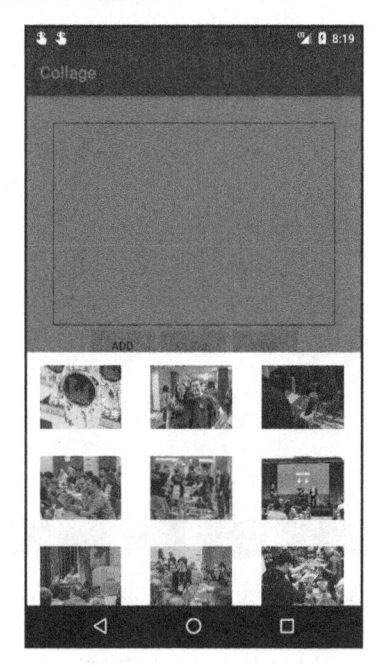

This is the stage in which you'd normally use an interface to have the PhotosBottomDialogFragment communicate that the user selected a photo. However, that's not very reactive — so, instead, you'll use an observable.

Navigate to **PhotosBottomDialogFragment** and create a new PublishSubject<Photo> variable:

```
private val selectedPhotosSubject =
    PublishSubject.create<Photo>()

val selectedPhotos: Observable<Photo>
  get() = selectedPhotosSubject.hide()
```

You'll see this pattern employed often. You created a new `PublishSubject`, but you don't want to expose that subject to other classes because you want to make sure that you know what's being put into it. Instead of directly exposing `selectedPhotosSubject`, you create a new public `selectedPhotos` property that returns `selectedPhotosSubject.hide()`. The `hide()` method simply returns an `Observable` version of the same subject.

Add the following to the empty `photosClicked()` method:

```
selectedPhotosSubject.onNext(photo)
```

You're now forwarding a photo that a user selected through your subject.

All that's left to do is to subscribe to this new observable.

Navigate over to **SharedViewModel** and add the following method:

```
fun subscribeSelectedPhotos(selectedPhotos: Observable<Photo>) {
  selectedPhotos
    .doOnComplete {
      Log.v("SharedViewModel", "Completed selecting photos")
    }
    .subscribe { photo ->
      imagesSubject.value?.add(photo)
      imagesSubject.onNext(imagesSubject.value!!)
    }
    .addTo(disposables)
}
```

`subscribeSelectedPhotos()` takes an `Observable<Photo>` and subscribes to that observable, forwarding the photos it receives through to the `imagesSubject`.

Now, navigate back to **MainActivity** and add the following line in the bottom of the `actionAdd()` method:

```
viewModel.subscribeSelectedPhotos(
  addPhotoBottomDialogFragment.selectedPhotos)
```

You're ready to go!

Run the app and you should be able to add different photos to your collage:

Cleaning up observables: Review

The code seemingly works as expected, but try the following: Add few photos to a collage, go back to the main screen and inspect logcat.

Do you see a message saying "completed selecting photos"? No? You added a Log statement to that last subscription using the doOnComplete() operator that should notify you that the provided selectedPhotos has completed.

Since the selectedPhotos observable never completes, the memory it's utilizing will not be freed until the SharedViewModel is itself cleared.

If the user keeps going back and forth adding new photos and presenting that bottom dialog fragment, that means more and more observables will be created, since one's created for every instance of PhotosBottomDialogFragment. Those observables are taking up precious memory!

Open **PhotosBottomDialogFragment** and add the following method:

```
override fun onDestroyView() {
  selectedPhotosSubject.onComplete()
  super.onDestroyView()
}
```

Now, whenever the view is destroyed, the `selectedPhotosSubject` will be completed and its memory will be reclaimed. You can see that this is true if you run the app, select a photo, then dismiss the bottom sheet. The log statement now prints out.

Perfect! You're now ready for the last part of this chapter: taking a plain old boring function and converting it into a super-awesome and fantastical reactive one.

Creating a custom observable

You may have noticed that there's one aspect of the app that doesn't work yet – saving a photo. Time to fix that!

Open **SharedViewModel** and take a look at the `saveBitmapFromImageView()` method. It's pretty simple — it just takes an `ImageView` and saves its bitmap to the external files directory.

There's only one problem: It's boring. Actually, the real problem is that, after you save the photo, there's no way to figure out where it was saved to — and it's a blocking call! Both problems that can be fixed by making this function an awesome reactive function.

First, change the return type of `saveBitmapFromImageView()` to `Observable<String>`. Then, wrap the existing function body in an `Observable.create` call like so:

```
fun saveBitmapFromImageView(
    imageView: ImageView,
    context: Context
): Observable<String> {
  return Observable.create { emitter ->
    // Body of the method
    // ...
  }
}
```

You're now returning an observable. However, that observable never emits anything and never finishes. Not all that useful.

Add this to the end of the `try` block:

```
emitter.onNext(tmpImg)
emitter.onComplete()
```

Then, add this to the end of the `catch` block:

```
emitter.onError(e)
```

You're emitting the name of the newly created file and then completing. If the file fails to save, you're instead emitting that error.

Navigate back to **MainActivity** and update the `actionSave()` method to the following:

```
viewModel.saveBitmapFromImageView(collageImage, this)
    .subscribeBy(
        onNext = { file ->
          Toast.makeText(this, "$file saved",
            Toast.LENGTH_SHORT).show()
        },
        onError = { e ->
          Toast.makeText(this,
            "Error saving file :${e.localizedMessage}",
            Toast.LENGTH_SHORT).show()
        }
    )
```

Build and run the App to test the **Save** functionality.

So you've created an observable that either emits one item and completes or emits an error. That sounds familiar…

Review: Single, Maybe, Completable

In Chapter 2, "Observables," you had the chance to learn about a few specialized RxJava types.

In this chapter, you'll do a quick review and see how you might use these types in an app, and then use one of the types in the **Combinestagram** project! Starting with `Single`:

Single

As you already know, `Single` is an `Observable` specialization. It represents a sequence, which can emit just once either a `success` event or an `error`.

This kind of type is useful in situations such as saving a file, downloading a file, loading data from disk or basically any asynchronous operation that yields a value.

You can categorize two distinct use-cases of `Single`:

1. For wrapping operations that emit exactly one element upon success, just like `saveBitmapFromImageView()` earlier in this chapter. You can directly create a `Single` instead of an `Observable`. In fact, you will update the `saveBitmapFromImageView()` method in `SharedViewModel` to create a `Single` shortly.

2. To better express your intention to consume a single element from a sequence and ensure if the sequence emits more than one element the subscription will error out. To achieve this, you can subscribe to any observable and use `singleOrError()` operator to convert it to a `Single`.

Maybe

Maybe is quite similar to Single with the only difference that the observable *may* or *may not* emit a value upon successful completion.

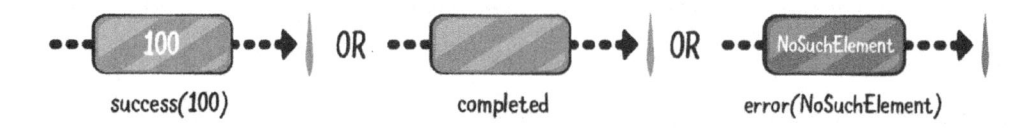

If you keep to the photograph-related examples, imagine this use-case for Maybe: your app is storing photos in its own custom photo album. You persist the album identifier in SharedPreferences and use that ID each time to "open" the album and write a photo inside.

You would design an open(albumId): Maybe<String> method to handle the following situations:

- In case the album with the given ID still exists, just emit a completed event.

- In case the user has deleted the album in the meanwhile, create a new album and emit a next event with the new ID, so you can persist it in SharedPreferences.

- In case something is wrong and you can't access the Photos library at all, emit an error event.

Just like other the specialized types, you can achieve the same functionality by using a "vanilla" Observable, but Maybe gives more context both to you as you're writing your code and to the programmers coming to alter the code later on.

Just as with Single, you can create a Maybe directly by using Maybe.create { ... }. Or, if you have an existing observable, you can use the firstElement() or lastElement() methods to get a Maybe of that element.

Completable

The final type to cover is `Completable`. This variation of `Observable` allows only for a single `completed` or `error` event to be emitted before the subscription is disposed of.

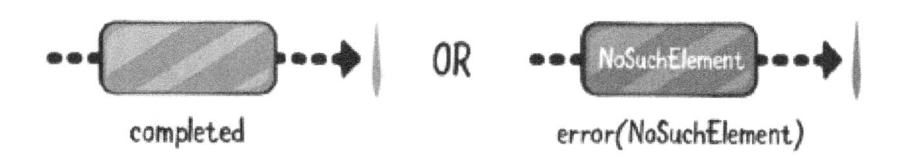

You can create a `Completable` sequence by using `Completable.create { ... }` with code very similar to that which you'd use to create other observables. You can also use the `ignoreElements()` method on an `Observable` to get a completable version of it that ignores all the elements.

You might notice that `Completable` simply doesn't allow for emitting any values and wonder why would you need a sequence like that. You'd be surprised at the number of use-cases in which you only need to know whether an asynchronous operation succeeded or not.

Here's an example before going back to Combinestagram. Let's say your app auto-saves a document while the user is working on it. You'd like to asynchronously save the document in a background queue, and when completed, show a small notification or an alert box onscreen if the operation fails.

Let's say you wrapped the saving logic into a function `fun saveDocument()`: `Completable`. This is how easy it is to then express the rest of the logic:

```
saveDocument()
  .andThen(Observable.just(createMessage))
  .subscribeBy(onNext = { message ->
    message.display()
  }, onError = { e ->
    showError(e.localizedDescription())
  })
```

The `andThen()` operator allows you to chain more completables or observables upon an event and subscribe for the final result. In case, any of them emits an error, your code will fall through to the final `onError` lambda.

Having *completed* (:]) a review of the specialized observable types, you can now update `saveBitmapFromImageView()` to return a more specialized and appropriate type.

Back to **Combinestagram** and the problem at hand!

Using Single in the app

Update `saveBitmapFromImageView()` to return a `Single<Photo>` and replace the relevant calls to `Observable` with the sibling calls to `Single`:

```
fun saveBitmapFromImageView(imageView: ImageView, context:
Context): Single<String> {
  return Single.create { emitter ->
    // ...
    try {
      // ..
      emitter.onSuccess(tmpImg)
    } catch(e: IOException) {
      Log.e("MainActivity", "Problem saving collage", e)
      emitter.onError(e)
    }
  }
}
```

Fancy!

All that's left is to change the subscription to this single and save the photo.

Navigate back to **MainActivity** and update the `actionSave()` method to the following:

```
viewModel.saveBitmapFromImageView(collageImage, this)
    .subscribeBy(
        onSuccess = { file ->
          // ...
        },
        onError = { e ->
          // ...
        }
    )
```

You're utilizing the new reactive version of the `saveBitmapFromImageView()` method and subscribing to the `Single` that it produces. If the single succeeds, you're showing a toast indicating that it finished. If it fails, you're showing a toast with the error message.

Give the app one last triumphant run to save the collage.

To see the saved file, use the **Device File Explorer** accessed from the **View ▸ Tool Windows** menu in Android Studio:

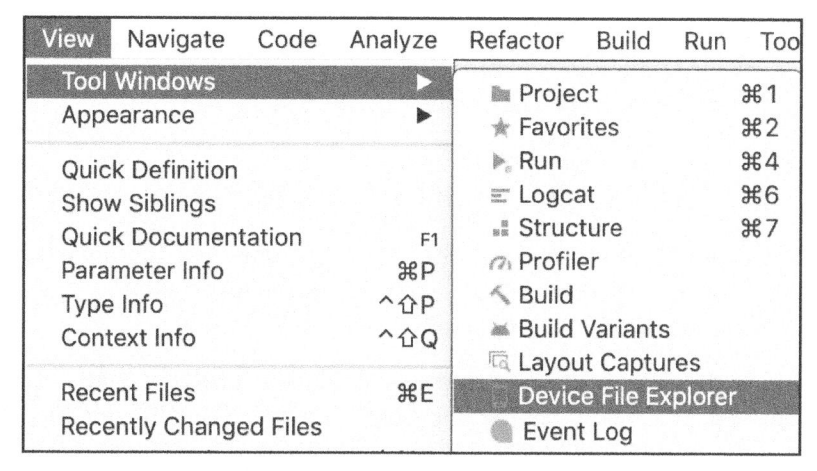

Then navigate to the app **data** directory in the device **sdcard** folder to see the file. You can double-click the image file to open it.

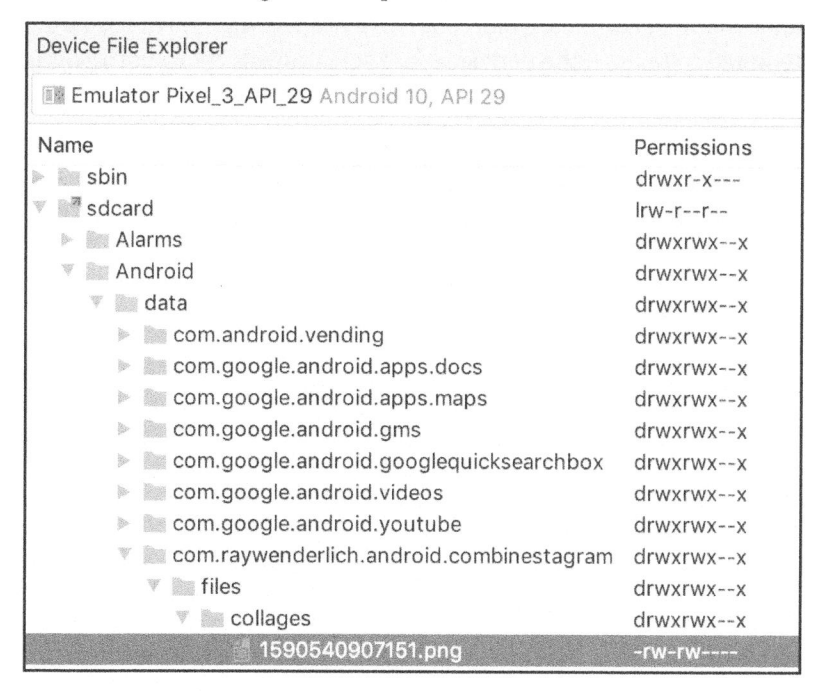

Before we move on, there's still one more issue to tackle.

You may have noticed that, when you saved a collage, the **Save** button freezes in the tapped state and the UI stopped responding. Saving a photo to storage can take a long time, and is best done on a background thread.

To achieve this, you'll see a sneak peek of one of the cooler parts of Rx: **Schedulers**.

In the `actionSave()` method, add the following code after the call to `saveBitmapFromImageView()` and before the call to `subscribeBy()`:

```
.subscribeOn(Schedulers.io())
.observeOn(AndroidSchedulers.mainThread())
```

The `subscribeOn()` method instructs the `Single` to do its subscription work on the IO scheduler. The `observeOn()` method instructs the single to run the `subscribeBy()` code on the Android main thread.

You'll learn much more about schedulers in Chapter 13, "Intro to Schedulers". For now, run the app. You should see the save button immediately return to its normal state after being tapped, and the UI should no longer be blocked.

With that, you've completed Section I of this book — congratulations!

You are not a young Padawan anymore, but an experienced RxJava Jedi. However, don't be tempted to take on the dark side just yet. You will get to battle networking, thread switching, and error handling soon enough!

Before that, you must continue your training and learn about one of the most powerful aspects of RxJava. In Section 2, "Operators and Best Practices," operators will allow you to take your `Observable` superpowers to a whole new level!

Key points

- **Observables** and **Subjects** exist not just for theory: you use them in real apps!
- RxJava observables can be combined with **LiveData** to pass events from a view model along to the UI.
- RxJava can be used to create **complex-UI interactions** with a small amount of **declarative** code.
- It's possible and useful to refactor existing non-Rx code into **custom observables** using `Observable.create`.
- The specialized observable types `Single`, `Maybe`, and `Completable` should be used when possible to make your intentions clear to both future you and your teammates.

Where to go from here?

Next up, back to some theory as you start Section II.

With your first Rx-enabled app project behind you, it's time to dig deeper into RxJava and look at how you can manipulate observable streams using **operators**.

Section II: Operators & Best Practices

Operators are the building blocks of Rx, which you can use to transform, process, and react to events emitted by Observables.

Just as you can combine simple arithmetic operators like +, -, and / to create complex math expressions, you can chain and compose together Rx's simple operators to express complex app logic.

In this chapter, you are going to:

- Start by looking into filtering operators, which allow you to process some events but ignore others.

- Move on to transforming operators, which allow you to create and express complex data transformations. You can for example start with a button event, transform that into some kind of input, process that and return some output to show in the app UI.

- Look into combining operators, which allow for powerful composition of most other operators.

- Explore operators that allow you to do time based processing: delaying events, grouping events over periods of time, and more. Work though all the chapters, and by the end of this section you'll be able to write simple RxJava apps!

Chapter 5: Filtering Operators

By Alex Sullivan & Scott Gardner

Learning a new technology stack is a bit like building a skyscraper: You've got to build a solid foundation before you can kiss the sky. By now, you've established a solid RxJava foundation, and it's time to start building up your knowledge base and skill set, one floor at a time.

This chapter will teach you about RxJava's filtering operators that you can use to apply conditional constraints to `next` events, so that the subscriber only receives the elements it wants to deal with. If you've ever used the `filter` method in the Kotlin Standard Library, you're already half way there. But if not, no worries; you're going to be an expert at this filtering business by the end of this chapter.

Getting started

The starter project for this chapter is an IntelliJ project. Open it up and give it a build. You won't see anything in the console yet.

Ignoring operators

Without further ado, you're going to jump right in and look at some useful filtering operators in RxJava, beginning with `ignoreElements`. As depicted in the following marble diagram, `ignoreElements` will do just that: ignore `next` event elements. It will, however, allow through stop events, i.e., `complete` or `error` events. Allowing through stop events is usually implied in marble diagrams.

It's just explicitly called out this time by the dashed line because that's *all* `ignoreElements` will let through.

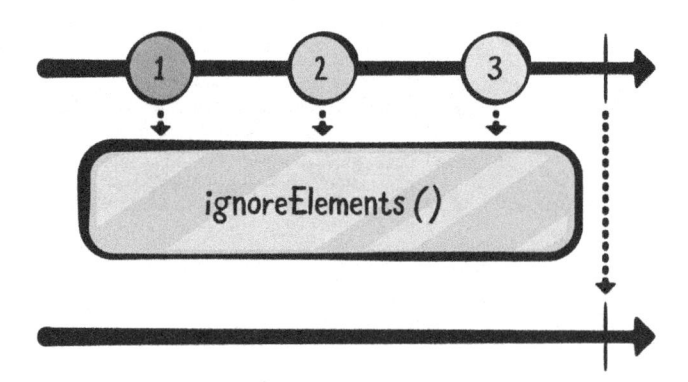

> **Note**: Up until now you've seen marble diagrams used for observable types. The marble diagram shown here instead helps to visualize how **operators** work. The top line is the observable that is being subscribed to. The box represents the operator and its parameters, and the bottom line is the subscriber, or more specifically, what the subscriber will *receive* after the operator does its thing.

See one, now do one, by adding this example to your `main` function:

```
exampleOf("ignoreElements") {

  val subscriptions = CompositeDisposable()
  // 1
  val strikes = PublishSubject.create<String>()
  // 2
  subscriptions.add(
      strikes.ignoreElements()
          // 3
          .subscribeBy {
             println("You're out!")
          })
}
```

Here's what you're doing:

1. Create a `strikes` subject.

2. Subscribe to *all* `strikes` events, but ignore all `next` events by using `ignoreElements`.

3. Since this observable now has no elements, `ignoreElements` converts it into a `Completable`. There is no `onNext` in `subscribeBy` for a `Completable`.

`ignoreElements` is useful when you only want to be notified when an observable has terminated, via a `complete` or `error` event. Add this code to the example:

```
strikes.onNext("X")
strikes.onNext("X")
strikes.onNext("X")
```

Even though this batter can't seem to hit the broad side of a barn and has clearly struck out, nothing is printed, because you're ignoring all `next` events. It's up to you to add a `complete` event to this subject in order to let the subscriber be notified. Add this code to do that:

```
strikes.onComplete()
```

Now, the subscriber will receive the `complete` event, and print that catchphrase *no batter ever wants to hear*.

```
--- Example of: ignoreElements ---
You're out!
```

> **Note**: If you don't happen to know much about strikes, batters and the game of baseball in general, you can read up on those when you decide to take a little break from programming: https://simple.wikipedia.org/wiki/Baseball.

elementAt operator

There may be times when you only want to handle the *nth* (ordinal) element emitted by an observable, such as the third strike. For that you can use `elementAt`, which takes the index of the element you want to receive, and it ignores everything else.

In the marble diagram, `elementAt` is passed an index of 1, so it only allows through the second element. Remember: observables, just like lists, are zero-indexed.

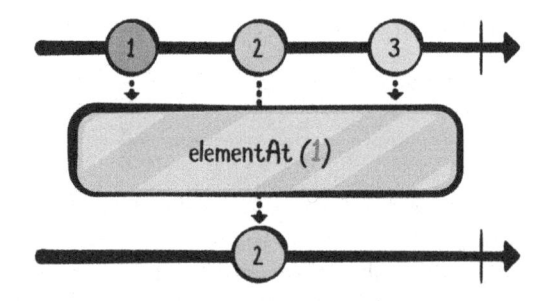

Add this new example:

```
exampleOf("elementAt") {

    val subscriptions = CompositeDisposable()
    // 1
    val strikes = PublishSubject.create<String>()
    // 2
    subscriptions.add(
        strikes.elementAt(2)
            // 3
            .subscribeBy(
                onSuccess = { println("You're out!") }
            ))
}
```

Here's the play-by-play:

1. You create a `strikes` subject.

2. You subscribe to the `strikes` observable, ignoring every element other than the third item.

3. Since this observable may not have a third item, `elementAt` returns a `Maybe`. Because it's a `Maybe` will subscribe with `onSuccess` instead of `onNext`.

Now you can simply add new strikes onto the subject, and your subscription will take care of letting you know when the batter has struck out. Add this code inside the example block:

```
strikes.onNext("X")
strikes.onNext("X")
strikes.onNext("X")
```

"Hey batta, batta, batta, swing batta!"

Now you can build and run and imagine the game:

```
--- Example of: elementAt ---
You're out!
```

filter operator

`ignoreElements` and `elementAt` are filtering elements emitted by an observable. When your filtering needs go beyond all or one, there's `filter`. `filter` takes a predicate lambda, which it applies to each element, allowing through only those elements for which the predicate resolves to `true`.

Check out this marble diagram, where only 1 and 2 are let through, because the filter's predicate only allows elements that are less than 3.

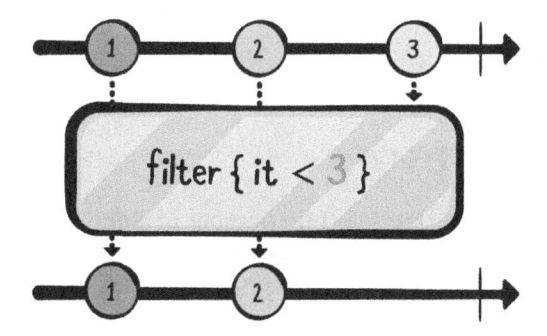

Add this example to your `main` function:

```
exampleOf("filter") {

  val subscriptions = CompositeDisposable()

  subscriptions.add(
      // 1
      Observable.fromIterable(
```

```
            listOf(1, 2, 3, 4, 5, 6, 7, 8, 9, 10))
    // 2
    .filter { number ->
        number > 5
    }.subscribe {
        // 3
        println(it)
    })
}
```

From the top:

1. You create an observable of some predefined integers.

2. You use the `filter` operator to apply a conditional constraint to prevent any number less than five from getting through. `filter` takes a predicate that returns a `Bool`. Return `true` to let the element through or `false` to prevent it. `filter` will filter elements for the life of the subscription.

3. You subscribe and print out the elements that passed the filter predicate.

The result of applying this filter is that only numbers greater than five are printed:

```
--- Example of: filter ---
6
7
8
9
10
```

Skipping operators

It might be that you need to skip a certain number of elements. Consider observing a weather forecast, where maybe you don't want to start receiving hourly forecast data until later in the day, because you're stuck in a cubicle until then anyway. The `skip` operator allows you to ignore from the first to the number you pass as its parameter. All subsequent elements will then pass through.

This marble diagram shows `skip` being passed 2, so it ignores the first 2 elements.

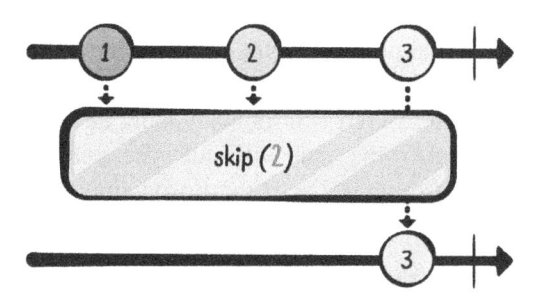

Enter this new example in your `main` function:

```
exampleOf("skip") {
  val subscriptions = CompositeDisposable()

  subscriptions.add(
      // 1
      Observable.just("A", "B", "C", "D", "E", "F")
          // 2
          .skip(3)
          .subscribe {
            println(it)
          })
}
```

With this code, you:

1. Create an observable of letters.

2. Use `skip` to skip the first 3 elements and then subscribe to `next` events.

After skipping the first three elements, only D, E, and F are printed like so:

```
--- Example of: skip ---
D
E
F
```

skipWhile operator

There's a small family of `skip` operators. Like `filter`, `skipWhile` lets you include a predicate to determine what should be skipped. However, unlike `filter`, which will filter elements for the life of the subscription, `skipWhile` will only skip up until something is *not* skipped, and then it will let everything else through from that point on. Also, with `skipWhile`, returning `true` will cause the element to be skipped, and returning `false` will let it through: it uses the return value in the opposite way to `filter`.

In this marble diagram, 1 is prevented because 1 % 2 equals 1, but then 2 is allowed through because it fails the predicate, and 3 (and everything else going forward) gets through because `skipWhile` is no longer skipping.

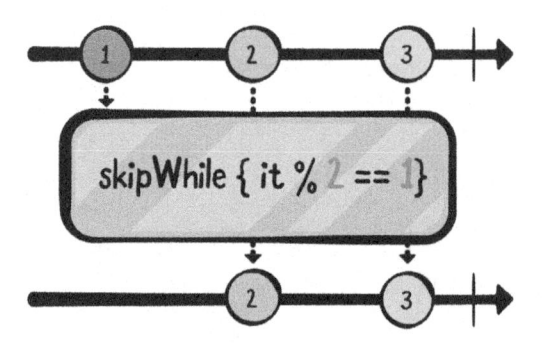

Add this new example to your `main` function:

```
exampleOf("skipWhile") {

    val subscriptions = CompositeDisposable()

    subscriptions.add(
        // 1
        Observable.just(2, 2, 3, 4)
            // 2
            .skipWhile { number ->
                number % 2 == 0
            }.subscribe {
                println(it)
            })
}
```

Here's what you did:

1. Create an observable of integers.
2. Use `skipWhile` with a predicate that skips elements until an odd integer is emitted.

`skipWhile` only skips elements up until the first element is let through, and then *all* remaining elements are allowed through.

```
--- Example of: skipWhile ---
3
4
```

If you were developing an insurance claims app, you could use `skipWhile` to deny coverage until the deductible is met. If only the insurance industry were that straightforward here in the United States.

skipUntil operator

So far, the filtering has been based on some static condition. What if you wanted to dynamically filter elements based on some other observable? There are a couple of operators that you'll learn about here that can do this. The first is `skipUntil`, which will keep skipping elements from the source observable (the one you're subscribing to) until some other **trigger** observable emits.

In this marble diagram, `skipUntil` ignores elements emitted by the source observable (the top line) until the trigger observable (second line) emits a `next` event.

Then it stops skipping and lets everything through from that point on.

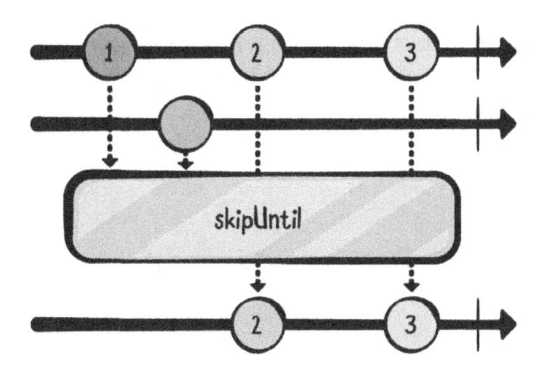

Add this example to see how `skipUntil` works in code:

```
exampleOf("skipUntil") {

    val subscriptions = CompositeDisposable()
    // 1
    val subject = PublishSubject.create<String>()
    val trigger = PublishSubject.create<String>()

    subscriptions.add(
        // 2
        subject.skipUntil(trigger)
            .subscribe {
                println(it)
            })
}
```

In this code, you:

1. Create a subject to model the data you want to work with, and another subject to model a `trigger` to change how you handle things in the first subject.

2. Use `skipUntil`, passing the `trigger` subject. When `trigger` emits, `skipUntil` will stop skipping.

Add a couple of next events onto `subject`:

```
subject.onNext("A")
subject.onNext("B")
```

Nothing is printed out, because you're skipping. Now add a new next event onto trigger:

```
trigger.onNext("X")
```

Doing so causes `skipUntil` to stop skipping. From this point onward, all elements will be let through. Add another next event onto `subject`:

```
subject.onNext("C")
```

Sure enough, it's printed out.

```
--- Example of: skipUntil ---
C
```

Taking operators

Taking is the opposite of skipping. When you want to only take certain elements, RxJava has you covered. The first taking operator you'll learn about is `take`. As shown in this marble diagram, the result will take the first of the number of elements you specified and ignore everything that follows.

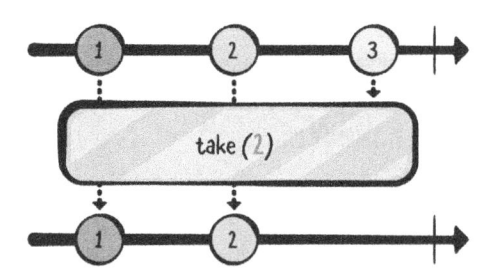

Add this example to your `main` function to explore the first of the take operators:

```
exampleOf("take") {
   val subscriptions = CompositeDisposable()

   subscriptions.add(
       // 1
       Observable.just(1, 2, 3, 4, 5, 6)
           // 2
           .take(3)
           .subscribe {
              println(it)
           })
}
```

Here's what you did:

1. Create an observable of integers.

2. Take the first three elements using `take`.

What you take is what you get. The output this time is:

```
--- Example of: take ---
1
2
3
```

takeWhile operator

There's also a `takeWhile` operator that works similarly to `skipWhile`, except you're taking instead of skipping. `takeWhile` works like `take`, but uses a predicate instead of a number of `next` events, as in this marble diagram:

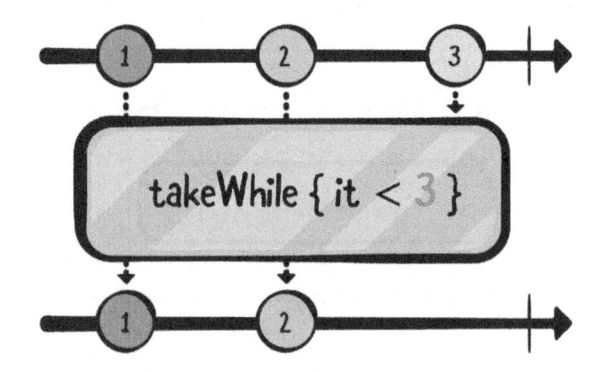

Enter this new example in your `main` function:

```
exampleOf("takeWhile") {
  val subscriptions = CompositeDisposable()

  subscriptions.add(
      // 1
      Observable.fromIterable(
        listOf(1, 2, 3, 4, 5, 6, 7, 8, 9, 10, 1))
          // 2
          .takeWhile { number ->
            number < 5
          }.subscribe {
            println(it)
          })
}
```

From the top:

1. Create an observable of integers counting up from 1 to 10, and then finally emitting another 1 value.

2. Use the `takeWhile` operator and take any number that's less than 5.

The output from the `takeWhile` example is:

```
--- Example of: takeWhile ---
1
2
3
4
```

You only receive integers that are less than five and came before any integer that was greater than 5. The 1 value at the end isn't emitted because the `takeWhile` operator already hit a value greater than 5.

takeUntil operator

Like `skipUntil`, there's also a `takeUntil` operator, shown in the next marble diagram. It takes from the source observable until the trigger observable emits an element.

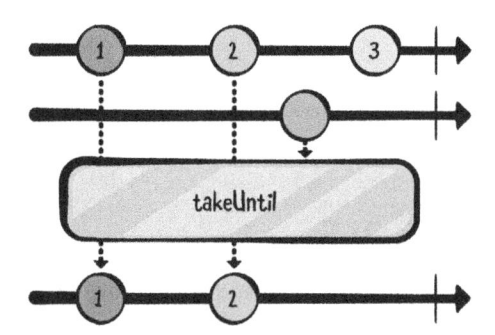

Add this new example, which is just like the `skipUntil` example you created earlier:

```
exampleOf("takeUntil") {
  val subscriptions = CompositeDisposable()
  // 1
  val subject = PublishSubject.create<String>()
  val trigger = PublishSubject.create<String>()

  subscriptions.add(
      // 2
      subject.takeUntil(trigger)
          .subscribe {
            println(it)
          })
  // 3
  subject.onNext("1")
  subject.onNext("2")
}
```

Here's what you did:

1. Create a primary subject and a `trigger` subject.

2. Use `takeUntil`, passing the `trigger` that will cause `takeUntil` to stop taking once it emits.

3. Add a couple of elements onto `subject`.

The console shows those elements, but `takeUntil` is in taking mode because the `trigger` did not emmit yet.

```
--- Example of: takeUntil ---
1
2
```

Now add an element onto `trigger`, followed by another element onto `subject`:

```
trigger.onNext("X")

subject.onNext("3")
```

The X stops the taking, so 3 is not allowed through and nothing more is printed.

Distinct operators

The next couple of operators you're going to learn about let you prevent duplicate items one-after-another from getting through. As shown in this marble diagram, `distinctUntilChanged` only prevents duplicates that are right next to each other. The second 2 does not emit but second 1 gets through since it is a change relative to what came before it.

Distinct operators can be visualized like this:

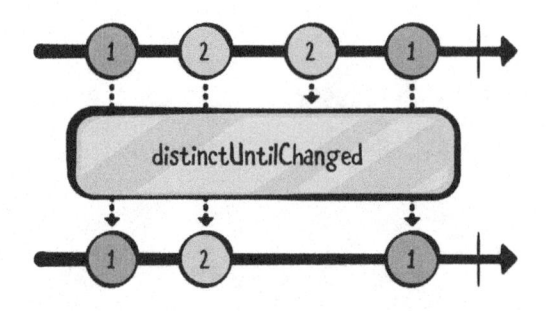

Add this new example to your `main` function:

```
exampleOf("distinctUntilChanged") {
  val subscriptions = CompositeDisposable()

  subscriptions.add(
      // 1
      Observable.just("Dog", "Cat", "Cat", "Dog")
          // 2
          .distinctUntilChanged()
          .subscribe {
            println(it)
          })
}
```

What you're doing, here:

1. Create an observable of our fluffy friends.

2. Use `distinctUntilChanged` to prevent sequential duplicates from getting through.

`distinctUntilChanged` only prevents contiguous duplicates. So the third element is prevented because it's the same as the second, but the last item, a Dog, *is* allowed through, because it comes after a different pet (Cat).

The resulting printout only includes the first Dog, first Cat, and then the Dog at the end:

```
--- Example of: distinctUntilChanged ---
Dog
Cat
Dog
```

The default behavior of `distinctUntilChanged` uses the `equals` method to determine that two items are equal. That may not be what you want, so you can use a variant of `distinctUntilChanged` that accepts a predicate comparing two items that are emitted one after another.

In the following marble diagram, objects with a property named `value` are being compared for distinctness based on `value`:

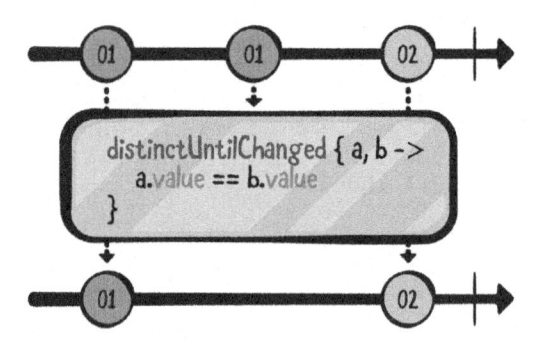

Add this new example to your project to use the new version of `distinctUntilChanged` in a slightly more elaborate way:

```kotlin
exampleOf("distinctUntilChangedPredicate") {
  val subscriptions = CompositeDisposable()

  subscriptions.add(
      // 1
      Observable.just(
        "ABC", "BCD", "CDE", "FGH", "IJK", "JKL", "LMN")
        // 2
        .distinctUntilChanged { first, second ->
          // 3
          second.any { it in first }
        }
        // 4
        .subscribe {
          println(it)
        }
  )
}
```

From the top, you:

1. Create an observable of strings representing chunks of the English alphabet.

2. Use `distinctUntilChanged(comparer: BiPredicate)`, which takes a lambda that receives each sequential pair of elements.

3. Return `true` if any character in the second string is also in the first string.

4. Subscribe and print out elements that are considered distinct based on the comparing logic you provided.

As a result, only distinct letters are printed in each pair of next events; that is, in each pair of strings, one does not contain any of the characters of the other:

```
--- Example of: distinctUntilChangedPredicate ---
ABC
FGH
IJK
```

So, this version of `distinctUntilChanged` is useful when you want to distinctly prevent duplicates for types that do not have a useful `equals` implementation.

Challenge

Challenge: Create a phone number lookup

Open the challenge starter project and have a look at what's to be found inside!

Breaking down this challenge, you'll need to use several filter operators. Here are the requirements, along with a suggested operator to use:

1. Phone numbers can't begin with 0 — use `skipWhile`.

2. You an only input a single-digit number at a time; use `filter` to only allow elements that are less than `10`.

3. This is limited to U.S. phone numbers, which are 10 digits, so take only the first 10 numbers inputted; use `take` and `toList`.

Review the setup code in the starter project. There's a simple contacts dictionary:

```
val contacts = mapOf(
    "603-555-1212" to "Florent",
    "212-555-1212" to "Junior",
    "408-555-1212" to "Marin",
    "617-555-1212" to "Scott")
```

There's a utility function that will return a formatted phone number for the list of `10` values you pass to it:

```
fun phoneNumberFrom(inputs: List<Int>): String {
    val phone = inputs.map { it.toString() }.toMutableList()
    phone.add(3, "-")
    phone.add(7, "-")
    return phone.joinToString("")
}
```

There's a `PublishSubject` to start you off:

```
val input = PublishSubject.create<Int>()
```

And there's a series of `onNext` calls to test that your solution works:

```
input.onNext(0)
input.onNext(603)

input.onNext(2)
input.onNext(1)

// Confirm that 7 results in "Contact not found", and then
// change to 2 and confirm that Junior is found
input.onNext(2)

"5551212".forEach {
  // Need toString() or else Char conversion is done
  input.onNext(it.toString().toInt())
}

input.onNext(9)
```

Because this challenge focuses on using the filter operators, here is code that you can use in the subscription's next event handler. It takes the result from `phoneNumberFrom` and print out the contact if found or else `"Contact not found"`:

```
if (contact != null) {
  println("Dialing $contact ($phone)...")
} else {
  println("Contact not found")
}
```

Add your code right below the comment `// Add your code here`.

Once you've implemented your solution, follow the instructions in the comment beginning `// Confirm that 7 results in...` to test that your solution works.

Key points

- **Ignoring** operators like `ignoreElements`, `elementAt`, and `filter` let you remove certain elements from an observable stream.

- **Skipping** operators let you skip certain elements and then begin emitting.

- Conversely, **taking** operators let you take certain elements and then stop emitting.

- **Distinct** operators let you prevent duplicates from being emitted back-to-back in an observable stream.

Where to go from here?

You've seen the theory behind filttering operators in an IntelliJ project. Next up, transfer that knowledge into a real Android app by going back to the **Combinestagram** photo collage app.

Chapter 6: Filtering Operators in Practice

By Alex Sullivan & Marin Todorov

In the previous chapter, you began your introduction to the *functional* aspect of RxJava. The first batch of operators you learned about helped you filter the elements of an observable sequence. As explained previously, the operators are simply methods on `Observable` and other associated RxJava types.

The operators operate on the elements of their `Observable` class and produce a new observable sequence as a result. This comes in handy because, as you saw previously, this allows you to **chain** operators, one after another, and perform several transformations in sequence:

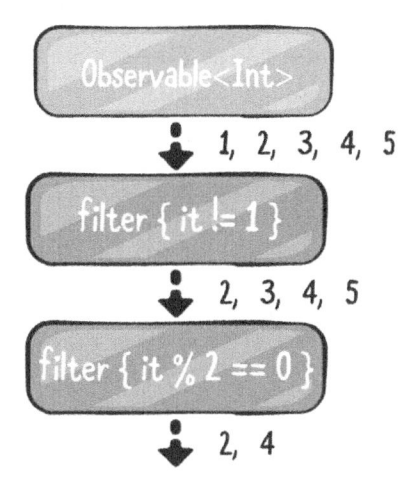

The preceding diagram looks great in theory. In this chapter, you're going to try using the filtering operators in a real-life app. In fact, you are going to continue working on the **Combinestagram** app that you already know and love from Chapter 4, "Observables & Subjects in Practice".

> **Note**: In this chapter, you will need to understand the theory behind the filtering operators in RxJava. If you haven't worked through Chapter 5, "Filtering Operators," do that first and then come back to the current chapter.

Improving the Combinestagram project

In this chapter, you will:

- Work through series of tasks, which (surprise!) will require you to use various filtering operators.
- Use different ones and see how you can use counterparts like `skip` and `take`.
- Take care of a few of the issues in the current **Combinestagram** project.

> **Note**: Since this book has only covered a few operators so far, you will not write the "best possible" code. For this chapter, don't worry about best practices or proper architecture yet, but instead focus on truly understanding how to use the filtering operators. In this book, you're going to slowly build up towards writing good RxJava code. It's a process!

Refining the photos sequence

Currently, the main screen of the app looks like this:

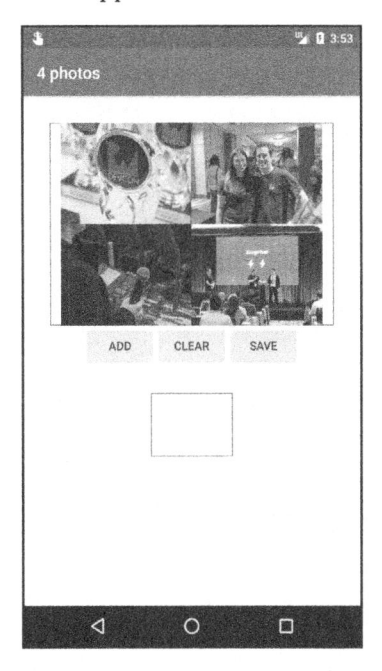

Right now, the app works by opening up an instance of
PhotosBottomDialogFragment whenever the user clicks the add button. Then, when the user clicks one of the photos, a photo object is added to the selectedPhotosSubject publish subject. The SharedViewModel subscribes to the selectedPhotosSubject and adds the newly emitted photo object onto its own imagesSubject. Whenever imagesSubject emits, the selectedPhotos live data object is updated and the MainActivity class receives the new photo.

That's all well and good, but **Combinestagram** could use a few new features. For example, wouldn't it be nice if you could view a thumbnail of the image collage? I'll answer that for you. It'd be great!

You could just add more code to the subscribe block in the subscribeSelectedPhotos method, but that would be messy and that subscribe block will quickly become too complex if you go that route.

Another option would be to create another subscription to the selectedPhotos observable. That would actually work here, but there's an important consideration to make before you go down that path.

Sharing subscriptions

Is there anything wrong with calling `subscribe(...)` on the same observable multiple times? Turns out there might be!

You've already seen that observables are lazy, pull-driven sequences. Simply calling a bunch of operators on an `Observable` doesn't involve any actual work. The moment you call `subscribe(...)` directly on an observable or on one of the operators applied to it, *that's* when the `Observable` livens up and starts producing elements.

Take a look at the code below:

```
val numbers = Observable.create<Int> { emitter ->
  val start = getStartNumber()
  emitter.onNext(start)
  emitter.onNext(start + 1)
  emitter.onNext(start + 2)
  emitter.onComplete()
}
```

The code creates an `Observable<Int>`, which produces a sequence of three numbers: `start, start + 1, start + 2`.

Now see what `getStartNumber()` looks like:

```
var start = 0
private fun getStartNumber(): Int {
  start++
  return start
}
```

The function increments a variable and returns it; nothing can go wrong there. Or can it? Add a subscription to `numbers` in one of the earlier IntelliJ projects and see for yourself:

```
numbers
  .subscribeBy(
      onNext = { println("element [$it]") },
      onComplete = { println(("--------------"))}
  ))
```

You will get the exact output you expected. Yay!

```
element [1]
element [2]
element [3]
--------------
```

Copy and paste the exact same subscription code one more time though, and this time the output is different.

```
element [1]
element [2]
element [3]
--------------
element [2]
element [3]
element [4]
--------------
```

The problem is that each time you call `subscribe(...)`, this creates a new `Observable` for that subscription — and each copy is not guaranteed to be the same as the previous. And even when the `Observable` *does* produce the same sequence of elements, it's overkill to produce those same duplicate elements for each subscription. Imagine if your observable wraps a network call - by subscribing twice, you'd end up making that same network call twice. Wasteful!

It's worth noting that `Subjects` don't have this problem - since every subscriber will get new items as they're emitted (depending on the subject type) you don't need to worry about the initial work done in the `create` block being repeated.

To share a subscription, you can use the `share()` operator. A common pattern in Rx code is to create several sequences from the same source `Observable` by filtering out different elements in each of the results.

You'll use `share` in a practical example in **Combinestagram** to understand its purpose a bit better.

Open the project and select **SharedViewModel**. Scroll to `subscribeSelectedPhotos()` and add this line as the first line in the method:

```
val newPhotos = fragment.selectedPhotos.share()
```

Then, instead of subscribing to the `fragment.selectedPhotos` observable, subscribe to the `newPhotos` observable:

```
subscriptions.add(newPhotos
    .doOnComplete {
      Log.v("SharedViewModel", "Completed selecting photos")
    }
    .subscribe { photo ->
      imagesSubject.value?.add(photo)
      imagesSubject.onNext(imagesSubject.value ?:
        mutableListOf())
    }
)
```

It's no longer true that each subscription is creating a new `Observable` instance like this:

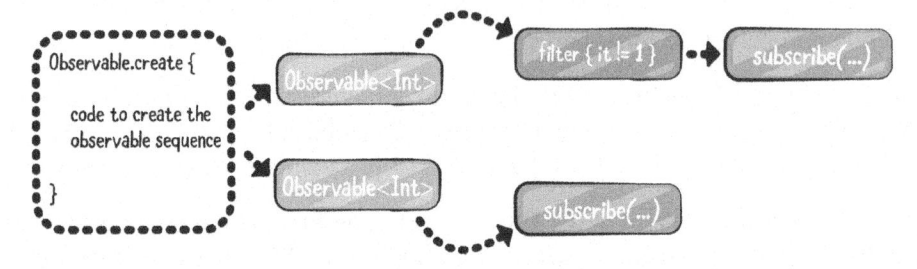

Instead, with `share()`, you allow for multiple subscriptions to consume the elements that a single `Observable` produces for all of them, like so:

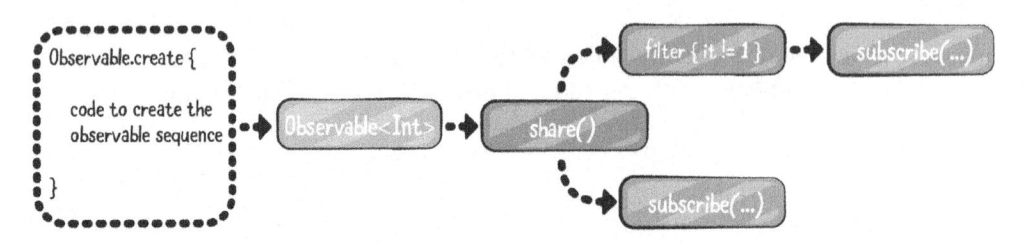

Now you can create a second subscription to `newPhotos` and filter out some of the elements you don't need.

Before moving on though, it's important to learn a bit more about how `share` works.

`share` creates a subscription only when the number of subscribers goes from 0 to 1 (e.g., when there isn't a shared subscription already). When a second, third and so on subscriber starts observing the sequence, `share` uses the already created subscription to share with them. If all subscriptions to the shared sequence get disposed (e.g. there are no more subscribers), `share` will *dispose the shared sequence as well*. If another subscriber starts observing, `share` will create a *new* subscription for it just like described above.

> **Note**: `share()` does not provide any of the subscriptions with values emitted before the subscription takes effect.

The rule of thumb about sharing operators is that it's safe to use `share()` with observables that do not complete, or if you guarantee no new subscriptions will be made after completion.

Ignoring all elements

You will start with the simplest filtering operator: the one that filters out all elements. No matter your value or type, `ignoreElements()` says "You shall not pass!"

Recall that `newPhotos` emits a `Photo` element each time the user selects a photo. In this section, you are going to add a small thumbnail of the collage in the middle of the screen.

Since you would like to update that icon only once, when the user dismisses the photo dialog fragment, you need to ignore all `Photo` elements and act only on a `completed` event.

`ignoreElements()` is the operator that lets you do just that: it discards all elements of the source sequence and lets through only `complete` or `error`.

Inside `subscribeSelectedPhotos()` at the bottom of the method, add the following:

```
subscriptions.add(newPhotos
    .ignoreElements()
    .subscribe {

    })
```

Before you flesh out the `subscribe` block you need to create a new enum class to represent the thumbnail status.

Add a new file called **ThumbnailStatus.kt**.

Add the following to the new file:

```
enum class ThumbnailStatus {
  READY,
  ERROR
}
```

A thumbnail can be READY, or something may have gone wrong, so it might be in an ERROR state.

Now add a new `MutableLiveData` variable that will notify the `MainActivity` to update the thumbnail image. Add the following `val` to the top of `SharedViewModel`:

```
private val thumbnailStatus = MutableLiveData<ThumbnailStatus>()
```

And add a corresponding getter:

```
fun getThumbnailStatus(): LiveData<ThumbnailStatus> {
    return thumbnailStatus
}
```

Finally, head back to the `subscribeSelectedPhotos` method and finish up the empty new `subscribe` block you added earlier:

```
subscriptions.add(newPhotos
  .ignoreElements()
  .subscribe {
    thumbnailStatus.postValue(ThumbnailStatus.READY)
  }
)
```

This subscription to `newPhotos` will ignore all images and will run the `subscribe` lambda when the user returns to the main activity.

Last but not least, you need to actually consume the new `thumbnailStatus` live data object in `MainActivity`. Add the following to the bottom of the `onCreate` method:

```
viewModel.getThumbnailStatus().observe(this,
    Observer { status ->
      if (status == ThumbnailStatus.READY) {
        thumbnail.setImageDrawable(collageImage.drawable)
      }
    }
)
```

If the thumbnail status is READY, the activity will update the `thumbnail ImageView` with whatever image is in the `collageImage ImageView`.

Run the app. Whenever you come back from selecting a photo, you should see the thumbnail box updated with the current collage:

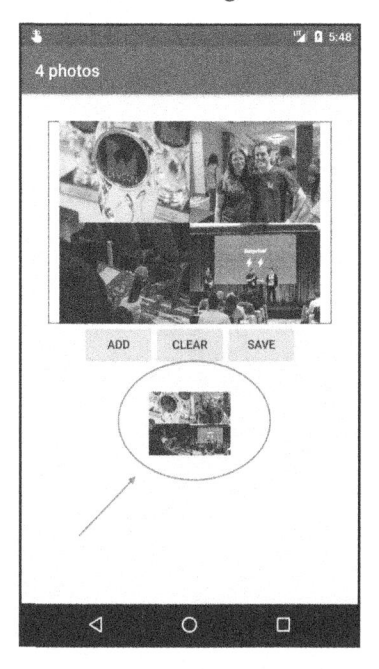

Filtering elements you don't need

Of course, as great as `ignoreElements()` is, sometimes you will need to ignore just *some* of the elements — not all of them.

In those cases, you will use `filter()` to let some elements through and discard others.

For example, you might have noticed that photos in portrait orientation do not fit very well in the collages in **Combinestagram**.

Of course, you could write smarter collage-building code... but in this chapter you're going to discard portrait photos and only include landscapes instead. That's one way to solve the issue. Pretend it's a feature, and not a bug!

Scroll to the top of `subscribeSelectedPhotos` and then add following operator after the `doOnComplete` call:

```
subscriptions.add(newPhotos
  .doOnComplete {
    // ..
  }
  .filter { newImage ->
    val bitmap = BitmapFactory.decodeResource(
    fragment.resources, newImage.drawable)
    bitmap.width > bitmap.height
  }
  .subscribe { photo ->
    // ..
  }
)
```

Now each photo that `newPhotos` emits will have to pass a test before it gets to `subscribe(...)`. Your `filter` operator will check if the width of the image is larger than its height, and if so, it will let it through. Photos in portrait orientation will be discarded.

Run the app and try adding the portrait photo at the bottom of the photo dialog fragment (scroll down if you don't see it). No matter how many times you tap on the photo in portrait orientation, it will not be added to the collage.

Implementing a basic uniqueness filter

Combinestagram, in its current form, has another controversial "feature": you can add the same photo more than once. That doesn't make for very interesting collages, so in this section you'll add some advanced filtering to prevent the user from adding the same photo multiple times.

> **Note:** There are better ways to achieve the required result than what you are going to implement below. It is, however, a great exercise to build a solution with your current RxJava skill set.

In order to check for duplicate collage images, you need a way to keep track of all the images that have been added so far. Luckily, you're using a `BehaviorSubject` with a list of photo objects, and since `BehaviorSubject` exposes its current value you can just check against that!

Add the following code below the `filter` operator you just added:

```
subscriptions.add(newPhotos
  .doOnComplete {
    // ..
  }
  .filter { newImage ->
    // ..
    // 1
  }
  .filter { newImage ->
    // 2
    val photos = imagesSubject.value ?: mutableListOf()
    // 3
    !(photos.map { it.drawable }
      // 4
      .contains(newImage.drawable))
  }
  .subscribe { photo ->
```

```
    // ..
  }
)
```

Here's a breakdown of the above code:

1. You're again using the `filter` operator to filter out duplicates images

2. You're getting the latest list of photos from `imagesSubject`. Since a `BehaviorSubject` could be in a state where an initial value hasn't been supplied, `value` is nullable. If you get a `null` value, which you shouldn't in this app, you'll instead use an empty list.

3. Next up you're calling `map` on the list of photos to turn it into a list of `int` values. Remember that the `int` drawable value on a photo represents a drawable ID that Android can use to fetch a real drawable.

4. Finally, you're checking to see if this list of drawable ids contains the new images drawable id. If it does, you return `false`, so the filter fails.

Run the app. You won't be able to add duplicate images anymore.

Keep taking elements while a condition is met

One of the "best" bugs in **Combinestagram** is that the **Add** button is disabled if you add six photos, which prevents you from adding any more images. But if you are in the photos bottom dialog fragment, you can add as many as you wish. There ought to be a way to limit those, right?

Well, believe it or not, you can easily filter all elements after a certain condition has been met by using the `takeWhile()` operator. You provide a `boolean` condition, and `takeWhile()` discards all elements when this condition evaluates to `false`.

Scroll again towards the top of `subscribeToSelectedPhotos` and add the following operator, again after `doOnComplete`:

```
subscriptions.add(newPhotos
  .doOnComplete {
    // ..
  }
  .takeWhile {
    imagesSubject.value?.size ?: 0 < 6
  }
  .filter { newImage ->
    // ..
  }
```

```
    .filter { newImage ->
      // ..
    }
    .subscribe { photo ->
      // ..
    }
)
```

`takeWhile(...)` will let photos through as long as the total number of images in the collage is less than six. You use the `?:` Elvis operator to default to 0 if `imagesSubject.value?.size` is null.

Run the app and try to add lots of photos to the collage. Once you add six photos, you won't be able to add any more. Mission accomplished!

Improving the photo selector

One common source of bugs in Android applications is what happens when a user quickly taps on a button multiple times. My guess is you've been in an app before where you quickly tapped a button and saw the application display multiple new activities.

A similar bug can happen in **Combinestagram**. If a user quickly taps two photos, the app will add those two photos. That might have been a mistake from the user's perspective. Luckily, you can use RxJava to quickly take care of that pesky issue!

Add the following new operator to the observable chain in `subscribeToSelectedPhotos` right before the actual `subscribe` call:

```
.debounce(250, TimeUnit.MILLISECONDS,
    AndroidSchedulers.mainThread())
```

There's two interesting things happening above. The first is the use of the `debounce` operator, the second is the use of the `AndroidSchedulers.mainThread()` call. Schedulers can be complex, but you'll learn all about them in more detail in a future chapter. For this example all you need to know is that to keep this code executing on the Android `main` thread you need to pass in the `AndroidSchedulers.mainThread()` scheduler.

debounce is an extremely handy operator that limits the number of events that get through to your `subscribe` block. debounce takes in an amount of time, 250 milliseconds in the above example, and makes sure that no new items are emitted until that time window runs out. If a new `next` event is emitted before that time period elapses, the old item will be dropped and the a new timer will start.

Timing operators can be challenging to understand, so here's an example.

Imagine you have an observable that emits A after one second, B after another second, and then C after 5 more seconds. If you were to call `debounce` on that observable and gave it a time period of two seconds you'd only receive two values in your `subscribe` block. You'd receive B after four seconds and then C after one more second. The A would be dropped since the B value came quickly after it.

Go ahead and run the app again. You'll find that if you quickly tap two photos only the latest one will be added. Nice!

Challenge

Challenge: Combinestagram's source code

Your challenge is to notify the user that they've reached the photo limit once they add 6 photos. Here's a few hints on how to proceed with this challenge.

First, you'll need some way to tell the `Activity` class that the photo limit has been reached. A good way to signal that information would be to create a new enum class called `CollageStatus` that could be exposed in a new `LiveData` instance.

Second, you'll need some way to figure out what the current `CollageStatus` is. Luckily you have `imagesSubject`, which you can subscribe to and check to see if 6 images have been selected. If you're feeling fancy, you can use the `share` operator on the `imagesSubject` to practice your sharing skills. Sharing is caring after all! However, since `imagesSubject` is a `Subject`, the `share` operator is a bit redundant so feel free to skip that step.

Key points

- You can share subscriptions to a single observable using `share()`.
- `ignoreElements` comes in handy when you want to only look for stop events.
- Filtering out elements in an observable using `filter` lets you prevent certain elements from coming through the stream, like allowing only landscape and not portrait photos.
- Implementing a **uniqueness** filter can be achieved by combining `filter` with the current value of a `BehaviorSubject`.
- **Debouncing** with the `debounce` operator helps you to get around pesky bugs that occur in apps due to rapid user interactions with the interface.

Where to go from here?

You now have a handle on the first type of RxJava operators we'll examine, filtering operators, and have used them in an Android app.

Next up, you'll learn about our second type of RxJava operators, transforming operators, which let you modify the data being sent through the observable stream.

Chapter 7: Transforming Operators

By Alex Sullivan & Scott Gardner

Before you decided to buy this book and commit to learning RxJava, you might have felt that RxJava was some esoteric library; elusive, yet strangely compelling you to master it. And maybe that reminds you of when you first started learning Android or Kotlin. Now that you're up to Chapter 7, you've come to realize that RxJava isn't magic. It's a carefully constructed API that does a lot of heavy lifting for you and streamlines your code. You should be feeling good about what you've learned so far.

In this chapter, you're going to learn about one of the most important categories of operators in RxJava: transforming operators. You'll use transforming operators all the time, to prepare data coming from an Observable for use by your Subscriber. Once again, there are parallels between transforming operators in RxJava and the Kotlin standard library, such as map() and flatMap(). By the end of this chapter, you'll be transforming everything!

Getting started

This chapter will use a normal IntelliJ project, so go ahead and open the starter project now.

Transforming elements

Observables emit elements individually, but you will frequently want to work with collections. One typical use case is when you're emitting a list of items to show in a `RecyclerView`.

A convenient way to transform an Observable of individual elements into a list of all those elements is by using `toList`.

As depicted in this marble diagram, `toList` will convert an observable sequence of elements into a list of those elements, and emit a `next` event containing that array to the subscribers.

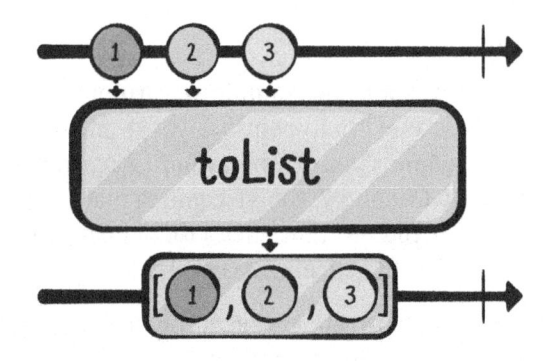

Add this new example to your project:

```
exampleOf("toList") {

  val subscriptions = CompositeDisposable()
  // 1
  val items = Observable.just("A", "B", "C")

  subscriptions.add(
      items
          // 2
          .toList()
          .subscribeBy {
            println(it)
          }
  )
}
```

Here's what you just did:

1. Create an `Observable` of letters.

2. Use `toList` to transform the elements in a list.

A list of the letters is printed.

```
--- Example of: toList ---
[A, B, C]
```

map operator

RxJava's map operator works just like Kotlin's standard map function, except it operates on observables instead of a collection. In the marble diagram, map takes a lambda that multiplies each element by 2.

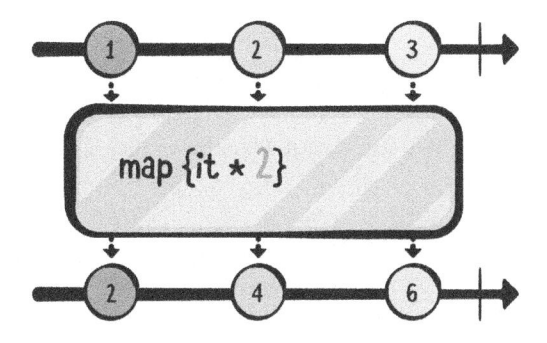

Add this new example to your project:

```
exampleOf("map") {

  val subscriptions = CompositeDisposable()

  subscriptions.add(
      // 1
      Observable.just("M", "C", "V", "I")
          // 2
          .map {
            // 3
            it.romanNumeralIntValue()
          }
          // 4
          .subscribeBy {
            println(it)
          })
}
```

Here's the play-by-play:

1. You create an `Observable` of Roman numerals, in this case `M` which stands for 1000, `C` which stands for 100, `V` which stands for 5, and `I` which stands for 1.

2. You use `map` to transform the Observable, passing in a lambda.

3. You take each of the Roman numeral items emitted by the observable and then use a `romanNumeralIntValue` method to convert it into its corresponding integer value.

4. You subscribe to the Observable to print the transformed values.

> **Note**: The `romanNumeralIntValue` method is defined in the **SupportingCode.kt** file. The implementation is pretty straightforward, but feel free to have a look if you are curious.

Go ahead and run the code. You should see the following output:

```
--- Example of: map ---
1000
100
5
1
```

Using the map operator, you have *mapped* each element of the original Observable to a new value as it passes through the stream.

Transforming inner observables

You may have wondered at some point, "How do I work with observables that are properties of observables?" Get ready to get your mind **blown**.

In the **SupportCode.kt** file in your project, add the following class which you'll use in the upcoming examples:

```
class Student(val score: BehaviorSubject<Int>)
```

`Student` is a class which has a `score` property that is a `BehaviorSubject<Int>`. RxJava includes a few operators in the `flatMap` family that allow you to reach into an Observable and work with its observable properties. You're going to learn how to use the two most common ones here.

> **Note**: A heads up before you begin: These operators have elicited more than their fair share of questions (and groans and moans) from the RxJava's newcomers. They may seem complex at first but you are going to walk through detailed explanations of each one. By the end of the section you'll be ready to put these operators into action with confidence!

flatMap operator

The first one you'll learn about is `flatMap`. The documentation for `flatMap` states that it "Projects each element of an observable sequence to an observable sequence and merges the resulting observable sequences into one observable sequence." Makes perfect sense, right?

Not!

That description, and the following marble diagram, may feel a bit overwhelming at first. Read through the play-by-play explanation that follows, referring back to the marble diagram, and you'll get it.

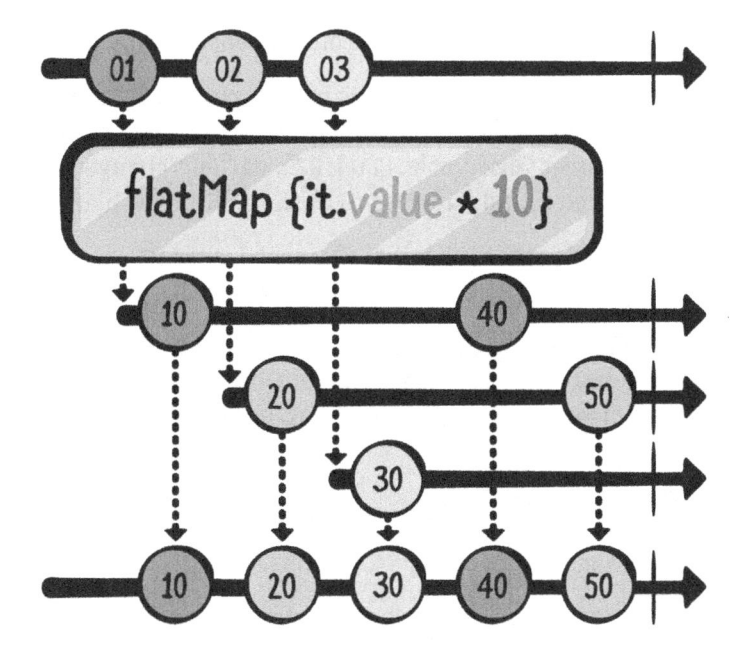

The easiest way to follow what's happening in this marble diagram is to take each path from the source observable (the top line) all the way through to the target Observable. The target Observable is represented by the bottom line, and it delivers elements to the Subscriber. The source observable is a type of object that has a `value` property that *itself* is an observable of type `Int`. To put it another way, the source observable emits observables. The *initial* value of each emitted observable is the number of the object: O1's initial `value` is 1, O2's is 2, and O3's is 3.

Starting with O1, `flatMap` receives the object and reaches in to access its `value` property and multiply it by 10. It then projects the transformed elements from O1 onto a new Observable. This is just what a regular `map` would do.

The first line below `flatMap` on the diagram is just for O1. That Observable is flattened down to the target Observable that will deliver elements to the Subscriber (the bottom line).

Later, O1's `value` property changes to 4, which is not visually represented in the marble diagram (otherwise the diagram would become even more congested).

But the evidence that O1's `value` has changed is that it is transformed to 40 and then projected onto the existing Observable for O1. As with the initial value, it is then flattened down to the target observable. This all happens in a time-linear fashion.

The next value in the source observable, O2, is received by `flatMap`. Now its initial value 2 is transformed to 20, projected onto a new observable for O2, and then flattened down to the target Observable. Later, O2's `value` is changed to 5. It is transformed to 50, projected, and flattened to the target Observable.

Finally, O3 is received by `flatMap`, its initial `value` of 3 is transformed, projected, and flattened.

`flatMap` transforms and projects all the values from all the Observables that it receives. It then flattens them all down to a target Observable. Simple, isn't it? Time to go hands-on with `flatMap` and really see how to use it. Add this example to your project:

```
exampleOf("flatMap") {

  val subscriptions = CompositeDisposable()
  // 1
  val ryan = Student(BehaviorSubject.createDefault(80))
  val charlotte = Student(BehaviorSubject.createDefault(90))
  // 2
  val student = PublishSubject.create<Student>()

  student
```

```
        // 3
        .flatMap { it.score }
        // 4
        .subscribe { println(it) }
        .addTo(subscriptions)
}
```

Here's the play-by-play:

1. You create two instances of Student, ryan and charlotte.
2. You create a source subject of type Student.
3. You use flatMap to reach into the student subject and access its score. You don't modify score in any way. Just pass it through.
4. You print out next event elements in the Subscription.

There's nothing in the console, yet. Add this code to the example:

```
student.onNext(ryan)
```

ryan's score is now printed out.

```
--- Example of: flatMap ---
80
```

Now change ryan's score by adding this code to the example:

```
ryan.score.onNext(85)
```

ryan's new score is printed.

```
--- Example of: flatMap ---
80
85
```

Next, add a different Student instance, charlotte, onto the source subject by adding the following code:

```
student.onNext(charlotte)
```

`flatMap` does its thing and `charlotte`'s `score` is printed.

```
--- Example of: flatMap ---
80
85
90
```

Here's where it gets interesting. Change `ryan`'s score by adding this line of code:

```
ryan.score.onNext(95)
```

`ryan`'s new `score` is printed.

```
--- Example of: flatMap ---
80
85
90
95
```

This is because `flatMap` keeps up with each and every Observable it creates, one for each element added onto the source observable.

Now change `charlotte`'s `score` by adding the following code, just to verify that `flatMap` monitors both Observables and projects the changes:

```
charlotte.score.onNext(100)
```

Sure enough, her new `score` is printed out.

```
--- Example of: flatMap ---
80
85
90
95
100
```

To recap, `flatMap` keeps projecting changes from each Observable. There will be times when you want this behavior and there will be times when you only want to keep up with the latest element in the source observable. Luckily, RxJava has an operator just for that situation called `switchMap`.

switchMap operator

According to the documentation, `switchMap`: "Applies the given io.reactivex.functions.Function to each item emitted by a reactive source, where that function returns a reactive source, and emits the items emitted by the most recently projected of these reactive sources."

So basically, `switchMap` takes a function which returns some type of reactive source (a `Completable`, `Observable`, `Single` and so on) and applies that function to each item emitted by some source observable. The observable returned by `switchMap` then emits only the items from whatever reactive source was the last emitted. Take a look at the following marble diagram:

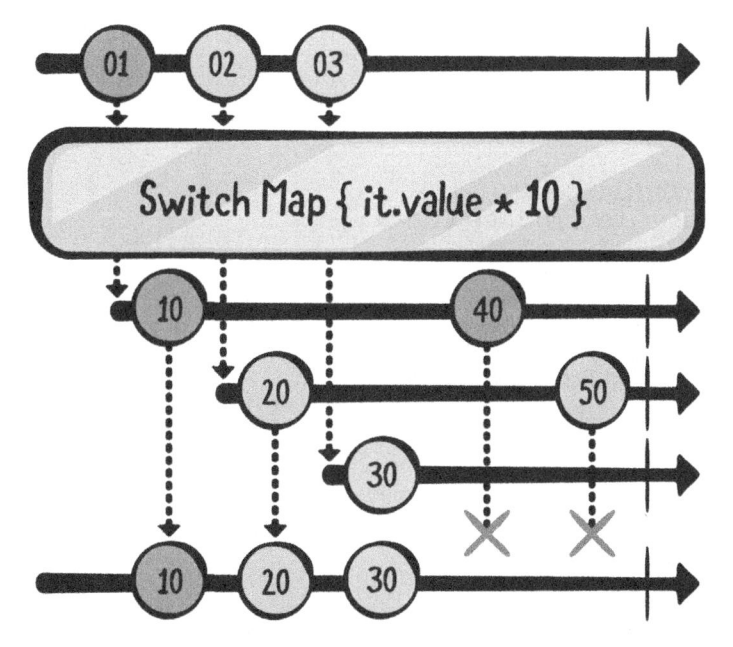

The top line represents the source observable that emits three separate items - 01, 02, and 03.

01 is received by switchMap, it transforms its value by a factor of 10, projects it onto a new observable for 01, and flattens it down to the target observable. Just like before.

But then `switchMap` receives 02 and does its thing, switching to 02's observable because it's now the latest. When 01 emits a value that is transformed to 40, that value does not get emitted by the target observable, since it has been *switched* to 02.

The process repeats when O3 is received by `switchMap`: it switches to the O3 stream and ignores the previous one (O2). So when O2 emits a value that is transformed to 50, the 50 is not emitted by the overall stream.

In summary, the result of using `switchMap` is that the target observable only receives elements from the latest source observable that has emitted. It's ok if things are still confusing—`flatMap` and `switchMap` tend to be some of the hardest operators for people to understand. But another example will help clear things up!

Add the following example to your project, which is a clone of the previous example except for changing `flatMap` to `switchMap`:

```
exampleOf("switchMap") {

  val ryan = Student(BehaviorSubject.createDefault(80))
  val charlotte = Student(BehaviorSubject.createDefault(90))

  val student = PublishSubject.create<Student>()

  student
      .switchMap { it.score }
      .subscribe { println(it) }

  student.onNext(ryan)

  ryan.score.onNext(85)

  student.onNext(charlotte)

  ryan.score.onNext(95)

  charlotte.score.onNext(100)
}
```

Now run the example. You should see the following output:

```
--- Example of: switchMap---
80
85
90
100
```

The only thing that's "missing" here compared to the `flatMap` example is that the last call to the ryan subject, i.e. `ryan.score.onNext(95)`, isn't being emitted. That's because the `charlotte` subject has already emitted and now the `switchMap` only emits its values! Since `charlotte` is a `BehaviorSubject` it will immediately emit its latest value, which is 90 in this case.

So you may be wondering when would you use `flatMap` or `switchMap`? Probably the most common use case for using `switchMap` is with networking operations. You will go through examples of this later in the book, but for a simple example, imagine that you're implementing a type-ahead search. As the user types each letter, e.g. k, o, t, l, i, n, you'll want to execute a new search and ignore results from the previous one. `switchMap` is how you do that.

Observing events

There may be times when you want to convert an Observable into an Observable of its events. One typical scenario where this is useful is when you do not have control over an Observable that has Observable properties, and you want to handle error events to avoid terminating outer sequences. Don't worry, it will get clearer in a couple of moments, just hang in there.

materialize operator

The `materialize` operator can do exactly that. It takes a normal Observable and turns it into an Observable that emits **Notification** objects that wrap the event type - whether it's onNext, onComplete or onError.

Enter this new example into the project:

```
exampleOf("materialize/dematerialize") {

  val subscriptions = CompositeDisposable()

  val ryan = Student(BehaviorSubject.createDefault(80))
  val charlotte = Student(BehaviorSubject.createDefault(90))

  val student = BehaviorSubject.create<Student>(ryan)
}
```

This code should look pretty familiar—just like before you're creating two new Student objects, ryan and charlotte, each of which contain a BehaviorSubject with an initial value. You're then also creating a BehaviorSubject named student of type Student with the initial value of ryan.

Similar to the previous two examples, you want to subscribe to the inner `score` property of `Student`. Add this code to the example:

```
// 1
val studentScore = student
    .switchMap { it.score }
// 2
subscriptions.add(studentScore
    .subscribe {
      println(it)
    })
// 3
ryan.score.onNext(85)

ryan.score.onError(RuntimeException("Error!"))

ryan.score.onNext(90)
// 4
student.onNext(charlotte)
```

Continuing this example, you:

1. Create a `studentScore` observable using `switchMap` to reach into the `student` Observable and access its `scoreObservable` property.

2. Subscribe and print out each `score` as it's emitted.

3. Add a score, an error, and another score onto the current student.

4. Add the second student `charlotte` onto the `student` Observable. Because you used `switchMap`, this will switch to this new student and subscribe to her `score`.

The error you added is unhandled. As a result, the `studentScore` observable terminates, and you get a very gnarly stack trace in the console.

```
--- Example of: materialize and dematerialize ---
80
85
io.reactivex.exceptions.OnErrorNotImplementedException: Error!
```

Using the `materialize` operator, you can wrap each event emitted by an Observable *in* a `Notification`.

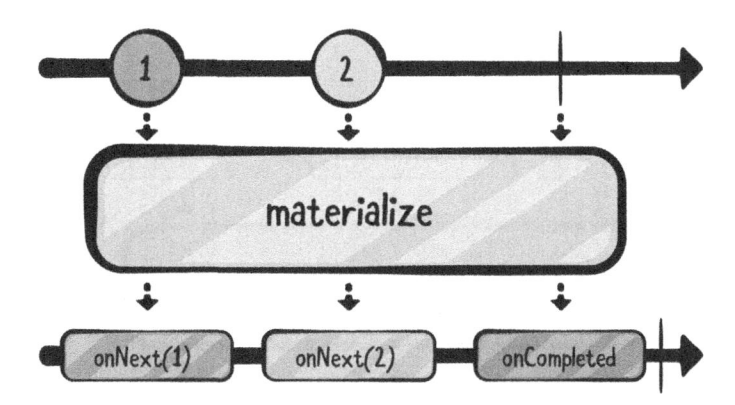

In the marble diagram, `Int` elements emitted by an observable are transformed to `Notification<Int>` values when emitted.

Change the `studentScore` implementation to the following:

```
val studentScore = student
    .switchMap { it.score.materialize() }
```

If you check the type of `studentScore` you'll see it is now an `Observable<Notification<Int>>`. And the Subscription to it now emits notifications. The error still causes the `studentScore` to terminate, but not the outer `student` Observable.

This way, when you switch to the new student, its `score` is successfully received and printed.

```
--- Example of: materialize/dematerialize ---
OnNextNotification[80]
OnNextNotification[85]
OnErrorNotification[java.lang.RuntimeException: Error!]
OnNextNotification[90]
```

However, now you're dealing with `Notifications`, not the `Int` elements of the original Observables.

dematerialize operator

That's where `dematerialize` comes in. It will convert a materialized Observable back into its original form.

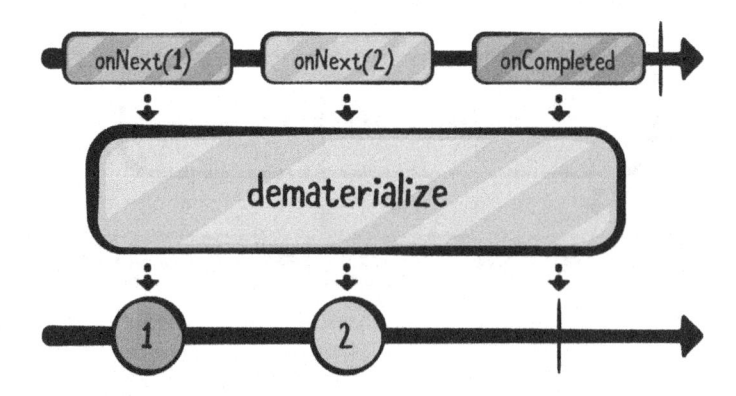

In the marble diagram, `Notification<Int>` values are transformed back into `Int` elements.

Change the Subscription in the example to the following:

```
studentScore
    // 1
    .filter {
      if (it.error != null) {
        println(it.error)
        false
      } else {
        true
      }
    }
    // 2
    .dematerialize { it }
    .subscribe {
      println(it)
    }
    .addTo(subscriptions)
```

Wrapping things up:

1. You print and filter out any errors.

2. You use `dematerialize` to return the `studentScore` Observable to its original form, emitting scores and stop events, not notifications of scores and stop events. Since this `Observable` is emitting `Notifications` directly you're simply returning it to dematerialize.

As a result, your `student` Observable is protected by errors on its inner `score` Observable. The error is printed and ryan's `score` Observable is terminated, so adding a new score onto him does nothing.

But when you add `charlotte` onto the `student` subject, her score is printed.

```
--- Example of: materialize/dematerialize ---
80
85
java.lang.RuntimeException: Error!
90
```

Challenge

Challenge: Sending alpha-numeric characters

In Chapter 5's challenge, you created a phone number lookup using filtering operators. You added the code necessary to look up a contact based on a 10-digit number entered by the user.

Your goal for this challenge is to modify the implementation to be able to take *letters* as well, and convert them to their corresponding number based on a standard phone keypad (abc is 2, def is 3, and so on).

The starter project includes a helper lambda to do the conversion:

```
val convert: (String) -> Int = { value ->
  val number = try {
    value.toInt()
  } catch (e: NumberFormatException) {
    val keyMap = mapOf(
        "abc" to 2, "def" to 3, "ghi" to 4, "jkl" to 5,
        "mno" to 6, "pqrs" to 7, "tuv" to 8, "wxyz" to 9)

    keyMap.filter { it.key.contains(value.toLowerCase()) }
```

```
        .map { it.value }.first()
  }
  if (number < 10) {
    number
  } else {
    // RxJava 2 does not allow null in stream, so return
    // sentinel value
    sentinel
  }
}
```

Since RxJava 3 doesn't allow `null` in an Observable stream, we will use a **sentinel** value of -1 to mark a number that exceeds 10 digits.

And there are lambdas to format and "dial" the contact if found (really, just print it out):

```
val format: (List<Int>) -> String = { inputs ->
  val phone = inputs.map { it.toString() }.toMutableList()
  phone.add(3, "-")
  phone.add(7, "-")
  phone.joinToString("")
}

val dial: (String) -> String = { phone ->
  val contact = contacts[phone]
  if (contact != null) {
    "Dialing $contact ($phone)..."
  } else {
    "Contact not found"
  }
}
```

These lambda values allow you to move the logic out of the Subscription, where it really doesn't belong. So what's left to do then? You'll use multiple `maps` to perform each transformation along the way. You'll use `skipWhile` just like you did in Chapter 5 to skip 0s at the beginning.

The starter project also includes code to test your solution. Just add your solution right below the comment `// Add your code here`.

Key points

- **Transforming operators** let you transform observable items from their original type to another type or value.

- You can use `toList` to turn a normal observable into an observable that emits a single list.

- The `map` operator will transform individual elements in an observable to some other value or type.

- You can use `flatMap` to flatten an observable stream of observables into one stream of items.

- Similarly, `switchMap` will also flatten a stream of observables, but this time only listening to the observable in the source that has most recently emitted.

- You use `materialize` to make observables emit notifications of events rather than the events themselves, and `dematerialize` to transform from the notification type back to the original type.

Where to go from here?

Just like for the earlier chapters on filtering operators, you'll want to gain experience using transforming operators in a real Android app project. That's up next!

Chapter 8: Transforming Operators in Practice

By Alex Sullivan & Marin Todorov

In the previous chapter, you learned about the real workhorses behind reactive programming with RxJava: the map and flatMap dynamic duo. Of course, those aren't the only two operators you can use to transform Observables, but a program can rarely do without using those two at least few times. The more experience you gain with these two, the better (and shorter) your code will be.

You've already gotten to play around with transforming operators in the safety of an Kotlin project, so hopefully you're ready to take on a real-life project. Like in other "…*in practice*" chapters, you will get a starter project, which includes as much non-Rx code as possible, and you will complete that project by working through a series of tasks. In the process, you will learn more about map and flatMap, and in which situations you should use them in your code.

> **Note**: In this chapter, you will need to understand the basics of transforming operators in RxJava. If you haven't worked through Chapter 7, "Transforming Operators," do that first and then come back to this chapter.

Without further ado, it's time to get this show started!

Getting started with GitFeed

I wonder what the latest activity is on the RxKotlin repository? In this chapter, you'll build a project to tell you this exact thing.

The project you are going to work on in this chapter, named **GitFeed**, displays the activity of a GitHub repository, such as all the latest likes, forks or comments. To get started with GitFeed, open the starter project for this chapter.

In the chapter, you'll use `Retrofit`, a networking library, and `Gson`, a JSON serialization library. `Retrofit` has a several nifty utilities that allow it to work particularly well with RxJava.

If you're not familiar with `Retrofit`, it's a simple networking library that allows you to declare your API in an `interface` and instantiate that API using `Retrofits` magical annotation processor. You'll see more about it in Chapter 18, "Retrofit".

Run the app. You'll see the following blank screen:

Start off by opening the app module **build.gradle** file and looking at the Retrofit and Gson dependencies:

```
def retrofit_version = "2.9.0"
implementation "com.squareup.retrofit2:retrofit:
$retrofit_version"
implementation "com.squareup.retrofit2:adapter-
rxjava3:$retrofit_version"
implementation "com.squareup.retrofit2:converter-gson:
$retrofit_version"
implementation "com.squareup.okhttp3:logging-interceptor:4.3.1"
```

There are four dependencies to note:

1. The actual Retrofit dependency.
2. An adapter that Retrofit provides that makes working with RxJava seamless.
3. A converter that allows you to use Gson.
4. An interceptor from the **OkHttp** library (on which Retrofit is built) that allows you to easily log all network output.

Fetching data from the web

Open **GithubService.kt**. All that's there now is a companion object `create` method that builds up an instance of the `GitHubApi` Retrofit interface. There's no actual networking code in here—yet.

Add the following method in the interface. Make sure the method is defined outside the companion object.

```
@GET("repos/ReactiveX/{repo}/events") // 1
fun fetchEvents(@Path("repo") repo: String) // 2
    : Observable<Response<List<AnyDict>>> // 3
```

Take care to import the `Observable` from the ReactiveX package and the `Response` class from Retrofit.

If you're not familiar with Retrofit, the above code can be intimidating. Here's a breakdown:

1. Retrofit allows you to use HTTP method type annotations on your methods to specify what type of HTTP action should be taken (POST, PUT, GET, etc). You also specify the path to the endpoint in this header. You can even add variables in the path, which is what {repo} is doing in this example.

2. After the annotation you create the actual method. In the method annotation you accept the name of the repo you want to fetch events for. By using the @Path annotation on the repo parameter, you're telling Retrofit that the passed in value should replace the {repo} variable you specified in the method annotation.

3. Retrofit integrates very nicely with RxJava. By specifying the return type as an Observable, Retrofit will create your network call in a way that allows the result to be propagated out via an Observable. Pretty nifty! The Response type is a Retrofit type that contains all the information about your network call, like the status code and any errors. The last interesting thing about this code is the AnyDict type. AnyDict is a simple typealias for a Map<String, Any>. In typical usage you'd specify a concrete modal class here instead of a map, but for this app a simple map is fine.

> **Note:** Normally it makes more sense for a API function to use the Single type instead of Observable. This is because REST API requests can only respond once. However this complicates the code later in this chapter, so here we use Observable for simplicity.

Now, navigate to MainViewModel and add the following line in the empty fetchEvents method:

```
val apiResponse = gitHubApi.fetchEvents(repo)
```

You're using the fetchEvents method you defined earlier in GitHubService to get an Observable<Response<List<AnyDict>>>, that is, an Observable of Response objects, each of which contains a List<AnyDict> representing the list of things that happened on the provided repo.

Transforming the response

It's time to start doing some transformations! And you'll mix in some filtering operators too.

Add the following below the `apiResponse` declaration:

```
apiResponse.filter { response ->
  (200..300).contains(response.code())
}
```

You're using the `filter` operator to filter out any response whose status code isn't in the 200 to 300 range — i.e., any response that isn't successful. In a production app you'd want to also handle any error that might occur, but for our purposes ignoring error codes is fine.

> **Note**: You can read more about HTTP response codes in this *Wikipedia* article, List of HTTP status codes https://en.wikipedia.org/wiki/List_of_HTTP_status_codes.

Now continue the chain by adding the following `map` call:

```
.map { response ->
  response.body()!!
}
```

Remember that `map` transforms the item emitted by your Observable. In the above code, you're transforming the `Response` object into a `List<AnyDict>?` by using the body method on `Response`. It's safe to use `!!` here but take care that there are times when the body of a request is `null`.

Continue the chain with the following `filter` call:

```
.filter { objects ->
  objects.isNotEmpty()
}
```

You're filtering out any response that provides an empty list of GitHub actions. Last but not least, add the following `map` call:

```
.map { objects ->
  objects.mapNotNull { Event.fromAnyDict(it) }
}
```

In this block, you're converting the `AnyDict` objects into `Events`, which are model objects that represents GitHub API events. The companion object `fromAnyDict` method on `Event` just converts from an `AnyDict` into an `Event`. That code isn't particularly interesting so it's already been written in the starter project.

Note that you're using the `mapNotNull` method on `List` that the Kotlin Standard library provides because `AnyDict` could contain `null` values if the API returns something we're not expecting.

> **Note**: In a production app, you'd be able to skip a few of these steps by having `Retrofit` directly convert the API response into an `Event` object. However, leaving that out helps demonstrate using the map operator and makes the Rx chain more substantial, which is a great way to learn about these operators.

Processing the response

Finish this chain up with the following code:

```
// 1
.subscribeOn(Schedulers.io())
// 2
.observeOn(AndroidSchedulers.mainThread())
.subscribeBy(
    // 3
    onNext = { events -> processEvents(events) },
    // 4
    onError = { error ->
      println("Events Error ::: ${error.message}") }
)
// 5
.addTo(disposables)
```

There's a bit of magic in this code, so let's see what it does:

1. You use `subscribeOn` to make sure the networking code happens off the `main` thread.

2. You use `observeOn` to get the results in `subscribeBy` on the `main` thread.

3. In the onNext lambda you're passing the events over to the processEvents method. processEvents takes the first 50 events provided by the API and sends them over to MainActivity via the eventLiveData object. Just like in the **Combinestagram** app from earlier chapters, the MainActivity class observes the eventLiveData object and updates its list adapter when it gets new items.

4. In the onError block, you're simply printing out the error. Again, in a production app you'd want to handle this error in a smart handy way, but for now this will do.

5. Finally, you're adding the disposable that is created by calling subscribeBy into a handy CompositeDisposable object that's already defined. You're using the RxKotlin extension function addTo that lets you add the disposable to the composite as part of the operator chain.

Build and run the app. You should see a healthy list of GitHub actions for the RxKotlin repo.

Persisting objects to disk

It'd be great to be able to persist these GitHub actions to app storage, so you can view them without a network connection. Ideally, the app should first load events up from the local database, then show those saved events in the app `RecyclerView`. In parallel, the app can fetch new events, show them, and finally save them off to be loaded next time the user opens the app.

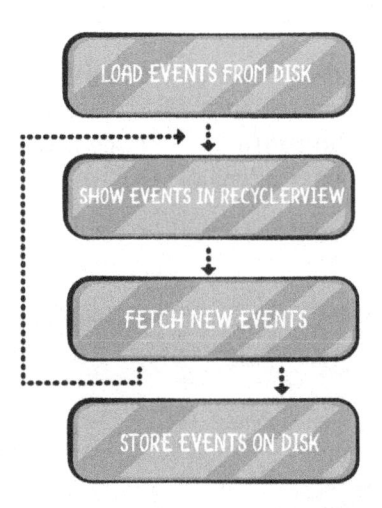

Add the following line to save the actions at the bottom of the `processEvents` method in `MainViewModel`:

```
EventsStore.saveEvents(events)
```

`EventStore.saveEvents` is a simple method that uses `Gson` to convert a list of `Event` instances into JSON and then saves those events to a file. Again, that code is straightforward enough that it's not worth spending time on it.

Now that you're saving events in the `processEvents` method, you can read the events and send them off to the Activity before the network provides a fresh set of events. Add the following to the top of `fetchEvents`:

```
eventLiveData.value = EventsStore.readEvents()
```

`EventsStore.readEvents` predictably pulls any saved events from the device storage and returns them.

You're now serving up a list of events saved to the device. To test this new feature, first uninstall the app. Then build and run the app again. After the items are pulled down from the server the events will be saved to the disk. Run the app once more, and you should see events instantly loaded on screen.

You may not see any new events, since what was saved could be whatever the API has to offer at this point in time, but the events should be loaded nice and quick.

Adding a last-modified header

GitFeed is looking pretty good, but there's still a few issues to iron out. One issue is that the app is being very wasteful when it comes to using a user's network data. Even if the app already has events saved, it requests all of the events every time it makes a network request.

That's about to change. You're going to update the app to only download events that it hasn't yet seen. And in the process you're going to see flatMap used in a real app. Riveting, right?!

First, head over to GithubService and replace the fetchEvents method with the following:

```
@GET("repos/ReactiveX/{repo}/events")
fun fetchEvents(
  @Path("repo") repo: String,
  @Header("If-Modified-Since") lastModified: String
): Observable<Response<List<AnyDict>>>
```

Notice that fetchEvents now takes a new parameter, a String representing the last date that the app accessed the API. Instead of being a Path parameter like repo, lastModified will be added as a header parameter. Specifically, the GitHub API utilizes the If-Modified-Since header to specify the last time the client tried to access that resource. Retrofit exposes the @Header annotation to specify that an argument should be added as a header value. Retrofit truly is an amazing library!

Open up MainViewModel. You should now notice that the line declaring the apiResponse variable has an error in it. That's because it's not passing in the lastModified value. Add the following code, replacing the apiResponse line:

```
val lastModified = EventsStore.readLastModified()

val apiResponse = gitHubApi.fetchEvents(repo,
  lastModified?.trim() ?: "")
```

You're fetching the `lastModified` value and passing it through to the `fetchEvents` method, making sure to trim any whitespace and defaulting to an empty string if there is no last-modified value. `EventsStore.readLastModified` hides some boilerplate around reading a last modified value from a text file you'll write to next.

Next up you'll want to reach into the `Response` object you get when you make the `fetchEvents` call and save the last modified value, which exists as a header object.

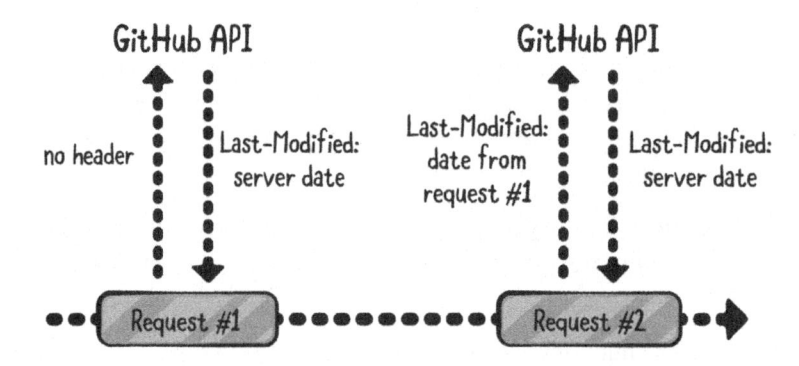

You have a few options, here. You could add a `doOnNext` operator to the Rx chain in `fetchEvents` and try to save off the last-modified value there. But that adds mutation into the Rx chain and muddies the purpose of that individual `Observable`.

Alternatively, you could make another call to the API and create a new Rx chain to get that last-modified value. That feels a bit better, but making a whole new API call is incredibly wasteful.

You may now be wondering: "Why not just use the `share` operator?"

THAT'S A GREAT IDEA!

Update the `apiResponse` value one more time, this time utilizing the `share` operator to share the API response:

```
val apiResponse =
  gitHubApi.fetchEvents(repo, lastModified?.trim() ?: "")
    .share()
```

Now that you have a shared Observable, you can start building up a new Rx chain to get and save that last modified value.

Add the following code below the previous Rx chain:

```
apiResponse
  .filter { response ->
    (200 until 300).contains(response.code())
  }
```

You're again filtering out any failed calls.

Now you want to pull the last-modified value out of the Response object. Response exposes its headers, and the GitHub API utilizes the Last-Modified header to send down the last-modified date. Unfortunately, it's **nullable** and RxJava doesn't allow you to emit null values.

Again, there are a few options for how to handle this situation. One would be to create a wrapper class that itself either contains null or the last-modified value, and then use the map operator to map from Response to that new wrapper class. There's an Optional type in Java just for this kind of situation. But that's a lot of boilerplate just to get around a possibly nullable value.

Instead, you can use flatMap!

Add the following to the new chain:

```
.flatMap { response ->
  // 1
  val value = response.headers().get("Last-Modified")
  if (value == null) {
    // 2
    Observable.empty()
  } else {
    // 3
    Observable.just(value)
  }
}
```

Since `flatMap` is so tricky, here's a breakdown of the above code:

1. Pull the last-modified value out of the `Response` objects headers. This value could be `null`.

2. If the value is `null`, return an empty `Observable`. If there's no last-modified value then there's nothing left for this Observable to do, so returning an empty Observable will just finish the chain.

3. If the value is present, return a new `Observable` that contains the last-modified value. This new `Observable` will now emit that last-modified value and finish. Perfect!

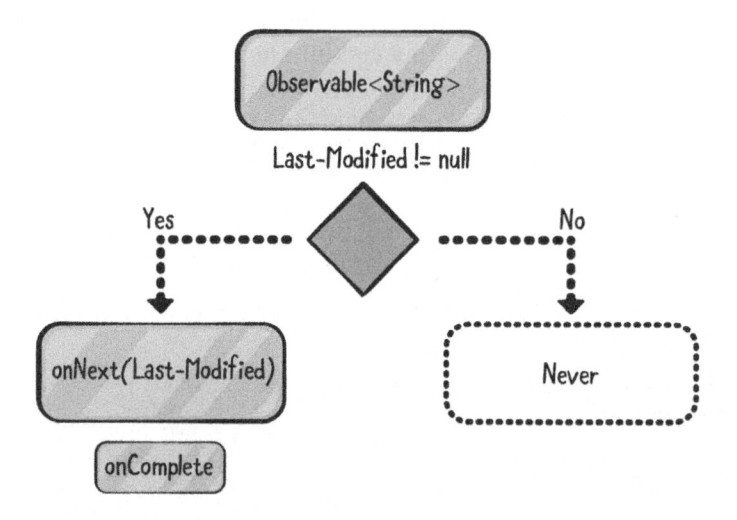

You've now got an `Observable` that's emitting the last modified value from the API. All that's left is to subscribe to it and save off that value. Add the following code to finish off the chain:

```
.subscribeOn(Schedulers.io())
.observeOn(AndroidSchedulers.mainThread())
.subscribeBy(
  onNext = { EventsStore.saveLastModified(it) },
  onError = { error ->
    println("Last Modified Error ::: ${error.message}") }
)
.addTo(disposables)
```

You're again using a background scheduler to do the actual work of making the API call and the `main` thread scheduler to run the `subscribeBy` code.

In the `onNext` lambda, you're saving off the last modified value. In the `onError` lambda you're simply logging an error.

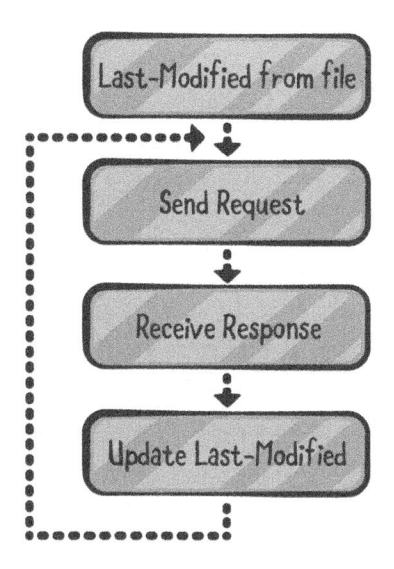

Challenge

Challenge: Fetch top repos and spice up the feed

In this challenge, you will go through one more `map`/`flatMap` exercise. You will spice up **GitFeed** a little bit: instead of always fetching the latest activity for a given repo like RxKotlin, you will find the top trending Kotlin repositories and display their combined activity in the app.

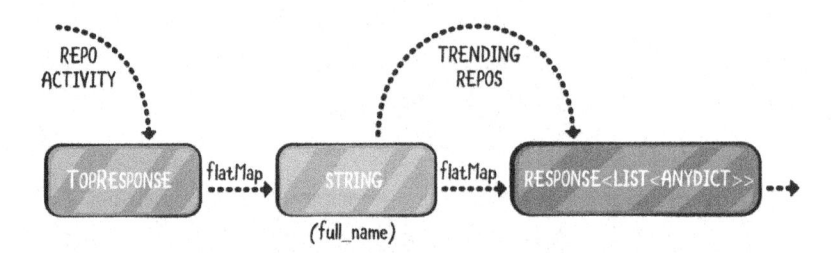

At first sight, this might look like a lot of work, but in the end you'll find it's only about a dozen lines of code.

Here's the general structure of the `flatMap` that you'll use:

```
apiResponse
  .flatMap { response: TopResponse ->
    if (response.items == null) {
      Observable.empty()
    } else {
      Observable.fromIterable(
        response.items.map { it["full_name"] as String })
    }
  }
```

To get you started, here's the `Retrofit` code you'll need to add to `GithubService` to fetch the top Kotlin repos and their associated activities:

```
@GET("repos/{repo}/events")
fun fetchEvents(@Path("repo", encoded = true) repo: String)
    : Observable<Response<List<AnyDict>>>

@GET("search/repositories?q=language:kotlin&per_page=5")
fun fetchTopKotlinRepos(): Observable<TopResponse>
```

You'll also want to create a new `TopResponse` class to handle the top Kotlin repositories. It should look like this:

```
class TopResponse(val items: List<AnyDict>?)
```

You'll use another `flatMap` to convert the JSON `items` value you get in the `Response` into a list of repo names using the `full_name` property of each repo. You'll want to check that `items` is not `null`, or else return an empty `Observable` — just as you've done before.

If you'd like to play around some more, you can sort the combined list of events by date and other interesting ways. What other types of sorting or filtering can you come up with?

When you've completed the challenge, your results will look something like this:

If you wrapped up this challenge successfully, you can consider yourself a transformation pro! Oh... if you could only use a map in real life to turn lead into gold, that would really be something! But data transformation with RxJava comes a close second — and that's great, too.

> **Note**: The GitHub JSON API is a great tool to play with. You can grab a bunch of very interesting data such as trending repositories, public activity, and more. If you are interested to learn more, visit the API homepage at https://developer.github.com/v3/.

Key points

- GitHub has a nice API to play with. It's a good place to experiment with transforming operators and Rx in general.

- Retrofit and Gson are a great networking duo for Android. The fact that Retrofit can return `Observables` and `Singles` makes it a good choice for learning Rx.

- Transforming operators can be chained in a flexible way. Experiment without fear! Sometimes, there's a better way of chaining them to get the result you want.

- Always handle errors in network requests to prevent crashes. There can be a number of errors that are out of control. Don't forget to use the `onError` case to prevent the app from crashing with an exception.

- You can easily filter out HTTP Status codes with Rx. Success codes are in the 2xx range, others status codes are mostly errors.

- Network requests in Android must be subscribed to on a background thread and observed on the `main` thread.

- `map` and `flatMap` let you transform the data in a server response to something that the app understands.

Where to go from here?

You've now seen filtering and transforming operators in action in an Android app. There's one more type of operator that we'll consider in detail: combining operators. So, back to IntelliJ in the next chapter to begin your look at how to use combining operators in RxJava.

Chapter 9: Combining Operators

By Alex Sullivan & Florent Pillet

In earlier chapters, you learned how to create, filter and transform Observable sequences. RxJava filtering and transformation operators behave much like Kotlin's standard collection operators. You got a glimpse into the true power of RxJava with flatMap, the workhorse operator that lets you perform a lot of tasks with very little code.

This chapter will show you several different ways to assemble sequences, and how to combine the data within each sequence. Some operators you'll work with are very similar to Kotlin collection functions. They help combine elements from asynchronous sequences, just as you do with Kotlin lists.

Getting started

This chapter uses IntelliJ to demonstrate some of the concepts. It also uses the exampleOf method you've become so familiar with. Open the starter project and run the **Main.kt** file. It's empty, so you won't see any output other than a "process finished" message in the run tab.

RxJava is all about working with and mastering asynchronous sequences. But you'll often need to make order out of chaos! There is a lot you can accomplish by combining Observables.

Prefixing and concatenating

One of the more obvious needs when working with Observables is to guarantee that an observer receives an initial value. There are situations where you'll need the "current state" first. Good use cases for this are "current location" and "network connectivity status." These are some Observables you'll want to prefix with the current state.

Using startWith

The diagram below should make it clear what this operator does:

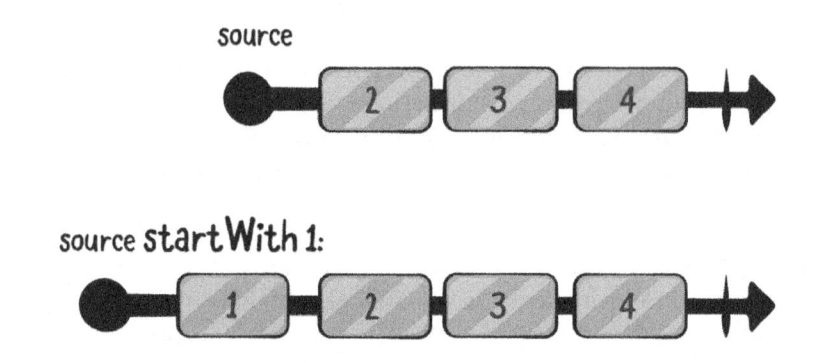

Add the following code to the `main()` function:

```
exampleOf("startWith") {

  val subscriptions = CompositeDisposable()
  // 1
  val missingNumbers = Observable.just(3, 4, 5)
  // 2
  val completeSet =
    missingNumbers.startWithIterable(listOf(1, 2))

  completeSet
    .subscribe { number ->
      println(number)
    }
    .addTo(subscriptions)
}
```

The `startWithIterable()` and `startWithItem()` operators prefix an Observable sequence with the given initial value. This value must be of the same type as the Observable elements. For `startWithItem()`, this is a single item, while `startWithIterable()` can be a list of initial items that will the stream will emit individually.

Here's what's going on in the code above:

1. Create an Observable of numbers.
2. Create an Observable starting with the missing values 1 and 2, then continue with the original sequence of numbers.

Don't get fooled by the position of the `startWithIterable()` operator! Although you chain it to the `missingNumbers` stream, the Observable it creates emits the initial values, followed by the values from the original `missingNumbers` Observable.

Run the code and look at the run area in the project to confirm this:

```
--- Example of: startWith ---
1
2
3
4
5
```

This is a handy tool you'll use in many situations. It fits in well with the deterministic nature of RxJava and guarantees observers they'll get an initial value right away, and any updates later.

Using concat

As it turns out, the `startWith` operators are a simple variant of the more general `concat` family of operators. Your initial value is a stream of one or more elements, to which RxJava appends the sequence that `startWith` chains to. The `Observable.concat` static function chains two sequences.

Have a look:

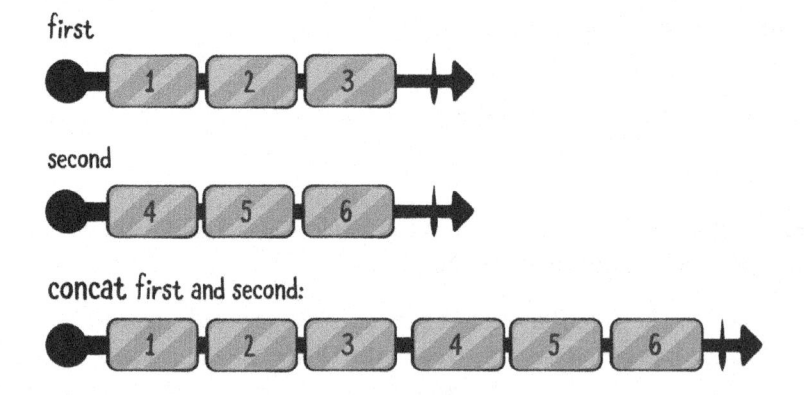

first

second

concat first and second:

Add this code to the `main()` function:

```
exampleOf("concat") {

  val subscriptions = CompositeDisposable()
  // 1
  val first = Observable.just(1, 2, 3)
  val second = Observable.just(4, 5, 6)
  // 2
  Observable.concat(first, second)
    .subscribe { number ->
      println(number)
    }
    .addTo(subscriptions)
}
```

Written this way, the concatenation order is more obvious to the untrained reader than when using one of the `startWith` operators. Run the example to see elements from the first stream: 1 2 3, followed by elements of the second stream: 4 5 6.

The `Observable.concat` static function takes a `vararg` number of Observables (i.e. an array). It subscribes to the first Observable of the collection, relays its elements until it completes, then moves to the next one. The process repeats until it uses all the Observables in the collection. If at any point an inner Observable emits an error, the concatenated Observable in turns emits the error and terminates.

Using concatWith

Another way to append sequences together is the `concatWith` operator (an instance method of `Observable`, not a class method). Add this code to the function:

```
exampleOf("concatWith") {
  val subscriptions = CompositeDisposable()

  val germanCities =
    Observable.just("Berlin", "Münich", "Frankfurt")
  val spanishCities =
    Observable.just("Madrid", "Barcelona", "Valencia")

  germanCities
    .concatWith(spanishCities)
    .subscribe { number ->
      println(number)
    }
    .addTo(subscriptions)
}
```

This variant applies to an existing Observable. It waits for the source Observable to complete, then subscribes to the parameter Observable. Aside from instantiation, it works just like `Observable.concat()`. Run the code and check the output; you'll see a list of German cities followed by a list of Spanish cities.

> **Note:** Observable sequences are strongly typed. You can only concatenate sequences whose elements are of the same type!
>
> If you try to concatenate sequences of different types, brace yourself for compiler errors. The Kotlin compiler knows when one sequence is an `Observable<String>` and the other an `Observable<Int>`, so it will not allow you to mix them up.

Using concatMap

A final operator of interest is `concatMap`, closely related to `flatMap` which you learned about in Chapter 7, "Transforming Operators." The lambda you pass to `flatMap` returns an `Observable` sequence which is subscribed to, and the emitted Observables are all merged. `concatMap` guarantees that each sequence produced by the lambda will run to completion before the next is subscribed to. `concatMap` is therefore a handy way to guarantee sequential order.

Try it in the project:

```
exampleOf("concatMap") {
  val subscriptions = CompositeDisposable()
  // 1
  val countries = Observable.just("Germany", "Spain")
  // 2
  val observable = countries
    .concatMap {
    when (it) {
      "Germany" ->
        Observable.just("Berlin", "München", "Frankfurt")
      "Spain" ->
        Observable.just("Madrid", "Barcelona", "Valencia")
      else -> Observable.empty<String>()
      }
    }
  // 3
  observable
    .subscribe { city ->
      println(city)
    }
    .addTo(subscriptions)
}
```

This example:

1. Creates an Observable of two country names.

2. Uses `concatMap` to produce another Observable depending on what country name it receives.

3. Outputs the full sequence of cities for a given country before starting to consider the next one.

Run the project. You should see this output:

```
--- Example of: concatMap ---
Berlin
München
Frankfurt
Madrid
Barcelona
Valencia
```

The German cities are all printed out, followed by the cities from Spain.

Now that you know how to *append* sequences together using the various concatenating operators, it's time to move on to *combining* elements from multiple sequences.

Merging

RxJava offers several ways to combine sequences. The easiest to start with is merge.

Using merge

Can you picture what merge does from the diagram below?

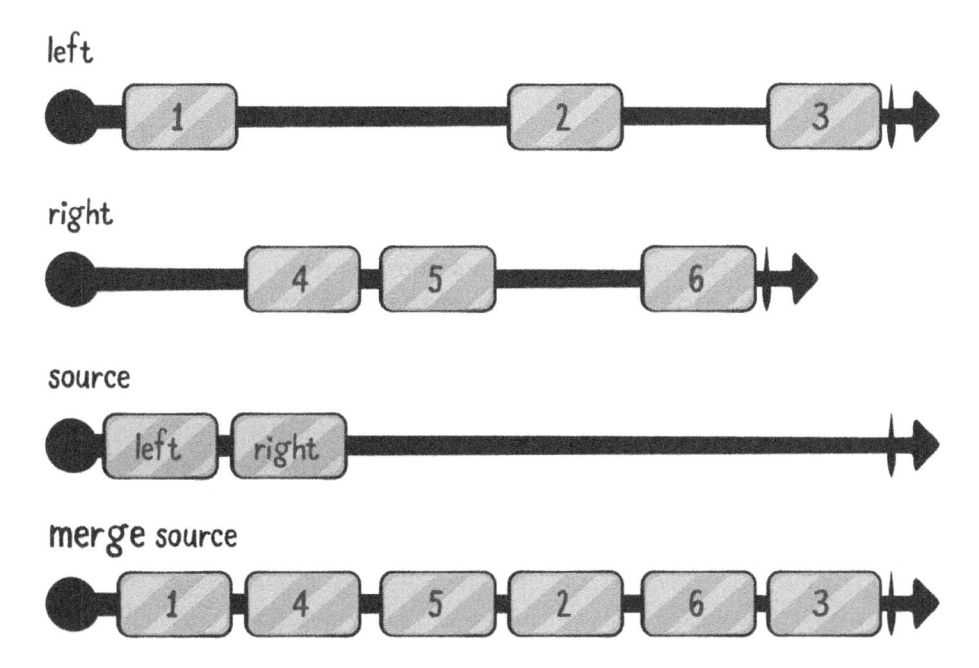

Your next task is to add a new exampleOf block, and prepare two subjects to which you can push values. You learned about Subject in Chapter 3, "Subjects". Start by adding this block:

```
exampleOf("merge") {
  val subscriptions = CompositeDisposable()

  val left = PublishSubject.create<Int>()
  val right = PublishSubject.create<Int>()
}
```

You'll now merge `left` and `right` together. Add the following to the example:

```
Observable.merge(left, right)
  .subscribe {
    println(it)
  }
  .addTo(subscriptions)
```

Now it's time to start emitting items. Add the following below the above code, within the example block:

```
left.onNext(0)
left.onNext(1)
right.onNext(3)
left.onNext(4)
right.onNext(5)
right.onNext(6)
```

You emit 0 and 1 from the `left` subject, then 3 from the `right` subject, and so on. If you were using concat here, you'd expect to see the following (assuming you called onComplete on both of the subjects): 0, 1, 4, 3, 5, 6. But since you're using merge, you see the following:

```
--- Example of: merge ---
0
1
3
4
5
6
```

Merge emits the items in the order that they come in. Pretty handy, right?

A `merge()` Observable subscribes to each of the sequences it receives and emits the elements as soon as they arrive — there's no predefined order.

You may be wondering when and how `merge()` completes. Good question! As with everything in RxJava, the rules are well-defined:

- `merge()` completes after its source sequence completes **and** all inner sequences have completed.
- The order in which the inner sequences complete is irrelevant.
- If any of the sequences emit an error, the `merge()` Observable immediately relays the error, then terminates.

Using mergeWith

Just like for `concat` and `concatWith`, there's also a `mergeWith` method you can use instead of the statically resolved `Observable.merge` method. Add the following example:

```
exampleOf("mergeWith") {

  val subscriptions = CompositeDisposable()

  val germanCities = PublishSubject.create<String>()
  val spanishCities = PublishSubject.create<String>()

  germanCities.mergeWith(spanishCities)
    .subscribe {
      println(it)
    }
    .addTo(subscriptions)
}
```

You're again using city names, this time via the `mergeWith` operator.

Now add the following:

```
germanCities.onNext("Frankfurt")
germanCities.onNext("Berlin")
spanishCities.onNext("Madrid")
germanCities.onNext("Münich")
spanishCities.onNext("Barcelona")
spanishCities.onNext("Valencia")
```

Just like before you're sending cities through on the different subjects in a mixed manner.

Run the project and you should see the following output:

```
--- Example of: mergeWith ---
Frankfurt
Berlin
Madrid
Münich
Barcelona
Valencia
```

The cities are received in the same order they are emitted by the merged subjects.

Combining elements

Using combineLatest

An essential operator in RxJava is the `combineLatest` operator. It combines values from several sequences:

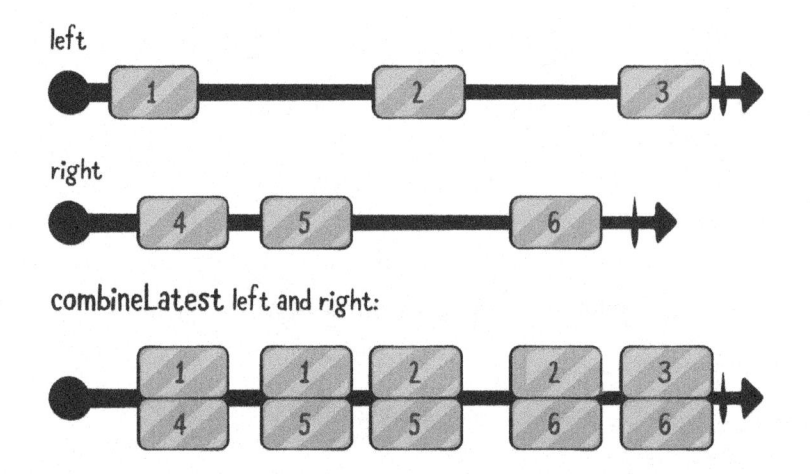

Every time one of the inner (combined) sequences emits a value, it calls a lambda you provide. You receive the last value from each of the inner sequences. This has many concrete applications, such as observing several text fields at once and combining their values, watching the status of multiple sources, and so on.

Does this sound complicated? It's actually quite simple! You'll break it down by working through an example.

First, create two subjects to push values to. Add this example to your `main()` function:

```
exampleOf("combineLatest") {

  val subscriptions = CompositeDisposable()

  val left = PublishSubject.create<String>()
  val right = PublishSubject.create<String>()
}
```

Next, create an Observable that combines the latest value from both sources. Don't worry; you'll understand how the code works once you've finished adding everything together:

```
Observables
  .combineLatest(left, right) { leftString, rightString ->
    "$leftString $rightString"
}.subscribe {
  println(it)
}.addTo(subscriptions)
```

Now add the following code to start pushing values to the Observables:

```
left.onNext("Hello")
right.onNext("World")
left.onNext("It's nice to")
right.onNext("be here!")
left.onNext("Actually, it's super great to")
```

Run the complete example from above. You'll see four sentences show up in the output of the project:

```
--- Example of: combineLatest ---
Hello World
It's nice to World
It's nice to be here!
Actually, it's super great to be here!
```

A few notable points about this example:

1. You **combine** Observables using a lambda receiving the latest value of each sequence as arguments. In this example, the combination is the concatenated string of both left and right values. It could be anything else that you need, as the **type** of the elements emitted by the combined Observable is the return type of the lambda.

2. In practice, this means you can combine sequences of heterogeneous types. `combineLatest` is the only core operator that permits using Observables of differing types.

3. Nothing happens until each of the combined Observables emits one value. After that, each time one of the combined observables emits a new value, the lambda receives the **latest** value of each of the Observables and produces its element.

> **Note**: Remember that `combineLatest` waits for all its Observables to emit one element before starting to call your lambda. It's a frequent source of confusion! It's also a good opportunity to use the `startWith` operator to provide an initial value for the sequences, which could take time to update. Like the `map` operator covered in Chapter 7, "Transforming Operators", `combineLatest` creates an `Observable` whose type is the lambda return type. You can use this to switch to a new type alongside a chain of operators!

A common pattern is to combine values to a tuple then pass them down the chain. For example, you'll often want to combine values and then call `filter` on them like so:

```
val observable = Observables
  .combineLatest(left, right) {
    leftString: String, rightString: String ->

    leftString to rightString
  }
  .filter { !it.first.isEmpty() }
```

One other interesting thing here is that you're actually using the `Observables.combineLatest` method exposed by **RxKotlin** here, not the one exposed by **RxJava**. **RxKotlin** provides several convenience methods that make them easier to call from Kotlin. For example, if you didn't have **RxKotlin**, the `combineLatest` call from the example would instead have to look like this:

```
Observable.combineLatest<String, String, String>(left, right,
    BiFunction { leftString, rightString ->
  "$leftString $rightString"
})
```

There are several variants in the `combineLatest` family of operators. They take between two and eight Observable sequences as parameters. As mentioned above, sequences don't need to have the same element type.

> **Note:** Last but not least, `combineLatest` completes only when the last of its inner sequences completes. Before that, it keeps sending combined values. If some sequences terminate, it uses the last value emitted to combine with new values from other sequences.

Using zip

Another combination operator is the `zip` family of operators. Like the `combineLatest` family, it comes in several variants:

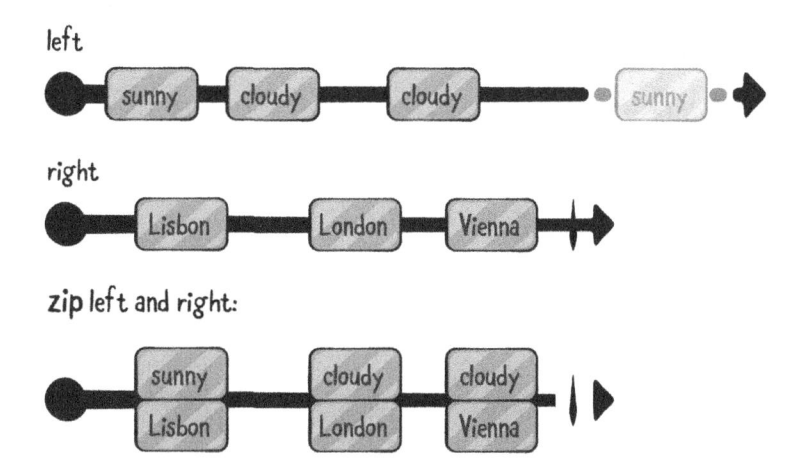

Add a new example:

```
exampleOf("zip") {

  val subscriptions = CompositeDisposable()

  val left = PublishSubject.create<String>()
  val right = PublishSubject.create<String>()
}
```

Then create a zipped Observable of both sources. Note that you're again using the **RxKotlin** version of the `zip` method. You can tell because it's namespaced with `Observables` rather than `Observable`:

```
Observables.zip(left, right) { weather, city ->
  "It's $weather in $city"
}.subscribe {
  println(it)
}.addTo(subscriptions)
```

Finally, feed some values into your subjects:

```
left.onNext("sunny")
right.onNext("Lisbon")
```

```
left.onNext("cloudy")
right.onNext("Copenhagen")
left.onNext("cloudy")
right.onNext("London")
left.onNext("sunny")
right.onNext("Madrid")
right.onNext("Vienna")
```

Run the code and check the output:

```
--- Example of: zip ---
It's sunny in Lisbon
It's cloudy in Copenhagen
It's cloudy in London
It's sunny in Madrid
```

Here's what `zip` did for you:

- Subscribed to the Observables you provided.

- Waited for each to emit a new value.

- Called your lambda with both new values.

Did you notice how `Vienna` didn't show up in the output? Why is that?

The explanation lies in the way `zip` operators work. They wait until each of the inner Observables emits a new value. If one of them completes, `zip` completes as well. It doesn't wait until all of the inner Observables are done! This is called **indexed sequencing**, which is a way to walk though sequences in lockstep.

> **Note:** Kotlin also has a `zip` collection operator. It creates a new collection of pairs with items from both collections.

Triggers

Apps have diverse needs and must manage multiple input sources. You'll often need to accept input from several Observables at once. Some will simply trigger actions in your code, while others will provide data. RxJava has you covered with powerful operators that will make your life easier. Well, your *coding* life at least!

Using withLatestFrom

You'll first look at `withLatestFrom`. Often overlooked by beginners, it's a useful companion tool when dealing with user interfaces, among other things.

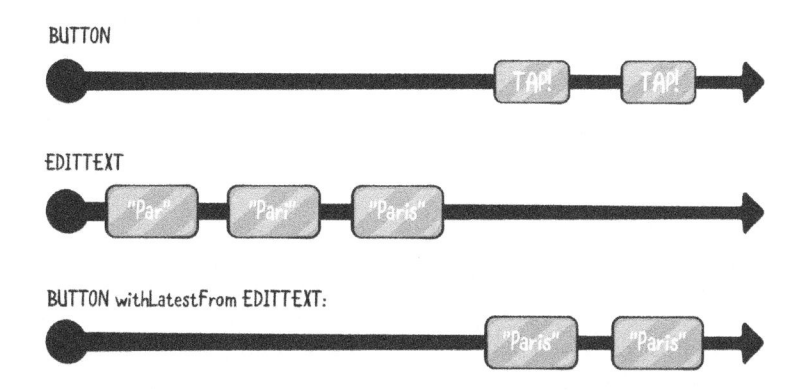

Add this code to the `main()` function. You may need to import `withLatestFrom` using `io.reactivex.rxkotlin.withLatestFrom`:

```
exampleOf("withLatestFrom") {
  val subscriptions = CompositeDisposable()

  // 1
  val button = PublishSubject.create<Unit>()
  val editText = PublishSubject.create<String>()

  // 2
  button.withLatestFrom(editText) { _: Unit, value: String ->
    value
  }.subscribe {
    println(it)
  }.addTo(subscriptions)

  // 3
  editText.onNext("Par")
  editText.onNext("Pari")
  editText.onNext("Paris")
  button.onNext(Unit)
  button.onNext(Unit)
}
```

This example simulates an Android `EditText` and `Button`.

Run this example and you'll see this output:

```
--- Example of: withLatestFrom ---
Paris
Paris
```

Let's go through what you just did:

1. Create two subjects simulating button presses and edit text input. Since the button carries no real data, you can use `Unit` as an element type.

2. When `button` emits a value, ignore it but instead emit the latest value received from the simulated `EditText`. The `Button` is acting as a *trigger* for getting values from the `EditText`.

3. Simulate successive inputs to the `EditText`, with values that are then emitted by the two successive button presses.

Simple and straightforward! `withLatestFrom` is useful in all situations where you want the current (latest) value emitted from an Observable, but only when a particular trigger occurs.

Using sample

A close relative to `withLatestFrom` is the `sample` operator.

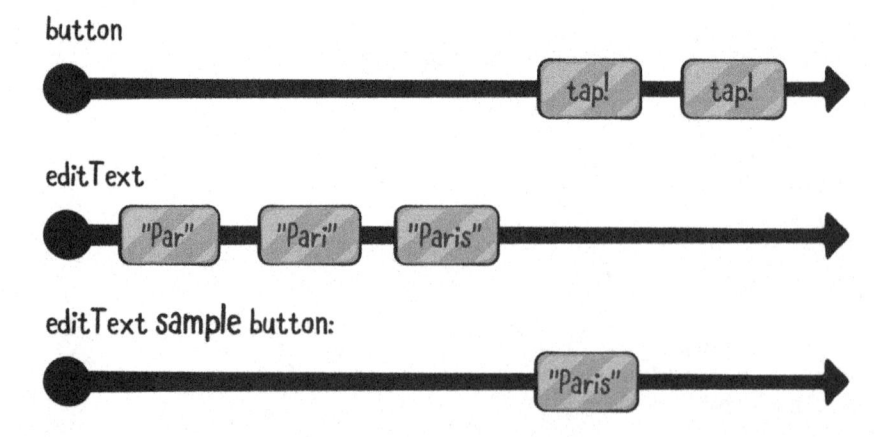

It does nearly the same thing with just one variation: each time the trigger Observable emits a value, `sample` emits the latest value from the "other" Observable, but only if it arrived since the last "tick". If no new data arrived, `sample` won't emit anything.

Try it in the project. Duplicate the previous example of `withLatestFrom`, using `sample` instead:

```
exampleOf("sample") {
  val subscriptions = CompositeDisposable()

  val button = PublishSubject.create<Unit>()
  val editText = PublishSubject.create<String>()

  editText.sample(button)
    .subscribe {
      println(it)
    }.addTo(subscriptions)

  editText.onNext("Par")
  editText.onNext("Pari")
  editText.onNext("Paris")
  button.onNext(Unit)
  button.onNext(Unit)
}
```

Run the project.

Notice that `"Paris"` now prints only once! This is because no new value was emitted by the text field between your two fake button presses. You could have achieved the same behavior by adding a `distinctUntilChanged` to the `withLatestFrom` Observable, but the smallest possible operator chains are the **Zen of Rx™**.

> **Note**: Don't forget that `withLatestFrom` takes the *data observable* as a parameter, while `sample` takes the *trigger observable* as a parameter. This can easily be a source of mistakes — so be careful!

Waiting for triggers is a great help when doing UI work. In some cases your "trigger" may come in the form of a sequence of observables (I know, it's *Inception* once again). Or maybe you want to wait on a pair of observables and only keep one. No matter — RxJava has operators for this!

Switches

Using amb

RxJava comes with one main so-called "switching" operator: amb. It allows you to produce an Observable sequence by switching between the events of the combined source sequences. This allows you to decide which sequence's events the subscriber will receive at runtime.

Think of "amb" as in "ambiguous".

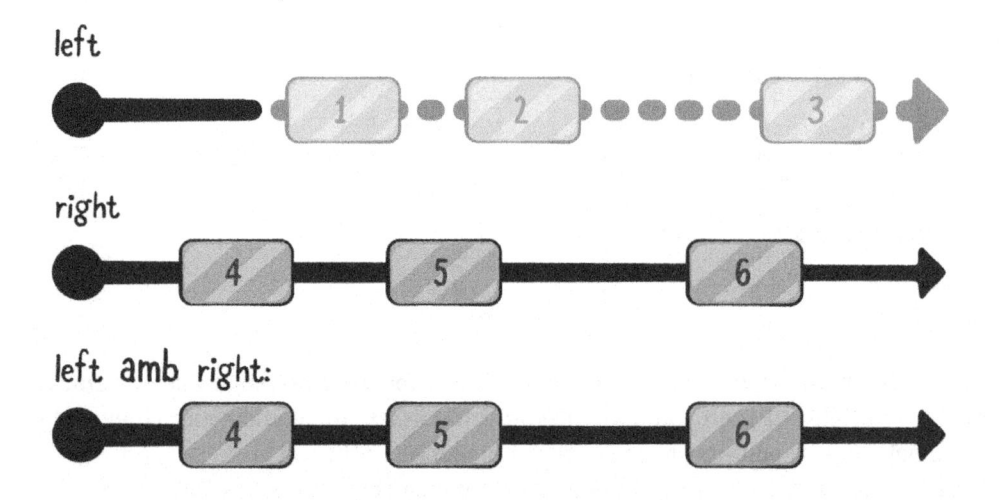

Add this code to the project:

```
exampleOf("amb") {

  val subscriptions = CompositeDisposable()

  val left = PublishSubject.create<String>()
  val right = PublishSubject.create<String>()

  // 1
  left.ambWith(right)
    .subscribe {
      println(it)
```

```
    }
    .addTo(subscriptions)
  // 2
  left.onNext("Lisbon")
  right.onNext("Copenhagen")
  left.onNext("London")
  left.onNext("Madrid")
  right.onNext("Vienna")
}
```

If you run the project, you'll notice that the output only shows items from the `left` subject. Here's what you did:

1. Create an Observable using `ambWith` which resolves *ambiguity* between left and right.
2. Have both Observables send data.

The `ambWith` operator combines the left and right Observables. It waits for any of them to emit an element, then unsubscribes subscriptions from the *other* one. After that, it only relays elements from the first active Observable. It really does draw its name from the term *ambiguous*: at first, you don't know which sequence you're interested in, and want to decide only when one fires.

This operator is often overlooked. It has a few select practical applications, like connecting to redundant servers and sticking with the one that responds first.

Combining elements within a sequence

All cooks know that the more you reduce, the tastier your sauce will be. Although not aimed at chefs, RxJava has the tools to reduce your sauce to its most flavorful components!

Using reduce

Through your coding adventures in Kotlin, you may already know about its `reduce` collection operator. If you don't, here's a great opportunity to learn about it, as this knowledge applies to pure Kotlin collections as well.

To get started, add this code to the project:

```
exampleOf("reduce") {

  val subscriptions = CompositeDisposable()

  val source = Observable.just(1, 3, 5, 7, 9)
  source
    .reduce(0) { a, b -> a + b }
    .subscribeBy(onSuccess = {
      println(it)
    })
    .addTo(subscriptions)
}
```

This is much like what you'd do with Kotlin collections, but instead with `Observable` sequences. The code above uses a lambda to add two items together. Run the code and see this reflected in the result:

```
--- Example of: reduce ---
25
```

The `reduce` operator "accumulates" a summary value. It starts with the initial value you provide (in this example, you start with 0). Each time the source Observable emits an item, reduce calls your lambda to produce a new summary by combining the current value with the newly emitted value per the lambda. When the source Observable completes, reduce emits the summary value, then completes.

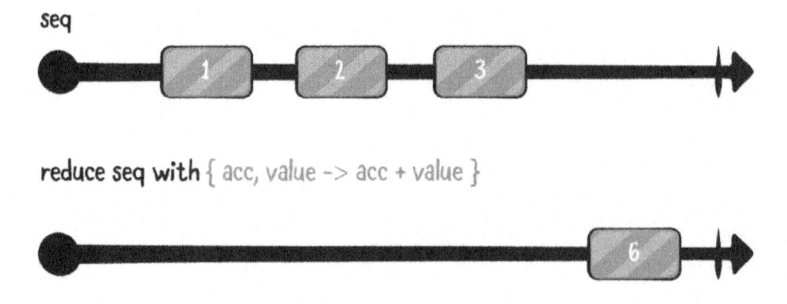

> **Note**: reduce produces its summary (accumulated) value only when the source Observable completes. Applying this operator to sequences that never complete won't emit anything. This is a frequent source of confusion and hidden problems.

Using scan

A close relative to reduce is the scan operator. Can you spot the difference in the diagram below, comparing to the last one above?

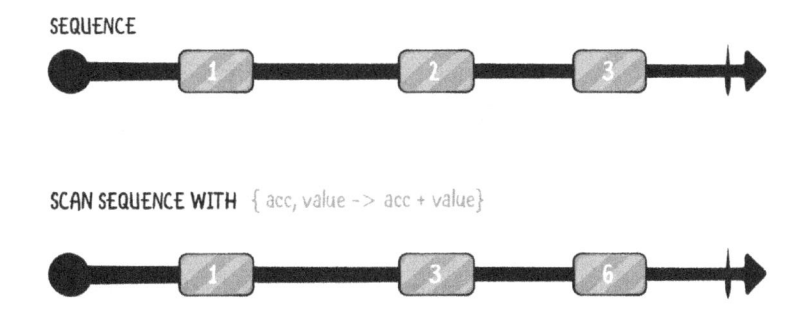

Add some code to the project to experiment:

```
exampleOf("scan") {

  val subscriptions = CompositeDisposable()

  val source = Observable.just(1, 3, 5, 7, 9)

  source
    .scan(0) { a, b -> a + b }
    .subscribe {
      println(it)
    }
    .addTo(subscriptions)
}
```

Now run it and look at the output:

```
--- Example of: scan ---
1
4
9
16
25
```

You get one output value per input value. As you may have guessed, this value is the running total accumulated by the lambda. Each time the source Observable emits an element, `scan` invokes your lambda. It passes the running value along with the new element, and the lambda returns the new accumulated value. Like `reduce`, the resulting Observable type is the lambda return type.

The range of use cases for `scan` is quite large; you can use it to compute running totals, statistics, states and so on. Encapsulating state information within a `scan` Observable is a good idea; you won't need to use local variables, and it goes away when the source Observable completes.

Challenge: The zip case

You learned a great deal about many combining operators in this chapter. But there is so much more to learn (and more fun to be had) about sequence combination!

You've learned about the `zip` family of operators that let you go through sequences in lockstep — it's time to start using them.

Take the code from the `scan` example above and improve it so as to display both the current value and the running total at the same time.

There are several ways to do this — and not necessarily with `zip`. Bonus points if you can find more than one method.

The solutions to this challenge, found in the project files for this chapter, show two possible implementations. Can you find them both?

Key points

- You can **prepend** or **append** Observable sequences to one another using operators like `startWith`, `concatWith`, and `concatMap`.

- The `merge` family of operators lets you **merge** sequences together so that items are received in the order that they are emitted.

- The `combineLatest` operator lets you combine heterogeneous observables into a type that gets emitted each time one of the inner observables emits.

- The `zip` operators emit only when each of the inner Observables have **all** emitted a new value, called **indexed sequencing**; the overall Observable completes when any of the inner Observables complete.

- In combined sequences, if an inner sequence emits an error, then generally the overall Observable emits the error and the sequence terminates.

- **Triggering** operators like `withLatestFrom` and `sample` let you limit the emitting of elements to only when certain triggering events occur.

- The `amb` or "ambiguous" operator lets you **switch** between multiple Observables by sticking to the first one that is active.

- The `reduce` and `scan` operators let you combine the elements in a sequence based on an input lambda; `reduce` only emits the final value when it receives the `complete` event, whereas `scan` emits intermediate accumulated values.

Where to go from here?

Having been introduced to combining operators, in the next chapter you'll see them in action in an Android app. The app project will retrieve data from a NASA API that you will combine in various ways. Despite being Earth-based data, it's sure to be out of this world!

Chapter 10: Combining Operators in Practice

By Alex Sullivan & Florent Pillet

In the previous chapter, you learned about combining operators and worked through increasingly more detailed exercises on some rather mind-bending concepts. Some operators may have left you wondering about the real-world application of these reactive concepts.

In this *"... in practice"* chapter, you'll have the opportunity to try some of the most powerful operators. You'll learn how to solve problems similar to those you'll face in your own applications.

> **Note**: This chapter assumes you've already worked your way through Chapter 9, "Combining Operators," and are familiar with both filtering (Chapter 5) and transforming operators (Chapter 7). At this point in the book, it is important that you are familiar with these concepts, so make sure to review these chapters if necessary!

You'll start with a new project for this chapter and build a small application with an ambitious name: **Our Planet**.

Getting started

The project will tap into the wealth of public data exposed by NASA. You'll target EONET, NASA's *Earth Observatory Natural Event Tracker*. It is a near real-time, curated repository of natural events of all types occurring on the planet. Check out https://eonet.sci.gsfc.nasa.gov/ to learn more!

To get started with **Our Planet**, open the starter project for this chapter in Android Studio 4.0 or newer.

Build and run the starter application; the default screen is empty.

Your tasks with this application are as follows:

- Gather the event categories from the EONET public API https://eonet.sci.gsfc.nasa.gov/docs/v2.1 and display them on the first screen.

- Download events and show a count for each category.

- When user taps a category, display a list of events for this category.

You'll learn how useful combineLatest can be in several situations, but you'll also exercise concat, merge, and scan. Of course, you'll also rely on operators you are already familiar with, like map and flatMap.

Preparing the EONET API class

Good applications have a clear architecture with well-defined roles. The code that talks with the EONET API shouldn't live in any of the activities. Instead, it will live in an object that you'll reference from a ViewModel.

Expand the **model** package in the **OurPlanet** project; you'll find a Retrofit interface ready for the app to utilize in **EONETApi.kt**. That interface will be used by the EONET object. You'll also find EOCategoriesResponse, EOCategory and EOEvent classes that map to the content delivered by the API.

Open the EONET object; it's already fleshed out with the basic structure of the class, including the API URL, endpoints, and some date formats you'll use later on.

Fetching categories

Now open the EONETApi file and add a fetchCategories method to the bottom of the class, after the companion object block.

```
@GET(EONET.CATEGORIES_ENDPOINT)
fun fetchCategories(): Observable<EOCategoriesResponse>
```

fetchCategories will fetch the different event categories from the EONET API. It returns an Observable<EOCategoriesResponse>. EOCategoriesResponse is a simple wrapper class for a list of categories, which are represented here via the AnyMap typealias.

Just like in previous projects, you're using AnyMap to represent a simple Map<String, Any> for objects returned from the network. You'll deserialize that AnyMap later on.

Next, open the EONET object and add the following method:

```
fun fetchCategories(): Observable<EOCategoriesResponse> {
  return eonet.fetchCategories()
}
```

This exposes the fetchCategories method you just created to other consumers of the EONET object.

Updating the CategoriesViewModel

Open CategoriesViewModel and add the following to the empty startDownload method:

```
// 1
EONET.fetchCategories()
  // 2
  .map { response ->
    val categories = response.categories
      categories.mapNotNull { EOCategory.fromJson(it) }
  }
  // 3
  .share()
  // 4
  .subscribeOn(Schedulers.io())
  .observeOn(AndroidSchedulers.mainThread())
  // 5
  .subscribe {
    categoriesLiveData.value = it
```

```
}
.addTo(disposables)
```

In this block you're doing the following:

1. Use the new `fetchCategories` method you added above to query the EONET API for event categories

2. Use the `map` operator to turn the response object you received from the previous call into a `List<EOCategory>`

3. Use the `share` operator so you can re-use this Observable later on.

4. Use the `subscribeOn` and `observeOn` methods to make sure you're querying the network off the `main` thread and observing the results on the `main` thread (you'll learn more about these operators in Chapter 13: "Intro to Schedulers")

5. Finally, `subscribe` to the Observable and update the `categoriesLiveData` with the data coming through.8Run the app. You should see a list of events, each of which show as having zero events listed.

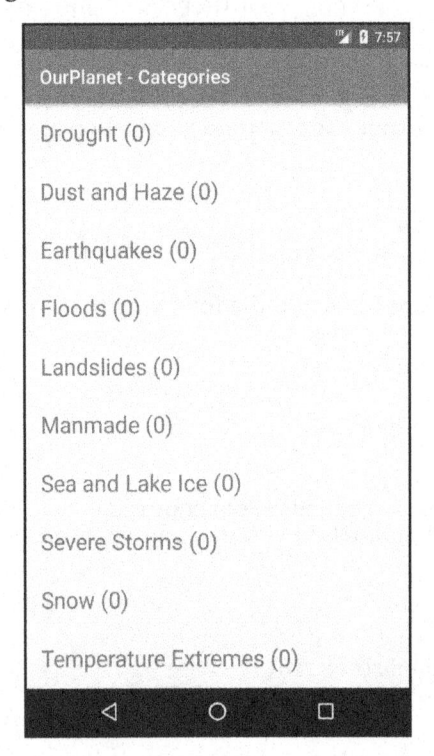

Add events into the mix

Now that you've got the categories loading, it's time to update the app to actually display the number of events in the category.

Add a new `EOEventsResponse` class in the `model` package:

```
class EOEventsResponse(val events: List<AnyMap>)
```

`EOEventsResponse` will model the top level response you get back from the EONET API.

Open the `EONETApi` class and add the following method below the `fetchCategories` method:

```
@GET(EONET.EVENTS_ENDPOINT)
fun fetchEvents(
  @Query("days") forLastDays: Int,
  @Query("status") status: String
): Observable<EOEventsResponse>
```

`fetchEvents` queries the EONET API for events that have happened within a certain number of days, and that have a status of either opened or closed.

Now that you have your Retrofit method set up, it's time to expose it in the `EONET` object. But before you expose the `fetchEvents` method publicly, you'll write a small helper method to help ease the process of returning both open and closed events. Open `EONET` and add the following `events` method:

```
// 1
private fun events(forLastDays: Int, closed: Boolean):
  Observable<List<EOEvent>> {
  // 2
  val status = if (closed) "closed" else "open"
  // 3
  return EONET.eonet.fetchEvents(forLastDays, status)
    //4
    .map { response ->
      val events = response.events
      events.mapNotNull { EOEvent.fromJson(it) }
    }
}
```

The events helper method works as follows:

1. It takes two parameters. The first parameter represents how many days back you want to go when fetching events from the EONET API. The second is a Boolean representing whether you want to look up closed or open events.

2. You're transforming the Boolean closed variable into a String that the EONET API can understand.

3. You're then using the fetchEvents method you just wrote to fetch events for a set number of days back and with the status that you just determined.

4. You're then taking the response from that network call and using the map operator to transform it into a List<EOEvent>, similar to what you did earlier with the EOCategory.

Now that you have the helper method out of the way, you can create the public fetchEvents method that will expose the events API to a consumer.

Add the following empty method above the events method:

```
fun fetchEvents(forLastDays: Int = 360):
Observable<List<EOEvent>> {

}
```

You're supplying a default number of days to make consumption of this API easier.

When you fetch events from the EONET API, you want to fetch both the closed and open events, so you get the full picture.

Add the following code at the top of the empty fetchEvents method:

```
val openEvents = events(forLastDays, false)
val closedEvents = events(forLastDays, true)
```

You're using the helper events method you just implemented to create two new Observables - one for the closed events and one for the open events.

Now that you have two Observables you want to combine them together. Funny how that would be the case in this chapter! You're going to use a concat method to combine openEvents and closedEvents. Add the following code below the two Observable declarations:

```
return openEvents.concatWith(closedEvents)
```

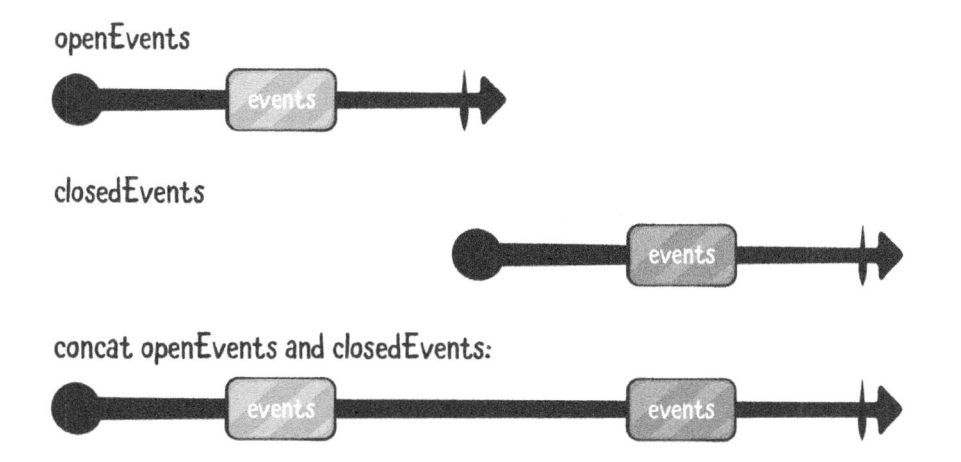

openEvents

closedEvents

concat openEvents and closedEvents:

Here's what's going on in the code you just added:

concatWith combines the openEvents Observable with the closedEvents Observable by first emitting all the events from the openEvents Observable and then following up with the events from the closedEvents Observable. If either of them emit an error, the whole Observable will terminate and emit that error. This is an OK solution for now, but you'll improve on it later on.

Combining events and categories

You've got a fancy `fetchEvents` method that fetches all of your events, so now it's time to utilize it in the `CategoriesViewModel` class.

You're going to update the `startDownload` method to combine the categories you're currently fetching with the events associated with each category.

First off, you're going to stop subscribing to the Observable produced by the `fetchCategories` method and instead save it off in a variable named `eoCategories`, making sure to remove all the operators after the `map` operator. You're new trimmed down method should look like this:

```
fun startDownload() {
  val eoCategories = EONET.fetchCategories()
    .map { response ->
      val categories = response.categories
      categories.mapNotNull { EOCategory.fromJson(it) }
    }
}
```

Now you're going to create a new Observable utilizing the `fetchEvents` method you just added. Add the following to the bottom of the `startDownload` method:

```
val downloadedEvents = EONET.fetchEvents()
```

You're using the default number of days to create your `downloadedEvents` Observable.

Next you're going to use another combining trick you learned about in the last chapter to combine `downloadedEvents` and `eoCategories`: the `combineLatest` method. Add the following to the `startDownload` method below the `downloadedEvents` declaration:

```
// 1
val updatedCategories = Observables
  .combineLatest(eoCategories, downloadedEvents)
    { categoriesResponse, eventsResponse ->
      // 2
      categoriesResponse.map { category ->
        // 3
        val cat = category.copy()
        // 4
        cat.events.addAll(eventsResponse.filter {
          it.categories.contains(category.id)
        })
        // 5
```

```
            cat
        }
    }
}
```

Wow, that's a hearty block of code! Here's a breakdown:

1. You're using the `combineLatest` method to combine the latest emission from `eoCategories` with the latest emission from `downloadedEvents`. Take a look at the diagram below this explanation for some visual help on making sense of `combineLatest`.

2. `combineLatest` takes a function that receives one item from the first Observable and one item from the second Observable as an argument. So in this lambda block you have `categoriesResponse`, which is a `List<Category>`, and `eventsResponse`, which is a `List<EOEvent>`.

   You're using the Kotlin standard library map method on the `categoriesResponse` list to transform each element.

3. Within the map lambda, you're creating a new copy of the current `EOCategory` you're looping through.

4. You're then adding every event from the `eventsResponse` list that has an associated category with the same id as the current `EOCategory` into the new `cat` copy. In other words, you're adding every event that belongs to `category` to your copy `cat`.

5. Finally, you're using Kotlin lambda implicit returns to return the new category copy. Remember though that the `cat` line at the bottom of the block is the return value for the `categoriesResponse.map` line, which is itself the return value for the `combineLatest` lambda. There's some lambda inception going on here!

See below:

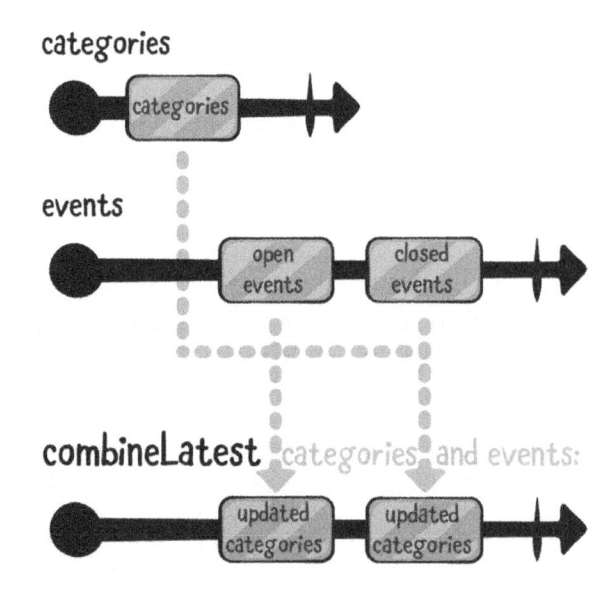

Diagram: marble diagram showing "categories" stream emitting categories, "events" stream emitting open events then closed events, and combineLatest of categories and events producing updated categories and updated categories.

Last but not least, you're going to combine the Observable of empty categories, i.e. `eoCategories`, with the new Observable of populated categories, `updatedCategories`. To do this, you'll use the `concatWith` operator. Finally, you will subscribe to the resulting Observable:

```
eoCategories.concatWith(updatedCategories)
  .subscribeOn(Schedulers.io())
  .observeOn(AndroidSchedulers.mainThread())
  .subscribe({
    categoriesLiveData.value = it
  }, {
    Log.e("CategoriesViewModel", it.localizedMessage)
  })
  .addTo(disposables)
```

Just like before you're using `subscribeOn` and `observeOn` to handle your threading needs. By using `concatWith` to combine the empty and populated categories, you'll be able to quickly show some data, the empty categories, while downloading new events to then combine with the categories.

There's one more small update to make before you can run the app. Open the `CategoriesAdapter` class and add the following line to the top of the `updateCategories` method:

```
this.categories.clear()
```

This will clear out the existing list of categories when you get a new list. Build and run the app.

You should see the categories listed and quickly updated to show the real count of events associated with that category.

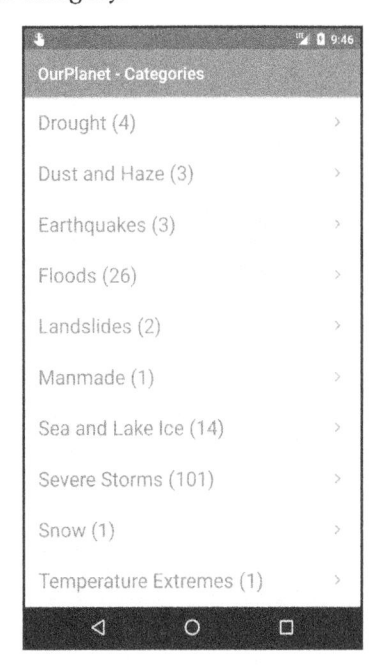

Downloading in parallel

Recall that the app is currently calling the EONET events endpoint twice. Once for closed events and once for open events. Since you're using the `concat` operator, it first downloads the open events and then the closed events.

Wouldn't it be great if you could parallelize that and download both events at once? With RxJava, not only can you achieve that parallelization, but you can do it without touching any of your UI code.

The EONET API allows you to download events in two ways. The first approach, which the app is currently taking, is to download all of the events at once. The second approach is to download events by category.

You'll refactor the app to download events by category rather than all at once. It'll be more complicated than the current approach, but you're already an RxJava ninja, so you'll get through it fine!

First, open the `EONETApi` class and update the `fetchEvents` method to take in its GET end point as a parameter:

```
@GET("{endpoint}")
fun fetchEvents(
  @Path("endpoint", encoded = true) endpoint: String,
  @Query("days") forLastDays: Int,
  @Query("status") status: String
): Observable<EOEventsResponse>
```

Retrofit makes this easy, since you can use the `@Path` annotation to update the endpoint in the `@GET` annotation.

Next, update the private `events` method in the `EONET` object to utilize the changed `fetchEvents` method:

```
private fun events(
  forLastDays: Int,
  closed: Boolean,
  endpoint: String
): Observable<List<EOEvent>> {
  val status = if (closed) "closed" else "open"
  return EONET.eonet.fetchEvents(endpoint, forLastDays, status)
    .map { response ->
    val events = response.events
    events.mapNotNull { EOEvent.fromJson(it) }
    }
}
```

You're now passing in an endpoint, which is a String, into the events helper method. You're then passing the endpoint through to the fetchEvents method you updated earlier.

Now update the public fetchEvents method in the EONET object to take in an EOCategory and pass its endpoint value into the open and closed events Observables:

```
fun fetchEvents(category: EOCategory, forLastDays: Int = 360):
    Observable<List<EOEvent>> {
  val openEvents =
    EONET.events(forLastDays, false, category.endpoint)
  val closedEvents =
    EONET.events(forLastDays, true, category.endpoint)

  return Observable.concat(openEvents, closedEvents)
}
```

Since you want the two network calls to be made in parallel, you should use the Observable.merge method to merge the two observables together instead of concat. Update the return statement of the fetchEvents method to use merge:

```
return Observable.merge(openEvents, closedEvents)
```

Incrementally updating events

You've done a lot of great work to parallelize downloading closed and open events, but there's still a bit farther to go.

Open CategoriesViewModel. In the startDownload method you'll notice that there's an error on the line declaring downloadedEvents. That's because you're not passing in an EOCategory to the fetchEvents method.

You may not have an instance of EOCategory lying around, but you've got the next best thing. The eoCategories Observable defined at the top of the startDownload method emits lists of EOCategory objects. All you need to do is tie into the eoCategories Observable to get your EOCategory instance!

Replace the original downloadedEvents Observable with the following two Observables:

```
// 1
val eventsObservables = eoCategories.flatMap { categories ->
  // 2
  val categoryEventObservables = categories.map { category ->
    EONET.fetchEvents(category)
```

```
  }
  // 3
  Observable.fromIterable(categoryEventObservables)
}
// 4
val downloadedEvents = Observable.merge(eventsObservables, 2)
```

That's a dense chunk of code. Here's a breakdown:

1. You're calling flatMap on the eoCategories Observable. eoCategories emits values of type List<EOCategory>, so categories here is a list of categories. Remember that flatMap expects you to return an Observable from its lambda.

2. You're then using the Kotlin standard library map method and the EONET.fetchEvents method to transform each EOCategory in categories into an Observable<List<EOEvent>>. That means the type of categoryEventObservables is actually List<Observable<List<EOEvent>>>. That's an intimidating type signature!

3. Next up you're using Observable.fromIterable to transform your List<Observable<List<EOEvent>>> into an Observable<Observable<List<EOEvent>>>. This is the ultimate type of eventsObservables. It's hard to reason about Observables inside Observables, but luckily you can flatten things out…

4. By using the merge operator! merge has a plethora of helpful versions. Rather than providing merge with a set number of Observables, you can instead give it an Observable that emits Observables and it will combine them all together. Merge them, if you will :].

   Merge also allows you to pass in a maximum number of concurrent subscriptions to those Observables. You don't want your app to make too many network requests at once, so by passing in an upper limit on the number of Observables being subscribed to you can help lessen the load.

The end result of the above code is that you get an Observable<List<EOEvent>> just like before, except now each category that comes through the eoCategories Observable triggers a call to get that category's associated EOEvent objects.

Head back to the `EONET` object and add the following function at the bottom of the object:

```kotlin
fun filterEventsForCategory(
    events: List<EOEvent>,
    category: EOCategory
): List<EOEvent> {
  // 1
  return events.filter { event ->
    // 2
    event.categories.contains(category.id) &&
        // 3
        !category.events.map { it.id }.contains(event.id)
    // 4
  }.sortedWith(EOEvent.compareByDates)
}
```

The above method is used to get a list of `EOEvent` objects that are associated with, but not already added to, an `EOCategory`. Here's a breakdown:

1. Call the Kotlin standard library `filter` operator on the passed in list of events. The `filter` lambda expects either `true` or `false` to determine if it should include the object in the list it returns.

2. Check if the list of category ids on the event contains the id of the category passed into this `filterEventsForCategory` function.

3. Also check to see if the passed in category already contains the event that `filter` is currently operating on. If the event belongs to the passed in category, and that category doesn't already contain the event, return `true` so the filter will include this event in its return list.

4. Last but not least, sort the resulting `List<EOEvent>` based off their dates.

Back in the `startDownload` method in the `CategoriesViewModel`, replace the `updatedCategories` declaration with the following:

```kotlin
// 1
val updatedCategories = eoCategories.flatMap { categories ->
  // 2
  downloadedEvents.scan(categories) { updated, events ->
    // 3
    updated.map { category ->
      val eventsForCategory =
        EONET.filterEventsForCategory(events, category)

      if (!eventsForCategory.isEmpty()) {
        val cat = category.copy()
        cat.events.addAll(eventsForCategory.filter {
```

```
            it.closeDate != null
        })
        cat
    } else {
        category
    }
}
}
}
```

Broken down, the above code:

1. Again calls `flatMap` on the `eoCategories` Observable. Since `eoCategories` emits objects of type `List<EOCategory>`, the `categories` argument to the `flatMap` lambda is also of type `List<EOCategory>`.

2. Then use the `scan` operator on the `downloadedEvents` Observable to progressively build up fully populated instances of `EOCategory`. Recall that the `scan` operator takes in an initial value and then runs a function you provide every time an item is emitted from the Observable, updating that initial value you provided as it goes. In this case the initial value that you provide is a `List<EOCategory>`. Each `EOCategory` in the list, however, has no associated `EOEvents`.

3. In the `scan` operators accumulator function, you're mapping through the list of `EOCategorys` and creating a new list of events that are associated with that category, using the `filterEventsForCategory` method you wrote earlier. You're then creating a copy of the category and adding all of its associated events to its own internal list of events and returning that copy. If there are no new events for the category, you're just returning the original category without modifying its events.

By using the `scan` combining operator, you're able to slowly but surely get a fully populated list of `EOCategory` objects without waiting for every network call to finish.

Phew! That was a lot of very complex Rx code.

Build and run the app now. You'll see that the counts for the categories increase as new network calls are made to populate each category.

Click into one of the categories and you'll see a screen that shows your progress.

Interacting with the slider doesn't do anything. Yet. You'll change that next.

Wiring up the days seek bar

Open the `EventsActivity` class and add the following at the top of the class:

```
private val days = BehaviorSubject.createDefault(360)
private val subscriptions = CompositeDisposable()
```

You'll be using a `BehaviorSubject` to represent the number of days currently selected in the days slider.

Next add the following to the bottom of the `onCreate` function:

```
seekBar.setOnSeekBarChangeListener(
  object : SeekBar.OnSeekBarChangeListener {
    override fun onProgressChanged(
      seekBar: SeekBar?, progress: Int, fromUser: Boolean) {
        days.onNext(progress)
      }

      override fun onStartTrackingTouch(seekBar: SeekBar?) {}
      override fun onStopTrackingTouch(seekBar: SeekBar?) {}
  })
```

You're using an `OnSeekBarChangeListener` to forward the current seek bar position to the days `BehaviorSubject`. Now whenever you scroll, the subject days will emit the new seekbar progress.

Next add the following below the `OnSeekBarChangeListener` code:

```
val allEvents = intent
  .getParcelableExtra<EOCategory>(CATEGORY_KEY).events
val eventsObservable = Observable.just(allEvents)
```

You're retrieving the `EOCategory` from the Activity `intent` and creating a new `eventsObservable` from the category events.

Now it's time for the Rx magic. Add the following below the `eventsObservable` declaration:

```
// 1
Observables
  .combineLatest(days, eventsObservable) { days, events ->
    // 2
    val maxInterval = (days.toLong() * 24L * 3600000L)
    // 3
    events.filter { event ->
      val date = event.closeDate
      if (date != null) {
        abs(date.time - Date().time) < maxInterval
      } else {
        true
      }
    }
  }
  // 4
  .observeOn(AndroidSchedulers.mainThread())
  .subscribe {
    adapter.updateEvents(it)
  }
  .addTo(subscriptions)
```

Here's a breakdown of the code:

1. You're using the `combineLatest` factory method to combine the `days` subject with the `eventsObservable`. Recall that `combineLatest` combines the last emitted value from each passed in Observable. Since `eventsObservable` only emits one item, that means that every time the `days` subject emits, its value will be combined with the full list of events.

2. Now you're taking the number of days emitted by the `days` subject and converting it into a number of milliseconds. Specifically, you're multiplying the number of days by 24 hours and then the number of hours by 3,600,000 milliseconds.

3. You're then filtering out any events that haven't happened within the time period entered on the seek bar.

4. Last but not least, you're applying the appropriate schedulers and sending the events that passed the filter to the `RecyclerView` adapter for this page.

Now add the following below the code you just wrote:

```
days
    .observeOn(AndroidSchedulers.mainThread())
    .subscribe {
      daysTextView.text =
        String.format(getString(R.string.last_days_format), it)
    }
    .addTo(subscriptions)
```

You're again observing the `days` subject and updating `daysTextView` to show the proper value.

There's only one thing missing. You need to clean up after yourself! Implement the `onDestroy` method and dispose of your subscriptions:

```
override fun onDestroy() {
  subscriptions.dispose()
  super.onDestroy()
}
```

Now run the app and click into a category. As you slide the seek bar you'll notice the events displayed become filtered down to only those that have happened in the time frame you've selected.

Magic, right?

Challenge: Adding a progress bar

Start from the final project in this chapter. Place an indeterminate horizontal progress bar below the toolbar and above the list of categories on the main screen. The progress bar should show while the categories and events are being downloaded and be hidden as soon as the downloads finish.

You'll need to update the layout in the **activity_categories.xml** file to include a horizontal progress bar. You'll also need to add a few constraints to it to get everything working correctly within the containing `ConstraintLayout`.

Hiding the progress bar will be a side effect of your reactive code. You should also use a `LiveData` object in your `CategoriesViewModel` class to communicate hiding and showing the progress bar with the `CategoriesActivity`.

Key points

- The `concatWith` method can be used to combine two Observables to emit one after the other. Watch out for your error handling though, since one Observable encountering an error will end the whole chain!

- If you need to parallelize multiple Observables, you can use the `merge` method to interweave the Observables. You can also limit the number of concurrent subscriptions happening!

- `combineLatest` can be effectively used to combine the last values of multiple Observables. It's particularly useful if you have one Observable that may not update often and another that updates frequently. Combining the two Observables with `combineLatest` can save you from writing a lot of stateful code!

- The `merge` method has a ton of overloads. If you have a collection of Observables, there's almost certainly a merge overload out there to merge your collection together. It even works if you have an Observable of Observables!

- The `scan` operator can be used to continuously emit items as you build up progress in some process. For this chapter, the progress was fetching events for a certain type of category. If you need to build up to a final product, `scan` or `reduce` are both great options.

Where to go from here?

That wraps up our chapters focusing on filtering, transforming and combining operators. You've seen them all in action in Android apps.

Before moving on to Section III of the book, you'll spend a chapter learning about another type of operator: time-based operators. And you'll do so while working within another Android app project.

Chapter 11: Time-Based Operators

By Alex Sullivan & Florent Pillet

Timing is everything. The core idea behind reactive programming is to model asynchronous data flow *over time*.

In this respect, RxJava provides a range of operators that allow you to deal with time and the way that sequences react and transform over time. As you'll see throughout this chapter, managing the time dimension of your sequences is easy and straightforward.

To learn about **time-based operators**, you'll practice with an animated app that demonstrates visually how data flows over time. This chapter comes with a basic app with several buttons that lead to different pages. You'll use each page to exercise one or more related operators. The app also includes a number of ready-made classes that'll come in handy to build the examples.

Getting started

Open the starter project for this section, then build and run the app. You should see a white screen with five gray buttons:

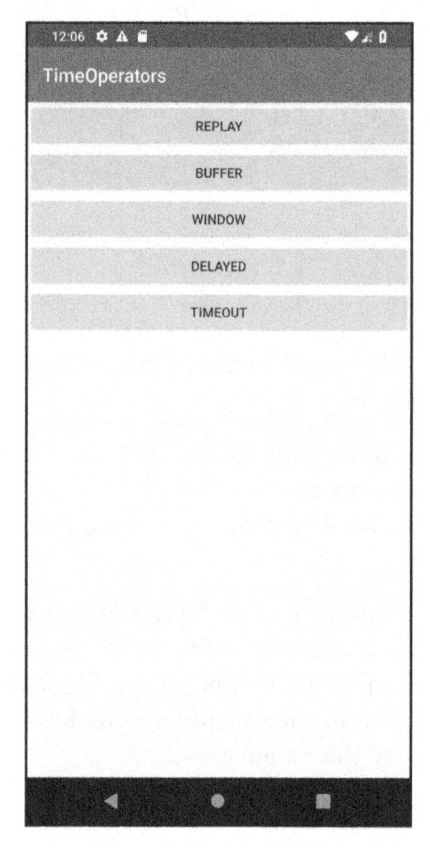

Clicking any of these buttons will send you to another screen that, for now, just has some text. As you work through this chapter, you'll flesh out each page to demonstrate a different set of time-based reactive operators.

Buffering operators

The first group of time-based operators deal with **buffering**. They will either replay past elements to new subscribers, or buffer them and deliver them in bursts. They allow you to control how and when past and new elements get delivered.

Replaying past elements

When a sequence emits items, you'll often need to make sure that a future subscriber receives some or all of the past items. This is the purpose of the `replay` and `replayAll` operators.

To learn how to use them, you'll start coding in the **replay** page of the app. To visualize what `replay` does, you'll display elements on a marble diagram-like view. The app contains custom classes to make it easy to display animated timelines.

Open **ReplayActivity.kt**.

> **Note**: For this chapter, you'll forgo the usual `ViewModel` + `Activity` approach takes elsewhere in the app. Since this app is meant to demonstrate different time-oriented operators, you don't need to worry about using a proper architecture.

Start by adding some definitions above the `class ReplayActivity : AppCompatActivity()` line:

```
val elementsPerSecond = 1
val replayedElements = 1
val replayDelayInMs = 3500L
val maxElements = 5
```

You'll create an Observable that emits elements at a frequency of `elementsPerSecond`. You'll also cap the total number of elements emitted, and control how many elements are "played back" to new subscribers. Build this emitting Observable in `onCreate()`, by using the `timer` function:

```
val sourceObservable = Observable.create<Int> { emitter ->
  var value = 1
  val disposable = timer(elementsPerSecond) {
    if (value <= maxElements) {
      emitter.onNext(value)
      value++
    }
  }
}
```

The `timer` function is a helper function defined in **TimerUtils.kt**. It helps to create simple repeating timers. Feel free to look at its implementation, but it may not make sense until later in the chapter, when you cover the `interval` method. Suffice to say it uses **RxJava** under the hood and returns a `Disposable`.

In the lambda passed to the `timer` function, you're using the `emitter` object to emit the next `value` and then incrementing `value`. At the end of the day, this Observable should now emit increasing values at the frequency you defined earlier.

Note that, for the purpose of this example, you don't care about *completing* the Observable. It simply emits as many elements as instructed and never completes.

Now, add the replay functionality to the end of the `sourceObservable` declaration:

```
.replay(replayedElements)
```

This operator creates a new sequence that records the last `replayedElements` number of elements emitted by the source Observable. Every time a new observer subscribes, it immediately receives these elements (if any) and then keeps receiving any new element like a normal subscription does.

To visualize the actual effects of `replay`, you're going to use a custom UI widget created for this chapter called `MarbleView`. The `MarbleView` class shows elements as they're emitted on a timeline, similar to the marble diagrams you've seen in previous chapters.

For this page, there are two `MarbleView`s already included in the `activity_replay` layout file. You'll use these two views to visualize the `replay` operators.

Add the following at the bottom of the `onCreate` method:

```
sourceObservable.subscribe(replay_1)
```

`replay_1` is the name of the first `MarbleView` for this screen.

The `MarbleView` class implements the `Observer` RxJava interface. Therefore, you can subscribe it to an Observable sequence and it will receive the sequence's events. Every time a new event occurs (element emitted, sequence completed or errored out), `MarbleView` displays it on the timeline.

Next, you want to subscribe again to the source Observable, but with a slight delay. Add the following again at the bottom of the `onCreate` method:

```
dispatchAfter(replayDelayInMs) {
  sourceObservable.subscribe(replay_2)
}
```

> `dispatchAfter` is another special function to make it easier to perform one-off actions.

This displays elements received by the second subscription in another marble view. You'll see the marble view shortly, I promise!

Now, since `replay` creates a **connectable Observable**, you need to connect it to its underlying source to start receiving items. If you forget this, subscribers will never receive anything.

> **Note**: Connectable Observables are a special class of Observables. Regardless of their number of subscribers, they won't start emitting items until you call their `connect()` method. While this is beyond the scope of this chapter, remember that a couple of operators return `ConnectableObservable`, not `Observable`. Specifically, the `replay` and `publish` operators.
>
> Replay operators are covered in this chapter. The publish operator is advanced, and only touched on briefly in this book. It allows sharing a single subscription to an Observable, regardless of the number of observers.

So add this code to connect, at the end of `onCreate()`:

```
sourceObservable.connect()
```

Now, build and run the app and navigate to the replay page.

You'll see two timelines. The top marble view reflects an observer named `connect()` that subscribes before you.

The bottom marble view is the one where subscription occurs after a delay. The source Observable emits numbers for convenience.

This way you can see the progress of emitted elements.

> **Note:** As exciting it is to see a live Observable diagram, it might confuse at first. **Static timelines** usually have their elements aligned to the left, but if you think twice about it, they also have the most recent ones on the right side just as the animated diagrams you observe right now.

In the settings you used, `replayedElements` is equal to 1. It configures the `replay` operator to only buffer the last element from the source Observable. The animated marble view shows that the second subscriber receives element **3** and then quickly receives element **4** afterwards. That's because the **3** element was the one being replayed. Then the **4** element was emitted normally.

Try raising the `replayedElements` constant to two instead of one. You'll see a much more noticeable impact on the `MarbleView`:

Since two elements were buffered, they were all emitted at the same time. The `MarbleView` class will group items emitted at (or around) the same time in a column to make them more visible.

> **Note**: You can now play with the `replayDelay` and `replayedElements` constants. Observe the effect of tweaking the number of replayed (buffered) elements. You can also tweak the total number of elements emitted by the source Observable using `maxElements`. Set it to a very large value for "continuous" emission.

Unlimited replay

In addition to the `replay` operator that takes in a maximum number of elements, there's an overloaded version of `replay` that takes no arguments. If used with no arguments, the `replay` operator will ensure that every item in your Observable is replayed. This one should be used with caution: Only use it in scenarios where you know the total number of buffered elements will stay reasonable. For example, it's appropriate to use `replay` with no arguments in the context of HTTP requests. You know the approximate memory impact of retaining the data returned by a query. On the other hand, using it on a sequence that may not terminate and may produce a lot of data will quickly clog your memory. This could grow to the point where you see an `OutOfMemoryException`!

To experiment with this new behavior, replace:

```
.replay(replayedElements)
```

With:

```
.replay()
```

Watch the effect on the marble view. You will see all buffered elements emitted instantly upon the second subscription.

Controlled buffering

Now that you touched on replayable sequences, you can look at a more advanced topic: **controlled buffering**. You'll first look at the `buffer` operator. Switch to the second page in the app called **BUFFER**. As in the previous example, you'll begin with some constants. Add the following to the top of the **BufferActivity.kt** file:

```
private val bufferMaxCount = 2
private val bufferTimeSpan = 4L
```

These constants define the behavior for the `buffer` operator you'll soon add to the code. For this example, you'll manually feed a subject with values. At the bottom of the `onCreate` method add:

```
val sourceObservable = PublishSubject.create<String>()
```

You will push short strings (a single emoji) to this Observable. You'll again use two predefined `MarbleView` widgets contained in the **activity_buffer.xml** layout file.

Subscribe to fill the top marble view with events, like you did in the **REPLAY** page:

```
sourceObservable
  .subscribe(buffer_1)
```

The buffered marble view will display the number of elements contained in each buffered array:

```
sourceObservable
  .buffer(bufferTimeSpan, TimeUnit.SECONDS, bufferMaxCount)
  .map { it.size }
  .subscribe(buffer_2)
```

What's happening here? Breaking it down:

- You want to receive lists of elements from the source Observable.

- Each list can hold **at most** bufferMaxCount elements.

- If that many elements are received before bufferTimeSpan expires, the operator will emit buffered elements and reset its timer.

- In a delay of bufferTimeSpan after the last emitted group, **buffer** will emit a list. If no element has been received during this time frame, the list will be empty.

Try building and running the app and navigating to the **BUFFER** page now.

Even though there is no activity on the source Observable, you can witness empty buffers on the buffered marble view. The buffer operator emits empty lists at regular intervals if nothing has been received from its source Observable. The 0s mean that zero elements have been emitted from the source Observable.

You can start feeding the raw Observable with data and observe the impact on the buffered Observable. First, try pushing three elements after five seconds. Append this to the bottom of the onCreate() method:

```
dispatchAfter(5000) {
  sourceObservable.onNext("🐱")
  sourceObservable.onNext("🐱")
  sourceObservable.onNext("🐱")
}
```

Can you guess what the effect will be? Build and run, and look how the marble view moves:

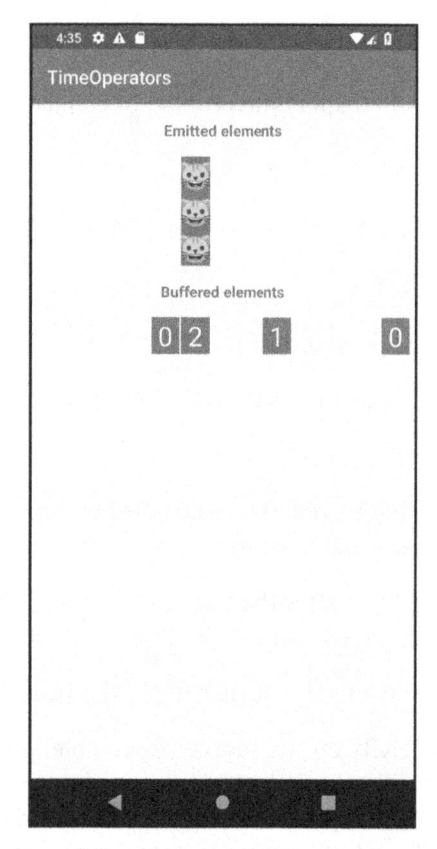

Each box shows the number of elements in each emitted array:

- At first, the buffered marble view emits an empty array — there's no element in the source Observable yet and the `bufferTimeSpan` amount of time has passed.

- Then you push three elements on the source Observable.

- The buffered marble view immediately gets an array of two elements because it's the maximum count you specified (due to the `bufferMaxCount` constant).

- Four seconds elapse, and a list with just one element is emitted. This is the last of the three elements that have been pushed to the source Observable.

As you can see, the buffer immediately emits an array of elements when it reaches full capacity, then waits for the specified delay, or until it's full again, before it emits a new array.

You can play a bit more with different buffering scenarios. Remove the
`dispatchAfter` that emits elements, and add this instead:

```
val elementsPerSecond = 1

timer(elementsPerSecond) {
  sourceObservable.onNext("😀")
}.addTo(disposables)
```

The marble view is very different! As before, you can tweak the constants (buffering time, buffering limit, elements per second) to see how grouping works.

Windows of buffered Observables

A last buffering technique very close to `buffer` is `window`. It has roughly the same signature and nearly does the same thing. The only difference is that it emits an `Observable` of the buffered items, instead of emitting an array.

You're going to build a slightly more elaborate `MarbleView`. Since windowed sequences emit multiple Observables, it will be beneficial to visualize them separately. Get started in the `WindowActivity`, which is the root of the **WINDOW** page by adding several constants to just after the class declaration of `WindowActivity`:

```
private val elementsPerSecond = 3
private val windowTimeSpan = 4L
private val windowMaxCount = 10L
```

You're going to look at how timed output is grouped in windowed Observables by pushing strings to a subject. Start off by adding another `PublishSubject<String>` to the bottom of the `onCreate()` method:

```
val sourceObservable = PublishSubject.create<String>()
```

Now, add a timer to push new strings into the `sourceObservable`:

```
timer(elementsPerSecond) {
  sourceObservable.onNext("😀")
}.addTo(disposables)
```

Then fill up the source marble view:

```
sourceObservable.subscribe(windowSource)
```

You're now at a point where you want to see each emitted Observable separately. To this end, you'll insert a new `MarbleView` every time `window` emits a new Observable.

Previous Observables will move downwards. Just before the end of `onCreate()`, append the following:

```
sourceObservable.window(windowTimeSpan, TimeUnit.SECONDS,
AndroidSchedulers.mainThread(), windowMaxCount)
```

This is your windowed Observable. How can you handle emitted Observables? Using your trusted `flatMap` operator of course! Chain this under the `window` operator:

```
.flatMap { windowedObservable ->
  val marbleView = MarbleView(this)
  marble_views.addView(marbleView)
  windowedObservable
    .map { value -> value to marbleView}
    .concatWith(Observable.just("" to marbleView))
}
```

This is the tricky part. Try to figure out the code yourself first, and then fall back on the following:

- Every time `flatMap` gets a new Observable, you insert a new `MarbleView` into the already existing `marble_views` layout.

- You then map the Observable of items to an Observable of pairs. The goal is to transport both the value and the marble view in which to display it.

- Once this inner Observable completes, you `concatWith` a single pair with an empty first value, so you can mark the timeline as complete.

- You `flatMap` the sequence of resulting observables of pairs to a single sequence of tuples.

- You subscribe to the resulting Observable and fill up timelines as you receive tuples.

> **Note**: In trying to keep the code short, you're doing something that is generally not advisable in Rx code: You're adding side effects to an operator that's supposed to just be transforming data. The right solution would be to perform side effects using a `doOnNext` operator. This is left as an exercise in this chapter's challenges!

Finally, you need to subscribe and display elements in each marble view. Since you mapped the elements to the actual marble view they belong to, this becomes easy. Chain this code to the previous:

```
.subscribe { (value, marbleView) ->
  if (value.isEmpty()) {
    marbleView.onComplete()
  } else {
    marbleView.onNext(value)
  }
}
.addTo(disposables)
```

The value in the tuple is a String: The convention here is that if it is empty, then it means the sequence completed. The code pushes either a next or a completed event to the marble view.

Build and run the app, and navigate to the window page. Things very quickly get interesting as new observables are emitted:

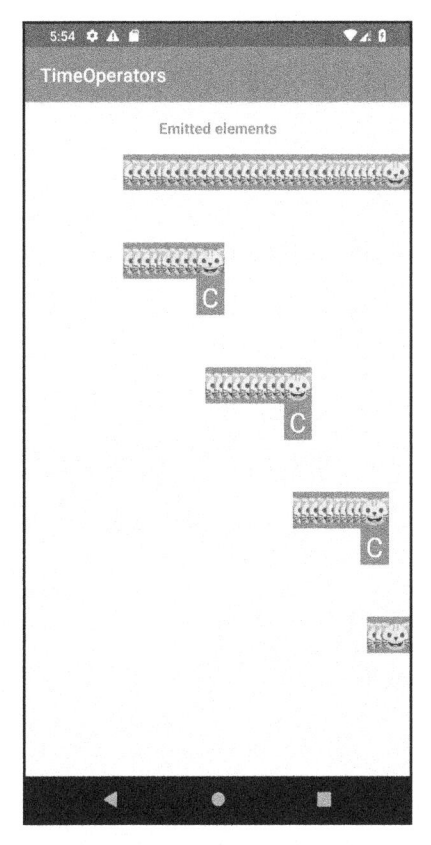

The `C` value at the bottom of some of the `MarbleViews` represent that Observable completing.

Starting from the second timeline, all the timelines you see are "most recent first." This screenshot was taken with a setting of ten elements maximum per windowed Observable, and a four-second window. This means that a new observable is produced at least every four seconds. It will emit, at most, ten elements before completing.

If the source Observable emits more than nine elements during the window time, a new Observable is produced, and the cycle starts again.

Time-shifting operators

Every now and again, you need to travel in time. While RxJava can't help with fixing your past relationship mistakes, it has the ability to freeze time for a little while to let you wait until self-cloning is available.

Next, you'll look into two time related operators. Navigate to **DelayActivity.kt** to get started.

Delayed subscriptions

Start off by adding the constants to the top of the class:

```
private val elementsPerSecond = 1
private val delayInSeconds = 3L
```

Next up, add a new `PublishSubject` at the bottom of the `onCreate()` method:

```
val sourceObservable = PublishSubject.create<Int>()
```

Now, add the code to add items to the `sourceObservable` below the previous declaration:

```
var current = 1
timer(elementsPerSecond) {
  sourceObservable.onNext(current)
  current++
}
```

And subscribe to `sourceObservable` with the `source MarbleView`:

```
sourceObservable.subscribe(source)
```

You're going to start off the delay section by using the `delaySubscription` operator. Append the following:

```
sourceObservable
  .delaySubscription(delayInSeconds, TimeUnit.SECONDS,
AndroidSchedulers.mainThread())
  .subscribe(delayed)
```

The idea behind the `delaySubscription` operator is, as the name implies, to delay the time a subscriber starts receiving elements from its subscription. Run the app and navigate to the **DELAYED** page, you can observe that the second marble view starts picking up elements after the delay specified by `delayInSeconds`.

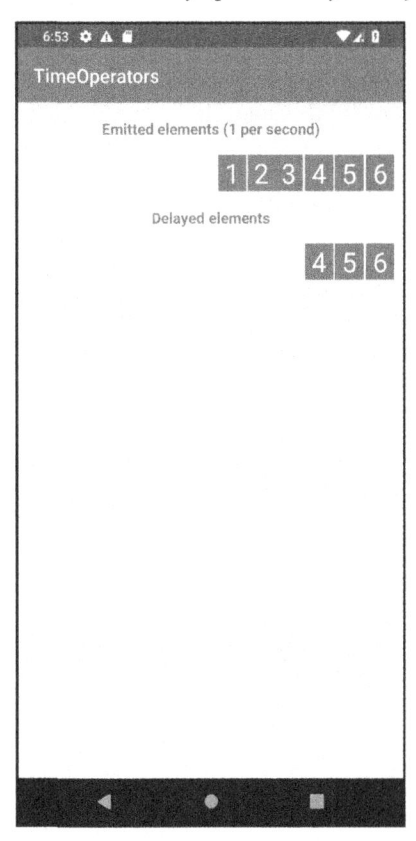

> **Note**: In Rx, some observables are called **cold** while others are **hot**. Cold Observables start emitting elements when you subscribe to them. Hot Observables are more like permanent sources you happen to subscribe to, at some point (think of broadcasts received in a `BroadcastReceiver`). When delaying a subscription, it won't make a difference if the Observable is cold. If it's hot, you may skip elements, as in this example.
>
> Hot and cold Observables are a tricky topic that can take some time getting your head around. Remember that cold Observables emit events only when subscribed to, but hot Observables emit events independent of being subscribed to.

Delayed elements

The other kind of delay in RxJava lets you time-shift the whole sequence. Instead of subscribing late, the operator subscribes *immediately* to the source observable, but delays every emitted element by the specified amount of time. The net result is a concrete time-shift.

To try this out, stay in the `DelayActivity`. Replace the delayed subscription (that you just added) with:

```
sourceObservable
  .delay(delayInSeconds, TimeUnit.SECONDS,
    AndroidSchedulers.mainThread())
  .subscribe(delayed)
```

As you can see, the code is similar. You just replaced `delaySubscription` with `delay`. Run the app and look at the marble views. Can you spot the difference?

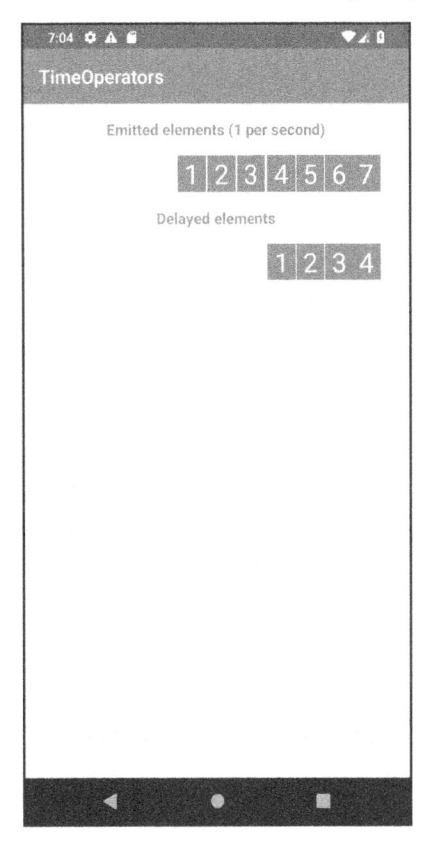

In the previous example, delaying the subscription made you miss the first three elements from the source Observable. When using the `delay` operator, you time-shift the elements and won't miss any. Again, the *subscription* occurs immediately. You simply "see" the items with a delay.

Timer operators

A common need in any kind of application is a *timer*. Android comes with a few methods to accomplish timing tasks. Typically, Android developers use the `Handler` class to accomplish this sort of task. `Handler` works OK, but the API is somewhat complicated unless you wrap it, like we did in this app with the `dispatchAfter` function.

RxJava provides a simple and efficient solution for both one-shot and repeating timers. It integrates perfectly with sequences and offers both cancellation and composability with other sequences.

Intervals

This chapter used the `timer` function several times to create interval timers through a handy custom function. In fact, the `timer` function uses another special RxJava function to achieve its timing tasks. Specifically, it uses the `Observable.interval` function. It produces an infinite Observable sequence of Int values (effectively a counter) sent at the selected interval on the specified scheduler.

In order to get some practice with the `Observable.interval` function, you're going to go back through some of the work you did previously and replace instances of the `timer` function with a direct call to `Observable.timer`. Go back to **ReplayActivity.kt** class. Towards the beginning of the code, you created a source Observable. You used `timer` to create a timer and feed observers with values.

Delete the declaration of `sourceObservable` (including the `replay()`) and replace it with this instead:

```
val sourceObservable = Observable.interval(1L /
elementsPerSecond,
  TimeUnit.SECONDS,
  AndroidSchedulers.mainThread()).replay(replayedElements)
```

And. That's. All.

Interval timers are incredibly easy to create with RxJava. Not only that, but they are also easy to cancel: Since `Observable.interval` generates an Observable sequence, subscriptions can simply `dispose()` the returned disposable to cancel the subscription and stop the timer. Very cool!

It is notable that the first value is emitted at the specified duration after a subscriber starts observing the sequence, not immediately. Also, the timer won't start before this point. The subscription is the trigger that kicks it off.

> **Note**: As you can see in the marble view if you run the app, values emitted by `Observable.interval` are integers starting from 0. Should you need different values, you can simply map them, or use the `Observable.intervalRange` function, which allows you supply both a starting value and a total number of items to emit. In most real life use-cases, the value emitted by the timer is simply ignored. But it can make a convenient index.

One-shot or repeating timers

You may want a more powerful timer Observable. You can use the `Observable.timer` operator that is very much like `Observable.interval` but adds the following features:

- You can specify a "due date" as the time that elapsed between the point of subscription and the first emitted value.

- The repeat period is *optional*. If you don't specify one, the timer Observable will emit once, then complete.

Can you see how handy this can be? Give it a go. Open the **DelayActivity.kt** again. Locate the place where you used the `delay` operator. Replace the whole block of code with:

```
Observable.timer(3, TimeUnit.SECONDS)
  .flatMap {
    sourceObservable.delay(delayInSeconds, TimeUnit.SECONDS)
  }
  .subscribe(delayed)
```

A timer triggering another timer? This *is* Inception! There are several benefits to using this over `Handler`:

- The whole chain is more readable (more "Rx-y").

- Since the subscription returns a `Disposable`, you can cancel at any point before the first or second timer triggers with a single Observable.

- Using the `flatMap` operator, you can produce timer sequences without having to jump through hoops with `Handler` lambdas.

Timeouts

You'll complete this roundup of time-based Operators with a special one: **timeout**. Its primary purpose is to semantically distinguish an actual timer from a timeout (error) condition. Therefore, when a timeout operator fires, it emits an `TimeoutException` error event; if not caught, it terminates the sequence.

Open the **TimeoutActivity.kt** file. The associated **activity_timeout.xml** layout file contains a single `MarbleView` and a `Button`.

You're going to use an extension from RxBindings that turns button taps into an Observable sequence. You'll learn more about RxBindings in the following chapters. For now, the goal is to:

- Capture button taps.

- If the button is pressed within five seconds, print something and terminate the sequence.

- If the button is not pressed, print the error condition.

In `onCreate()`, set up the Observable and connect it to the marble view:

```
button.clicks()
  .map { "•" }
  .timeout(5, TimeUnit.SECONDS)
  .subscribe(timeout)
```

Build and run, and click the "Timeout" button on the landing page. If you click the button within five seconds (and within five seconds of subsequent presses), you'll see your taps on the marble view. Stop clicking, and five seconds after that, the timeout fires! The marble view will stop with an error donated by a big E.

An alternate version of `timeout` takes an Observable and, when the timeout fires, switches the subscription to this Observable instead of emitting an error.

There are many uses for this form of timeout, one of which is to emit a value (instead of an error) then complete normally.

To try this, change the `timeout` call to the following:

```
.timeout(5, TimeUnit.SECONDS, Observable.just("X"))
```

Now, instead of the error indicator, you see the "X" element and a regular completion. Mission accomplished!

Challenge

Challenge: Circumscribe side effects

In the discussion of the `window` operator, you created timelines on the fly inside the closure of a `flatMap` operator. While this was done to keep the code short, one of the guidelines of reactive programming is to "not leave the monad". In other words, avoid side effects except for specific areas created to apply side effects. Here, the "side effect" is the creation of a new marble view in a spot where only a transformation should occur.

Your task is to find an alternate way to do this. You can consider several approaches; try to pick the one that seems the most elegant to you. When finished, compare it with the proposed solution!

There are several possible approaches to tackle this challenge. The most effective will be to split the work into multiple Observables then join them later.

Make the windowed Observable a separate one that you use to produce two separate sequences.

1. The first one prepares the marble views (remember that side effects can be performed with the `doOnNext` operator).

2. The second one takes both the produced marble view and the source sequence element to generate a contextual value, every time `window` emits a new sequence. You might want to use a combination of `zip` and `flatMap` for this.

Key points

- When a sequence emits items, you'll often need to make sure that a future subscriber receives some or all of the past items. This is the purpose of the `replay` and `replayAll` operators.
- **Buffering operators** are a group of time-based operators that deal with **buffering**. They will either replay past elements to new subscribers, or buffer them and deliver them in bursts. They allow you to control how and when past and new elements get delivered.
- `dispatchAfter` is a special function to make it easier to dispatch one-off actions. This displays elements received by the second subscription in another marble view.
- `delaySubscription` operators delay the time a subscriber starts receiving elements from its subscription. `delay` operators push the elements to they arrive later.
- The `Observable.interval` function produces an infinite Observable sequence of `Int` values (effectively a counter) sent at the selected interval on the specified scheduler.
- **Timeout** is an operator that semantically distinguishes an actual timer from a timeout (error) condition. Therefore, when a timeout operator fires, it emits an `TimeoutException` error event; if not caught, it terminates the sequence.

Section III: Intermediate RxJava

Once you start writing complete apps with RxJava, you will also need to take care of more intermediate topics than simply observing for events and processing them with Rx.

In a full production-quality app, you will need to build an error handling strategy, do more advanced multi-threading processing, create a solid test suite, and more.

In this part of the book, you will work through five challenging chapters, which will lift your Rx status from a rookie level to a battle-tested warrior.

Chapter 12: Error Handling in Practice

By Alex Sullivan & Junior Bontognali

Life would be great if we lived in a perfect world, but unfortunately things frequently don't go as expected. Even the best RxJava developers can't avoid encountering errors, so they need to know how to deal with them gracefully and efficiently. In this chapter, you'll learn how to deal with errors, how to manage error recovery through retries, or just surrender yourself to the universe and let the errors go.

Getting started

The app you'll be creating for this chapter is a weather app. It will allow a user to type in a city name and see the weather for that city. It will also allow the user to use their current location as the trigger to fetch weather details. To accomplish all of this, you'll use the **OpenWeatherMap API**.

Before continuing, make sure you have a valid **OpenWeatherMap** API Key http://openweathermap.org. If you don't already have a key, you can sign up for one at https://home.openweathermap.org/users/sign_up.

Once you've completed the sign-up process, visit the dedicated page for API keys at https://home.openweathermap.org/api_keys and generate a new one.

Open the starter project in Android Studio. In the starter project, open the **WeatherApi.kt** file, take the key you generated above and replace the placeholder in the following location:

```
val apiKey =
    BehaviorSubject.createDefault("INSERT_YOUR_API_KEY_HERE")
```

Once that's done, run the app. When prompted, grant the app permission to use the device's location. After you grant permission, you'll see the following screen:

Try entering some text into the top `EditText` box at the top of the screen where it says **Current Location**. You should see the weather details change. You should also see a nice image in the center of the app indicating what the current weather is. For example, if it's snowing outside, you'll see a cloud with some snow underneath. Brrrr!

If you instead see nothing show up, then that might mean you hit an error. Make sure the API key you entered is valid and that the city name you entered is a real city. If you just created your account, make sure you check your email to confirm your email address. You'll have to re-run the app if it did experience an error when making the initial API call. Not a great user experience, right?

This good news is you're going to fix that user experience!

Before you start diving into managing errors, it's a good idea to get acquainted with the code for the app. Open the `WeatherViewModel` and look around. It takes one argument:

```
private val lastKnownLocation: Maybe<Location>
```

`lastKnownLocation` is a `Maybe` representing the last known location of the user. If you're interested in learning about how the app creates a `Maybe` out of the last known location, take a look at the `lastKnownLocation` method in the **X.kt** file.

In addition to the `lastKnownLocation` constructor parameter, `WeatherViewModel` exposes two public methods that `WeatherActivity` uses to notify the `ViewModel` of clicks on the location button and text change events:

```
fun locationClicked() = locationClicks.onNext(Unit)

fun cityNameChanged(name: CharSequence) =
  cityNameChanges.onNext(name)
```

These methods pipe their relevant values into a couple of `PublishSubjects` that are defined at the top of the file:

```
private val locationClicks = PublishSubject.create<Unit>()
private val cityNameChanges =
  PublishSubject.create<CharSequence>()
```

Now you can easily represent users actions as streams. Hooray!

In the `init` block, `WeatherViewModel` uses the `Observable.merge` function to merge the two subjects built from `locationClicks` and `cityNameChanges` to create a final Observable that will emit `Weather` updates to the `weatherLiveData` object.

Notice that the `locationObservable` declaration uses the `onErrorReturnItem()` method to default to an empty instance of the `Weather` object if the stream emits any errors.

Sure, it's a nice, compact, single line, but it doesn't make for a great UX. You can do way better!

Managing errors

Errors are an inevitable part of any app. Unfortunately, no one can guarantee an app will never error out, so you will always need some type of error-handling mechanism.

Some of the most common errors in apps:

- **No internet connection**: This is quite common. If the app needs an internet connection to retrieve and process the data, but the device is offline, you need to be able to detect this and respond appropriately.

- **Invalid input**: Sometimes you require a certain form of input, but the user might enter something entirely different. Perhaps you have a phone number field in your app, but the user ignores that requirement and enters letters instead of digits.

- **API error or HTTP error**: Errors from an API can vary widely. They can arrive as a standard HTTP error (response code from 400 to 500), or as errors in the response, such as using the `status` field in a JSON response.

In RxJava, error handling is part of the framework and it handles them in two ways:

- **onError**: Return a default value.

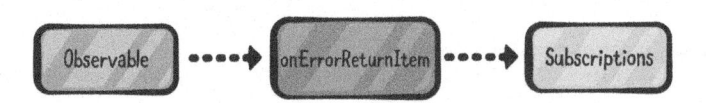

- **Retry**: Retry for a limited (or unlimited!) number of times.

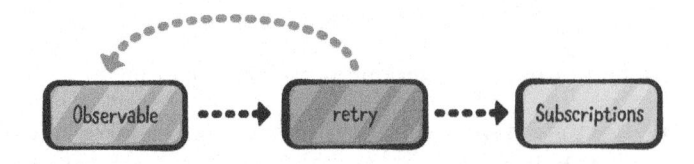

The starter version of this chapter's project doesn't have any real error handling. All the errors are caught with a single `onErrorReturnItem()` operator that returns a dummy version of the weather. This might sound like a handy solution, but there are better ways to handle this in RxJava. A consistent and informative error-handling approach is expected in any app.

At this point, it's worth noting that there's nothing magical about how RxJava propagates errors. For example, if you're in an operator and you want to signal an error that ends the rest of the Observable chain, all you have to do is throw an error just like you would in normal Kotlin code. That error will then propagate down to the subscriber, who may or may not handle it.

Handling errors with catch

Now that you know about the types of errors you can encounter, it's time to see how to handle those errors. The most basic way is to use one of the onError. operators. The onError operators works much like the try-catch flow in plain Kotlin.

When an Observable performs, and if something goes wrong, you can return an event that wraps an error. In RxJava there are two main operators to catch errors. The first is onErrorResumeWith().

onErrorResumeWith() allows you to return a different Observable when your Rx chain encounters an error. The chain will then switch to emitting items from the Observable passed to onErrorResumeWith() whenever it encounters an error. Here's the method signature, written in Java:

```java
public final Observable<T> onErrorResumeWith(
  @NonNull ObservableSource<? extends T> fallback
)
```

Sometimes you may want to return a different type of Observable depending on the error. In that scenario, you can use onErrorResumeNext(). Instead of directly taking an Observable, onErrorResumeNext() takes in a function. That function is itself called by the RxJava library with an error whenever it encounters an error. You then return an Observable from the function, allowing you to customize what type of Observable you return based off the type of error you encountered.

If you can't quite see where you'd use this option, think about a caching strategy that returns a previously cached value if the Observable errors out. With this operator, you can then achieve the following flow:

The `onErrorResumeNext()` in this case returns values that were previously available and that, for some reason, aren't available anymore.

The second operator is `onErrorReturnItem()`:

```
public final Observable<T> onErrorReturnItem(final T item)
```

This operator is how the app is currently handling errors.

`onErrorReturnItem()` ignores errors and just returns a pre-defined value, as opposed to `onErrorResumeWith()` which returns a new Observable to switch to. Just like `onErrorResumeWith()`, there's a version of `onErrorReturnItem()` that takes in a function to produce an item given an error.

Avoiding a common pitfall

Errors propagate through the Observable's chain, so an Observable will forward an error that happens at the beginning of an Observable chain to the final subscription if there aren't any handling operators in place.

What does this mean exactly? When an Observable errors out, error subscriptions are notified and all subscriptions are then disposed. So when an Observable errors out, the Observable is essentially terminated and any events following the error will be ignored. This is a rule of the Observable contract.

You can see this plotted below on a timeline. Once the network produces an error and the Observable sequences errors out, the subscription updating the UI will stop working, effectively preventing future updates:

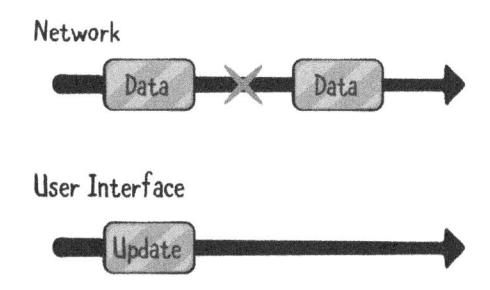

Network

Data —✗— Data →

User Interface

Update →

To translate this into the actual app, remove the `.onErrorReturnItem(Weather.empty)` line inside the `textObservable` in `WeatherViewModel`. Then update the `subscribe()` line in the `Observable.merge()` chain at the bottom of the `init` block to catch the error:

```
.subscribeBy(
  onError = {
    Log.e("Weather", "Error: $it")
  },
  onNext = {
    weatherLiveData.postValue(it)
  }
)
```

Run the app and type in a city that doesn't exist. Something gibberish like **asdf** works just fine. You should see something similar to this in the Logcat console:

```
E/Weather: Error: java.lang.IllegalStateException: Not Found
```

That Not Found message is the tip of a 404 iceberg. You will also notice that the search stops working after that 404! Even if you then enter a valid city name, no new weather data will show. That's because the Observable has terminated. Not exactly the best user experience, is it?

Even if you use the `onErrorReturnItem()` operator, the Observable will still end. Instead of calling its observer's `onError()` block, it will instead emit the item supplied to `onErrorReturnItem()` and call the observer's `onComplete()` method. One common mistake made by people who are new to RxJava error handling is that they expect the Observable to keep emitting items even if it encounters an error.

Catching errors

Now, revert the changes you just made so that the `Observable.merge()` call is using a single line `subscribe()` and the `textObservable` is again returning an empty instance of `Weather` if it encounters an error.

You're going to update the app so that, instead of returning an empty instance of a `Weather` object when encountering an error, you'll look for a cached value of that city's weather to use.

Add the following instance variable below the `disposables val`:

```
private val cache = mutableMapOf<String, Weather>()
```

Your cache will be a simple `Map<String, Weather>`. The key to the map will be the name of the city and the value will be the last `Weather` instance the app pulled down.

It's time to start filling up your cache.

Update the `textObservable` definition by replacing the existing `flatMapSingle()` call with the following:

```
.flatMapSingle { cityName ->
  WeatherApi.getWeather(cityName.toString())
    .doOnSuccess { cache[cityName.toString()] = it }
}
```

Now, every time you get the weather for a particular city, you'll store the results of that network request in the cache. Now, how do you actually pull items from the cache?

To return a cached value in the event of an error, you'll replace the `.onErrorReturnItem(Weather.empty)` operator in the `textObservable` declaration with something a bit more robust.

First, create a new function below the `init` block in `WeatherViewModel`. It will have a compiler error until you fill in the body in the next step:

```
private fun getWeatherForLocationName(
    name: String
): Single<Weather> {
}
```

This function will do the heavy lifting of actually fetching a `Weather` object for a given city name and will replace the existing `flatMapSingle()` call.

Now, add the following to the body of getWeatherForLocationName():

```
return WeatherApi.getWeather(name)
  .doOnSuccess { cache[name] = it }
```

Just like before, you're using the doOnNext() operator to update your cache with the latest and great data.

Now, chain the following after the doOnNext() call:

```
.onErrorReturn {
  cache[name] ?: Weather.empty
}
```

Here's where the magic happens. You're using the onErrorReturn() operator to supply a default item whenever the Observable encounters an error. If you have a cached value of the city's weather, you'll use that value. Otherwise, you'll return the Weather.empty value.

Now that you have the onErrorReturn() operator going in the getWeatherForLocationName() method, you can remove the existing onErrorReturnItem() operator from the textObservable declaration and start using getWeatherForLocationName(). Replace the flatMapSingle() block in the textObservable declaration with the following:

```
.flatMapSingle { getWeatherForLocationName(it.toString()) }
```

To test this, run the app and input three or four various cities such as "London," "Boston," and "Amsterdam," and load the weather for these cities. After that, disable your internet connection and perform a search for a different city, such as "Barcelona"; you'll receive an error and the screen will go blank.

Leave your internet connection disabled and search for one of the cities you just retrieved data for, and the app should return the cached version.

This is a very common usage of onErrorReturn(). You can definitely extend this to make it a general and powerful caching solution.

Retrying on error

Catching an error is just one way you can handle errors in RxJava. You can also handle errors with `retry()`.

When you use a `retry()` operator and an Observable errors out, the Observable will repeat itself. It's important to remember that `retry()` means repeating the *entire* task inside the Observable.

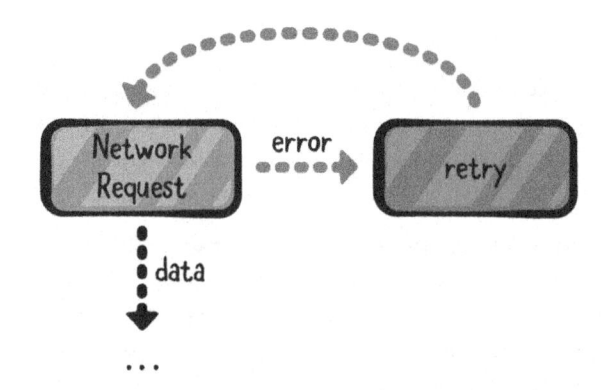

This is one of the main reasons it's recommended to avoid side effects that change the user interface inside an Observable, as you can't control who will retry it!

Retry operators

There are three basic types of `retry()` operators. The first one is the most basic:

```
public final Observable<T> retry()
```

This operator will repeat the Observable an unlimited number of times until it returns successfully. For example, if there's no internet connection, this would continuously retry until the connection was available.

This might sound like a robust idea, but it's resource-heavy, and it's seldom recommended to `retry()` for an unlimited number of times if there's no valid reason for doing it.

To test this operator, comment the complete `onErrorReturn()` block in the `getWeatherForLocationName()` method you recently created:

```
//.onErrorReturn {
//   cache[name] ?: Weather.empty
//}
```

In its place, insert a `retry()`:

```
.retry()
```

Next, run the app, disable the internet connection and try to perform a search. You'll see a lot of output in Logcat, showing the app is trying to make the requests. After a few seconds, re-enable the internet connection, and you'll see the result displayed once the app has successfully processed the request.

> **Note**: Remember that `retry()` will keep retrying a failed call *forever*. That means that if you accidentally searched for an invalid city, the app will forever be stuck trying to get the weather for that city! If you're not seeing the results you expect, take a look at the Logcat output. You should see a line that looks something like this `GET https://api.openweathermap.org/data/2.5/weather?q=Boston&appid=<appId>&units=metric`. Make sure the q=MyCity parameter is what you'd expect!

The second operator lets you vary the number of retries:

```
public final Observable<T> retry(long times)
```

With this variation, the Observable is repeated for a specified number of times. To give it a try, do the following:

- Remove the `retry()` operator you just added.
- Uncomment the previously commented code block.
- Just before `onErrorReturn`, insert a `.retry(3)`.

The complete `getWeatherForLocationName` method should now look like this:

```
private fun getWeatherForLocationName(name: String):
Single<Weather> {
  return WeatherApi.getWeather(name)
    .doOnSuccess { cache[name] = it }
    .retry(3)
    .onErrorReturn {
      cache[name] ?: Weather.empty
    }
}
```

If the Observable is producing errors, it will be retried three times in succession. If it errors a fourth time, that error will not be handled and execution will move on to the `onErrorReturn()` operator.

Run the app and try searching for the weather with the internet connection disabled again. This time, there should only be four requests made before it stops trying: one initial and three retries.

Advanced retries

The last operator, `retryWhen()`, is suited for advanced retry situations. This error handling operator is considered one of the most powerful:

```
public final Observable<T> retryWhen(
    Function<? super Observable<Throwable>,
        ? extends ObservableSource<?>> handler
)
```

`retryWhen()` takes in a function that when given an Observable of throwables returns a new Observable. That new Observable acts as a type of "trigger" for `retryWhen()`. Whenever it emits a value, `retryWhen()` will retry the original source Observable. Whenever that new trigger Observable calls `onComplete()` or `onError()`, `retryWhen()` will then signal to the original source Observable that the Observable has completed or an error has occurred.

`retryWhen()` is one of the most complicated operators you will experience in this book, so don't worry if the above was confusing.

This is the operator you will include in the current application, using a smart trick to retry if the internet connection is not available, or if there's an error from the API. The goal is to implement an incremental back-off strategy if the original search errors out.

The desired result is as follows:

```
subscription -> error
delay and retry after 1 second

subscription -> error
delay and retry after 2 seconds

subscription -> error
delay and retry after 3 seconds

subscription -> error
delay and retry after 4 seconds
```

It's a smart yet complex solution. In regular imperative code, this would imply the creation of some abstractions, perhaps using `AsyncTasks` with `Handler` to run a loop and checking if the task failed or not. But with RxJava, it's a small (albeit complex) block of code.

Before creating the final result, consider what the inner Observable (the trigger Observable) should return. Since `retryWhen()` only looks at the fact that trigger Observable has emitted and not *what* it has emitted, the type can be ignored, and the trigger can be of any type.

The goal is to retry four times with a given sequence of delays. First, inside `WeatherViewModel`, add a new instance variable representing the maximum number of attempts to get the weather the app should make:

```
private val maxAttempts = 4
```

After this many retries, the error should be forwarded on.

Now, replace `.retry(3)` in the `getWeatherForLocationName()` method with the following. There will be a compiler error until you fill in the lambda:

```
.retryWhen { errors: Flowable<Throwable> ->

}
```

You'll learn more about `Flowables` in **Chapter 14, "Flowables & Back Pressure"**, but for now you can think of a `Flowable` in the exact same way you think of an `Observable`. Here's the flow that you want to achieve: Whenever `errors` emits a value, that means a new error has been emitted from the original source Observable. In this scenario you want to emit some value (it doesn't matter what value) after one second, then two seconds, then three seconds, and then four seconds.

So first things first: You need a way to emit items only after a certain amount of time. Luckily, you learned about `Observable.timer()` in the previous chapter! In case you need a quick recap, `Observable.timer()` takes in an amount of time and emits 0L after that amount of time. Then it finishes. Perfect for your needs here!

Add the following code in the currently empty lambda being supplied to the `retryWhen()` operator:

```
errors.flatMap { Flowable.timer(1, TimeUnit.SECONDS) }
```

You need to use a `Flowable` instead of an `Observable` here to satisfy the RxJava type system. Again, for now you can think of a `Flowable` in the same way you think of an `Observable`. Now, every time the `errors` Flowable emits, meaning a new error has been encountered, you'll send a trigger value (in this case 0L) after one second, telling `retryWhen()` to retry the source Observable.

That's great and all, but there are two problems:

1. You're emitting after one second every time. Remember that the goal is to create a sort of back-off strategy in which you wait longer after each network attempt.

2. Every time an error is produced, `Flowable.timer()` will send out an `onNext()` value, triggering another retry. That means that this code effectively retries the network request infinitely. No good!

So you need a way to signal to `Flowable.timer()` that it needs to wait longer and that after a certain number of retries it should just give up.

One way you could achieve the first part about waiting longer is by using `flatMap()` to convert an Observable that emits increasing values into a timer.

Replace the code you just added with the following:

```
errors
  .scan(1) { count, _ ->
    count + 1
  }
  .flatMap { Flowable.timer(it.toLong(), TimeUnit.SECONDS) }
```

Recall that the `scan()` operator works by taking in an initial seed value and a function that, when given an accumulating value and the item emitted by the source Observable, returns a new accumulated value. You can use the `scan()` operator to begin counting up integers and then use `flatMap()` to convert those increasing integers into timers by again using `Flowable.timer()`.

In this manner, you're now waiting longer and longer between network requests.

Last but not least, you need to make sure that you're only retrying the network request a certain number of times. This can be done when combined with the `scan()` method you just wrote. Replace the body of the `scan()` lambda, which currently contains this code:

```
.scan(1) { count, _ ->
  count + 1
}
```

With the following:

```
.scan(1) { count, error ->
  if (count > maxAttempts) {
    throw error
  }
  count + 1
}
```

Now, once you've tried more than `maxAttempts` times, you'll throw the error produced by the errors Observable, indicating to `retryWhen()` that you're done retrying and it's time to give up.

Now, build and run. Disable your internet connection and perform a search. If you look at the Logcat logs, you should see OkHttp making network requests after one second, then two seconds, then three seconds and so on until you hit the maximum number of retries you've specified with `maxAttempts`.

```
GET https://api.openweathermap.org/data/2.5/weather?q=Chicago&appid=5...&units=metric
END GET
HTTP FAILED: java.net.UnknownHostException: Unable to resolve host "api.openweathermap.org": No address associated with hostname
GET https://api.openweathermap.org/data/2.5/weather?q=Chicago&appid=5...&units=metric
END GET
HTTP FAILED: java.net.UnknownHostException: Unable to resolve host "api.openweathermap.org": No address associated with hostname
GET https://api.openweathermap.org/data/2.5/weather?q=Chicago&appid=5...&units=metric
END GET
HTTP FAILED: java.net.UnknownHostException: Unable to resolve host "api.openweathermap.org": No address associated with hostname
GET https://api.openweathermap.org/data/2.5/weather?q=Chicago&appid=5...&units=metric
END GET
HTTP FAILED: java.net.UnknownHostException: Unable to resolve host "api.openweathermap.org": No address associated with hostname
GET https://api.openweathermap.org/data/2.5/weather?q=Chicago&appid=5...&units=metric
END GET
HTTP FAILED: java.net.UnknownHostException: Unable to resolve host "api.openweathermap.org": No address associated with hostname
```

Here's a good visualization of what's going on:

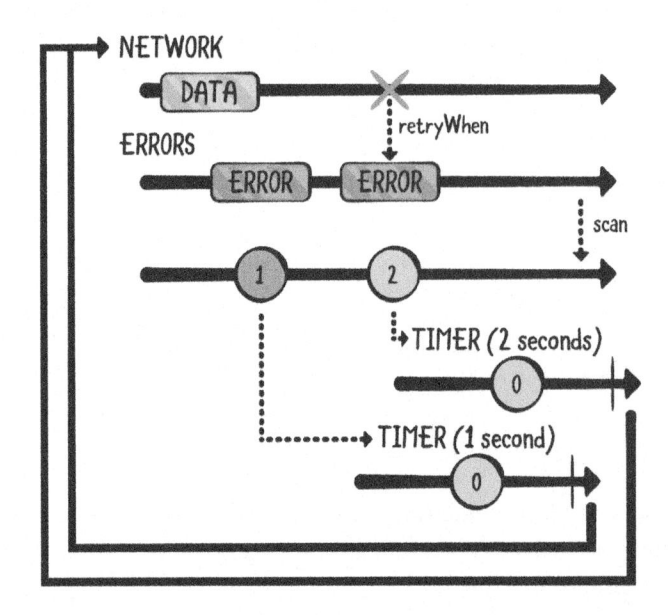

You've only scratched the surface of using `retryWhen()`. To get even fancier, you can inspect the types of errors that you're seeing coming through the `errors` Observable to execute different logic depending on what error you're seeing. We won't go that deep into the rabbit hole in this book, but it's worth exploring on your own!

Errors as objects

As you go deeper into the world of reactive and functional programming, it can become painful to keep dealing with `Throwables` and exceptions for expected results. It often makes more sense to treat an exception as something that your program could not have imagined, and thus does not know how to handle.

For instance, you know that if you type in an invalid city that the OpenWeatherMap API will return a `404` status code. Should that really be modeled as an exception? You know it may happen, and as a matter of fact you know it **will** happen.

Everyone mistypes every now and then, so people are bound to type in an invalid city name in the app. It often makes more sense to model behavior that you know it can happen, but may not be the desired path as an object to be handled later on instead of an exception.

Modeling a network error

Open `WeatherApi` and look at the bottom of the file. You should see two unused sealed classes:

```
sealed class NetworkResult {
  class Success(val weather: Weather) : NetworkResult()
  class Failure(val error: NetworkError) : NetworkResult()
}

sealed class NetworkError : Exception() {
  object ServerFailure : NetworkError()
  object CityNotFound : NetworkError()
}
```

You'll soon update the networking portion of the app such that all network requests that successfully get to the server and come back are mapped to a `NetworkResult` object. Remove the existing `weatherResponseObservable()` and replace it with the following:

```
private fun mapWeatherResponse(
    response: Response<WeatherNetworkModel>
): NetworkResult {
  return when (response.code()) {
    // 1
    in 200..300 -> {
      val body = response.body()
      if (body != null) {
        NetworkResult.Success(
            body.toWeather().copy(icon = iconNameToChar(
                body.weather.first().icon)))
      } else {
        NetworkResult.Failure(NetworkError.ServerFailure)
      }
    }
    // 2
    in 400..500 -> NetworkResult.Failure(
        NetworkError.CityNotFound)
    // 3
    else -> NetworkResult.Failure(NetworkError.ServerFailure)
  }
}
```

That's a big chunk of code! Here's a breakdown:

1. The retrofit interface you're using specifies a Response object as a return type for your network calls. That Response object has a status code attached to it that you're inspecting. If the status code is anywhere in the 200–300 range, that means the call was successful. In this scenario you're attempting to pull out the data from the response and construct a NetworkResult.Success object. If you can't pull the data out, you're instead returning a NetworkResult.Failure with a NetworkError of ServerFailure.

2. You're interpreting any error in the 400–500 range as meaning that the city couldn't be found. This isn't strictly true, but you'll update it later on to be closer to the truth.

3. If you see any response code that's over 500, you're returning a generic server failure, since that usually means something has gone wrong on the server's end.

Now update the two getWeather() calls to produce an Observable<NetworkResult> and use the new mapWeatherResponse() method:

```
fun getWeather(city: String): Single<NetworkResult> {
  return weather.getWeather(city, apiKey.value)
      .map(this::mapWeatherResponse)
}

fun getWeather(location: Location): Single<NetworkResult> {
  return weather.getWeather(
      location.latitude, location.longitude, apiKey.value)
      .map(this::mapWeatherResponse)
}
```

Nice! You've updated your API.

Now, open the WeatherViewModel class. Since you changed the return type of your network Observable from Single<Weather> to Single<NetworkResult>, there are quite a few errors, here.

First off, update the onErrorReturnItem() call in both the locationObservable and textObservable declaration from this:

```
.onErrorReturnItem(Weather.empty)
```

To a version that returns a `NetworkResult`:

```
.onErrorReturnItem(
    WeatherApi.NetworkResult.Success(Weather.empty))
```

Next up, change the return type of `getWeatherForLocationName()` to the following:

```
Single<WeatherApi.NetworkResult>
```

Remove the `doOnSuccess()` operator from `getWeatherForLocationName()`. You'll re-implement the caching strategy in a moment.

Now, replace the `onErrorReturn()` operator with a version that uses the `NetworkResult` class:

```
.onErrorReturn {
  val cachedItem = cache[name] ?: Weather.empty
  WeatherApi.NetworkResult.Success(cachedItem)
}
```

Only one change left! Now that you're returning a `NetworkResult` instead of a `Weather` object, you need to handle that new object in the subscribe block of your merged Observable in the `init` block at the top of the class.

Add the following method to the `WeatherViewModel` class:

```
private fun showNetworkResult(
    networkResult: WeatherApi.NetworkResult
) {
  when (networkResult) {
    // 1
    is WeatherApi.NetworkResult.Success -> {
      cache[networkResult.weather.cityName] =
          networkResult.weather
      weatherLiveData.postValue(networkResult.weather)
    }
    // 2
    is WeatherApi.NetworkResult.Failure -> {
      when (networkResult.error) {
        WeatherApi.NetworkError.ServerFailure ->
            errorLiveData.postValue("Server Failure")
        WeatherApi.NetworkError.CityNotFound ->
            errorLiveData.postValue("City Not Found")
      }
    }
  }
}
```

The above code may seem beefy, but it's not too bad when broken down:

1. You're checking what the actual type of your networkResult is. If it's a successful call to get the weather, you're updating your cache with the new weather and emitting it in your weatherLiveData.

2. If it's a failure, you're checking what the type of failure is and sending a message in your errorLiveData to notify the user of the issue.

Last but not least, replace the subscribe() block on your merged Observable at the bottom of the init block with the following:

```
.subscribe(this::showNetworkResult)
```

You're now ready to rock! Run the app and enter an invalid city name. You should see a snackbar appear above the keyboard indicating the city name was invalid.

Challenges

Challenge 1: Reacting to an invalid API key

Recall that, earlier in the chapter, you started using the NetworkResult object to encapsulate both success and errors from the network. You're currently interpreting values between 400 and 500 as "city not found" errors, but that's not actually the case.

A 401 error means that the auth token that you're using is invalid. Since this project comes with an invalid API key by default, it would be wise to handle this case specifically and let the user know. For this:

1. Update the project so that there's one more possible NetworkError called InvalidKey.

2. mapWeatherResponse() in **WeatherApi.kt** should return a NetworkFailure with the InvalidKey error if it encounters a 401 status code.

3. Update showNetworkResult() in WeatherViewModel to handle the new error type.

To test your implementation, try hitting the key icon in the bottom-right corner of the app and entering an invalid API key. Then search for a city and see if your new error shows up.

Challenge 2: Use retryWhen on restored connectivity

In this challenge you need to handle the condition of an unavailable internet connection.

To start, take a look at `connectivityStream()` in the **X.kt** file. Given a `Context`, it will return an `Observable<NetowrkState>` indicating that the network is connected or disconnected. For this:

1. You'll need to pass an instance of this connectivity stream into the **WeatherViewModel** class.

2. You'll need to update `WeatherViewModel` to take a new argument of type `Observable<NetworkState>`.

3. You can then pass in an Observable in the **WeatherActivity** `ViewModelProviderFactory` code by using the `connectivityStream()` function.

Once these things are done, extend the `retryWhen()` handler to handle the connectivity situation. Remember that when the internet connection is up, you have to fire a retry.

To achieve this:

1. Update the lambda in the `retryWhen()` block in **WeatherViewModel.kt**.

2. You'll want to use the `flatMap()` method on the `errors` Observable. In the `flatMap()` block you'll want to check what type of error is being emitted. If the error is an `UnknownHostException` you know the error is being caused by a lack of internet.

3. In that case, you'll want to return the `connectivityStream` Observable but filtered so that it only emits when the network state changes to `CONNECTED`. Otherwise, you'll want to use the existing logic to slowly back off repeated retries.

The final goal is to have the system automatically retry once the internet is back, if the previous error was due to the device being offline.

As always, you can peek into the challenges folder and see the solution provided.

Key points

- Errors are an inevitable part of any app. You will always need some type of error-handling mechanism.

- **No internet connection** is a common error. If the app needs an internet connection to retrieve and process the data, but the device is offline, you need to be able to detect this and respond appropriately.

- **Invalid input** is a common error. Sometimes you require a certain form of input, but the user might enter something entirely different. Perhaps you have a phone number field in your app, but the user ignores that requirement and enters letters instead of digits.

- **API error or HTTP error** is a common error. Errors from an API can vary widely. They can arrive as a standard HTTP error (response code from 400 to 500), or as errors in the response, such as using the `status` field in a JSON response.

- In RxJava, error handling is part of the framework and can be handled in two ways: **onError** (return a default value) and **retry** (Retry for a limited or unlimited number of times).

Where to go from here?

In this chapter, you were introduced to error handling using `retry()` and `onErrorReturn()`. The way you handle errors in your app really depends on what kind of project you're building. When handling errors, design and architecture come in play, and creating the wrong handling strategy might compromise your project and result in re-writing portions of your code.

You should spend some time playing with `retryWhen()`. It's a non-trivial operator, so the more you play with it, the more you'll feel comfortable using it in your applications.

Chapter 13: Intro to Schedulers

By Alex Sullivan & Junior Bontognali

Until now, you've managed to work with schedulers, while avoiding any explanation about how they handle threading or concurrency. In earlier chapters, you used methods, which implicitly used some sort of concurrency/threading level, such as the `buffer` or `interval` operators.

You probably have a feeling that schedulers have some sort of magic under the hood, but before you understand schedulers, you'll also need to understand what those `observeOn` and `subscribeOn` functions are all about.

This chapter is going to cover the beauty behind schedulers. You'll learn why the Rx abstraction is so powerful and why working with asynchronous programming is far less painful than using `AsyncTasks`, `IntentHandlers` and the myriad of other asynchronous tools Android development offers.

> **Note**: Creating custom schedulers is beyond of the scope of this book. Keep in mind that the schedulers and initializers provided by RxJava generally cover 99% of cases. Always try to use the built-in schedulers.

What is a scheduler?

Before getting your hands dirty with schedulers, it's important to understand what they are — and what they are not. To summarize, a **scheduler** is an abstraction introduced by the RxJava library to schedule work at some point in time. The work happens in some asynchronous context. That context could be custom Threads, an event loop, Executors and so on.

While the Scheduler abstract class is a powerful abstraction over different ways of executing asynchronous code, for Android apps you can usually think of schedulers in relation to threads and thread pools. You'll learn more about the different types of schedulers and how they allow you to switch between threading contexts later on.

Here's a good example as to how schedulers can be used:

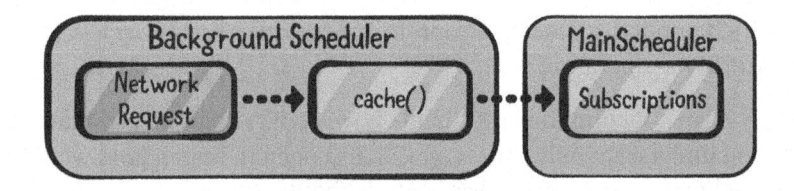

In this diagram, you have the concept of a **cache operator**. An Observable makes a request to a server and retrieves some data. This data is processed by a custom operator named cache, which stores the data somewhere. After this, the data is passed to all subscribers in a different scheduler, most likely the main scheduler, which sits on top of the Android main thread. Remember that anytime you update a UI element in an Android app it *must* be done on the main thread.

Setting up the project

Time to write some code! In this project, you are going to work with an Android app called **Schedulers** that has a profoundly beautiful user interface. That user interface is one TextView in the center of a white screen.

You'll work on this project in Android Studio instead of IntelliJ IDEA, because, in this chapter, you'll also be introduced to the **RxAndroid** library, which requires Android dependencies.

To gaze upon the beginnings of this magnificent app, Open Android studio to its initial screen and select "Open existing project":

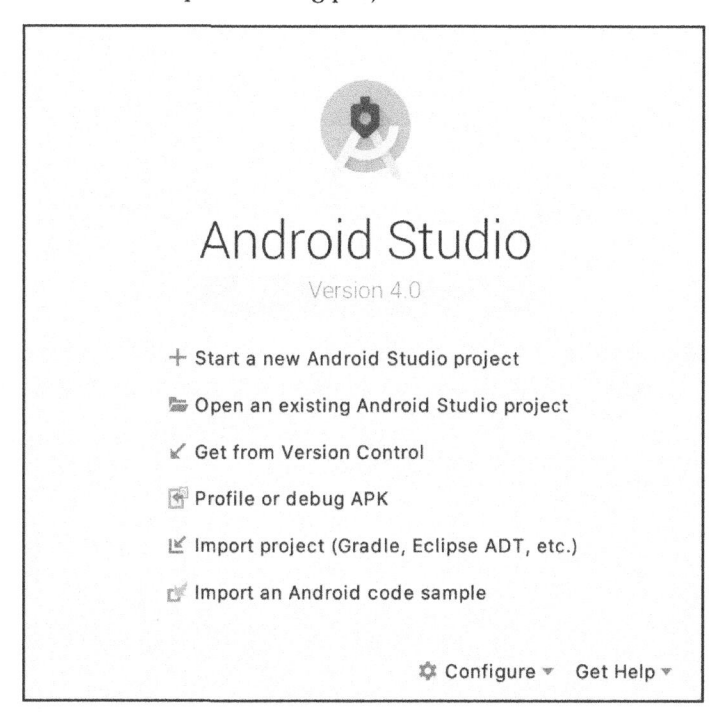

This will cause Android studio to load up and build the project. When it finishes (be patient), you'll see a Play button appear in the top toolbar next to the connected device (or emulator), that's after a litte Android icon and the word app:

Now, use the **Play** button in the top toolbar to build and run the app. You'll see a very basic interface when it runs:

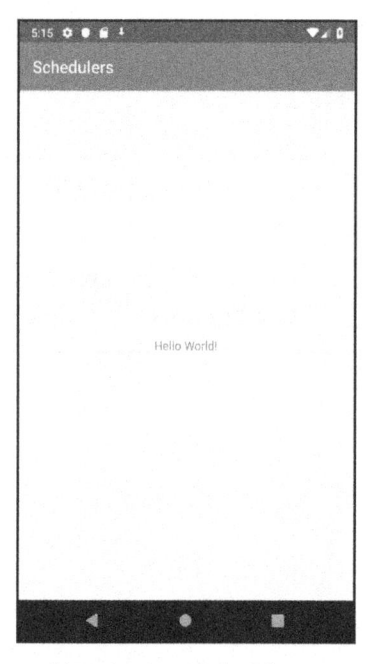

While you'll technically be working on an Android app, you'll be focused almost entirely on the **Logcat** output, which you can find in the bottom console of Android Studio:

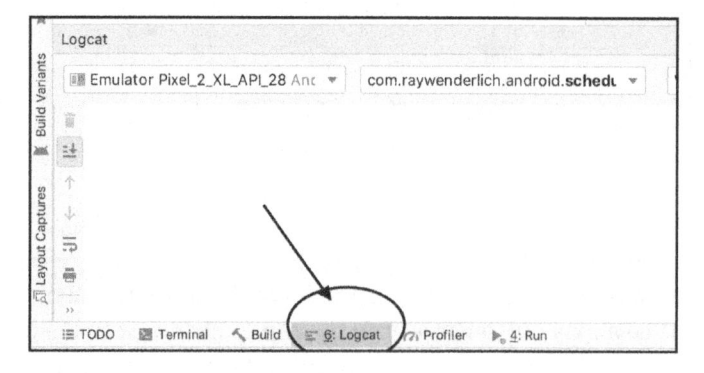

Logcat can get pretty noisy, so you should make sure that you're filtering the output to the **Schedulers** app and filtering it further by including the main `TAG` used by the app when logging. The `TAG` is "SchedulerLogging" and you can filter based off that tag by adding the string in the search box at the top right of the Logcat window:

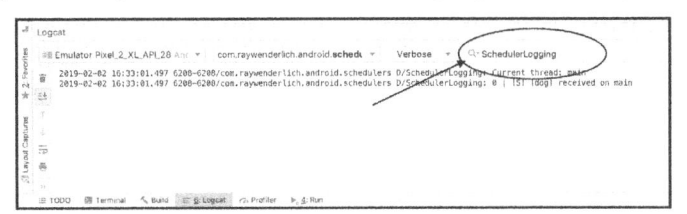

Inspect the filtered Logcat output, and you should see the following:

```
0s | [D] [dog] received on Thread: main
0s | [S] [dog] received on Thread: main
```

Before proceeding, open **X.kt** and take a look at the implementation of `dump` and `dumpingSubscription`.

The first method dumps the element and the current thread information inside a `doOnNext` operator using the `[D]` prefix. The second does the same using the `[S]` prefix, but calls subscribe. Both methods indicate the elapsed time, so the 0s above stand for "0 seconds elapsed."

Switching schedulers

One of the most important things in Rx is the ability to switch schedulers at any time, without any restrictions except for ones imposed by the inner process generating events.

> **Note**: An example of that type of restriction is if the Observable emits non-thread safe objects, which cannot be sent across threads. In that case, RxJava will allow you to switch schedulers, but you would be violating the logic of the underlying code.

To understand how schedulers behave, you'll create a simple Observable to play with that provides some fruit.

Add the following code to the bottom of the `onCreate` method in
SchedulersActivity.kt:

```
val fruit = Observable.create<String> { observer ->
  observer.onNext("[apple]")
  Thread.sleep(2000)
  observer.onNext("[pineapple]")
  Thread.sleep(2000)
  observer.onNext("[strawberry]")
}
```

This Observable features a `Thread.sleep` function. While this is not something you'd usually see in real apps, in this case, it will help you understand how subscriptions and observations work.

Add the following code to subscribe to the Observable you created:

```
fruit
  .dump()
  .dumpingSubscription()
  .addTo(disposables)
```

Build and run, and check out the logging in the console:

```
0s | [D] [dog] received on Thread: main
0s | [S] [dog] received on Thread: main
0s | [D] [apple] received on Thread: main
0s | [S] [apple] received on Thread: main
2s | [D] [pineapple] received on Thread: main
2s | [S] [pineapple] received on Thread: main
4s | [D] [strawberry] received on Thread: main
4s | [S] [strawberry] received on Thread: main
```

The starter project already contained code creating a `animal` behavior subject and subscribing and dumping the contents. So here you have the original subject, followed by a fruit every two seconds after that.

The fruit is generated on the `main` thread, but it would be nice to move it to a background thread. Growing fruit takes time after all, and you wouldn't want to block your `main` thread while it's growing! To create the fruit in a background thread, you'll have to use `subscribeOn`.

Using subscribeOn

In some cases, you might want to change on which scheduler the Observable **computation** code runs — *not* the code in any of the subscription operators, but the code that is actually emitting the Observable events.

> **Note**: For the custom Observable that you have created, the code that emits events is the one you supply as the trailing lambda for `Observable.create { ... }`.

The way to set the scheduler for that computation code is to use the `subscribeOn` operator. It might sound like a counterintuitive name at first glance, but after thinking about it for a while, it starts to make sense. When you want to actually *observe* an Observable, you *subscribe* to it. This determines where the original processing will happen. If `subscribeOn` is not called, then RxJava automatically uses the current thread:

This process is creating events on the `main` thread using the main scheduler. The `AndroidSchedulers.mainThread()` that you've used in previous chapters sits on top of the `main` thread. All the tasks you want to perform on the `main` thread have to use this scheduler, which is why you used it in previous examples when working with the UI. To switch schedulers, you'll use `subscribeOn`.

As noted previously, the `subscribeOn` operator allows you to provide a `Scheduler` to change what thread the Observable creation code is called on. However, before you can use the operator, you need an instance of `Scheduler`.

RxJava provides a `Schedulers` (notice the trailing s in that class name) utility class that contains several instances of predefined schedulers, as well as a few utility methods to create new schedulers from existing Java concepts like `Executor`.

For this example, you'll use the `io` scheduler that you've used in past projects. You'll see a detailed breakdown of the different types of default schedulers you can use later on in the chapter.

To use the scheduler, replace the previous subscription to `fruits` you created with this new one:

```
fruit
  .subscribeOn(Schedulers.io())
  .dump()
  .dumpingSubscription()
  .addTo(disposables)
```

Now that your new scheduler is in place, build and run and check the result:

```
0s | [D] [dog] received on Thread: main
0s | [S] [dog] received on Thread: main
0s | [D] [apple] received on Thread: RxCachedThreadScheduler-1
0s | [S] [apple] received on Thread: RxCachedThreadScheduler-1
2s | [D] [pineapple] received on Thread: RxCachedThreadScheduler-1
2s | [S] [pineapple] received on Thread: RxCachedThreadScheduler-1
4s | [D] [strawberry] received on Thread: RxCachedThreadScheduler-1
4s | [S] [strawberry] received on Thread: RxCachedThreadScheduler-1
```

Under the hood, the `Schedulers.io()` method is returning a scheduler that works off of a thread pool. Those threads are cached and the library names them accordingly.

Now, both the Observable and the subscribed observer from the `fruit` Observable are processing data in the same thread.

Since you didn't use the `subscribeOn` operator on the `animal` subscribing code, its objects are still being emitted on the `main` thread.

That's cool, but what can you do if you want to change where the observer performs the code of your operators? You have to use `observeOn`.

Using observeOn

Observing is one of the three fundamental concepts of Rx. It involves an entity producing events and an observer for those events. In this case, and in opposition to `subscribeOn`, the operator `observeOn` changes the scheduler where the *observation* happens.

Once an event is pushed by an `Observable` to all the subscribed observers, this operator will ensure that the event is handled by the correct scheduler.

To switch from the `io` scheduler to the `main` thread, you need to call `observeOn` before subscribing.

There's only one issue. RxJava has no idea what a `main` scheduler is. The `animal` subscription code is running on the `main` thread, but that's just because RxJava defaults to using whatever thread calls the subscribing code if there's no `observeOn` operator.

Remember, RxJava is a Java library that has no knowledge of Android. Since the `main` thread is specific to your Android app, you need some way of creating a scheduler that always routes work to the Android `main` thread.

You could write the logic yourself to wrap the Android `main Looper` in an RxJava scheduler. Luckily for you, someone else has already done that work!

Open the **build.gradle** file and add a new dependency for the **RxAndroid** library in the dependencies block:

```
implementation "io.reactivex.rxjava3:rxandroid:3.0.0"
```

RxAndroid is an extremely small library whose entire purpose is to expose the Android `main` looper as a scheduler via the `AndroidSchedulers.mainThread()` static utility function.

While the name of the library would imply that it interacts with all things Android, the maintainers of the library felt that it would be better to whittle the project down to only the most crucial element of using Rx on Android.

One more time, replace your `fruits` subscription code:

```
fruit
  .subscribeOn(Schedulers.io())
  .dump()
  .observeOn(AndroidSchedulers.mainThread())
  .dumpingSubscription()
  .addTo(disposables)
```

Run the project and check the Logcat output once more (you will need to wait a few seconds until the app stops printing):

```
0s | [D] [dog] received on Thread: main
0s | [S] [dog] received on Thread: main
0s | [D] [apple] received on Thread: RxCachedThreadScheduler-1
0s | [S] [apple] received on Thread: main
2s | [D] [pineapple] received on Thread: RxCachedThreadScheduler-1
2s | [S] [pineapple] received on Thread: main
4s | [D] [strawberry] received on Thread: RxCachedThreadScheduler-1
4s | [S] [strawberry] received on Thread: main
```

You've achieved the result you wanted: All the events are now processed on the correct thread. The Observable is processing and generating events on the background thread, and the subscribing observer is doing its job on the `main` thread.

This is a very common pattern: You often use a background process to retrieve data from a server and process the data received, only switching to the `AndroidSchedulers.mainThread` scheduler to process the final event and display the data in the user interface.

Pitfalls

The ability to switch schedulers and threads looks amazing, but it comes with some pitfalls. To see why, you'll push some events to the subject using a new thread. Since you need to track on which thread the computation takes place, a good solution is to use Thread.

Right after the `fruit` Observable, add the following code to generate some animals:

```
val animalsThread = Thread {
  Thread.sleep(3000)
  animal.onNext("[cat]")
  Thread.sleep(3000)
  animal.onNext("[tiger]")
  Thread.sleep(3000)
  animal.onNext("[fox]")
  Thread.sleep(3000)
  animal.onNext("[leopard]")
}
```

Then name the thread, so you will be able to recognize it, and start it up:

```
animalsThread.name = "Animals Thread"
animalsThread.start()
```

Run the app. You should see your new thread in action:

```
...
3s  | [D] [cat] received on Thread: Animals Thread
3s  | [S] [cat] received on Thread: Animals Thread
4s  | [D] [strawberry] received on Thread:
RxCachedThreadScheduler-1
4s  | [S] [strawberry] received on Thread: main
6s  | [D] [tiger] received on Thread: Animals Thread
6s  | [S] [tiger] received on Thread: Animals Thread
9s  | [D] [fox] received on Thread: Animals Thread
9s  | [S] [fox] received on Thread: Animals Thread
12s | [D] [leopard] received on Thread: Animals Thread
12s | [S] [leopard] received on Thread: Animals Thread
```

Perfect — you have animals created on the dedicated thread. Next, process the result on `io` scheduler.

> **Note**: It might seem repetitive to keep adding code and then replacing it with something else, but the goal here is to compare the differences between the various schedulers.

Replace the original subscription to the animal subject with the following code:

```
animal
  .dump()
  .observeOn(Schedulers.io())
  .dumpingSubscription()
  .addTo(disposables)
```

Build and run, and the new result is as follows:

```
...
3s  |  [D] [cat] received on Thread: Animals Thread
3s  |  [S] [cat] received on Thread: RxCachedThreadScheduler-1
4s  |  [D] [strawberry] received on Thread: RxCachedThreadScheduler-2
4s  |  [S] [strawberry] received on Thread: main
6s  |  [D] [tiger] received on Thread: Animals Thread
6s  |  [S] [tiger] received on Thread: RxCachedThreadScheduler-1
9s  |  [D] [fox] received on Thread: Animals Thread
9s  |  [S] [fox] received on Thread: RxCachedThreadScheduler-1
12s |  [D] [leopard] received on Thread: Animals Thread
12s |  [S] [leopard] received on Thread: RxCachedThreadScheduler-1
```

Now you're switching threads from the animals thread where the items are actually pushed to the subject, to one of the cached `io` threads provided by the `Schedulers.io` function.

What if you want the observation process on the `io` scheduler, but you want to handle the subscription on the `main` thread? For the first case, the `observeOn` is already correct, but for the second, it's necessary to use `subscribeOn`.

Replace the `animal` subscription, this time with the following:

```
animal
  .subscribeOn(AndroidSchedulers.mainThread())
  .dump()
  .observeOn(Schedulers.io())
  .dumpingSubscription()
  .addTo(disposables)
```

Build and run, and you'll get the following result:

```
3s  |  [D] [cat] received on Thread: Animals Thread
3s  |  [S] [cat] received on Thread: RxCachedThreadScheduler-2
4s  |  [D] [strawberry] received on Thread: RxCachedThreadScheduler-1
4s  |  [S] [strawberry] received on Thread: main
6s  |  [D] [tiger] received on Thread: Animals Thread
```

```
6s  | [S] [tiger] received on Thread: RxCachedThreadScheduler-2
9s  | [D] [fox] received on Thread: Animals Thread
9s  | [S] [fox] received on Thread: RxCachedThreadScheduler-2
12s | [D] [leopard] received on Thread: Animals Thread
12s | [S] [leopard] received on Thread:
RxCachedThreadScheduler-2
```

Wait?! What? Why isn't the computation happening on the correct scheduler? Since you're using the `subscribeOn` operator, you should be seeing the items being computed on the `main` scheduler, right? This is a common and dangerous pitfall that comes from thinking of Rx as asynchronous or multi-threaded by default — which isn't the case.

Rx and the general abstraction is free-threaded; there's no magic thread switching taking place when processing data. The computation is always performed on the original thread if not specified otherwise.

> **Note:** Any thread switching happens after an explicit request by the programmer using the operators `subscribeOn` and `observeOn`.

Thinking Rx does some thread handling by default is a common trap to fall into. What's happening above is a misuse of the `Subject`. The original computation is happening on a specific thread, and those events are pushed in that thread using `Thread() { ... }`. Due to the nature of `Subject`, Rx has no ability to switch the original computation scheduler and move to another thread, since there's no direct control over where the subject is pushed.

Why does this work with the fruit thread though? That's because using `Observable.create` puts Rx in control of what happens inside the `Thread` block so that you can more finely customize thread handling.

This unexpected outcome is commonly known as the **Hot and Cold** Observables problem.

In the case above, you are dealing with a **hot** Observable. The Observable doesn't have any side-effect during subscription, but it does have its own context in which events are generated and RxJava can't control it (namely, it sports its own `Thread`).

A **cold** Observable in contrast doesn't produce any elements before any observers subscribe to it. That effectively means it doesn't have its own context until, upon subscription, it creates some context and starts producing elements.

Hot vs. cold

The section above touched on the topic of hot and cold Observables. The topic of hot and cold Observables is quite opinionated and generates a lot of debate, so let's briefly look into it, here. The concept can be reduced to a very simple question:

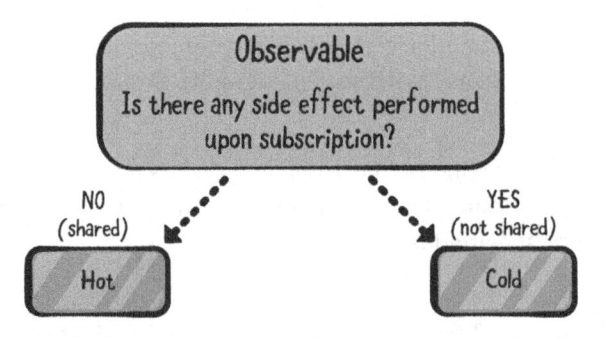

Some examples of side effects are:

- Fire a request to the server
- Edit the local database
- Write to the file system
- Launch a rocket

The world of side effects is endless, so you need to determine whether your `Observable` instance is performing side effects upon subscription. If you can't be certain about that, then perform more analysis or dig further into the source code. Launching a rocket on every subscription might *not* be what you're looking to achieve…

Another common way to describe this is to ask whether or not the `Observable` shares side-effects. If you're performing side effects upon subscription, it means that the side effect is *not* shared. Otherwise, the side effects are shared with all subscribers.

This is a fairly general rule, and applies to any RxJava object like a subject and related subtypes.

As you've certainly noticed, we haven't spoken much about hot and cold Observables so far in the book. It's a common topic in reactive programming, but in Rx you encounter the concept only in specific cases like the Thread example above or when you need greater control, such as when you run tests.

Keep this section as a point of reference, so in case you need to approach a problem in terms of hot or cold Observables, you can quickly open the book to this point and refresh yourself on the concept.

Best practices and built-in schedulers

Schedulers are a non-trivial topic, so they come with some best practices for the most common use cases. In this section, you'll get a quick introduction to serial and concurrent schedulers, learn how they process the data and see which type works better for a particular context.

Android main scheduler

AndroidSchedulers.mainThread() sits on top of the main thread. This scheduler is used to process changes on the user interface and perform other high-priority tasks.

As a general practice when developing applications on Android, long-running tasks should not be performed using this scheduler, so avoid things like database requests or other heavy tasks. If you try and execute a network request from this scheduler you'll receive a NetworkOnMainThreadException.

Additionally, if you perform side effects that update the UI, you must switch to this scheduler to make sure all UI updating logic happens on the main thread. If you don't, you may see exceptions about modifying UI code from a different thread.

io scheduler

The scheduler returned by Schedulers.io() should be used whenever you're doing work that's IO bound. Specifically, if you're making any network calls, accessing items from a database, or reading lines from a file, this is the scheduler for you.

Under the hood, it's backed by thread pool that will grow as needed, so make sure not to do strict computational work while using the IO scheduler.

Computation scheduler

If you do need to heavy computational work, like crunching large data sets or handling event loops, you can use the scheduler returned by `Schedulers.computation()`.

In opposition to the IO scheduler, the computation scheduler will not spawn more threads as needed. Instead, the number of threads it works with is normally limited to the number of cores the CPU has.

If you think about it this makes sense: If you're doing computationally heavy work and you have more threads than number of cores in the CPU, you won't be able to process the work any faster since all cores are occupied. Instead, you'd just be creating more memory overhead by creating new threads.

Single threaded scheduler

Sometimes, you need to work off the `main` thread but you also need guarantees that the work you're doing is happening sequentially. This isn't a problem if you're only working in the confines of one RxJava chain, since, for the most part, those chains will always happen sequentially.

However, if you have multiple distinct chains and you want to know that you're continually adding new work to a queue, you can use the `Schedulers.single` scheduler.

The `single` scheduler is potentially the simplest of all the schedulers. It's ultimately backed by one thread. That means that, whenever you queue up new work on that thread, it's queued to the bottom so you know it happens after other work you've added before.

Trampoline scheduler

Similar to the `single` scheduler, the scheduler returned by `Schedulers.trampoline()` always operates on a single thread. Unlike the `single` scheduler, that thread isn't a background thread. Instead, it's the main thread that created the trampoline scheduler. You'll see in Chapter 15, "Testing RxJava Code," that the `trampoline` scheduler can be very useful while writing unit tests.

Test scheduler

`TestScheduler` is a special kind of beast. It's meant only to be used in testing, so make sure **not** to use this scheduler in production code. This special scheduler simplifies operator testing. You will have a look into using this scheduler in the dedicated chapter about testing, but let's have a quick look since you're doing the grand tour of schedulers.

Open the **SchedulerTest.kt** file. It's a simple unit test that attempts to test the `Observable.timer` method. As any good developer knows, testing code that interacts with time can be extremely challenging. Without `TestScheduler`, you may be forced to block the test from finishing until a certain amount of time has passed. That makes for very slow unreliably tests, which is a big no-no in the testing world.

`TestScheduler` allows you to control how much "time" has passed and how actions and events are triggered.

Take a look at the following code:

```
val scheduler = TestScheduler()
val observable = Observable.timer(2, TimeUnit.SECONDS,
  scheduler)
```

You're creating an instance of `TestScheduler` and then passing that schedule in to the `Observable.timer` method. You have seen the `Observable.timer` factory method, but you may not have used the version that takes in a scheduler yet.

Command-click into the `Observable.timer` method and scroll up one method signature to the version of `Timer` that doesn't take a scheduler. In that methods JavaDocs, you'll see the following:

```
 * <dd>{@code timer} operates by default on the {@code
computation} {@link Scheduler}.</dd>
```

By default, most timing oriented operators will operate on the computation scheduler you saw earlier. That can create problems if you want to test the code later on or if you expect the code to be run on whatever thread it was started on.

Going back to the example unit test, you see the following code:

```
val testTimer = observable.test()

testTimer.assertNotComplete()

scheduler.advanceTimeBy(2, TimeUnit.SECONDS)

testTimer.assertComplete()
```

You'll learn about the `test` method on Observables in Chapter 15, "Testing RxJava Code." All you need to know for now is thatu it allows you to assert certain events have happened on yor Observable. In the above example you're first asserting that the Observable has not completed yet, which makes sense because the Observable only completes after two seconds.

Then you're using the `TestScheduler.advanceTimeBy` method to artificially advance what that scheduler thinks of as the current time. Kind of like time traveling, except it makes for a far less interesting sci-fi television series.

Since you've advanced time by two seconds, that means the Observable should have emitted its value and completed.

Sure enough, if you run the unit test by clicking the small green arrow next to the test method, you'll see that it passed.

```
@Test
fun `Test Scheduler utilities`() {
    val scheduler = TestScheduler()
    val observable = Observable.timer( delay: 2, TimeUnit.SECONDS, scheduler)

    val testTimer = observable.test()

    testTimer.assertNotComplete()

    scheduler.advanceTimeBy( delayTime: 2, TimeUnit.SECONDS)

    testTimer.assertComplete()
}
```

You'll learn more about how amazing `TestScheduler` is later on.

Key points

- A `Scheduler` is an abstract context upon which RxJava executes work. In other words, `Scheduler`s let you choose to do work on different threads.

- You can use the `subscribeOn` operator to control on what thread your Observable is created. That allows you to, for example, execute the actual networking portion of an API call off the `main` thread.

- After using `subscribeOn`, you can use the `observeOn` operator to then choose a different thread to actually receive the emitted objects on. You'll often use this operator to switch back to the `main` thread to update UI objects.

- While `subscribeOn` and `observeOn` are extremely powerful operators, they're not magic. If you call the `onNext` method of a subject on a different thread, RxJava can't honor your `subscribeOn` call and you'll see the item emitted on the original thread.

- There are both `hot` Observables and `cold` Observables. `cold` Observables create some special side effect when they're subscribed to. A network call that returns an Oobservable is an example of a `cold` stream. A `hot` Observable is always running and emitting items, even if no one is listening. Subscribing to a `hot` Observable will not cause any special side effects.

- There are several built in schedulers for you to use. The `io` scheduler is great for network and database calls, while the `computation` scheduler is good for event loops and computationally expensive code.

- The **RxAndroid** library exposes another special scheduler you can use to emit items on the Android `main` thread.

- Finally, the `TestScheduler` class assists in testing RxJava code and should not be used in production code.

Where to go from here?

Schedulers are a non-trivial topic in the Rx space; they're responsible for computing and performing all tasks in RxJava.

Before proceeding, invest some time in playing around with the examples in this chapter and test some schedulers to see what impact they have on the final result. Understanding schedulers will make life easier with RxJava, and will improve your confidence when using `subscribeOn` and `observeOn`.

Chapter 14: Flowables & Backpressure

By Alex Sullivan

You've been using **Observables** to do some pretty powerful stuff — but there's one problem that you still need to cover. What happens if a subscriber can't keep up with the next events that the Observable is emitting?

Backpresssure

That thorny scenario where operators or subscribers can't consume next events as fast as an Observable may produce them is called **backpressure**, and you'll explore it thoroughly in this chapter!

To start, open up the starter project for this chapter using IntelliJ IDEA. Navigate to **SupportCode.kt** and take a look around. You'll find:

- The tried and true exampleOf method, a safeSleep method that simply calls Thread.sleep and catches any InterruptedExceptions.

- A freeMemory method that calculates the total mount of free memory the system has.

Fancy, right?

Now, head over to **Main.kt** and add the following code in main():

```
exampleOf("Zipping observable") {
   val fastObservable = Observable.interval(1, TimeUnit.MILLISECONDS)
   val slowObservable = Observable.interval(1, TimeUnit.SECONDS)
}
```

With the above, you're creating two new `Observables` using the `Observable.interval` static factory method. The `interval` method creates an `Observable` that counts up from the provided number at a frequency you provide, forever, so it never terminates.

The two Observables are almost exactly the same, except one will emit a `next` event with a new number every millisecond, and the other will only emit every second.

Now, add the following right below the `slowObservable` line:

```
// 1
val disposable =
  Observables.zip(slowObservable, fastObservable)
    .subscribeOn(Schedulers.io())
    .subscribe { (first, second) ->
      // 2
      println("Got $first and $second")
    }
// 3
safeSleep(5000)
// 4
disposable.dispose()
```

That's a solid chunk of code, so breaking it down step by step:

1. Create a new `Observable` by using the `zip` function, which, as you know, combines two Observables together. You're using the RxKotlin factory function to keep everything neat. It also makes a `Pair` from the two emitted items for you.

2. Subscribe to the zipped Observable and print out both items.

3. Sleep the thread for five seconds. Since you're subscribing to the zipped Observable on the `io` scheduler, the "Zipping Observable" example block would finish immediately if you didn't sleep the thread. You'd never do this in a real application since the application would never terminate naturally like this one, but it's necessary for the examples in this chapter.

4. As the Rx guru that you are by now, you never forget to dispose the subscriptions.

Run the **Main.kt** file. You should see the following:

```
--- Example of: Zipping observable ---
Got 0 and 0
Got 1 and 1
Got 2 and 2
Got 3 and 3
```

The next events are being zipped together, but it leaves one question unanswered: What's happening to all the items that the fast Observable is emitting?

It took about five seconds to print out those four numbers, but we know in that time the fast Observable should have emitted thousands of items, since it should be emitting every millisecond.

It turns out that RxJava **buffers** those items under the hood. That means that it keeps a list of items that keeps growing until the **downstream** operators and subscribers can consume them.

Buffering danger!

Most of the time buffering next events is exactly what you want, but sometimes that buffering approach eats too much memory and can lead to OutOfMemoryError crashes!

You'll create a new example that results in an OutOfMemoryError.

Copy the following code after the previous example:

```
exampleOf("Overflowing observer") {
  // 1
  val disposable = Observable.range(1, 10_000_000)
      // 2
      .subscribeOn(Schedulers.io())
      .observeOn(Schedulers.computation())
      // 3
      .subscribe {
        println("Free memory: ${freeMemory()}")
        safeSleep(100)
      }
  // 4
  safeSleep(20_000)
  disposable.dispose()
}
```

That's a lot of code, so again we'll break it down by section:

1. Create a new `Observable` using the `range` static factory method. The `range` method returns an `Observable` that emits integers starting from the first argument until the second argument — so between 1 and `10_000_000` in this example.

2. Subscribe on the `io` scheduler and observe on the `computation` scheduler. It's important that you subscribe and observe on different threads for this example. You'll see why later.

3. Subscribe to the `Observable`. In the `subscribe` lambda, print out the total amount of remaining free memory in the system and sleep the thread for 100 seconds. Sleeping for 100 milliseconds allows you to mimic a situation where the subscribing code is slower than the emitting code.

4. Sleep the thread for 20 seconds, so that the example has enough time to finish.

Run the code. You should see something like this:

```
--- Example of: Overflowing observer ---
Free memory: 3793645960
Free memory: 3769377888
Free memory: 3701230888
Free memory: 3608875976
...
```

But you probably won't see an `OutOfMemoryError`. What gives, you may ask? RxJava is buffering integers, but an `Int` is so tiny that it doesn't make much of a dent in your JVMs memory. So instead, you need to buff up the memory intensity of each item. Add the following code after the `subscribeOn` operator and before the `observeOn` operator:

```
.map {
  LongArray(1024 * 8)
}
```

Now, you're taking each integer emitted by the `range` Observable and turning into a `LongArray` with a size of 8192. Now that's a beefy object!

Run the code again. You should see some **fireworks**:

```
--- Example of: Overflowing observer ---
Free memory: 3793645432
Free memory: 3595255472
...
Free memory: 276971776
```

```
Free memory: 277053320
io.reactivex.exceptions.UndeliverableException:
java.lang.OutOfMemoryError: Java heap space
```

As you consume more and more memory, and RxJava buffers more and more items, you'll see the total amount of free memory decreasing and, eventually, you should see an `OutOfMemoryError`. Isn't making software blow up the best?

Natural backpressure

Now, backpressure isn't *always* a problem. In the previous example, try removing the `observeOn` line and run the example again.

No fireworks! What gives?

Since you removed the `observeOn` call, it means the subscribing code *and* the observing code are now both running on the same thread — the scheduler thread that you told it to run on with the `subscribeOn` call.

That means that, when you call `safeSleep(100)` in the subscribing lambda, the whole Rx chain stops for 100 milliseconds. The subscribing code is consuming items as fast as the Observable is emitting them — so there's no backpressure!

What that means is that, if you're not mucking about with `observeOn` and `subscribeOn` calls, you really don't need to worry about backpressure.

Introduction to Flowables

But since you usually **are** mucking about with threading in your RxJava chains, the RxJava library has got your back.

`Flowables` are backpressure-aware versions of `Observables` that allow you to specify how you want to handle backpressure. A `Flowable` is distinct from an `Observable`, but they both share all of the operators and fun jazzy static constructors you've grown to love. You don't need to worry about learning a whole new set of operators to go along with your new `Flowable` type.

Copy the following code for a new example into your `main` method below the previous examples:

```
exampleOf("Zipping flowable") {
  val slowFlowable = Flowable.interval(1, TimeUnit.SECONDS)
  val fastFlowable = Flowable.interval(1, TimeUnit.MILLISECONDS)
  val disposable =
    Flowables.zip(slowFlowable, fastFlowable)
      .subscribeOn(Schedulers.io())
      .observeOn(Schedulers.newThread())
      .subscribe { (first, second) ->
        println("Got $first and $second")
      }

  safeSleep(5000)
  disposable.dispose()
}
```

Hopefully, this code looks pretty familiar. It's exactly the same code as you wrote in the "Zipping observable" example, except this time it's using `Flowable` instead of `Observable`!

Just like `Observable`, `Flowable` has a static `interval` factory method that creates an instance of `Flowable` that counts up when subscribed to.

And just like in the previous example, you're combining two `Flowables` — one fast and one slow. In the subscribe lambda you're printing out both values from the `Flowables`.

There's only one problem: You haven't told your `Flowables` how to react to backpressure. Unlike `Observable`, `Flowable` won't automatically buffer items. If you run this code, it'll crash.

Since blowing up code is super fun, run it! You should see the following at least once in the resulting stack trace:

```
io.reactivex.exceptions.MissingBackpressureException: can't
deliver value 128 due to lack of requests
```

Since your `Flowable` won't automatically buffer items like `Observable` does, you need to tell it how to handle that backpressure. Since the fast flowable is the one that will encounter backpressure, modify the `fastFlowable` value to look like the following example:

```
val fastFlowable = Flowable.interval(1, TimeUnit.MILLISECONDS)
  .onBackpressureDrop { println("Dropping $it") }
```

You're using the `onBackPressureDrop` operator on your fast Flowable to instruct it how on how to handle backpressure. `onBackPressureDrop` can optionally take a `Consumer` function that lets you do something with the dropped item. Here, you're just printing out the dropped value.

Run the code. It won't crash this time and you should see the following:

```
--- Example of: Zipping flowable ---
Dropping 128
Dropping 129
Dropping 130
...
Got 0 and 0
...
```

No more crashing!

Why did the fast `Flowable` only start dropping items once it got to all the way up to the 128th value? that's because using the `observeOn` method actually creates a buffer of size 128 to be more performant for bursty `Flowable`s that can emit a lot of values at once and then stop.

Backpressure strategies

You've seen that you can remove back-pressured items from the stream by using the `onBackpressureDrop` method, but there's actually three different ways you can handle backpressure:

1. `onBackPressureDrop`: Remove items from the stream as they come if the downstream consumer can't handle them.

2. `onBackPressureBuffer`: Buffer the backpressured item up to a limit that you specify. You can then handle the case in which the buffer is overrun.

3. `onBackPressureLatest`: Hold onto the latest value and emit that value when the downstream consumer can handle it.

onBackPressureBuffer

Copy the following example into your project:

```kotlin
exampleOf("onBackPressureBuffer") {
  val disposable = Flowable.range(1, 100)
      .subscribeOn(Schedulers.io())
      .observeOn(Schedulers.newThread(), false, 1)
      .doOnComplete { println("We're done!") }
      .subscribe {
        println("Integer: $it")
        safeSleep(50)
      }
  safeSleep(1000)
  disposable.dispose()
}
```

Everything here should look pretty normal, with one exception. What's going on with that observeOn line?

```
observeOn(Schedulers.newThread(), false, 1)
```

observeOn actually has an overloaded version of the operator that can take a boolean to delay the error across thread boundaries and, more interesting for this backpressure example, an int representing the internal buffer you learned about earlier in the chapter.

You're setting that internal buffer value to **1** so you can clearly see the backpressure operator at play!

> **Note**: In a real project you'd **never** want to set the buffer that low. Chances are that you'll never actually want to change that buffer size either. But, if you do, make sure to give it a value of at least 16, so the performance of bursty sources doesn't go down the tubes!

Now, it's time to hook up the backpressure! Add the following line below the
`subscribeOn` operator:

```
.onBackpressureBuffer(
  // 1
  50,
  // 2
  { println("Buffer overrun; dropping latest") },
  // 3
  BackpressureOverflowStrategy.DROP_LATEST
)
```

That's a chunky operator, so breaking it down section by section:

1. `onBackpressureBuffer` takes in a maximum buffer count, which you've set to 50. If you end up needing to buffer more than 50 items, you'll want a way to handle that situation. Which is good news because…

2. You're also passing in a lambda to take an action if your buffer overruns. In this example, you're just printing a message.

3. Since the buffer can overflow, you need to tell RxJava what to do in that scenario. Right now, you're telling it to drop items that come in after the buffer overruns. You can instead use `BackpressureOverflowStrategy.DROP_OLDEST` to drop the oldest items in the buffer. Last but not least, you can use `BackpressureOverflowStrategy.ERROR` if you want to run into your old friend `MissingBackpressureException`.

If you run the example, you should see the following:

```
Integer: 1
Buffer overrun; dropping latest
Buffer overrun; dropping latest
...
Integer: 2
Integer: 3
...
```

The first item comes in without issue. Then, since the subscribing code is sleeping for 50 milliseconds, backpressure starts creeping up and you quickly overrun the size 50 buffer.

Since you're using the DROP_LATEST overflow strategy, the later elements are dropped and the first items to be buffered are held onto, so once the upstream starts emitting again you get those buffered items.

onBackPressureLatest

Copy the following example into your project:

```
exampleOf("onBackPressureLatest") {
  val disposable = Flowable.range(1, 100)
    .subscribeOn(Schedulers.io())
    .observeOn(Schedulers.newThread(), false, 1)
    .doOnComplete { println("We're done!") }
    .subscribe {
      println("Integer: $it")
      safeSleep(50)
    }
  safeSleep(1000)
  disposable.dispose()
}
```

This code looks pretty familiar, huh? But, as you've seen before, it's missing a backpressure operator! Add the following line between `subscribeOn` and `observeOn`:

```
.onBackpressureLatest()
```

As mentioned before, `onBackpressureLatest()` instructs the `Flowable` to hold onto the latest back-pressured value and emit that when the downstream can handle it.

Run the example. you'll see the following:

```
--- Example of: onBackPressureLatest ---
Integer: 1
Integer: 100
We're done!
```

The first item is emitted just like it was before. Then the Flowable encounters backpressure, all the way up until the last item, which, again emits OK.

You can think of `onBackpressureLatest` as being equivalent to using `onBackpressureBuffer` with a buffer size of one and a `BackpressureOverflowStrategy` of `DROP_LATEST`.

Built-in backpressure support

You've done a fantastic job handling backpressure in several ways. But there's one more example to work through. It's a quick one though!

Copy the following example into your project:

```kotlin
exampleOf("No backpressure") {
  val disposable = Flowable.range(1, 100)
    .subscribeOn(Schedulers.io())
    .observeOn(Schedulers.newThread(), false, 1)
    .doOnComplete { println("We're done!") }
    .subscribe {
      println("Integer: $it")
      safeSleep(50)
    }
  safeSleep(1000)
  disposable.dispose()
}
```

Run the code. You should see the following:

```
--- Example of: No backpressure ---
Integer: 1
Integer: 2
Integer: 3
...
```

Now, you might be thinking, "Wait a minute. I thought that code would throw a `MissingBackpressureException` since there's no `onBackPressure...` operator?!" Great observation - some `Flowable`s actually support backpressure right out of the box!

The `range` operator will only produce new values when the downstream code requests them. That means that, if the subscribing code takes a long time, a new value will only be produced after it finishes its task and is ready for a new value.

Not all operators honor backpressure this way, so it's important to look at the Javadocs for operators to see how they handle backpressure. Every `Flowable` operator will have a section in the Javadocs explaining how they handle backpressure.

> **Backpressure:**
> The operator honors backpressure from downstream and signals values on-demand (i.e., when requested).
> **Scheduler:**
> range does not operate by default on a particular `Scheduler`.

JavaDocs for Flowable.range

Here's an example of the `range` operators JavaDocs. You can see the section on backpressure in the image above.

Now here's an example of the `zip` operators backpressure documentation.

> **Backpressure:**
> The operator expects backpressure from the sources and honors backpressure from the downstream. (I.e., zipping with `interval(long, TimeUnit)` may result in MissingBackpressureException, use one of the onBackpressureX to handle similar, backpressure-ignoring sources.
> **Scheduler:**
> `zip` does not operate by default on a particular `Scheduler`.

JavaDocs for Flowable.zip

You can see from the documentation that, as opposed to the `range` operator, `zip` expects you to handle the backpressure yourself.

Remember to check the documentation of all `Flowable` operators before using them to make sure you don't get caught with unexpected backpressure handling!

Flowables, Observables, Processors and Subjects — Oh, My!

You may be feeling a little overwhelmed since you've just been given a whole new reactive type — `Flowables`! But don't worry, `Flowables` are really just like `Observables`, but with more control over backpressure. You can even switch between the two types seamlessly.

`Observable` has an instance method on it called `toFlowable`. I know it's crazy, but that method *actually* converts an `Observable` to a `Flowable`.

Since you're moving from an `Observable` to a `Flowable`, you have to handle backpressure. `toFlowable` takes a `BackpressureStrategy`, which indicates how this Flowable should handle backpressure.

> **Note**: `BackpressureStrategy` is different from the `BackpressureOverflowStrategy` you saw earlier, so don't confuse them!

Choosing a BackpressureStrategy value

There's five different `BackpressureStrategy` values you can pick from:

1. `MISSING`: Use this strategy if you're planning to use one of the `onBackpressureX` strategies you saw earlier. If you don't use one of the backpressure operators, you may get a `MissingBackpressureException` if you encounter backpressure.

2. `ERROR`: Signals `MissingBackpressureException` if the downstream can't keep up.

3. `BUFFER`: Buffers **all** of the `next` events. This is similar to how an `Observable` handles backpressure by default.

4. `DROP`: Drops the most recent `next` events if the downstream can't keep up.

5. `LATEST`: Keeps the latest `next` event, overriding it if the downstream can't keep up.

You can see that many of the constants above are similar to the backpressure operators you saw earlier. If you need more fine-grained control when converting a `Flowable` to an `Observable`, you can always use one of the `onBackpressure...` methods you learned about in this chapter.

Add the following example at the bottom of the `main` class:

```
exampleOf("toFlowable") {
  val disposable = Observable.range(1, 100)
    .toFlowable(BackpressureStrategy.MISSING)
    .subscribeOn(Schedulers.io())
    .observeOn(Schedulers.newThread(), false, 1)
    .subscribe {
      println("Integer: $it")
      safeSleep(50)
    }
  safeSleep(1000)
  disposable.dispose()
}
```

Just like before you're using the `range` operator to create an `Observable` that emits integers. This time, however, you're using the `toFlowable` method to convert the `Observable` into a `Flowable`, passing in `MISSING` as your backpressure strategy.

Can you guess what will happen when you run this code?

Run the app. Since you're using the `MISSING` backpressure strategy and not applying one of the `onBackPressure...` operators, your `Flowable` blows up with a `MissingBackpressureException`.

Now swap out the `BackpressureStrategy` you're supplying to the `toFlowable` operator in the above example with the `BUFFER` strategy:

```
.toFlowable(BackpressureStrategy.BUFFER)
```

Run the project again. This time you'll see items printed normally. Try out the LATEST and DROP strategies as well. They should work exactly as you'd expect.

Processors

Since a `Subject` is just a fancy `Observable`, you could always use `toFlowable` on it to turn it into a `Flowable`. Just like before, you'll have to supply a `BackpressureStrategy`. Alternatively, if you want a backpressure-aware version of your favorite subject, you can use the `Processor` type. it's just like a `Subject`, except backpressure aware!

There's a `Processor` type for each `Subject` you know and love! For example, if you want a backpressure aware version of `BehaviorSubject`, you can just use `BehaviorProcessor`.

Add the following example to the bottom of the `main` class:

```
exampleOf("Processor") {
  // 1
  val processor = PublishProcessor.create<Int>()
  // 2
  val disposable = processor
    .observeOn(Schedulers.newThread(), false, 1)
    .subscribe {
      println("Integer: $it")
      safeSleep(50)
    }
  // 3
  Thread().run {
    for (i in 0..100) {
      processor.onNext(i)
```

```
      safeSleep(5)
    }
  }
  safeSleep(1000)
  disposable.dispose()
}
```

This code is a bit different, so here's a breakdown:

1. You're creating a `PublishProcessor`, which acts just like a `PublishSubject` except it won't buffer items if it experiences backpressure. `PublishProcessor` is to `PublishSubject` as `Flowable` is to `Observable`.

2. Just like before, you're calling the overloaded version of `observeOn` to avoid any internal scheduler buffering. You're subscribing directly to the processor and printing out the integer in the `subscribe` lambda. To simulate a slow subscriber, you're using the `safeSleep` method to sleep the thread for 50 milliseconds. Unlike before, you're not using the `subscribeOn` operator. Since you'll be manually calling `onNext` on the processor, the items will be initially created on whatever thread calls `onNext`, so a `subscribeOn` call would have no affect.

3. In order to simulate items being generated on a separate thread, you're creating a new `Thread` object and using the `onNext` method to send a range of integers into your processor. You're again using the `safeSleep` method to ensure that all values aren't delivered at once to emulate a more real world use case.

> **Note**: Refer to Chapter 13, "Intro to Schedulers" chapter for more information on how subjects (and by extension processors) handle schedulers.

Run the project. Since you didn't utilize one of the `onBackPressure...` methods, the project will crash with a `MissingBackpressureException`.

`Processors` will not buffer items delivered via the `onNext` method like a `Subject` would. You have to manually control the backpressure just like you do with a `Flowable`.

Update the example above to use the `onBackPressureDrop` operator:

```
val disposable = processor
  .onBackpressureDrop { println("Dropping $it") }
  .observeOn(Schedulers.newThread(), false, 1)
  .subscribe {
    println("Integer: $it")
    safeSleep(50)
  }
```

Now whenever an item is dropped due to backpressure you'll print out a quick message explaining that the item's been dropped.

Run the project. You should see output that looks like this:

```
--- Example of: Processor ---
Integer: 0
Dropping 1
Dropping 2
Dropping 3
Dropping 4
Dropping 5
Dropping 6
Dropping 7
Dropping 8
Dropping 9
Integer: 10
Dropping 11
...
```

Most items are dropped, and the ones that do make it through are printed out in your `subscribe` lambda. Processors are good to know about, but in the real world you'll rarely need to use them. One example that might warrant using a `Processor` is if you find yourself sending large objects, like `Bitmaps`, through a `Subject`.

In order to avoid buffering lots of heavy duty, high memory objects you could use a `Processor` with the `onBackpressureLatest` operator. That way, only the freshest data would be stored in memory.

Key points

- `Flowables` offer a powerful tool for handling **backpressure**, which is when a stream is producing values faster than they can be consumed by an `Observer`. Most of the time you can ignore backpressure and use `Observables`, but `Flowable` can be super-handy if you need it.

- You'd typically use a `Flowable` if you have really large (like over 1000 items) streams that come at variable speeds. For example, image you have a web socket that sends down tons of data at random times. You might want to only handle the latest item, so you could use the `onBackpressureLatest` method to achieve that.

- If you have an `Observable` that emits `Bitmaps` (or other types which can have a really huge memory footprint), you might want to be aware of the fact that all the emitted `Bitmaps` will buffer if you can't consume them fast enough, which could lead to an `OutOfMemoryError`. It might make sense to make use of one of the backpressure operators there as well.

- Similarly, if you are buffering high memory items into a `Subject`, consider using a `Processor` instead. Just make sure to add the proper `onBackPressure...` operator to ensure you aren't hit with a `MissingBackpressureException`!

`Flowables` are a powerful and sometimes intimidating part of RxJava. But with this chapter's help, you now have all the knowledge you need to tackle them in your own applications!

Where to go from here?

Backpressure is one of things that only show up when you least expect it. Before proceeding, invest some time in playing around with the examples in this chapter and test some operators to see what impact they have on the final result. Understanding backpressure will make your life easier with RxJava, and it will improve your confidence when working with `Flowables`.

Chapter 15: Testing RxJava Code

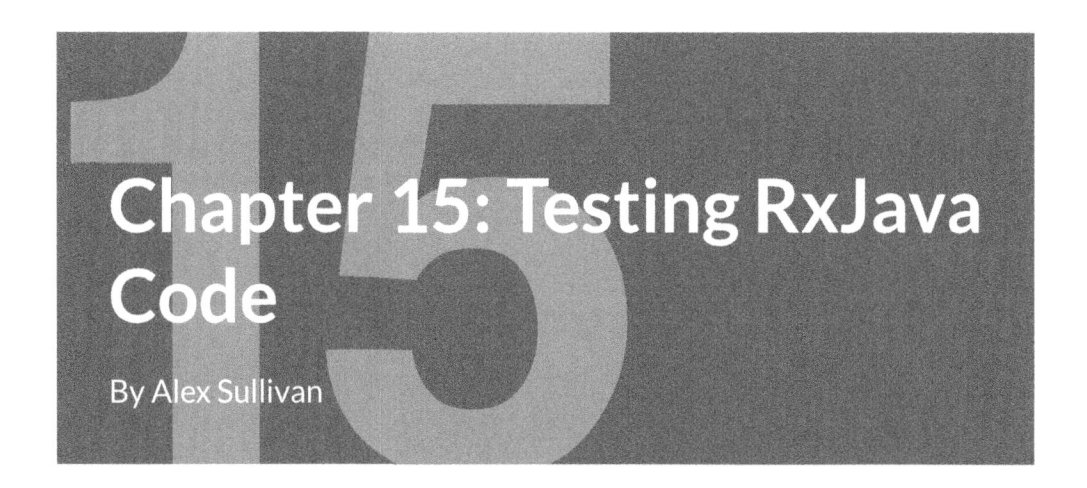

By Alex Sullivan

First and foremost — you're a hero for not skipping this chapter! Testing your code is at the heart of writing good software — RxJava comes with lots of nifty tricks for testing everything under the sun. In this chapter, you'll use JUnit to write unit tests to test a few operators and this chapter's app.

Getting started

You're going to be working on an app named **HexColor** for this chapter. **HexColor** is a nifty app that lets you input a hex color string. The app then shows you that color and (if it's within a set of known hex colors) tells you what the name of the color is. Open the starter project and run the app. You should see an app that looks like this:

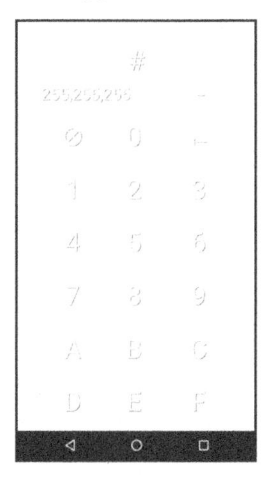

Enter a full hex string to see the app in action. It wouldn't be a color-based app if there wasn't some product placement, so try to enter the **Ray Wenderlich** green color: #006636

You should see the following screen:

In the top-left, you can see the color broken up by RGB values. On the right, you can see the name of the color.

Fancy, right?

Now that you're thoroughly impressed, take a look at the `ColorViewModel` class to see what's going on inside. Most of the logic for the app is actually contained in the init block:

```
// Send the hex string to the activity
hexStringSubject
  .subscribeOn(backgroundScheduler)
  .observeOn(mainScheduler)
  .subscribe(hexStringLiveData::postValue)
  .addTo(disposables)

// Send the actual color object to the activity
hexStringSubject
  .subscribeOn(backgroundScheduler)
  .observeOn(mainScheduler)
  .map { if (it.length < 7) "#FFFFFF" else it }
  .map { colorCoordinator.parseColor(it) }
  .subscribe(backgroundColorLiveData::postValue)
  .addTo(disposables)
```

```
// Send over the color name "--" if the hex string is less than
// seven chars
hexStringSubject
  .subscribeOn(backgroundScheduler)
  .observeOn(mainScheduler)
  .filter { it.length < 7 }
  .map { "--" }
  .subscribe(colorNameLiveData::postValue)
  .addTo(disposables)

// If our color name enum contains the given hex string, send
// that color name over.
hexStringSubject
  .subscribeOn(backgroundScheduler)
  .observeOn(mainScheduler)
  .filter {
    hexString -> ColorName.values().map { it.hex }
                 .contains(hexString)
  }
  .map { hexString -> ColorName.values().first {
      it.hex == hexString }
  }
  .map { it.toString() }
  .subscribe(colorNameLiveData::postValue)
  .addTo(disposables)

// Send the RGB values of the color to the activity.
hexStringSubject
  .subscribeOn(backgroundScheduler)
  .observeOn(mainScheduler)
  .map {
    if (it.length == 7) {
      colorCoordinator.parseRgbColor(it)
    } else {
      RGBColor(255, 255, 255)
    }
  }
  .map { "${it.red},${it.green},${it.blue}" }
  .subscribe(rgbStringLiveData::postValue)
  .addTo(disposables)
```

The hexStringSubject property is a BehaviorSubject, which receives hex string digits from the user as they come in via the digitClicked method. At any given moment, hexStringSubject has the whole hex string that the user has entered.

Each block in the above code subscribes to the hexStringSubject behavior subject, interprets the current string, and sends some information to the several live data objects contained in ColorViewModel.

The app is complete in its functionality — it just needs a few tests to make it perfect!

Weirdly enough, whoever wrote this app actually created two test classes with some plumbing already set up. How convenient!

Before you start writing tests for `ColorViewModel`, you need some background on testing in RxJava. To do that, you'll start by writing a few sample RxJava tests in the `OperatorTest` class.

Introduction to TestObserver

Have you ever tried to test asynchronous code? If you have, you probably know that it's no cake walk. It can be (very) difficult to both test all aspects of your asynchronous code and keep your unit tests running quickly. RxJava provides an extremely convenient set of test utilities to make testing Observables easier — the first of which is the `TestObserver` class.

Open up **OperatorTest.kt**, and add the following code to the `test concat` method, which is already in the file:

```
@Test
fun `test concat`() {
  val observableA = Observable.just(1)
  val observableB = Observable.just(2)
  val observableC = observableA.concatWith(observableB)
}
```

> **Note**: When offered an import for `Observable`, make sure to import `io.reactivex.rxjava3.core.Observable`, *not* the `java.util` version.

You've got two simple Observables that emit one integer and then complete. Then you've got a third Observable that uses the `concatWith` method to concatenate those two Observables together. As you've probably gathered from the name of the method, you want to test that that `concatWith` method returns what you'd expect — an Observable that emits two values: 1 followed by 2, and then it finishes.

You *could* subscribe to `observableC` and record what values are emitted and then assert against those values as they come in. But that would be messy and would quickly fall apart when you have more complicated streams.

You've got another option: the `test()` method.

Every RxJava type (`Observable`, `Maybe`, `Completable`, and so on) exposes a `test()` method that returns a `TestObserver`. You can use this `TestObserver` class to assert against different conditions on your Observable (or whatever other RxJava type you're using).

Add the following code below the line declaring `observableC`:

```
observableC.test()
   .assertResult(1, 2)
   .assertComplete()
```

You're using the `test()` method on `observableC` and asserting a couple of things: that the Observable returns two results, 1 and 2, and then completes.

Run this unit test by right-clicking the little green **Play** button in the left sidebar next to the test name:

```
          @Test
▶ Run Test   `test concat`() {
          val observableA = Ob
```

You should see the test pass.

If you're like me, you're always skeptical of a test that passes on the first try. Try updating the `assertResult` statement to remove one of the values:

```
.assertResult(1)
```

Run the test again, and good news — it does indeed fail! 👍 for failure!

The `TestObserver` class that the `test()` method returns has many more uses. One of the most convenient things that it offers is an insight into what values the Observer has received so far. You can use the `values()` method on it to get a list of all the items that Observable has emitted. You'll see a few more examples of what `TestObserver` can do as you progress through some other nifty testing utilities RxJava exposes.

Using a TestScheduler

In addition to `TestObserver`, the RxJava library exposes a special scheduler that you can use to control when your Observables emit items. That scheduler is called `TestScheduler`.

Add the following code below the concat test you wrote earlier:

```
@Test
fun `test amb`() {
  // 1
  val observableA = Observable.interval(1, TimeUnit.SECONDS)
    .take(3)
    .map { 5 * it }
  val observableB = Observable
    .interval(500, TimeUnit.MILLISECONDS)
    .take(3)
    .map { 10 * it }

  // 2
  val ambObservable = observableA.ambWith(observableB)

  // 3
  val testObserver = ambObservable.test()

  testObserver.assertValueCount(3)
  testObserver.assertResult(0L, 10L, 20L)
  testObserver.assertComplete()
}
```

Since that's a lengthy block of code, here's a breakdown to describe what's going on so far:

1. You're creating two Observables using the `interval` method. As a reminder, the `interval` factory method creates a new Observable that starts counting up at a frequency that you dictate. For `observableA`, that frequency is once every second. For `observableB`, that frequency is once every 500 milliseconds. You're then taking the first three results from each Observable and doing math on it. For `observableA`, you're multiplying that number by 5. For `observableB`, you're multiplying the number by 10.

2. You're then creating a new ambObservable using the ambWith method. The amb and ambWith methods are very handy — they take two or more Observables and combine them into a resulting Observable that mirrors the **first** Observable to fire. The other Observable is discarded. amb comes in very handy when you have two sources of information and you only care about whichever one is the fastest. Imagine reading from a database and pulling data from a network. You may only care about which source gets your users the information they care about fastest. Neat!

3. Finally, you're using the test() method you learned about earlier to create a testObserver. You're then asserting a few things about the ambObservable: it emitted three values, those values were longs with a value of 0, 10, and 20, and finally that the Observable completed after emitting those three values.

> **Note**: If you're confused about why 0, 10, and 20 are emitted by the ambObservable don't worry! amb can be a confusing method to wrap your head around. Since observableA emits every second and observableB emits every half second, observableB will be the first one to emit between the two. Since amb only mirrors the first Observable to emit a value, observableB will win out. Then, since observableB uses the map method to multiply its values by 10, the resulting observable will emit 0 * 10, 1 * 10, and 2 * 10 - so 0, 10, and 20.

Run the unit test by clicking the **Run test** button, which shows up in the left sidebar next to the top of the test amb method. You should see the following:

```
java.lang.AssertionError: Value counts differ; Expected: 3,
Actual: 0 (latch = 1, values = 0, errors = 0, completions = 0)
```

Uh, oh — that doesn't look like a success at all! It looks like the assertValueCount(3) call failed. assertValueCount asserts that the Observable has emitted a certain number of values. The error message shows that ambObservable has emitted zero items by the time you start asserting.

The reason that call failed is because the testing code hasn't waited enough time for the Observables to actually start emitting values. Remember that the first Observable only emits once a second (starting after the first second), and the second Observable only emits once every 500 milliseconds.

There are two options for handling these sorts of timing issues:

1. You could start adding `Thread.sleep` calls to make the test wait long enough for the Observable to start emitting. Good test design and sleeping threads are not two things that go together! In this case, you run the risk of hitting interrupted thread exceptions and it makes your tests take much longer to finish. Doesn't sound like a great option.

2. You could use a `TestScheduler` and use it to control time yourself!

It may be shocking, especially with the title of this section, but the best path forward is option number 2: using a `TestScheduler`.

At the very top of `test amb`, create a `TestScheduler` before creating any of the Observables:

```
val scheduler = TestScheduler()
```

Then, update both `Observable.interval` calls to take a third parameter — the new `TestScheduler`:

```
val observableA = Observable.interval(1, TimeUnit.SECONDS, scheduler)
    .take(3)
    .map { 5 * it }
val observableB = Observable
    .interval(500, TimeUnit.MILLISECONDS, scheduler)
    .take(3)
    .map { 10 * it }
```

This may seem weird. Usually, you use schedulers in either the `subscribeOn` or `observeOn` operators. However, most RxJava operators and factory methods that deal with time can actually take a scheduler as a parameter.

That scheduler is then responsible for reporting the time back to that observable so it can figure out when to emit a new item. By default, the `computation` scheduler is used for this time logic. In the above example, the `interval` method will ask the `TestScheduler` you passed in for time information.

This is great news because TestScheduler allows you to control what time it reports back to the interval method!

Remove the existing three assertions at the end of test amb, and replace that code with the following:

```
scheduler.advanceTimeBy(500, TimeUnit.MILLISECONDS)
testObserver.assertValueCount(1)
```

You're using the advanceTimeBy method on TestScheduler to advance the schedulers clock forward a certain amount of time; in this case, 500 milliseconds. Since observableB emits every 500 milliseconds, that means that after that call the ambObservable should have emitted one value.

Run the unit test again. You should see a successful test. Nice!

For completeness, add the following code below the assertValueCount call:

```
scheduler.advanceTimeBy(1000, TimeUnit.MILLISECONDS)

testObserver.assertValueCount(3)
testObserver.assertResult(0L, 10L, 20L)
testObserver.assertComplete()
```

You're again advancing time (can anyone say time travel?). This time you're moving forward one more second, which should give observableB the opportunity to emit two more items. Since you're using the take method the Observable should finish after the three values are emitted.

Run the test, again, and you should see another success. Nice!

In addition to the advanceTimeBy method, TestScheduler exposes a method called triggerActions, which triggers any actions that are due to be run by that point in time. You'll see an example later on.

Injecting schedulers

There will be many times in which you're attempting to unit test classes that don't directly expose an Observable. For example: Most of the `ViewModel` classes that you'll see in this book don't expose an Observable. Instead, they subscribe to those Observables internally and expose `LiveData` objects that work better with the Android lifecycle.

That makes for a great architecture, but it can make it more difficult to test that your Observables are doing what you expect.

Here's an example `Timer` class that uses the `interval` method to count time:

```
class Timer() {
  var elapsedTime: Int = 0

  init {
    val intervalObservable = Observable
      .interval(1, TimeUnit.SECONDS)
      .subscribeOn(Schedulers.io())
      .observeOn(AndroidSchedulers.mainThread())

    intervalObservable
      .subscribe {
        elapsedTime++
      }
  }
}
```

You can query the timer's `elapsedTime` variable to see how much time has passed since it was first instantiated.

Now imagine you wanted to unit test this class. Since `intervalObservable` isn't exposed, you can't use the `test()` method or supply a `TestScheduler` to the `subscribeOn` or `observeOn` operators.

This is where **Dependency Injection** comes in to play. Injection?! That sounds painful!

The good news is that Dependency Injection is a fancy term for passing parameters, which supply dependencies to your classes rather than having those classes create them internally.

With Dependency Injection, you can rewrite the `Timer` class as follows:

```
class Timer(backgroundScheduler: Scheduler,
  mainThreadScheduler: Scheduler, timerScheduler: Scheduler) {
  var elapsedTime: Int = 0

  init {
    Observable.interval(1, TimeUnit.SECONDS, timerScheduler)
      .subscribeOn(backgroundScheduler)
      .observeOn(mainThreadScheduler)
      .subscribe {
        elapsedTime++
      }
  }
}
```

Now you can easily pass in a `TestScheduler` when you create an instance of `Timer` to unit test. Everyone wins!

Using Trampoline schedulers

Now that you're injecting schedulers, there's another scheduler that can be very helpful when running unit tests.

Often times, when unit testing an Observable, you want a scheduler that will force the work of the Observable to happen on the current thread. You can achieve some of this behavior by using `TestScheduler`. However, if you're not working with Observables that interact with time it can be laborious to have to call `advanceTimeBy` or `triggerActions` all the time.

Instead, you can use the `TrampolineScheduler` class, which you saw in Chapter 13, "Intro to Schedulers."

In case you missed that chapter or it's been a while, here's a quick refresher: `TrampolineScheduler` is a scheduler that schedules work on the current thread at the end of an internal queue it holds. It's a great option when you're injecting a scheduler and you don't want to go through the ceremony of using a `TestScheduler`.

How about a quick example? Add the following unit test to the `OperatorTest` class:

```
@Test
fun `using trampoline schedulers`() {
  val observableA = Observable.just(1)
    .subscribeOn(TrampolineScheduler.instance())
```

```
  val observableB = Observable.just(1)
    .subscribeOn(Schedulers.io())
}
```

Here you see two Observables, both of which are using the just method to construct an Observable that emits the integer 1 then finishes.

observableA uses the subscribeOn operator with a TrampolineScheduler, whereas observableB uses the io scheduler.

If you were to run these two Observables, what do you think would happen?

Since observableA is using a TrampolineScheduler, it will be run on whatever the current thread is, thus blocking the method until it finishes. observableB, on the other hand, would run on a different thread and the test method would terminate before it finished!

Add the following code at the end of the method:

```
observableA.test().assertResult(1)
observableB.test().assertEmpty()
```

You're asserting that observableA does indeed finish while observableB does not, since it's run on a different thread and won't have time to finish before the assertion is called.

Run the unit test. You should see a dazzling success. Well, a success anyways!

Using subjects with mocked data

One thing that can be very helpful is **mocking** data — that is, replacing one real piece of the puzzle with a different one that appears the same but which you have direct control over. This allows you to check that the other pieces of the puzzle work the way you expect them to when you feed them specified data.

As an example, think of trying to create a button that allows the user to repeatedly tap to add a photo to a list, with a maximum of five photos. If you were to use a ViewModel to control that, you would want to keep adding incoming photos until the list reached its maximum, and then disable the button the ViewModel controlled.

Within the **test** package, create a new Kotlin file called **PhotoTest.kt**. In this file, add the following code to bring this example to life:

```kotlin
// 1
class Photo

// 2
interface PhotoProvider {
  fun photoObservable(): Observable<Photo>
}

// 3
class PhotoViewModel(provider: PhotoProvider) {

  var disableButton = false
  private var photoList = arrayListOf<Photo>()

  init {
    // 4
    provider.photoObservable()
      .subscribe {
        photoList.add(it)
        if (photoList.size >= 5) {
          disableButton = true
        }
      }
  }
}
```

What's happening here? Walking through this step by step:

1. Create the simplest possible Kotlin class — one that just has a name.

2. Declare an `interface`, which will provide an Observable that can be watched.

3. Create a ViewModel, which takes the `PhotoProvider` interface you just created as a parameter. Congratulations - you're now using dependency injection!

4. Take the passed in `PhotoProvider` and subscribe to its Observable. When a new photo is added, you add it to the list and then determine if the button should be disabled.

Next, below the existing code, add a new test class and the beginnings of a test:

```kotlin
class PhotosTest {
  @Test
  fun `button disabled after 5 photos`() {
    val photoProviderMock = object: PhotoProvider {
      override fun photoObservable(): Observable<Photo> {
        TODO("Return some data")
```

```
      }
    }
    val viewModel = PhotoViewModel(photoProviderMock)

    Assert.assertFalse(viewModel.disableButton)
  }
}
```

What value should the `photoObservable` method return? You could provide a simple Observable that immediately returns five photos. But then you can't accurately test the transition from the `disableButton` value going from `false` to `true`.

Instead, it's often beneficial to return a **PublishSubject** that you can control in the test by handing it objects one by one. Update your test to create one, then return it as the `photoObservable`:

```
val subject = PublishSubject.create<Photo>()
val photoProviderMock = object: PhotoProvider {
  override fun photoObservable(): Observable<Photo> {
    return subject
  }
}
```

Next, at the end of the test, add code to pass some photos through the Observable and check whether `disableButton` is still `false` or has been flipped to `true`:

```
subject.onNext(Photo())
Assert.assertFalse(viewModel.disableButton)
subject.onNext(Photo())
subject.onNext(Photo())
subject.onNext(Photo())
Assert.assertFalse(viewModel.disableButton)
subject.onNext(Photo())
Assert.assertTrue(viewModel.disableButton)
```

Run the test by clicking the **Run** button in the left sidebar, and it will pass — `disableButton` is still `false` after adding four photos, but `true` after adding a fifth!

Now, you can precisely control when the subject emits new values and be more confident in your tests. Wahoo!

Testing ColorViewModel

Now that you're an expert in testing, it's time to add some real unit tests to the ViewModelTest class.

Open **ViewModelTest.kt** and add the following empty unit test:

```
@Test
fun `color is red when hex string is FF0000`() {
}
```

This unit test is testing that when the user enters the hex color "FF0000", the view models colorNameLiveData live data object emits the "Red" color name.

If you go back into the ColorViewModel class you can pick out the relevant piece of code in the init block. It looks like this:

```
// If our color name enum contains the given hex string, send
that color name over.
hexStringSubject
  .subscribeOn(backgroundScheduler)
  .observeOn(mainScheduler)
  .filter { hexString ->
    ColorName.values().map { it.hex }.contains(hexString)
  }
  .map { hexString ->
    ColorName.values().first { it.hex == hexString }
  }
  .map { it.toString() }
  .subscribe(colorNameLiveData::postValue)
  .addTo(disposables)
```

You'll also notice that the ColorViewModel class is set up to take in schedulers for both background work and main thread work. Nice!

Since this block utilizes the subscribeOn and observeOn operators, and doesn't utilize any Observables that deal directly with time, it's a good candidate for using a TrampolineScheduler.

Go back to **ViewModelTest.kt**. In the empty unit test method you just added, add the following code:

```
val trampolineScheduler = TrampolineScheduler.instance()
val viewModel = ColorViewModel(trampolineScheduler,
  trampolineScheduler, colorCoordinator)
```

You're getting an instance of `TrampolineScheduler` and constructing a `ColorViewModel`, passing that trampoline scheduler in for both the background and main thread schedulers. You're also passing in a `ColorCoordinator` mock that's defined at the top of the file. `ColorCoordinator` is a simple class that parses out RGB values of a color and wraps a call to the `Color.parseColor` Android function to make testing the ViewModel easier.

Since you're passing in a `TrampolineScheduler`, you know all of the RxJava work will be done synchronously. All that's left is adding the business logic of the test! Add the following code below the ViewModel declaration:

```
viewModel.digitClicked("F")
viewModel.digitClicked("F")
viewModel.digitClicked("0")
viewModel.digitClicked("0")
viewModel.digitClicked("0")
viewModel.digitClicked("0")

Assert.assertEquals(ColorName.RED.toString(),
  viewModel.colorNameLiveData.value)
```

Boom! You're simulating the user clicking the relevant digits and then asserting that the `colorNameLiveData` current value is equal to the RED color name.

Run the test and you should see it pass.

That was easy enough with a `TrampolineScheduler`, but what would it look like using the `TestScheduler`? Add the following new unit test:

```
@Test
fun `color is red when hex string is FF0000 using test scheduler`() {
  val testScheduler = TestScheduler()
  val viewModel = ColorViewModel(testScheduler,
    testScheduler, colorCoordinator)

  viewModel.digitClicked("F")
  viewModel.digitClicked("F")
  viewModel.digitClicked("0")
  viewModel.digitClicked("0")
  viewModel.digitClicked("0")
  viewModel.digitClicked("0")

  Assert.assertEquals(null, viewModel.colorNameLiveData.value)
  Assert.assertEquals(ColorName.RED.toString(),
     viewModel.colorNameLiveData.value)
}
```

In this version of the unit test, you're doing the exact same thing as before except passing in a `TestScheduler` instead of a `TrampolineScheduler`.

Run the test. You should see the following:

```
java.lang.AssertionError:
Expected :RED
Actual   :null
```

As you saw earlier, `TestScheduler` requires more ceremony to use than `TrampolineScheduler`. You need to tell it to advance time or trigger its actions before any work done on that scheduler will actually happen.

Add the following line between the two assert calls:

```
testScheduler.triggerActions()
```

Run the test again and it should succeed. On to the next test!

Last but not least, it'd be good to test that the **Clear** button correctly clears the hex string display and replaces it with a single # character. Add the following new unit test:

```
@Test
fun `hex subject is reset after clear is clicked`() {
}
```

What kind of scheduler do you want to use for this test? Take a look at the `ColorViewModel` class again. Every time `digitClicked` is called, the view model calls `onNext` with the relevant character on the `hexStringSubject`.

In the top of the `init` block, you can see the code that determines what the app shows in the hex string field:

```
hexStringSubject
  .subscribeOn(backgroundScheduler)
  .observeOn(mainScheduler)
  .subscribe(hexStringLiveData::postValue)
  .addTo(disposables)
```

Pretty simple — the current string in `hexStringSubject` is just fed into the `hexStringLiveData` variable. That means that using a `TrampolineScheduler` in the test should be good enough; there's no need to use `TestScheduler`.

Back in the test, set up the code. Again, you'll want to use a `TrampolineScheduler` to create your ViewModel and feed it the digits of a hex color:

```
@Test
fun `hex subject is reset after clear is clicked`() {
  val trampolineScheduler = TrampolineScheduler.instance()
  val viewModel = ColorViewModel(trampolineScheduler,
    trampolineScheduler, colorCoordinator)

  viewModel.digitClicked("F")
  viewModel.digitClicked("F")
  viewModel.digitClicked("0")
  viewModel.digitClicked("0")
  viewModel.digitClicked("0")
  viewModel.digitClicked("0")
}
```

Next, add the following lines at the bottom of the test to validate both that the subject has fully updated and that clicking **Clear** actually does what you want it to:

```
Assert.assertEquals("#FF0000", viewModel.hexStringSubject.value)
viewModel.clearClicked()
Assert.assertEquals("#", viewModel.hexStringSubject.value)
```

Run the test. Everything works exactly as expected, and you've got a more resilient and tested app! Well done!

Key points

- You can use the `test()` method on any reactive type to easily test them.

- `TestObserver` provides a useful set of tools to test the values and state of your Observables.

- With `TestObserver`, you can assert that your Observable has completed, has emitted a few values, or has even thrown an error.

- In order to test classes that don't expose their internal Observables, you should use the Dependency Injection design pattern to inject your schedulers.

- If you need a synchronous scheduler that allows you to trigger new actions, you can use `TestScheduler`.

- If all you need is to make your Observables synchronous, use `TrampolineScheduler`.

- `Subjects` can be used to precisely control when elements are emitted and, combined with mocked data, make for great testing tools.

Where to go from here?

Testing is an important piece to writing great apps. Hopefully after reading this chapter, you've picked up some tricks to use the next time you need to test some reactive code. Happy testing!

Chapter 16: Creating Custom Reactive Extensions

By Alex Sullivan

After being introduced to RxJava and learning how to create tests, you have yet to see how to create wrappers using RxJava on top of frameworks created by Google or by third parties. Wrapping a Google or third party library component is instrumental in writing reactive applications, so you'll be introduced to the concept in this chapter.

In this chapter you'll create a reactive wrapper around an Android Widget, a request for a specific permission, and the process of getting location updates. It's worth noting here that in a real application you'd probably want to use libraries rather than write these specific wrappers yourself. Later chapters in this book will introduce you to a few of those libraries.

Getting started

You're going to be creating an app that allows a user to search for gifs through the API for Giphy https://giphy.com, one of the most popular GIF services on the web.

To start, you'll need a beta key. To get the beta key, navigate to the official docs https://developers.giphy.com/docs/api, and scroll down to "Create an App."

Follow the instructions there to create an app. You can pick the **API** key type when prompted. Name your app **BestGif**:

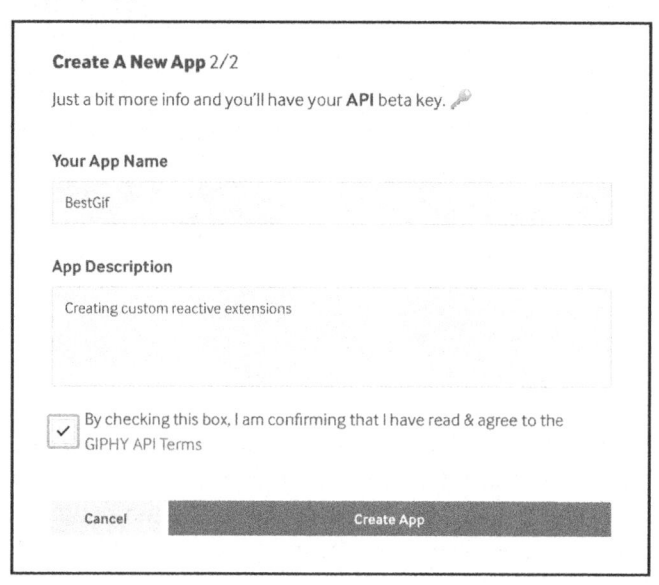

When you create an app on that page (via the "Create an App" button) you will get a development key, which will suffice to work through this chapter. The API key is displayed under the name of your newly created app like so:

Open the starter project in Android Studio. Then, open **GiphyApi.kt** and copy the key into the correct place:

```
private const val API_KEY = "YOUR API KEY HERE"
```

Once you've replaced the API key, run the app. You should see an empty screen with a simple `EditText` up top. It doesn't do much yet.

Extending a framework class

It's often useful to adapt existing framework classes to have a more reactive approach and styling. Luckily, Kotlin's extension methods allow for a fluid interface to achieve reactive framework classes.

You're going to start off by extending an `EditText` widget so you can observe text changes as the user writes them.

Open **EditTextUtils.kt** and take a look at the `EditText.textChanges()` method. Right now it returns an empty Observable, but once you're done it will return an Observable that emits whatever the user types.

To create the actual extension, you're going to rely on `Observable.create()` to create an Observable from an existing, non-reactive asynchronous API.

Replace the line returning the empty Observable with the following:

```
return Observable.create { emitter ->
}
```

As you'll recall from Chapter 2, "Observables", `Observable.create()` takes in an `ObservableOnSubscribe` source that allows you to pipe events into an `ObservableEmitter` object to control how your Observable emits items.

This is a common paradigm when moving from the callback world to the reactive world. `Observable.create()` provides a convenient interface to wrap existing, callback styled methods.

Now add the following in the `Observable.create()` block:

```
val textWatcher = object : TextWatcher {
  override fun afterTextChanged(text: Editable) {
    emitter.onNext(text.toString())
  }

  override fun beforeTextChanged(
    p0: CharSequence?, p1: Int, p2: Int, p3: Int) {}
  override fun onTextChanged(
    p0: CharSequence?, p1: Int, p2: Int, p3: Int) {}
}
addTextChangedListener(textWatcher)
```

`TextWatcher` is an Android framework interface that allows you to observe text changes on any `TextView` or `EditText`. It allows you to observe the current value before the text changes, as the text changes, and after the text has changed.

While the interface requires methods to do all three things, the only thing you care about is whatever the text is after the `EditText`s text has changed. If you wanted to manipulate the text, then you may care about the other two functions, but for now, you can just leave them with empty implementations.

Since all you care about is what the text is after it's changed, you're sending the new text received in `afterTextChanged()` into the Observable via the emitters `onNext` method. Pretty simple, right?

Last but not least, you're telling the `EditText` to use the object you created as a `onTextChangedListener`. Since you're creating an extension method, `this` represents the current instance of `EditText`.

At this point, you have a fully functioning reactive wrapper. Hooray!

However, it's not a very responsible wrapper. It never un-registers the text changed listener from the `EditText`. Since the `onTextChangedListener` has a strong reference to the `EditText`, it means your `EditText` won't be garbage collected until the Observable is garbage collected, even if the Observable finished long ago. Luckily, the `ObservableEmitter` class comes with a easy way to trigger cleaning up any resources.

Add the following below the line to add the `textChangedListener`:

```
emitter.setCancellable {
  removeTextChangedListener(textWatcher)
}
```

Now whenever the Observable you're returning finishes or disposes, it will call that cancellation block and the `TextWatcher` will be un-registered.

Remember, kids: Safe programming is fun programming. And always wear your seatbelt.

Wiring the extension up

It's time to use the new extension. Open up **GifActivity.kt**, and add the following to the bottom of `onCreate()`:

```
text_input
  // 1
  .textChanges()
  // 2
  .flatMapSingle { GiphyApi.searchForGifs(it) }
  // 3
  .onErrorReturnItem(listOf(GiphyGif(
      "https://media.giphy.com/media/SQ24FpNRW9yRG/giphy.gif")))
  // 4
  .subscribeOn(Schedulers.io())
  .observeOn(AndroidSchedulers.mainThread())
  // 5
  .subscribe { adapter.items = it }
  .addTo(disposables)
```

Here's what's happening in the above chain:

1. You're using the new `textChanges()` extension to get the changed text from the `EditText`
2. You're feeding that received text into `GiphyApi.searchForGifs()` via `flatMapSingle()`. Then, `searchForGifs()` queries the Giphy API and searches for gifs with the given string.
3. You're using the `onErrorReturnItem` operator to default to an adorable gif of two kittens if there are any errors.
4. You're using `subscribeOn()` and `observeOn()` to make sure you make the network call from the `io` thread pool, and you handle the callback on the main thread.
5. You're subscribing to the whole chain, and updating the adapter's items to the results received from the API.

Run the app and search for your favorite gif. It should work as expected now, and you should see a list of loading indicators followed by a list of gifs.

There's one more issue, though. Every time you type a character, the app does a network request for new gifs. In reality, you only really want to start searching once the user has stopped typing for a second or so.

You could update the code in Observable.create() method to add some sort of timer and only emit items every so often, but that sounds like a ton of work. Instead, you can utilize the debounce() operator you learned about in Chapter 6, "Filtering Operators in Practice."

In case you need a refresher, debounce() limits the items emitted by the source Observable and only emits an item if it isn't followed by another item after a certain amount of time. It's perfect for limiting actions taken after typing.

Add the following operator right below textChanges() in the Rx chain:

```
.debounce(500, TimeUnit.MILLISECONDS)
```

Now you'll only receive an item at most once every 500 milliseconds. Run the app again and search for a gif. You should see that you only start seeing loading indicators once you're done typing.

Wrapping the locations API

The app is looking pretty good, but it's a bit empty before the user types something in. This seems like a great excuse to wrap some more framework classes!

You're going to update the app so that it automatically searches for gifs with the name of whatever city the user is currently located in, so you'll be using the location APIs.

But before you start fetching the location, you need to be a good Android citizen and request permission. You'll be using a Subject to convert the existing permissions API into a reactive one.

Add the following as instance variables in `GifActivity`:

```
private val locationRequestCode = 500
private val permissionsSubject =
    BehaviorSubject.create<Boolean>()
```

Now add and implement `onRequestPermissionsResult()`, importing `android.Manifest`:

```
override fun onRequestPermissionsResult(
    requestCode: Int,
    permissions: Array<out String>,
    grantResults: IntArray
) {
  super.onRequestPermissionsResult(requestCode, permissions,
      grantResults)
  if (requestCode == locationRequestCode) {
    val locationIndex = permissions.indexOf(
        Manifest.permission.ACCESS_FINE_LOCATION)
    if (locationIndex != -1) {
      val granted = grantResults[locationIndex] ==
          PackageManager.PERMISSION_GRANTED
      permissionsSubject.onNext(granted)
    }
  }
}
```

Most of the above code is permissions boilerplate that checks the request code and checks that the location permission has been granted or denied. The one interesting piece is the part where you call `onNext()` on the `permissionsSubject` with a boolean indicating whether the location permission was granted or denied.

Now that the `permissionsSubject` is up and running, add the following to the bottom of `onCreate()`:

```
permissionsSubject
  .doOnSubscribe {
    if (Build.VERSION.SDK_INT >= Build.VERSION_CODES.M) {
      requestPermissions(arrayOf(
          Manifest.permission.ACCESS_FINE_LOCATION),
        locationRequestCode)
    } else {
      permissionsSubject.onNext(true)
    }
  }
  .filter { it }
```

You're building up a new Observable chain here, but not subscribing to it just yet. You're using `doOnSubscribe()` to actually kick off the call to request the location permission. If the API version of the device the app is running on is less than M, i.e. before the new permissions model came into effect, you can assume you already have the permission and forward a `true` event into the `permissionsSubject`.

You're also using `filter()` to filter out any instances where you didn't receive the location permission. You'll see why shortly.

You've got a new sleek permissions model. It's time to finish this feature off with a reactive wrapper around the locations API.

Open **LocationUtils.kt** and look at `locationUpdates()`. Its return type is `Observable<Location>`. The location API offers a perfect opportunity for a reactive wrapper, since it works with a constant stream of items in the form of location updates.

For this example you'll be using the fused location API rather than the raw `LocationManager` framework API.

To receive location updates, you need to create a `LocationRequest` object and a `FusedLocationProviderClient`. Add the following to the top of `locationUpdates()`, before the return statement:

```
val currentLocationRequest = LocationRequest()
  .setInterval(500)
  .setFastestInterval(0)
  .setMaxWaitTime(0)
  .setSmallestDisplacement(0f)
  .setPriority(LocationRequest.PRIORITY_HIGH_ACCURACY)

val client = FusedLocationProviderClient(context)
```

You're creating that `LocationRequest` and `FusedLocationProviderClient` with some configuration options.

Now replace the `return Observable.empty()` line with the old reliable `Observable.create()`:

```
return Observable.create { emitter ->
}
```

You're again using `Observable.create()` to create a bridge between the callback world and the reactive world.

You need to use `requestLocationUpdates()` on `FusedLocationProvider` to actually start the process of getting location updates. To get set up to do that, first add the following in the `Observable.create()` lambda block:

```
val callback = object : LocationCallback() {
  override fun onLocationResult(result: LocationResult?) {
    result?.lastLocation?.let { emitter.onNext(it) }
  }
}
```

This callback will be called whenever the system has a new location update for you, so that's where you call `onNext()` on the `ObservableEmitter`. `onLocationResult()` can deliver a `null` location, so that's why you're using `let`.

Below the `callback` declaration add the following:

```
client.requestLocationUpdates(currentLocationRequest, callback,
    null)
```

You learned earlier that you can use `setCancellable()` on `ObservableEmitter` to clean up any resources once the Observable terminates. Listening for location updates is an extremely battery intensive task, so it's doubly important to clean up after yourself when wrapping the location APIs. To that end, add the following right below the `requestLocationUpdates()` line:

```
emitter.setCancellable {
  client.removeLocationUpdates(callback)
}
```

Boom! You've wrapped the fused location API with minimal pain, and you're cleaning up after yourself like a responsible developer.

Time to utilize your newfound location powers.

Head back to `GifActivity`. It's time to finish up that Rx chain you started earlier.

Now that you have access to a reactive wrapper around location updates, you can use `flatMap()` to start receiving location updates after you receive the location permission. Add the following right after the `.filter { it }` line:

```
.flatMap { locationUpdates(this) }
```

Now the type of the Observable switches from `Observable<Boolean>` to `Observable<Location>`. Nice! This line of code really shows how powerful it is to create reactive wrappers around traditionally callback based APIs. You can now combine your permission logic and your location logic into one simple declarative stream.

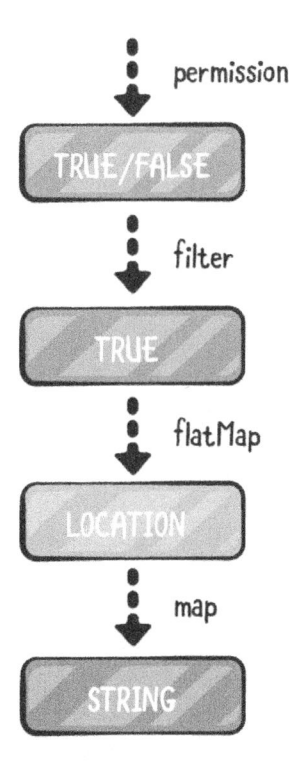

In this app you don't actually want to keep listening for location updates. All you really care about is the first location you get back. After that first location it will be up to the user to search for their own gif.

You've got a few options for limiting the number of location updates to just one. You could try and change up `locationUpdates()` to only return one `Location` object and then complete. But that limits the usefulness of `locationUpdates()`.

Instead, you can use `take()` to only take the first item emitted by your new `Observable<Location>` object. Add the following operator to the bottom of your chain, after `flatMap()`:

```
.take(1)
```

Now you'll only get one `Location` object, then the Observable will terminate. And since you were a responsible developer and you used `setCancellable()` on your `ObservableEmitter` the app will stop listening for location updates after that first object comes through.

The Giphy API doesn't accept a `Location` object. Instead, you want to convert that `Location` into a `String` representing the users city. Add the following operator to the bottom of the chain:

```
.map { cityFromLocation(this, it) }
```

`cityFromLocation()` is a method in `LocationUtils` that uses the `Geocoder` API to pull out a locality from a `Location` object.

It might be a good idea to give the user a heads up that the app is searching for their city. You can use the `hint` attribute on your `EditText` to show them what's been searched for. Add the following operator to the chain:

```
.doOnNext { text_input.hint = it }
```

It's time to make the actual network call to fetch some gifs from the city name. Add the following operator:

```
.flatMapSingle {
  GiphyApi.searchForGifs(it).subscribeOn(Schedulers.io())
}
```

You need to call `subscribeOn()` on the actual Observable returned from `flatMap()` to make sure this this nested Observable is also being run on the correct thread.

Add the following to finish the chain:

```
.observeOn(AndroidSchedulers.mainThread())
.subscribe { adapter.items = it }
.addTo(disposables)
```

You're setting the list of GiphyGifs on your RecyclerView adapter in your subscribe().

The app is ready to go! Give it a run and you should see the app immediately make a request to the Giphy API with whatever city your emulator is set to, after you grant location permissions:

The lift and compose functions

You may come across a few other functions in your Rx travels with regard to custom extensions, especially when interoperating with Java. Since Kotlin supports extension functions, you probably won't need to use these very often, but it's still a good idea to understand how they work in case you see them out in the wild in any Java code that you're interacting with.

The first is compose(), which allows you to write custom RxJava operators that fit inline with the Rx chain.

You will often find that you want to apply a certain set of schedulers when working on reactive apps. For instance, if you're doing a network call and then you want to display the results of that call to the user, you'll probably want to use the subscribeOn(Schedulers.io()) and observeOn(AndroidSchedulers.mainThread()) operators and schedulers to make sure you're running the task on the background thread and applying the results on the main thread. For example:

```
val observable: Observable<MyModelClass> =
  networkMethodThatReturnsAnObservable()
observable
  .subscribeOn(Schedulers.io())
  .observeOn(AndroidSchedulers.mainThread())
  .subscribe { displayMyResults(it) }
```

That subscribeOn() and observeOn() combination is so common that lots of people make a Kotlin extension function that applies those two operators:

```
fun <T> Observable<T>.applySchedulers(): Observable<T> {
  return subscribeOn(Schedulers.io())
    .observeOn(AndroidSchedulers.mainThread())
}
```

You can use that extension function like an operator in your code:

```
val observable: Observable<MyModelClass> =
  networkMethodThatReturnsAnObservable()
observable
  .applySchedulers()
  .subscribe { displayMyResults(it) }
```

However, if you're still using Java, the above won't look nearly as clean since Java doesn't support extension functions, and you have to access those functions through the file they're created in:

```
Observable<Integer> observable = Observable.just(1);
Observable<Integer> schedulersApplied =
    FileContaingFunctionKt.applySchedulers(observable);
```

Pretty gross, huh?

Instead, you can use `compose()` to keep the chain flowing. All you have to do is create a class that implements the `ObservableTransformer<T>` interface and override `apply()`:

```kotlin
class ApplySchedulers<T>: ObservableTransformer<T, T> {
  override fun apply(upstream: Observable<T>):
ObservableSource<T> {
    return upstream
        .subscribeOn(Schedulers.io())
        .observeOn(AndroidSchedulers.mainThread())
  }
}
```

Creating that class allows you to write Java code that looks like this:

```java
Observable<Integer> schedulersApplied =
  Observable.just(1).compose(new ApplySchedulers<>());
```

Much prettier and easier to follow, right?

Fortunately, since you're using Kotlin you shouldn't have to mess around with `compose()` too much!

The last piece of the reactive extensions puzzle is `lift()`. `lift()` is an extremely complicated method that many of the internal RxJava operators utilize.

The short explanation is that `lift()` allows you to create a new operator by reaching into the upstream `Observer` and directly manipulating its `onNext()` values.

It's not worth going too deep into how `lift()` works. What's important to know is that if you're finding yourself in a situation where you feel like you have to use `lift()`, you're probably overthinking things. It's almost always a better choice to make an extension function that utilizes existing RxJava operators.

Testing your custom reactive extension

Testing your custom reactive extensions is just like testing a normal Rx chain. You just need to make sure you're testing the right thing!

First off, you'll test the textChanges() extension to EditText you made earlier.

Open **EditTextUtilsKtTest.kt** and add the following in the body of newStringsReachObserver():

```
val view = EditText(context)
val testObserver = view.textChanges().test()
view.setText("Test 1")
view.setText("Test 2")
view.setText("Test 3")
view.setText("Test 4")
testObserver.assertValueCount(4)
testObserver
  .assertValues("Test 1", "Test 2", "Test 3", "Test 4")
```

You're using the test() method you learned about in Chapter 15, "Testing RxJava Code" to make sure textChanges() emits new text values as expected.

Run the test. It should pass.

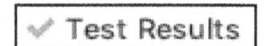

Pretty easy right?

Next up you're going to test that locationUpdates() stops listening for location updates after its associated Observable terminates, ensuring that the locationCallback object is not leaked.

Open **LocationUtilsKtTest.kt** and add the following to locationUpdatesRemoveOnComplete(). Note that it won't compile yet until you make some changes in the next step:

```
val context =
  InstrumentationRegistry.getInstrumentation().targetContext
// 1
val locationProvider =
  mockk<FusedLocationProviderClient>(relaxed = true)

val locationObservable =
  locationUpdates(context, locationProvider)

// 2
verify(exactly = 0) {
```

```
    locationProvider.removeLocationUpdates(any<LocationCallback>())
  }

  locationObservable
    // 3
    .take(0)
    .test()
    .assertComplete()

  // 4
  verify(exactly = 1) {
    locationProvider
      .removeLocationUpdates(any<LocationCallback>())
  }
```

1. You're using the **mockk** library to mock out the `FusedLocationProviderClient` class so you can verify the location updates are being removed when the Observable completes.

2. You're using **mockk**'s `verify()` to make sure that before the Observable has terminated, the method to remove location updates has not been called.

3. You're using `take(0)` to force the location Observable to complete immediately, then validating the Observable has completed.

4. You're using `verify()` again to validate that now that the Observable has been completed and the method to remove location updates has been called once (and only once).

> **Note**: For this test, you're not interested in whether the Observable actually emits any location objects. All you care about here is that the location provider stops listening for the location as soon as the Observable terminates.

You can't run this code yet because `locationUpdates()` doesn't currently accept a `FusedLocationProviderClient`. But you can fix that easily.

Open **LocationUtils.kt**, and update `locationUpdates()` so it takes in the client as a parameter:

```
fun locationUpdates(
  context: Context,
  client: FusedLocationProviderClient =
    FusedLocationProviderClient(context)
): Observable<Location> {
  ...
}
```

Next delete the line declaring `val client = FusedLocationProviderClient(context)` before creating the observer, since `client` is now being passed in as a parameter.

You should be ready to go. Run the `testLocationUpdates` test and you should see it pass.

Awesome, you're not leaking a location callback!

Key points

- You can wrap an existing Android component via `Observable.create()`.

- You should pay attention to any long-lived references inside extensions. Clean up after yourself and cancel any resources when an Observable is disposed.

- You explored `compose()` and `lift()` and when to use them (TL;DR avoid `lift()` unless you know what you're doing; use `compose()` if you're writing Java code).

- Test your reactive wrappers by writing unit tests and mocking any system component.

Where to go from here?

In this chapter, you saw how to implement and wrap the Android framework. Sometimes, it's very useful to abstract an official Android framework or third party library to better connect with RxJava.

There's no written rule about when an abstraction is necessary, but the recommendation is to apply this strategy if the code in question meets one or more of these conditions:

- Uses callbacks with success and failure information.
- Needs to inter-operate with other RxJava parts of the application.
- Uses lots of asynchronous constructs to return information.

You also need to know if the code in question has restrictions on which thread the data must be processed. For this reason, it's a good idea to read the documentation thoroughly before creating an RxJava wrapper.

And don't forget to look for existing community extensions. There's a lot of high quality existing reactive wrappers around common Android APIs, some of which you'll learn about in the next few chapters. If you do write your own wrapper, consider sharing it back with the community!

Section IV: RxJava Community Cookbook

RxJava's popularity keeps growing every day. Thanks to the friendly and creative community that formed around this library, a lot of community-driven Rx projects are being released on GitHub.

The advantage of the community-built libraries that use RxJava is that unlike the main repository, which needs to follow the Rx standard, these libraries can afford to experiment and explore different approaches, provide non multi-platform specializations, and more.

In this section you are going to look into just a few of the many community open source projects. The section contains four short cookbook-style chapters that look briefly into four community projects that help you with binding Android Views, talking to your server with Retrofit, persisting preferences data, and handling user permissions.

Chapter 17: RxBindings

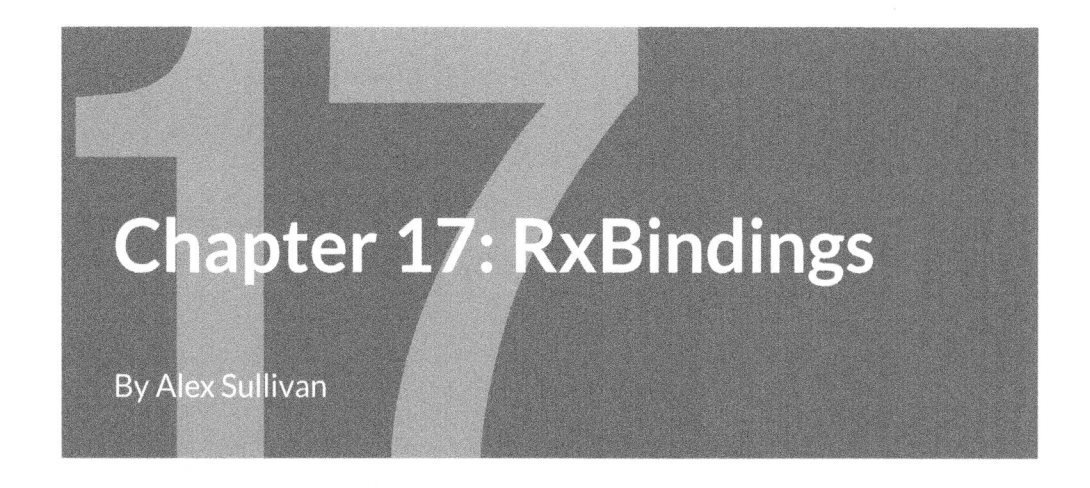

By Alex Sullivan

In the last chapter, you learned all about wrapping existing APIs to make them into Observables. Hopefully, you've realized how powerful it is to express a lot of the framework APIs in reactive terms. Unfortunately, it's a fair amount of repetitive work to wrap all of these frameworks.

It's not too bad to make a reactive extension for, say, a `Button`. And it's not too bad to make a reactive extension for an `EditText`. But, as you keep going, it starts to become a bit laborious to keep making these reactive wrappers.

There's an extremely handy library called `RxBindings`, which takes care of making reactive bindings for all of the Android view classes. So good news! You get to be lazy and rely on a library to make those extensions for you. And as we all know, programming is 1% creativity and 99% laziness.

In this chapter, you'll revisit the **HexColor** app and improve on it by using the `RxBindings` library.

Getting started

Open the starter project and run the app. You should see the **HexColor** app from Chapter 15, "Testing RxJava Code."

Feel free to tap around. You can type in a hex code, and the background will change to that color. It will also show the RGB value and if you type in one of the colors in the `ColorName` enum, the name will show, too.

There's a few limitations to the app, though. First off, most colors you enter don't have an associated color name in the `ColorName` enum. You can see this list in **X.kt**.

That's a hard nut to crack, since there's a near infinite number of color combinations you can use in the app. Next up, manually tapping the digits can be a bit burdensome. It'd be nice if you could also use the keyboard to enter a new hex color.

In this chapter, you'll work through solving both of these problems while also using the **RxBinding** library to make the Android view components a bit more reactive.

Extending ValueAnimator to be reactive

Speaking of making things more reactive, take a look at the `animateColorChange` method in `ColorActivity`. It's the method that's responsible for that fancy color changing animation. It's a pretty great method, but it's not very reactive. In the spirit of building on the work you did last chapter, you're going to wrap that call in a reactive wrapper to make it fit better with the rest of the reactive app.

Open the **AnimationUtils.kt** file and look at the `colorAnimator` method:

```kotlin
fun colorAnimator(fromColor: Int, toColor: Int): Observable<Int>
{
  return Observable.empty()
}
```

`colorAnimator` takes two arguments: an integer named `fromColor` representing the starting color and another integer named `toColor` representing the ending color. The idea, here, is to convert the `animateColorChange` method to use this `colorAnimator` Observable instead of using a `ValueAnimator` the way it does now.

Replace the `return Observable.empty()` line with the following:

```kotlin
// 1
val valueAnimator =
  ValueAnimator.ofObject(ArgbEvaluator(), fromColor, toColor)
valueAnimator.duration = 250 // milliseconds
// 2
val observable = Observable.create<Int> { emitter ->
  // 3
  valueAnimator.addUpdateListener {
    emitter.onNext(it.animatedValue as Int)
  }
}
```

Here's a breakdown of the previous code:

1. Create a new `ValueAnimator` using the `ArgbEvaluator` to go from the `fromColor` to the `toColor`. In case you're not familiar with `ValueAnimator`, it provides a handy way to get interpolated values between two values you provide, that you can later use to animate some view between them. The `ArgbEvaluator` interpolates two color `Int`s to make a smooth transition.

2. Create a new Observable via the `create` function. The Observable will emit `Int`s since that's what type the `ValueAnimator` declared above will output.

3. Add an `updateListener` to the `valueAnimator` and call `emitter.onNext` with the updated animated value. Now whenever the `valueAnimator` object calls its update listener with a new value, the Observable will emit that value.

Now, add the following line to finish up the reactive wrapper:

```
return observable.doOnSubscribe { valueAnimator.start() }
```

You're returning the `observable` object you created earlier. You're using the `doOnSubscribe` operator to actually start the `valueAnimator`. Now whenever someone subscribes to the Observable the `valueAnimator` will start emitting.

Nifty.

Head over to **ColorActivity.kt** and replace the `animateColorChange` method with the following:

```
private fun animateColorChange(newColor: Int) {
  val colorFrom = root_layout.background as ColorDrawable
  colorAnimator(colorFrom.color, newColor)
    .subscribe { color ->
      root_layout.setBackgroundColor(color)
      if (Build.VERSION.SDK_INT >= Build.VERSION_CODES.LOLLIPOP)
{
        window.statusBarColor = color
      }
    }
    .addTo(disposables)
}
```

Now, instead of directly using a `valueAnimator`, you're using the `colorAnimator` method you defined earlier and subscribing to the resulting Observable.

Now that this animation is represented via an Observable, you could easily chain together multiple animators and utilize the power of Rx.

Using RxBindings with Android widgets

Now that you've react-ified that animation code, it's time to move on to actually using `RxBindings`.

First off, open the app's **build.gradle** file (not the top-level one!).

Navigate to the dependencies section and take a look at the RxBindings dependencies:

```
implementation 'com.jakewharton.rxbinding4:rxbinding:4.0.0'
```

Open **ColorViewModel.kt** class. If you look at the structure of the class, you'll notice that there's two distinct "sections" to the class:

1. There's the `init` block, which is where the bulk of the actual logic is. This is where all of the Rx magic happens. It's declarative and simple to read. It's not stateful, and it's cohesive.

2. There's the several `xClicked` methods below the `init` block. These methods are primarily boilerplate to forward relevant data into the `hexStringSubject`.

If you think about it, these `xClicked` methods are acting as intermediaries for a stream-like flow. Take the `clearClicked` method for example. At any point in time, the app is listening for the user to click the **Clear** button. That event then triggers a call to `clearClicked`, which then maps that **Clear**-clicked event into a new value for the `hexStringSubject`.

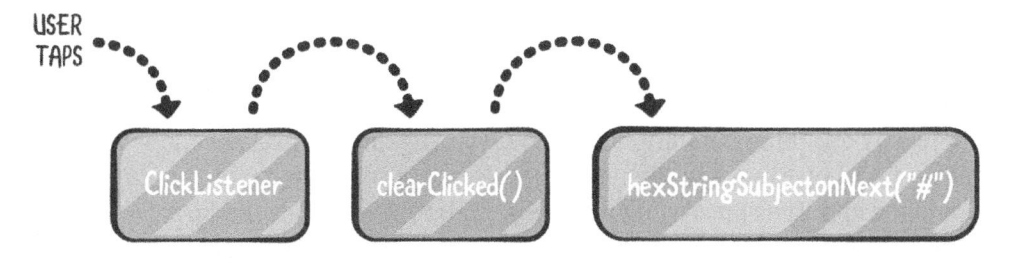

USER TAPS → ClickListener → clearClicked() → hexStringSubject.onNext("#")

Converting clearClicked() to use RxBindings

The `clearClicked` method is really just an impediment to the above flow. What the app really needs is another `Observable<Unit>` that represents the user clicking the **Clear** button — **RxBindings** provides that functionality, but there's a catch.

Update the `ColorViewModel` class header to add a `clearStream` Observable:

```
class ColorViewModel(
  backgroundScheduler: Scheduler,
  mainScheduler: Scheduler,
  colorCoordinator: ColorCoordinator,
  clearStream: Observable<Unit>
) : ViewModel() { ... }
```

Now, the `ColorViewModel` takes a `clearStream` object of type `Observable<Unit>`. The type of `clearStream` is `Unit` because the app doesn't actually care what the value emitted by the Observable is — all it cares about is that the Observable emitted **something**.

Head over to `ColorActivity`. If you look at the line declaring `viewModel`, you'll see that the `ColorViewmodel` is being instantiated inside a `ViewModelProvider.NewInstanceFactory` object. There's a fair amount of boilerplate here that isn't important. Update the actual line returning a `ColorViewModel`:

```
return ColorViewModel(
  Schedulers.io(),
  AndroidSchedulers.mainThread(),
  ColorCoordinator(),
  clear.clicks()
) as T
```

There's only one thing different here: You're passing one extra argument — `clear.clicks()`. `clear` is a reference to the big **X** button that clears the current color in the app. The app is using the Kotlin Android Extensions plugin to automatically generate view references, so no more `findViewById` boilerplate. `clicks()` is an extension method on `View` provided by **RxBindings** that turns a views click listener into an `Observable<Unit>`. It's that easy to get an Observable of click events using RxBindings. Isn't that magical?!

Remove the block of code setting a click listener on the `clear` view. Since you'll handle clear events via an Observable, you don't need to worry about setting a click listener on it anymore.

Back in `ColorViewModel`, you can also remove the `clearClicked` method. Again, you'll be handling clear events via an Observable, so it's unnecessary.

Now that all the plumbing is in place, it's time to actually utilize the `clearStream` to clear out the current color.

In the bottom of the `init` method, add the following:

```
clearStream
  .map { "#" }
  .subscribe(hexStringSubject::onNext)
  .addTo(disposables)
```

The code is dead simple: You're subscribing to the `clearStream` Observable and mapping each `Unit` event to the `"#"` string. Then you're forwarding that string to the `hexStringSubject` object using its `onNext` method. You're using a method reference to make the code nice and compact.

Notice that this code is almost identical to the code in `clearClicked`. Nothing is fundamentally changing, you're just consolidating the code and Rx-ifying the app!

Run the app. Enter your favorite color string (I know you've got favorites!) and click the clear button. It should be cleared.

Dangerzone!

There's actually a subtle but devious bug in the code you just wrote. To demonstrate the bug, run the app and then rotate the device. Input a hex string and hit the clear button. You'll notice that nothing happens - the color isn't cleared.

RxBindings works by generating a series of convenient helper functions on a plethora of different **View**s. However, when the app is rotated the actual **View** is destroyed and a new set of **View**s are created. But the `ViewModel` you're using survives the configuration change - that's the whole point of the `ViewModel` class!

That means that `ColorViewModel` is now holding onto a reference for an Observable that's firing for a **View** that no longer exists! Since the old `clear` button has been destroyed and there's a brand new `clear` button, **RxBindings** doesn't have a reference to the new button. That means you won't get any of the click effects that you'd expect.

Working around the issue

You can't just pass in an `Observable` generated by **RxBindings** into your `ViewModel` via the constructor, but you *can* emulate that reactive flow.

First, you need to go back a few steps. Remove `clearStream: Observable<Unit>` from the `ColorViewModel` constructor and in `ColorActivity`, delete `clear.clicks()` from the parameter list when creating the `viewModel` object.

Then, start fixing the problem by adding a new property to the top of `ColorViewModel`:

```
private val clearStream = PublishSubject.create<Unit>()
```

Now add back in the `clearClicked` method and trigger the new `clearStream` subject:

```
fun clearClicked() = clearStream.onNext(Unit)
```

You're now building up your own clear clicked Observable without the bugs discovered earlier. The last thing you need to do is trigger the `clearClicked` method. You can use **RxBindings** in your `ColorActivity` to keep things nice and reactive. Add the following below the `viewModel` creation block:

```
clear.clicks().subscribe { viewModel.clearClicked() }
  .addTo(disposables)
```

You're now getting all of the benefits of reactive views without the bug previously discovered.

Converting backClicked() to use RxBindings

Now that you've handled the **Clear** button, you're going to go through the same process for the **Back** button. Update the `ColorViewModel` with another `PublishSubject` to represent back clicks:

```
private val backStream = PublishSubject.create<Unit>()
```

And update the `backClicked` method to forward a value into `backStream`

```
fun backClicked() = backStream.onNext(Unit)
```

Finally, start listening to actual click events on the back button with **RxBindings** in ColorActivity:

```
back.clicks().subscribe { viewModel.backClicked() }
    .addTo(disposables)
```

Take a look at the old implementation of the backClicked method:

```
fun backClicked() {
    if (currentHexValue().length >= 2) {
        hexStringSubject.onNext(currentHexValue()
            .substring(0, currentHexValue().lastIndex))
    }
}
```

This method is a bit more complicated than the clearClicked method you replaced earlier. If the current hex value has a length greater than two — i.e., it's more than just the "#" string — then you want to add a new string onto the hexStringSubject. That new string is whatever the current string is minus the last character.

Add the following code at the bottom of the classes init block in ColorViewModel:

```
// 1
backStream
    // 2
    .map { currentHexValue() }
    // 3
    .filter { it.length >= 2 }
    // 4
    .map { it.substring(0, currentHexValue().lastIndex) }
    // 5
    .subscribe(hexStringSubject::onNext)
    .addTo(disposables)
```

Reactive programming is so different from imperative programming that it may be a good idea to break the above code down:

1. You're subscribing to the backStream Observable, which is an Observable<Unit>. Every time the user clicks the **Back** button, this Observable will emit a Unit value.

2. You don't actually care about the Unit value emitted by the Observable. You're just using it as a trigger. So you're immediately mapping that Unit object to the currentHexValue(), which you'll use later on in the stream.

3. You only want to proceed through the chain if the current hex values length is greater than or equal to two.

4. Next up you're getting a substring of the current hex value starting at zero and going up to, but not including, whatever the last index of the hexstring is. The last index is just the size of the string minus 1. Since you used the `filter` operator above, you can be confident that this string will have a length >= 2.

5. You're subscribing to the Observable and forwarding the emitted string to the `hexStringSubject`, so the rest of the code above this block can react to the new hex string value.

> **Note:** You may be tempted to avoid the first map call and instead just operate directly on whatever `currentHexValue()` provides in both the `filter` operator and the second `map` operator. While that may be tempting, it would also introduce a race condition and a potential crash! Between the first `filter` being executed and the second `map` being executed, another thread could update the current hex value and your assumption that the length of the string returned by `currentHexValue()` being greater than two is no longer certain. Chances are it wouldn't happen in this app, but it's always worth keeping those potential race conditions in mind.

Boom! You've replicated the code in `backClicked` in a more streamlined reactive style. Run the app. Tapping the **Back** key should work exactly the same.

Last but not least is the `digitClicked` method.

Converting digitClicked() to use RxBindings

Again, add a new subject representing digit clicks in the `ColorViewModel` class:

```
private val digitsStream = BehaviorSubject.create<String>()
```

This time you're using a `BehaviorSubject` so that every time you subscribe to the stream you'll get the latest and greatest digit clicks.

The incoming digits will be of type `String`. Each `String` will be a single character.

In `ColorActivity`, delete the line declaring `digits` and the `forEach` block setting click listeners on each digit.

Then, replace the `digits` declaration and the following `digits.forEach` with the following snippet:

```
// 1
val digits = listOf(zero, one, two, three, four, five, six,
  seven, eight, nine, A, B, C, D, E, F)
  // 2
  .map { digit ->
    // 3
    digit.clicks().map { digit.text.toString() }
  }
```

If the above is confusing, don't worry! Here's a breakdown:

1. Build up a list of each digit on the "keypad" in the app. Each object in this list is a `TextView`. Again, the app is using the Kotlin Android Extensions to provide easy reference to each view in the app. So this `listOf()` call returns a `List<TextView>`.

2. Call map on this list. `digit` in the lambda block is a `TextView`.

3. Call `clicks()` on each `digit` to turn it into an `Observable<Unit>`. Then, call a map on that Observable. Map the `Unit` value to the string representation of the text in the `digit` `TextView`. Don't be confused by the two maps — one is on the `List<TextView>`, the other is on the `Observable<Unit>`.

The result of the above code is that `digits` is now a `List<Observable<String>>`. How meta is that?!

Now, add the following below `digits`:

```
val digitStreams = Observable.merge(digits)
```

You're using the `merge` method you learned about in Chapter 9, "Combining Operators," to combine the `List<Observable<String>>` into a single `Observable<String>`.

Now, any time a user taps one of the digits in HexColor `digitStreams` will emit.

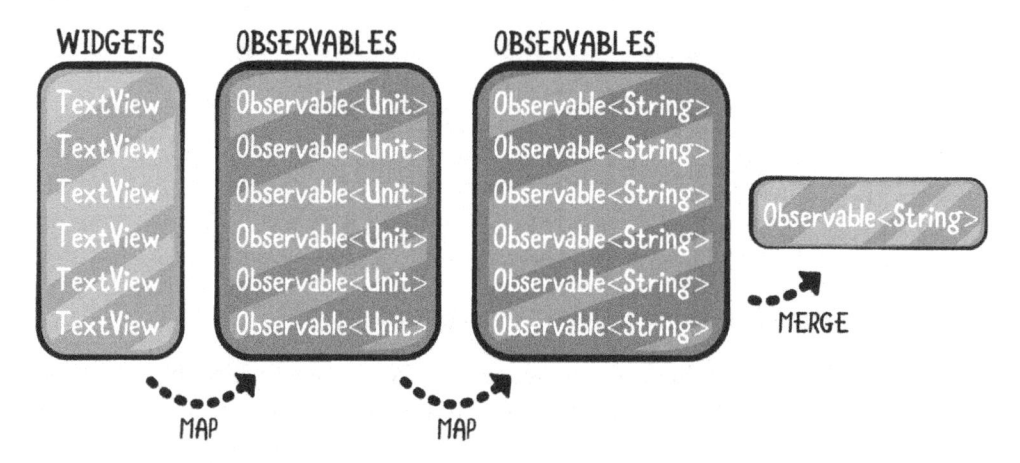

[Diagram showing WIDGETS (TextViews) → MAP → OBSERVABLES (Observable<Unit>) → MAP → OBSERVABLES (Observable<String>) → MERGE → Observable<String>]

Next, update the `digitClicked` method to forward your digit through to your subject:

```
fun digitClicked(digit: String) = digitsStream.onNext(digit)
```

Finally, subscribe to the `digitStream` stream you just created in `ColorActivity` and forward the result through to the `ColorViewModel`:

```
digitStreams.subscribe(viewModel::digitClicked)
    .addTo(disposables)
```

You're using a method reference to make the code even more concise.

Back in `ColorViewModel`, add the following at the bottom of the `init` file:

```
digitsStream
  // 1
  .map { it to currentHexValue() }
  // 2
  .filter { it.second.length < 7 }
  // 3
  .map { it.second + it.first }
  .subscribe(hexStringSubject::onNext)
  .addTo(disposables)
```

Here's another breakdown:

1. Take the `String` emitted by `digitsStream` and use `map` to combine it with whatever the current hex value is. The `to` infix function is a simple shorthand to create a `Pair` object.

2. Use `filter` to ignore any element emitted while the current hex values length is ≥ 7. If the current hex value is ≥ 7, you want to ignore any taps, since the full hex color string has already been input.

3. Now, combine the current hex value and the `String` the user just tapped, appending the new string onto the existing hex value.

Delete the old `digitClicked` method and run the app.

Now, take a step back and look at the `ColorViewModel` class. Doesn't it look fantastic? So sleek and declarative. Just a real beauty. Don't you wish all code could be this declarative and reactive?

Fetching colors from an API

The code for the app is looking a lot better. But the app itself is still fairly limited; it can only display names for a small list of colors. You're going to change that by integrating with the color API found here: www.thecolorapi.com.

Open the `ColorService` class and add the following method to the bottom of the interface **outside** the companion object:

```
@GET("id")
fun getColor(@Query("hex") hex: String): Single<ColorResponse>
```

The above code will fetch a lot of metadata for a color based off the hex string passed in.

Now add another constructor parameter at the bottom of the list of constructor parameters for the `ColorViewModel` class:

```
colorApi: ColorApi
```

In the `ColorActivity`, pass in `ColorApi` to the `ColorViewModel` constructor:

```
return ColorViewModel(
  Schedulers.io(),
  AndroidSchedulers.mainThread(),
  ColorCoordinator(),
  ColorApi
) as T
```

Now, open up **ColorApi.kt**. `ColorApi` is a simple object that wraps the `ColorService` class to make API calls. Replace the body of the `getClosestColor` method with the following:

```
return colorService.getColor(hexString)
```

Now, head back to **ColorViewModel.kt**. It's time to actually use the API.

Find the Observable chain that searches through the `ColorName` enum whenever a new hex string comes in. It looks like this:

```
hexStringSubject
  .subscribeOn(backgroundScheduler)
  .observeOn(mainScheduler)
  .filter { hexString -> ColorName.values()
    .map { it.hex }
    .contains(hexString) }
  .map { hexString -> ColorName.values()
    .first { it.hex == hexString } }
  .map { it.toString() }
  .subscribe(colorNameLiveData::postValue)
  .addTo(disposables)
```

Delete the whole chain and replace it with the following:

```
hexStringSubject
  .filter { it.length == 7 }
  .observeOn(mainScheduler)
  .flatMapSingle {
    colorApi.getClosestColor(it)
        .subscribeOn(backgroundScheduler)
  }
  .map { it.name.value }
  .subscribe(colorNameLiveData::postValue)
  .addTo(disposables)
```

You're again filtering out any hex strings that aren't yet at size seven. You're then using `flatMap` to fetch the color details from the color API making sure to subscribe to the network call off the `main` thread. Then you're using `map` to convert the `ColorResponse` object you get back from the API into a human readable color name. Finally you're posting that value to the `colorNameLiveData`.

Run the app. Try out any color combination, and you'll see a name. How cool is that?

My favorite is #555555. It makes me feel like a boss.

Displaying an information dialog

Next up on the docket is to allow the user to manually type out a color string without tapping the digits on the app. To do this, you're going to expose a bottom sheet dialog that includes an `EditText` widget that the user can input text in.

Add the following to the bottom of the `onCreate` method in `ColorActivity`:

```
color_name.clicks()
  .subscribe {
    val bottomSheetDialog =
      ColorBottomSheet.newInstance(hex.text.toString())
    bottomSheetDialog
        .show(supportFragmentManager, "Custom Bottom Sheet")
  }
  .addTo(disposables)
```

You're using the `clicks` extension method on the `color_name` widget to create an `Observable<Unit>` representing clicks. In the `subscribe` block you're creating an instance of the `ColorBottomSheet` fragment with the current hex color string value and showing it.

Run the app and input a color. If you click on the color name in the top-right, you should see a bottom dialog with an empty `EditText` appear.

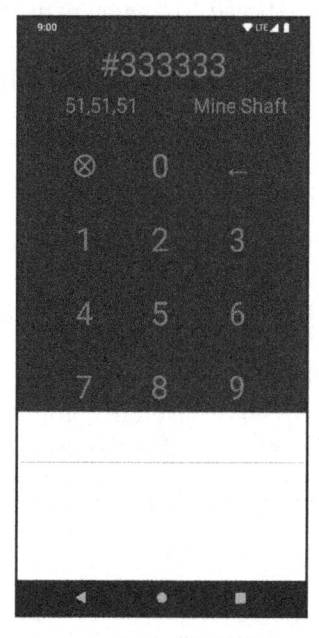

Open up the `ColorBottomSheetViewModel` class. It's pretty empty right now. It has three `LiveData` objects — one for showing a loading indicator, one for showing the name of the color input by the user, and a last one for showing the "closest" matching color to whatever color the user inputs.

> **Note**: The concept of a **difference** or **distance** between two colors is actually really interesting! You can use the distance formula you learned in algebra to get the "distance" between two colors. Wikipedia has a great article about it: https://en.wikipedia.org/wiki/Color_difference.

Before you can start using the color API in this new bottom sheet you need to access the string that the user types into the `EditText` at the top of the bottom sheet.

Normally, the way you'd listen for text changes on an `EditText` would be to create a new `TextWatcher` object and implement the `afterTextChanged` event. But that's a lot of boilerplate. You'll use **RxBindings** instead to get an `Observable<String>` representing the text changes.

First, update the `ColorBottomSheetViewModel` to have a `val` representing search strings. Add the following to the top of the class:

```
private val searchObservable = BehaviorSubject.create<String>()
```

And just like before add a method that will be called to forward a value into your new Observable:

```
fun onTextChange(text: String) = searchObservable.onNext(text)
```

Next, head to `ColorBottomSheet` and add the following below the line declaring the `viewModel` in `onViewCreated`:

```
hex_input.textChanges()
  .map { it.toString() }
  .subscribe { viewModel.onTextChange(it) }
```

`textChanges` is an **RxBindings** extension method on `TextView`. It turns an `Observable<Editable>`, so you're using `map` to convert the `Editable` into a `String`. You're then subscribing to the resulting Observable and forwarding it through to your `ViewModel`.

Since you're using the `subscribe` method, you need to make sure to dispose of the resulting `Disposable` at some point. Add a `CompositeDisposable` value at the top of the file:

```
private val disposables = CompositeDisposable()
```

Update the `textChanges` block you just wrote to add the `Disposable` into your newly created `disposables` object:

```
hex_input.textChanges()
    .map { it.toString() }
    .subscribe { viewModel.onTextChange(it) }
    .addTo(disposables)
```

You're now ready to use the text-changes Observable to fetch a color from the color API.

Head back to `ColorBottomSheetViewModel` and create an `init` block with the following code:

```
init {
  val colorObservable = searchObservable
    .filter { it.length == 7 }
    .flatMapSingle {
      ColorApi.getClosestColor(it).subscribeOn(Schedulers.io())
    }
    .map { it.name }
    .share()
}
```

Above:

- You're using the `Observable<String>` passed in from `ColorBottomSheet`, which you got via the **RxBindings** library, to construct a new Observable chain. It first filters out any inputs that aren't of length seven, since that's the correct length for a hex color string.

- Then you're using `flatMapSingle` to fetch the closest color to the input string from the color api, which returns a `Single` with the network response.

- Finally, you're using `map` to pull out the `ColorName` object from the `ColorResponse`.

- You're using the `share` operator to share the whole chain so you can have multiple subscribers listen to the same set of results.

The above block is great, but you're still not actually subscribing to the `colorObservable` or emitting anything into the `LiveData` objects. Add the following below the `colorObservable` chain:

```
colorObservable
  .subscribe { colorNameLiveData.postValue(it.value) }
  .addTo(disposables)
```

That's more like it! You're subscribing to `colorObservable` and pulling out the `value` object from the `ColorName` class, which maps to the name of the color, and pushing it through the `colorNameLiveData` object.

Before you run the app, finish off the functionality of the bottom sheet by adding one more subscriber:

```
colorObservable
  .subscribe {
    closestColorLiveData.postValue(it.closest_named_hex)
  }
  .addTo(disposables)
```

You're now pulling out the `closest_named_hex` value from the `ColorName` object and pushing it through the `closestColorLiveData` object. Nice!

> **Note:** `closest_named_hex` is named with underscores rather than the normal camelCase format to allow for automagical json deserializing from the GSON deserialization library.

Run the app, enter a color and tap the color name to show the bottom sheet. Input a hex value and you should see the name of the closest named color the API could find, as well as the hex value of that closest color. You may need to close the keyboard to see the output.

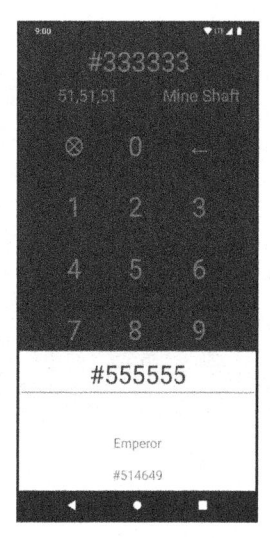

The app is almost perfect. The only issue is if you enter a value on the main screen and then click the color name you don't see the details of the color that you input. You only see the closest color and the name of that color if you type in something new. This is an easy one line fix.

In `ColorBottomSheetViewModel` utilize the `startsWithItem` operator before the `filter` operator in the `colorObservable` declaration (first chain):

```
.startWithItem(startingColor)
```

Now, run the app and tap around. You should see the details of whatever color you originally input on the bottom sheet when it first appears.

Challenges

Challenge 1

Start from the final project from this chapter and update the bottom color sheet to show a loading indicator while the `ColorBottomSheetViewModel` is loading a color from the color API.

You don't need to worry about adding a new view or hooking up a new live data. You can use the `showLoadingLiveData` to toggle whether the loading indicator should be shown or hidden.

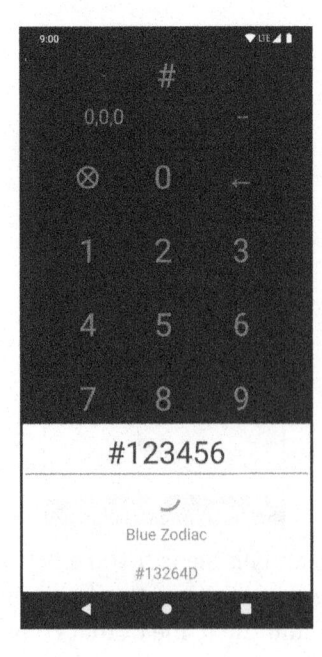

Challenge 2

Update the `ColorBottomSheet` so that the `EditText` input always includes a # character, is limited to seven characters, and only allows characters between 1-9 and A-F.

To accomplish this challenge, you'll want to use another **RxBindings** method on `EditText`, specifically the `afterTextChangesEvents` method. `afterTextChangesEvents` produces an `Observable<TextViewAfterTextChangeEvent>`. `TextViewAfterTextChangeEvent` includes an `Editable` object that you can manipulate to only include the strings that you want.

If you're having difficulties, take a look at the completed challenges project for a hint.

Key points

- Practicing creating reactive extensions around existing Android classes.
- Using the **RxBindings** library to create reactive streams from Android widgets.
- Using the `clicks` extension method to replace an Android click listener.
- Using the `textChanges` extension method to get a stream of `TextView` or `EditText` changes.
- Using the `afterTextChangeEvents` method to get a stream describing any changes that are happening to an `EditText`.

Where to go from here?

If you're hooked on RxJava, RxBindings is a great supplement to the regular classes. RxBinding is simple to use, provides a consistent API for consumption, and makes your application much more composable and reactive.

Chapter 18: Retrofit

By Alex Sullivan

Throughout this book, you've often used the popular **Retrofit** library to build your apps. In this chapter, you'll further explore how exactly Retrofit interfaces with the Rx world and how you can take advantage of all that it offers.

Getting started

For this chapter, you'll build a JSON-viewing app. The app you'll build will allow you to add rows to a JSON object, save that object to the JSONBlob (https://jsonblob.com/) storage API and then retrieve that saved JSON string.

While building the app, you'll explore the different options you have when interacting with Retrofit.

Open the starter project for the chapter and run the app. You'll see a white screen with an empty JSON object, signified with the {} text. You'll also see two EditTexts and a FloatingActionButton (FAB) at the bottom of the screen.

That's where you'll add the new rows for the JSON object.

Recap of Retrofit

Before you start exploring how Retrofit interacts with RxJava, it's worth taking a moment to recap what Retrofit is.

Retrofit is an open-source, networking library made and maintained by the **Square** team. It allows you to declare your networking interface via an `interface`. It abstracts away the tedious boilerplate of setting up HTTP connections and executing them. A typical Retrofit interface will look like this example from Chapter 8, "Transforming Operators in Practice":

```
// 1
interface GitHubApi {
  // 2
  @GET("repos/ReactiveX/{repo}/events")
  // 3
  fun fetchEvents(@Path("repo") repo: String,
      @Header("If-Modified-Since") lastModified: String)
      // 4
    : Observable<Response<List<AnyDict>>>
}
```

Here's a breakdown of the above code:

1. As mentioned earlier, Retrofit requires you to declare your API in an `interface`. You don't need to worry about implementing the interface, though; Retrofit provides a simple hook to create an instance for you.

2. Every method in a Retrofit interface must be annotated with both the HTTP method type (GET, POST, PUT etc) and the relative path to the APIs endpoint. This path doesn't declare the full API endpoint. Instead, you provide a root URL when using that Retrofit hook to create the interface. You can even make the relative path dynamic. In this example, the method expects to receive an argument that will ultimately fill in the {repo} section of the relative path.

3. You can name your Retrofit methods whatever you want. What's more important is how you annotate the arguments that will be passed in to the method. This example uses a dynamic path, so you need to use the @Path annotation to specify that this argument should fill in {repo} portion of the path. It also uses the @Header annotation to specify that this particular call should also include an If-Modified-Since header with the annotated argument being the value that corresponds to the header.

4. One of the beautiful parts about Retrofit, and the piece that you'll interact with the most for this chapter, is the fact that you can choose your return type for your API methods, and Retrofit will do it's best to give you objects that correspond to that type. The above code is telling Retrofit to provide an Observable instance that emits objects wrapped in Retrofit's Response object and that contains data corresponding to the type List<AnyDict>. Now that's a super-powered library!

While the above code specifies Observable as a return type for the fetchEvents method, if you're not using RxJava you'd typically use the Call<T> object as a return type. You could even just specify the actual model object as a return type. If, instead of Observable<Response<List<AnyDict>>> you specified List<AnyDict> as the return type, Retrofit would interpret that as a blocking network call.

Retrofit uses the OkHttp HTTP client under the hood and allows you to customize it to your heart's desire. This chapter's project will use a custom OkHttp instance to log all network calls.

Including Rx adapters

Open the `JsonBinService` class and look at the `create` method in the `companion object`. At the bottom of the method, you're declaring an instance of the `Retrofit` object with the following code:

```
val retrofit = Retrofit.Builder()
  .baseUrl(JsonBinApi.API)
  .client(client)
  .addConverterFactory(ScalarsConverterFactory.create())
  .addConverterFactory(GsonConverterFactory.create())
  .build()
```

Notice the two lines calling the `addConverterFactory` method on the Retrofit builder.

`addConverterFactory` takes an instance of `Converter.Factory`. This converter plugin architecture is how Retrofit serializes and deserializes the types that the network returns. In this block, you're specifying two different converters:

1. The `ScalarsConverterFactory`, enables Retrofit to convert JSON objects into simple Java primitive types and strings.

2. The `GsonConverterFactory`, allows you to plug Gson, a JSON serialization library, into the Retrofit converter architecture. Without this converter factory, you wouldn't be able to tell Retrofit to return complex model types since it would have no way of deserializing its JSON representation into the objects.

In addition to these converter factories, Retrofit also lets you specify custom call adapter factories that allow you to customize the return type of your interface methods.

To specify Rx return types in your Retrofit interface methods, you'll need one of these `CallAdapter.Factory` instances. Luckily, the square team provides a separate library that exposes just such a factory.

Open the `build.gradle` file and add the following dependency to the `dependencies` block:

```
implementation "com.squareup.retrofit2:adapter-rxjava3:$retrofit_version"
```

Open the `JsonBinService` class. Now, update the `Retrofit.Builder` to specify the new `CallAdapter.Factory`:

```
val retrofit = Retrofit.Builder()
  .baseUrl(JsonBinApi.API)
  .client(client)
  .addCallAdapterFactory(RxJava3CallAdapterFactory.create())
  .addConverterFactory(ScalarsConverterFactory.create())
  .addConverterFactory(GsonConverterFactory.create())
  .build()
```

You can now specify reactive return types for your Retrofit methods.

Creating a JSON object

Now that you've got Retrofit properly configured, it's time to create a JSON object and save it with the JSONBlob API.

Open the `JsonViewModel` class and look around. There's three important fields to look at:

```
private val clicks = PublishSubject.Create<Unit>()
private val keyChanges = BehaviorSubject.create<CharSequence>()
private val valueChanges =
    BehaviorSubject.create<CharSequence>()
```

Each of these arguments represents some action done by the user.

In the above:

- `clicks` is an `Observable<Unit>` representing clicks on the bottom FAB.

- `keyChanges` is an `Observable<CharSequence>` representing text changes to the left-most `EditText` object.

- `valueChanges` is an `Observable<CharSequence>` representing text changes to the right-most `EditText` object.

Add the following code to the `init` block of `JsonViewModel`:

```
val buttonObservable = clicks
  .flatMap {
    Observables.combineLatest(keyChanges, valueChanges)
  }
  .share()
```

You're using `flatMap` to create a new Observable every time the user clicks on the floating action button. The new Observable will combine the latest values emitted by the `keyChanges` and `valueChanges` Observables, thus emitting the current text in the left key `EditText` and the right value `EditText` every time the user clicks the FAB.

To accomplish this combination, you're using the `Observables.combineLatest` method exposed by the **RxKotlin** library. Finally, you're using the `share` operator so that you can subscribe to the resulting Observable multiple times.

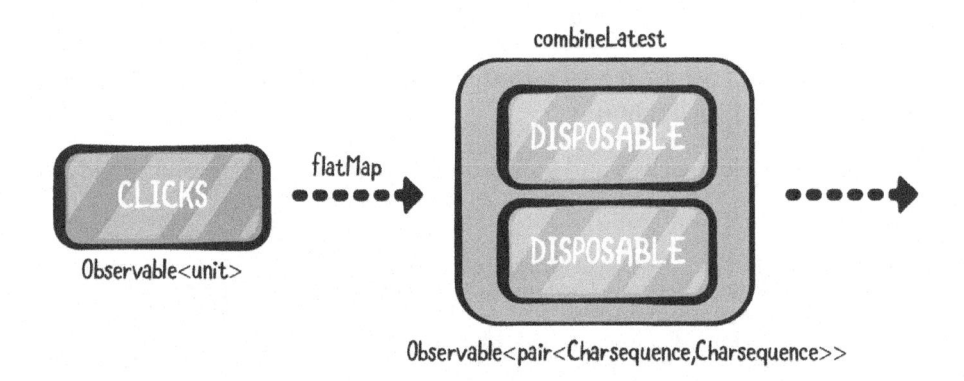

You've now got an Observable that will emit a `Pair<CharSequence, CharSequence>` representing the current text in the key `EditText` and the value `EditText`. You now want to use that Observable to create a new JSON object in the JSONBlob API.

Before you can wire up the creation logic in the `JsonViewModel`, you'll need to add a new Retrofit method that sends a JSON object to the JSONBlob API.

Open `JsonBinService` and add the following below the `companion object` declaration:

```
@POST("jsonBlob")
@Headers("Content-Type:application/json")
fun createJson(@Body json: String): Observable<Response<String>>
```

You're creating a new method that will POST a JSON string to the JSONBlob `jsonBlob` endpoint. The POST will deliver a payload of the initial JSON string. The return type of your `createJson` method will be `Observable<Response<String>>`.

Now that the Retrofit method has been created, you can update the `JsonBinApi` class to reference it.

Open `JsonBinApi` and replace the existing body of the `createJson` method with the following:

```
return service.createJson(json).map {
  it.headers().get("Location")
}
```

It calls the `createJson` method you just defined. It then inspects the `headers` object of the `Response` to find the URI of the bin where your newly created JSON is stored.

With the Retrofit method set up and your API ready to go, it's time to actually send some JSON to the API.

Open the `JsonViewModel` class and add the following code below the `buttonObservable` declaration:

```
val creationObservable = buttonObservable
  // 1
  .take(1)
  // 2
  .map { "{\"${it.first}\":\"${it.second}\"}" }
  .doOnNext { jsonTextLiveData.postValue(it) }
  // 3
  .flatMap {
    JsonBinApi.createJson(it).subscribeOn(Schedulers.io())
  }
  // 4
  .map { it.substringAfterLast("/") }
  .cache()
```

Here's a breakdown of the above code:

1. You're building a new `creationObservable` by chaining off of the `buttonObservable` you designed earlier. You only want to create a JSON object in the JSONBlob API once. After that, you'll update the object, so you're using the `take` operator to limit the number of items emitted by the `buttonObservable` to just one.

2. You're then constructing a JSON object by using the `map` operator and breaking apart the `Pair<CharSequence, CharSequence>` you received from `ButtonObservable`. The JSON object string may look a bit funky, but that's just because you need to use an escaping character, \, to include quotation marks in the string. After calling `map`, you're posting the new JSON object to the `jsonTextLiveData` object so the user can immediately see the JSON they constructed.

3. You're then using `flatMap` to create a new Observable by using the new `createJson` method you declared earlier.

4. The result of that last `flatMap` is that you're now operating on an `Observable<String>`. What you really care about is the ID of the new JSON object you created on the JSONBlob API. So you're using a `map` operator to pull out the ID portion of the URI on the result.

Now you're cooking with gas!

Add the following code at the bottom of the `init` method to subscribe to the creation Observable:

```
creationObservable
  .subscribe()
  .addTo(disposables)
```

You're using the `cache` method so that you can reference the ID of the JSON you created at a later point.

Now, run the app. Enter some text in both of the `EditText`s and click the FAB. You should see a JSON object appear on your screen.

Updating the JSON

After creating and storing a JSON object in the JSONBlob API, it's time to update that object with new values.

Add the following code to the `JsonViewModel init` method right below the `creationObservable` declaration but before subscribing to it:

```
val updateObservable = creationObservable
  .flatMap { buttonObservable }
  .map {
    createNewJsonString(it.first, it.second,
      jsonTextLiveData.value!!)
  }
```

You're creating a new `updateObservable` by calling `flatMap` on the cached `creationObservable` and returning the `buttonObservable` you defined earlier. You're then using the `map` operator to take the latest input from the `buttonObservable` and creating a new JSON string from it and the current JSON string, which is stored in the `jsonTextLiveData` object.

By subscribing to `updateObservable`, you'll ensure that the `creationObservable` is run and then after the initial JSON object is created you switch to just emitting new JSON strings. By using `flatMap` here, you're able to chain the creation of a JSON object into the updating of that object.

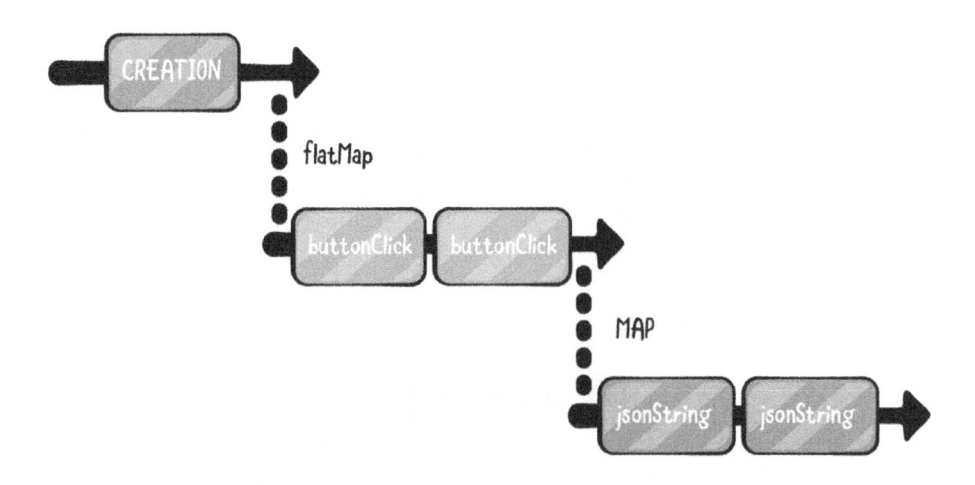

All that's left to do is to subscribe to the `updateObservable`. Remove the existing code that subscribes to `creationObservable` and replace it with the following:

```
updateObservable
  .subscribe {
    jsonTextLiveData.postValue(it)
  }
  .addTo(disposables)
```

Run the app. Add an initial key and value, and then tap the FAB. Next, try adding a different key and value, and then tap the FAB. You should see an ugly chunk of JSON.

Now, edit either the key or the value in preparation for adding another line.

Woah. Something weird is happening.

Every time you update the text, even if you don't click the FAB, the JSON blob is being updated. That certainly shouldn't happen. Spend a minute or so making cool pyramid designs.

After you're done playing around with the bug, look back at the creation of the `buttonObservable`:

```
val buttonObservable = clicks
  .flatMap {
    Observables.combineLatest(keyChanges, valueChanges)
  }
  .share()
```

`buttonObservable` is supposed to emit a `Pair<CharSequence, CharSequence>` whenever the button is clicked. However, that's not actually what the above code does!

Instead, `buttonObservable`, as it's currently defined, emits a `Pair<CharSequence, CharSequence>` when the button is entered and then **every time either EditText is changed**. The problem lies in the `combineLatest` call. `combineLatest` will emit a pair anytime either of the `EditText` objects change.

To fix the bug, update append a `take(1)` operator to the end of `combineLatest`:

```
val buttonObservable = clicks
  .flatMap {
    Observables.combineLatest(keyChanges, valueChanges)
      .take(1)
  }
  .share()
```

Now only the first pair of `CharSequences` will be emitted whenever the button is tapped. Run the app and confirm that you'll only see changes to the JSON on the screen when you tap the FAB.

You're now updating the JSON that the user sees, but you're not actually saving the updated JSON on the JSONBlob API.

Open the `JsonBinService` Retrofit interface and add the following method below the `createJson` method you added earlier:

```
@PUT("jsonBlob/{id}")
@Headers("Content-Type:application/json")
fun updateJson(@Path("id") binId: String, @Body json: String):
Completable
```

In the above, `updateJson` takes an ID of the JSON "bin" to update and a new JSON string. It uses the `PUT` HTTP method to update the JSON object at the given bin. You don't actually care about what the server returns when you hit the endpoint, so you're making the return type `Completable`. Now, you'll be able to call this method and be notified when it finishes without actually caring about any data that comes with it.

You'll often find that using the `Completable` return type pairs well with a REST `PUT` request, since it's entirely mutative. Retrofit's fluent call adapter functionality allows you the flexibility to declare the types that make the most sense for your HTTP calls.

Open the `JsonBinApi` class and replace the body of the `updateJson` method with the following:

```
return service.updateJson(bin, json)
```

Now that you've got your API calls ready to go, it's time to update the `JsonViewModel` to actually save off the new JSON.

Replace the existing `updateObservable` declaration with the following:

```
val updateObservable = creationObservable
  // 1
  .flatMap { binId ->
    buttonObservable
      // 2
      .map { createNewJsonString(it.first, it.second,
        jsonTextLiveData.value!!) }
      .map { binId to it }
  }
  // 3
  .flatMapCompletable {
    JsonBinApi.updateJson(it.first, it.second)
      .subscribeOn(Schedulers.io())
  }
```

Here's a breakdown of the above code:

1. Just like before, you're using `flatMap` to start streaming the events from the `buttonObservable`.

2. You're then using the `map` operator to build up a new JSON object that includes the latest values in the key and value `EditText`s. After that, you're using another `map` operator to create a `Pair<String, String>` by combining the `binId` value from the `creationObservable` with the new JSON string.

3. You're then using the `flatMapCompletable` operator to take the `Pair<String, String>` object produced earlier in the chain and sending both the bin id and the new JSON object through to the JSONBlob via the Retrofit method you implemented earlier. You're using `flatMapCompletable` because the return type for the `updateJson` method is `Completable`.

To complete the JSON updating flow, replace the existing code that subscribes to `updateObservable` with the following:

```
updateObservable
  .subscribe()
  .addTo(disposables)
```

You're now sending JSON updates through to the JSONBlob API.

There's only one issue: You're never actually printing the new JSON to the screen. Since the `jsonTextLiveData` object isn't being updated, the JSON you're generating and sending to the JSONBlob API isn't being built up. Instead, you're only ever sending up a JSON object with two lines: the first line when you created the object and the new values from your `EditText` streams.

You could simply add a doOnNext operator in the Observable chain you just wrote and emit the new JSON values. However, the JSONBlob API exposes an endpoint that allows you to fetch the current JSON object in a bin, so you can be confident that your JSON is actually saved.

That sounds like the best option moving forward.

Retrieving JSON

Open the JsonBinService class again and add the following method below the updateJson method you added earlier:

```
@GET("jsonBlob/{id}")
@Headers("Content-Type:application/json")
fun getJson(@Path("id") binId: String): Single<Response<String>>
```

This time, you're targeting the /jsonBlob/{id} endpoint, which returns whatever JSON is stored in that bin. Just like in the updateJson method, you're passing in a bin id that will be used to identify your JSON.

For this method, you're setting the return type as Single<Response<String>>. There's two interesting things at play, here:

1. The first is that you're using the Single reactive type. Once again Retrofit is amazingly flexible in what return types you can specify for your methods. Single is a fantastic choice when using Retrofit since your network calls will almost always return a single result and then finish. Setting the return type as Single<YourResponseObject> lets you more clearly specify the expected structure of your HTTP calls.

2. The second interesting piece is that you're using Retrofit's built-in Response object. You used the Response object earlier when creating the JSON, but it's worthwhile to dig in here. Retrofit always allows you to wrap your model object in its Response object. The Response object provides several nice to haves, such as HTTP status codes, access to header objects, and any errors that may have been encountered. If you didn't want to use the Response object, you could easily set the return type of this method to be Single<String>.

Handling errors

This is a good time to pause for a moment and consider how error handling works in Retrofits RxJava integration. No matter what reactive return type you specify, whether its `Observable`, `Single`, `Completable`, or `Maybe`, if you do not have internet access when you attempt to make a call through Retrofit you will hit the error block of your subscriber. Not particularly surprising but good to point out.

What may be slightly more surprising is that depending on what return type you use with Retrofit, and specifically depending on whether you include the `Response` object in that return type, you may or may not see HTTP server errors and non successful status calls in your error blocks.

You have two options when deciding on a return type for your Retrofit methods:

1. You could include the `Response` object as a wrapper to your model type in the return type. That means having a return type that looks like `Single<Response<MyObject>>`. In this scenario, if your server returns a non successful (i.e., non 2xx) status code, a `Response<MyObject>` will still be delivered to the success block of your subscriber, even though the server ultimately rejected the call. You can check the status code of the `Response` object to figure out if the call was successful or not. You'll see an example of this later on.

2. Alternatively, if you exclude the `Response` object and instead specify your return type to look something like `Single<MyObject>`, you'll then see non successful status codes going into the error block. So if your server returned a 404, meaning the resource wasn't found, your `Single<MyObject>` would report an error and you would need to make sure to handle that error.

Tying it all together

Now that you've got a method in your Retrofit interface to retrieve JSON, you need to update the `JsonBinApi` class to reference the new method. Replace the body of the `getJson` method with the following:

```
return service.getJson(bin)
```

Now, open the `JsonViewModel` class. After you call through to the `JsonBinApi.updateJson` method, you need to retrieve the newly updated JSON and send it through your `jsonTextLiveData` object.

Remove the existing `flatMapCompletable` block of the `updateObservable` and replace it with the following:

```
// 1
.flatMap { pair ->
  // 2
  JsonBinApi.updateJson(pair.first, pair.second)
    // 3
    .andThen(JsonBinApi.getJson(pair.first))
    .toObservable()
    .subscribeOn(Schedulers.io())
}
```

Here's a breakdown:

1. Instead of using `flatMapCompletable`, you're switching to use a normal `flatMap` method. That means the return object in your `flatMap` lambda will have to be an `Observable` instead of a `Completable`.

2. You're again calling the `JsonBinApi.updateJson` method, passing through the bin id and the new JSON object.

3. Instead of calling it quits after updating the JSON object through the API, you're chaining a call to `JsonBinApi.getJson` after the initial call to update the JSON object. Since `JsonBinApi.updateJson` returns a `Completable`, you can use the `andThen` method to execute another reactive type after the completable finishes. Finally, since `flatMap` expects an `Observable` to be returned in its lambda, you're using the `toObservable` method to turn the `Single<Response<String>>` object returned by `JsonBinApi.getJson` into an `Observable<Response<String>>`.

Now, update the code at the bottom of the `init` method that subscribes to the `updateObservable` and replace it with the following:

```
updateObservable
  .subscribe {
    if (it.isSuccessful) {
      val prettyJson = JSONObject(it.body()!!).toString(4)
      jsonTextLiveData.postValue(prettyJson)
    } else {
      errorLiveData.postValue("Whoops, we got an error!")
    }
  }
  .addTo(disposables)
```

In this block, you're checking the Response object to see if the HTTP call was successful. If it was, you're formatting your JSON to be nice and pretty and then sending the new JSON string returned by the API into the jsonTextLiveData. If it wasn't successful you're sending an error message through the errorLiveData.

Run the app. You should now be able to add as many rows to the JSON object as you want, and you should see a nicely formatted JSON blob.

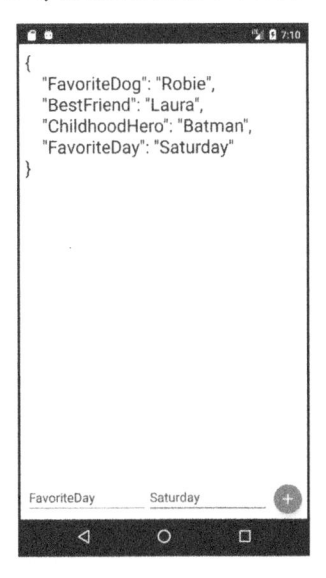

Key points

- In order to return any of the reactive types from a Retrofit interface, you have to make sure to include the RxJava3 call adapter library.

- Once you do include the call adapter library, you can return any of the reactive types you've seen in the book. `Observable`, `Flowable`, `Completable`, `Single`, `Maybe` — the whole gang's here!

- You can use the Observables (or other reactive types) you receive from Retrofit just like any other Observable. Make sure to use the `subscribeOn` and `observeOn` operators to do your network operations off the `main` thread.

- You can wrap your custom model types in the `Response` object to get access to HTTP status codes and errors. You can even nest those types inside your reactive types!

- Make sure to pay extra special attention to how you handle errors when using Retrofit. If you use the `Response` object you'll see fewer exceptions in your `subscribe` error handling code.

Where to go from here?

Retrofit is a great example of a library that makes use of RxJava in a very pragmatic way. Retrofit is a solid addition to any Android project, and even more so when coupled with RxJava.

Be sure to check out the Retrofit repository on GitHub github.com/square/retrofit if you're interested in taking a deeper dive into the library.

Chapter 19: RxPreferences

By Alex Sullivan

Every good Android developer is intimately familiar with SharedPreferences. You use it to store one-off values that you want to persist across the lifetime of the app.

Many developers will also be familiar with the tools you use to listen to changes in these preferences. The **RxPreferences** library provides a reactive wrapper around these preference notification listeners.

In this chapter, you'll learn how the library works and how you can use it to effectively stream preference changes.

Getting started

In this chapter, you're going to put the final touches on the **HexColor** app that you started in the Chapter 15, "Testing RxJava Code," code and expanded upon in Chapter 17, "RxBindings."

Open the starter project in Android Studio and run the app. You should see a familiar screen:

Try tapping out a hex color. You'll see the screen change to that color, and a color name will appear in the top right below the actual hex value. If you tap on that color name, you should see a new pop-up appear at the bottom of the screen with it's own edit text where you can enter a hex code.

At the bottom of that pop-up, there will be a small heart that should be the color of whatever hex code you input in the edit text at the top of the pop-up.

The goal for this last update to the **HexColor** app is to allow the user to tap that heart icon and have the main app's background update to that new color.

Right now, the app is using a `BottomSheetDialogFragment` to show the bottom dialog and an `Activity` to show the main keyboard and color view.

As you already know, communicating between fragments and activities is a painful process. It usually means defining an `interface` for the `Activity` to implement and then using `getActivity` from the `BottomSheetDialogFragment` to hopefully communicate any changes back up to the `Activity`. However, you need to be careful to make sure that the `Activity` you get back from `getActivity` isn't `null`, since that's always a possibility!

If only there was a better way to communicate this information...

Using SharedPreferences

There is! The Android SDK provides `SharedPreferences` as a means to save small amounts of information that the user may be interested in across app restarts. The Android SDK also provides a way to observe preference changes for individual preference keys using the `OnSharedPreferenceChangedListener` interface, allowing you to build up an app that reacts to preference changes.

You can use `SharedPreferences` to have the bottom sheet dialog save whatever color the user "loved" by tapping the heart. Then the activity (or the view model for the activity) can subscribe to those changes and update the app accordingly.

Start off by updating the `ColorBottomSheetViewModel` class to accept a new `SharedPreferences` argument:

```
class ColorBottomSheetViewModel(
  startingColor: String,
  colorCoordinator: ColorCoordinator,
  sharedPreferences: SharedPreferences
) : ViewModel()
```

Next, just like you did in the **RxBindings** chapter, you need to create a subject representing favorite clicks. Add the following `val` at the top of the class:

```
private val favoriteClicksObservable =
  PublishSubject.create<Unit>()
```

And add a new `onFavoriteClick` method at the bottom of the class:

```
fun onFavoriteClick() = favoriteClicksObservable.onNext(Unit)
```

`favoriteClicksObservable` is of type `PublishSubject<Unit>`. Every emission from the subject will represent a new click by the user.

Now, update the code creating the `ColorBottomSheetViewModel` object in the `ColorBottomSheet` class. The code creating the view model exists in `onViewCreated()`, in an anonymous object extending the `NewInstanceFactory` class. Add `SharedPreferences` as the final parameter for the `ColorBottomSheetViewModel` constructor.

```
return ColorBottomSheetViewModel(colorString,
  ColorCoordinator(),
    PreferenceManager
      .getDefaultSharedPreferences(requireContext())) as T
```

Next up, use the **RxBindings** `clicks` extension method to listen for clicks on the `favorite` button. Add the following below the block creating the `viewModel`:

```
favorite.clicks().subscribe {
  viewModel.onFavoriteClick()
}.addTo(disposables)
```

You've used the **RxBindings** `clicks()` to get an `Observable<Unit>` representing clicks to the `favorite` view. You're then forwarding that click event to the view model.

Now that you've got a way to react to Favorite clicks and an instance of `SharedPreferences`, it's time to update `ColorBottomSheetViewModel` to save the currently displayed color object whenever a user clicks the Favorite icon.

Add the following to the bottom of the `init` block in `ColorBottomSheetViewModel`:

```
favoriteClicksObservable
  .subscribe {
    sharedPreferences.edit()
      .putString("favoriteColor", closestColorLiveData.value)
      .apply()
  }
  .addTo(disposables)
```

You're now using the latest value from the `closestColorLiveData` object and saving it every time the user clicks the Favorite button.

Now you need to listen for this preference update in the activity and react accordingly.

Listening for preference updates

Just like before, you'll need to pass in an instance of `SharedPreferences` into the view model corresponding to the `ColorActivity`. Update the `ColorViewModel` class to accept an instance of `SharedPreferences`:

```
class ColorViewModel(
  backgroundScheduler: Scheduler,
  mainScheduler: Scheduler,
  colorApi: ColorApi,
  colorCoordinator: ColorCoordinator,
  sharedPreferences: SharedPreferences
) : ViewModel()
```

Now, update the `ColorActivity` to supply the `SharedPreferences` object. In `ColorActivity`'s `onCreate()`', update the line creating the new `ColorViewModel` to pass in `SharedPreferences` as the last parameter.

```
return ColorViewModel(Schedulers.io(),
  AndroidSchedulers.mainThread(),
  ColorApi, ColorCoordinator(),
  PreferenceManager
    .getDefaultSharedPreferences(this@ColorActivity)) as T
```

Now that you have an instance of `SharedPreferences` in `ColorViewModel`, you can start using it. Add the following to the bottom of the `init` block in `ColorViewModel`:

```
sharedPreferences.registerOnSharedPreferenceChangeListener {
  sharedPreferences, key ->
  if (key == "favoriteColor") {
    hexStringSubject.onNext(
        sharedPreferences.getString(key, ""))
  }
}
```

You're registering a shared preference change listener and checking if the key that's changed is the key you're interested in. If it is, you're forwarding the new color along to `hexStringSubject`. Recall that `hexStringSubject` drives the rest of the logic of the app, so pushing a new color string into `hexStringSubject` should update the color of the main activity view, the name of the color, and everything else you've come to expect from inputting a new color.

Build and run the app. Then, input a color and tap on the color name in the top-right. You should see the bottom sheet expand. Now, enter a new color in the edit text at the top of the bottom sheet and tap the Favorite icon.

Hmmmm. Nothing happened! The main color view behind the bottom sheet dialog didn't change!

If you try to debug the app, you'll see that the `OnSharedPreferenceChangeListener` you're supplying to `sharedPreferences` is never being called. What gives?

To find the culprit, take a look at the
`registerOnSharedPreferenceChangeListener` listeners documentation:

> Registers a callback to be invoked when a change happens to a
> preference.
>
> Caution: The preference manager does not currently store a
> strong reference to the listener. You must store a strong
> reference to the listener, or it will be susceptible to garbage
> collection. We recommend you keep a reference to the listener in
> the instance data of an object that will exist as long as you
> need the listener.

Under the hood, `registerOnSharedPreferenceChangeListener` uses a `WeakHashMap` to store its listeners. That means that if you don't store a strong reference to the listener, the JVM will garbage collect the listener and you'll lose out on any notifications you would otherwise receive.

This weak reference is a common point of pain for Android developers looking to use the `OnSharedPreferenceChangeListener` interface. Such is life when developing Android apps!

To create a strong reference to the preference change listener, you can add it as an instance variable on the `ColorViewModel` class:

```
private val listener =
  SharedPreferences.OnSharedPreferenceChangeListener {
    sharedPreferences, key ->
    hexStringSubject.onNext(
      sharedPreferences.getString(key, ""))
  }
```

Now, update the line where you register the preference change listener to reference the `listener` instance variable:

```
sharedPreferences
  .registerOnSharedPreferenceChangeListener(listener)
```

Run the app and enter a color. Click the color name and then enter a new color in the bottom sheet. Then, click the Favorite icon. You should now see the background of the main view change to be the new color. Fancy!

Using RxPreferences

Now that you've seen how to write reactive code using `SharedPreferences` on your own, it's time to take a look at the **RxPreferences** library to see an easier and more efficient way to use `SharedPreferences` reactively.

First, include the dependency in the apps `build.gradle` file, then sync the gradle file:

```
implementation 'com.f2prateek.rx.preferences2:rx-preferences:2.0.0'
```

Open `ColorBottomSheetViewModel` and replace the shared preferences class parameter:

```
sharedPreferences: SharedPreferences
```

With the Rx version:

```
sharedPreferences: RxSharedPreferences
```

RxPreferences introduces a new version of `SharedPreferences` called `RxSharedPreferences`. You'll use that class instead of `SharedPreferences` moving forward.

Now, replace the block of code at the bottom of the `init` block that subscribes to `favoriteClicksObservable` with the following:

```
val preference = sharedPreferences.getString("favoriteColor")
favoriteClicksObservable
  .map { closestColorLiveData.value!! }
  .subscribe(preference::set)
  .addTo(disposables)
```

The **RxPreferences** library exposes getX() methods you're accustomed to using with `SharedPreferences`. However, instead of returning a `String` or `Int`, or any of the other types, it returns a `Preference<X>`, where X is the `String` or `Int` or whatever else you can pull out of `SharedPreferences`. In this case, the preference object is of type `Preference<String>`. The `Preference` interface exposes several handy functions, one of which is setting a new value, which you're using in the `subscribe()` block using a method reference.

This code replaces the traditional `edit()`, `putString("myKey", "myString")` and `apply()` methods on the `sharedPreferences` object that you're used to seeing when setting a new shared preference; **RxPreferences** abstracts those away!

Now you need to update the `ColorBottomSheet` class to pass in an instance of `RxSharedPreferences` instead of `SharedPreferences` to the `ColorBottomSheetViewModel`. Replace the existing `SharedPreferences` class argument in the `onViewCreated` method with the following:

```
return ColorBottomSheetViewModel(colorString,
  ColorCoordinator(),
    RxSharedPreferences.create(
      PreferenceManager
        .getDefaultSharedPreferences(requireContext()))) as T
```

The `RxSharedPreferences` class wraps an existing instance of `SharedPreferences`, so you can pass whatever shared preferences object you want.

Subscribing to preference changes

You're properly saving the `favoriteColor` preference, so now it's time to start observing it using the **RxSharedPreferences** library. Just like before, you'll need to swap out the class arguments for `ColorViewModel`.

In the `ColorViewModel` class, replace the `sharedPreferences` class argument with the following:

```
private val sharedPreferences: RxSharedPreferences
```

You're using `val` here to make sure you have a strong reference.

Now, update the `ColorActivity` to pass in an instance of `RxSharedPreferences` into the `ColorViewModel` in the `onCreate` method:

```
return ColorViewModel(Schedulers.io(),
  AndroidSchedulers.mainThread(),
    ColorApi, ColorCoordinator(),
    RxSharedPreferences.create(
      PreferenceManager
        .getDefaultSharedPreferences(this@ColorActivity))) as T
```

Back in `ColorViewModel`, delete the instance variable `listener`. You'll use the **RxPreferences** Rx integration instead of listeners. Make sure to also delete the call to `registerOnSharedPreferenceChangeListener` at the bottom of the `init` block.

Add the following code at the bottom of the `init` block to replace the `registerOnSHaredPreferenceChangeListener()` call you deleted:

```
sharedPreferences.getString("favoriteColor")
  .asObservable()
  .filter { !it.isBlank() }
  .subscribe { hexStringSubject.onNext(it) }
```

Just like before, you're using `getString()` to get a `Preference<String>` from `RxSharedPreferences`. This time, you're also using `asObservable()` to turn that preference into an Observable representing any changes to the shared preference.

Run the app and try going through the flow. Everything should work perfectly!

> **Note**: Just like before, it's important to be mindful of the `WeakHashMap` that the Android SDK uses under the hood to store preference change listeners, which **RxSharedPreferences** utilizes. You need to make sure that you keep a strong reference to the `RxSharedPreferences` object to avoid your listeners' garbage being collected prematurely!

Try deleting the app and setting a breakpoint on the `filter()` line above. Run the app in debug mode, and you'll notice that the breakpoint pauses even without setting a value on the `Preference`. Each `Preference` will emit a default value if no value has been set yet. A common source of errors when using the **RxSharedPreferences** library is assuming that no value will be emitted if you haven't saved any shared preferences objects yet, so make sure to keep in mind that an initial default value will be emitted!

Dealing with old versions of RxJava

There's one thing missing with the Rx chain that you just wrote:

```
sharedPreferences.getString("favoriteColor")
  .asObservable()
  .filter { !it.isBlank() }
  .subscribe { hexStringSubject.onNext(it) }
```

You're not disposing of the Disposable that subscribe() returns!

Normally you'd use the addTo() **RxKotlin** extension function to add the disposable to your CompositeDisposable. Go ahead and give that a shot. You should see an error that looks something like this:

```
Unresolved reference. None of the following candidates is
applicable because of receiver type mismatch:
public fun Disposable.addTo(compositeDisposable:
CompositeDisposable): Disposable defined in
io.reactivex.rxjava3.kotlin
```

The problem is that the **RxPreferences** library is using RxJava2 under the hood, whereas you're using the newer **RxJava3** library. RxJava2 and 3 have different package structures - meaning you can't pass an RxJava2 Observable into a method that expects an RxJava3 Observable and vice versa!

Luckily, the Rx authors provide a bridging library to help ease the transition that you can use to solve this particular roadblock.

Add the following dependency in the **app/build.gradle** file and then sync:

```
implementation "com.github.akarnokd:rxjava3-bridge:3.0.0"
```

The **rxjava3-bridge** library exposes several methods to transition between RxJava2 and RxJava3 types.

Open the **X.kt** file and add the following method at the bottom of the file:

```
fun <T> io.reactivex.Observable<T>.toV3Observable():
    io.reactivex.rxjava3.core.Observable<T> {
  return RxJavaBridge.toV3Observable(this)
}
```

You're defining a new extension function on the RxJava2 version of `Observable` that converts it into an instance of the RxJava3 `Observable` using `toV3Observable()` from the bridging library.

Now head back to the `ColorViewModel` class and replace the shared preferences rx block you added earlier with the following:

```
sharedPreferences.getString("favoriteColor")
  .asObservable()
  .toV3Observable()
  .filter { !it.isBlank() }
  .subscribe { hexStringSubject.onNext(it) }
  .addTo(disposables)
```

You're now using `toV3Observable()`, which you defined earlier to convert the `Observable` returned by **RxSharedPreferences** to a RxJava3 `Observable`. Since it's now the right type of `Observable`, you can use the addTo **RxKotlin** method as expected.

Saving custom objects

You're now sending color data from the `ColorBottomSheet` to the `ColorActivity` seamlessly.

However, there's a major inefficiency. Every time you click the Favorite icon in the bottom sheet, the `ColorViewModel` class executes another network call to fetch the color data for the color you just favorited. That means that the same network call is being made twice: Once in the `ColorBottomSheetViewModel` when the user inputs the color and the once again in the `ColorViewModel`. It'd be great if you could share the whole `ColorResponse` object that the API returns rather than just the hex value of the color.

And you can! **RxPreferences** provides an easy mechanism with which to save custom object types into shared preferences. In this next section, you'll update the app to share the entire `ColorResponse` object returned by the API.

First, add a new file called `ColorResponseConverter` into the **hexcolor** package and add the following code, importing `com.f2prateek.rx.preferences2.Preference` when prompted:

```
class ColorResponseConverter:
    Preference.Converter<ColorResponse> {
  override fun deserialize(serialized: String): ColorResponse {
    TODO()
  }

  override fun serialize(value: ColorResponse): String {
    TODO()
  }
}
```

`ColorResponseConverter` is going to implement the `Preference.Converter` interface exposed by **RxSharedPreferences**. `Preference.Converter` is a simple conversion interface to serialize an object into a `String` and deserialize an object from a `String` into an object type, in this case a `ColorResponse`.

Now, replace the code in `serialize()` with the following:

```
val gson = Gson()
return gson.toJson(value)
```

To serialize an object, you'll use `Gson` to convert the object into a `String`.

Similarly, replace the contents of `deserialize()`:

```
val gson = Gson()
return gson.fromJson(serialized, ColorResponse::class.java)
```

You're again using `Gson`, this time to take a previously serialized object and convert it into an instance of `ColorResponse`.

> **Note**: It's trivial to make a generic abstract class that extends the `Preference.Converter` interface and uses `Gson` under the hood to deserialize any custom object type, so you don't need to write converters for each of your objects!

You'll also need a default, blank instance of `ColorResponse` to return in case the app hasn't yet saved any objects with that type — remember earlier when we discussed default values being returned? Custom objects are no exception!

Add the following as a **top level** value in the **ColorResponseConverter.kt**, outside of the class. You may need to import com.raywenderlich.android.hexcolor.networking.ColorName to make sure you're using the ColorName class instead of the enum:

```
val defaultColorResponse = ColorResponse(ColorName("#", "#"))
```

defaultColorResponse is a "blank" instance of ColorResponse.

Open ColorBottomSheetViewModel. Since you're now going to be saving the results of the last completed network call, you'll need to hold onto that value. Add the following as an instance variable in the view model:

```
private var previouslyFetchedColor: ColorResponse =
    defaultColorResponse
```

Now, delete the code declaring preference at the bottom of the init block and replace it with the following:

```
// 1
val preference = sharedPreferences.getObject(
    "favoriteColor",
    defaultColorResponse,
    ColorResponseConverter()
)
favoriteClicksObservable
  // 2
  .map { previouslyFetchedColor }
  // 3
  .subscribe(preference::set)
  .addTo(disposables)
```

Here's a breakdown:

1. You've switched from using getString() to using getObject(). getObject() takes two additional parameters: A default instance of whatever object you'll be operating on, which in this case is ColorResponse, and a Preference.Converter to convert to and from that object type.

2. You're then using the map operator to transform the Unit value emitted by favoriteClicksObservable into the previouslyFetchedColor object you defined earlier.

3. Finally, you're using set() like before!

All that's left to do in `ColorBottomSheetViewModel` is to actually save the last `ColorResponse` received from the server.

Update the `colorObservable` declaration towards the top of the `init` block such that it saves the last response from the server. Specifically, add the following line before the `map` call:

```
.doOnNext { previouslyFetchedColor = it }
```

Now that you're saving the value, it's time to respond to the new object type in the `ColorViewModel`

Observing a custom object

Open the `ColorViewModel` class. Delete the code observing the `"favoriteColor"` preference string and replace it with the following:

```
sharedPreferences.getObject(
      "favoriteColor",
      defaultColorResponse,
      ColorResponseConverter()
).asObservable()
  .toV3Observable()
  .map { it.name }
  .subscribe {
    colorNameLiveData.postValue(it.value)
    hexStringSubject.onNext(it.closest_named_hex)
  }
  .addTo(disposables)
```

Just like before, you're using `getObject()` to get a `Preference<ColorResponse>`. And like the earlier iteration you're using `asObservable()` to convert it into an Observable.

You're then using `map()` to convert the `ColorResponse` into a `ColorName`, which holds all the meaningful data. Finally, you're posting the color name to the `colorNameLiveData` and the hex string to the `hexStringSubject`.

However, you've now run into an issue. Whenever `hexStringSubject` receives a hex string of length 7, it runs the following Rx block:

```
hexStringSubject
  .filter { it.length == 7 }
  .observeOn(mainScheduler)
  .subscribe {
    colorNameDisposable?.dispose()
    colorNameDisposable = colorApi.getClosestColor(it)
```

```
      .subscribeOn(backgroundScheduler)
      .subscribe { response ->
          colorNameLiveData.postValue(response.name.value)
      }
  }
  .addTo(disposables)
```

This means that the code will still run a network request whenever the preference is updated.

To fix this issue, first delete the code block referenced above. You'll handle making the API request elsewhere.

Then, replace the existing `subscribe()` block in the Rx chain subscribing to the `digitsStream` with the following:

```
hexStringSubject.onNext(currentHexValue() + it)
if (currentHexValue().length == 7) {
  colorNameDisposable?.dispose()
  colorNameDisposable =
    colorApi.getClosestColor(currentHexValue())
      .subscribeOn(backgroundScheduler)
      .subscribe { colorResponse ->
          colorNameLiveData.postValue(colorResponse.name.value)
      }
}
```

You've moved the logic which executes the network request to be triggered based off of digits being input rather than the `hexStringSubject` being updated. That frees the code that subscribes to `hexStringSubject` to be entirely cosmetic. Now, whenever you change a preference, all the normal UI updates will happen without the network request.

Run the app and make sure the above is the case. You should see the color name updated in the main color view after you choose a favorite color via the bottom sheet.

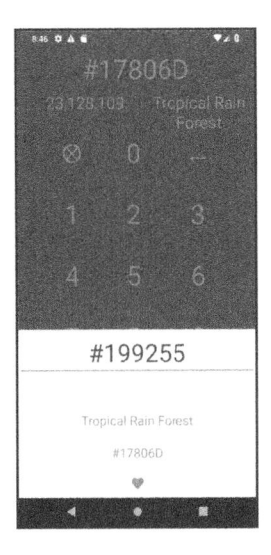

Key points

- You can use **RxPreferences** to create reactive streams out of individual preferences.

- **RxPreferences** provides type safe ways to access data stored in shared preferences.

- Make sure to keep a strong reference to the `RxSharedPreferences` class to avoid listeners being garbage collected prematurely!

- If you want to store and retrieve custom objects, use the `Converter` interface to convert between strings and your object type.

- You can use the **rxjava-bridge** library to bridge between RxJava2 and RxJava3 types

Where to go from here?

Now that you know all about making `SharedPreferences` reactive, you can move even farther Rx-ifying your apps! Hopefully you're starting to notice that for every core component needed to write an Android app, an existing Rx-ified library exists to keep your code base reactive.

In the upcoming chapters, you'll learn about a few more libraries, including some that were written by the Android platform team!

Chapter 20: RxPermissions

By Alex Sullivan

Starting in Android Marshmallow, Android developers need to ask for certain permissions at runtime to allow the user a chance to reject those permissions without rejecting the entire app. For the most part, it's been a great change to the Android ecosystem. However, it has also come with a non-trivial amount of developer pain.

Most Android developers are intimately familiar with the Android flow for requesting a permission. It requires you to request the permission and then handle the result of that permission request in another callback in the activity life cycle. This discrepancy between where you request a permission and where you learn if you've gotten it or not is the cause of a lot of headaches.

There's a helpful library called **RxPermissions** that you'll use in this chapter to help alleviate some of these pain points and give you a reactive flow when requesting permissions. What more could you want?

Getting started

Start off by opening the starter project for this chapter. You'll work on the **Wundercast** app that you started earlier in the book. Recall that **Wundercast** allows you to search for a city and see the temperature, humidity and other weather information.

In addition to the location and API key buttons you've come to love, there's also two new buttons at the bottom of the screen for this chapter. The Save icon towards the left will, once you're done with the chapter, save the currently displayed weather. The Clock icon to its right will then reload the last saved weather and display it in the app. Handy, right?

Wundercast uses the OpenWeatherMap API, so before continuing, make sure you have a valid OpenWeatherMap API key http://openweathermap.org. If you don't already have a key, you can sign up for one at https://home.openweathermap.org/users/sign_up.

Once you've completed the sign-up process, visit the dedicated page for API keys at https://home.openweathermap.org/api_keys and generate a new one.

Then, in the starter project, open the **WeatherApi.kt** file, take the key you generated above and replace the placeholder in the top of the file:

```
val apiKey =
  BehaviorSubject.createDefault("INSERT-API-KEY-HERE")
```

Once that's done, run the app and make sure you can fetch the weather for your favorite city or town.

Requesting the location permission

When you first started working on **Wundercast**, the app would immediately request the location permission as soon as the app launched. As we all know, that's not great user experience. It forces the user to make a quick decision about giving your app the location permission before they have a chance to see why you actually need it. In addition to that, requesting the permission without the proper context can make the user more likely to reject your permission. Instead, it'd be much better if you requested the location permission only after the user clicked the location button in the bottom-left.

The starter project for this chapter removed the code to request the location permission on app launch, so you'll add that back in now.

Start off by commenting out the locationObservable declaration at the top of the init method of WeatherViewModel.

Next up, comment out the Observable.merge block at the end of the init method.

Now, add the following code at the bottom of init, below the commented-out merge code:

```
textObservable
  .subscribeOn(Schedulers.io())
  .observeOn(AndroidSchedulers.mainThread())
  .subscribe(this::showNetworkResult)
  .addTo(disposables)
```

Now that you've removed the Rx-oriented location code, it's time to transition to the sad world of imperative programming. But don't worry, you'll be back soon!

Moving to **WeatherActivity.kt**, add the following code at the bottom of the `onCreate` method:

```
location.setOnClickListener {
  if (Build.VERSION.SDK_INT >= Build.VERSION_CODES.M) {
    requestPermissions(
      arrayOf(Manifest.permission.ACCESS_FINE_LOCATION),
      locationRequestCode)
  }
}
```

You're setting a click listener on the `location` `ImageView`. The click listener will request the location permission if the app is running on a phone with a version of Android at or after Android M. The app is using the Kotlin Android extensions plugin to automatically generate references to views in the layout file, so no need for any pesky `findViewById` calls.

Now, add the `locationRequestCode` constant at the top of your `MainActivity` class:

```
private val locationRequestCode = 101
```

You're now properly requesting the location permission whenever the user taps the Location button. However, you still need to listen for the permission callback and decide what to do from there.

Add the following below the `onCreate` method:

```
override fun onRequestPermissionsResult(requestCode: Int,
  permissions: Array<out String>, grantResults: IntArray) {
  super.onRequestPermissionsResult(requestCode, permissions,
    grantResults)
  if (requestCode == locationRequestCode) {
    val result = grantResults[0]
    if (result == PackageManager.PERMISSION_GRANTED) {
      TODO("Fetch the location!")
    }
  }
}
```

You're listening for the `onRequestPermissionResult` lifecycle method to be called and checking if the user granted the location permission.

Add the following method at the bottom of the `WeatherViewModel` class:

```
fun updateWeatherFromLocation() {
  cityLiveData.postValue("Current Location")
  lastKnownLocation
    .flatMapSingle {
      WeatherApi.getWeather(it).subscribeOn(Schedulers.io())
    }
    .onErrorResumeWith(Maybe.just(
      WeatherApi.NetworkResult.Success(Weather.empty)
    ))
    .subscribe(this::showNetworkResult)
    .addTo(disposables)
}
```

In this method, you're updating the text displayed to the user and using the `lastKnownLocation Maybe<Location>` object to fetch the last known location and then sending it through to the activity via the `showNetworkResult` method.

Head back to the `WeatherActivity` class. You'll use the new `updateWeatherFromLocation` method, but before you do that you'll need to update the code creating the `WeatherViewModel` to store the view model as an instance variable.

Before, all the business logic of the app was happening in the `onCreate` method, so you didn't need a class-wide reference to the view model. Now that you're interacting with the view model outside of `onCreate`, you'll need that view model reference at a broader scope — such is life in the imperative world.

Add the following line below the `locationRequestCode` value you added earlier at the top of the `WeatherActivity` class:

```
private lateinit var model: WeatherViewModel
```

Now, change the code creating the view model from this:

```
val model = ...
```

To this:

```
model = ...
```

You now have a reference to the view model, so you can replace the TODO function in the `onRequestPermissionsResult` callback with the following:

```
model.updateWeatherFromLocation()
```

You should be fetching the weather from the user's current location if they gave you the location permission. Run the app and ensure that, after clicking the Location button in the bottom-left the app, updates with your city's weather.

Using RxPermissions

You've got a working solution that incorporates permissions, but it took a lot of code, and you had to disrupt the existing reactive setup you had. It required storing more state, i.e., the view model, in your `WeatherActivity` class as well.

There's a better way! Add the following dependency to your `build.gradle` file:

```
implementation 'com.github.tbruyelle:rxpermissions:0.10.2'
```

The **RxPermissions** library provides a reactive wrapper around the permissions flow.

You're going to go back through the code you just wrote and replace it with the Rx-based version provided by **RxPermissions**. Head back to the `WeatherActivity` class and delete the `onRequestPermissionResult` method.

Also delete the `clickListener` you set on the `location` view in the bottom of `onCreate`.

Right below the block constructing the `WeatherViewModel` in `onCreate`, add the following line:

```
val permissions = RxPermissions(this)
```

The `RxPermissions` class is your window into the **RxPermissions** library. Through it you can request any type of permission, you could request normally via the `requestPermissions` method.

In order to stick with the reactive theme of the app, you're going to go back to utilizing the `clicks` RxBindings method on the `location` view.

Add the following block below the `permissions` declaration:

```
// 1
val locationObservable = location.clicks()
  // 2
  .flatMap {
    permissions
      .request(Manifest.permission.ACCESS_FINE_LOCATION)
  }
```

```
// 3
.filter { it }
// 4
.map { Unit }
```

Here's a breakdown of the above:

1. As mentioned earlier, you're using the clicks method to get an Observable<Unit> representing user taps on the location view.

2. You're then using the flatMap operator to start emitting objects from the permissions.request method. The request method takes in a permission and returns an Observable<Boolean>. If the resulting observable emits true, that means the permission was accepted. If it emits false, it means that the user did not grant the permission.

3. You're then using the filter operator to make sure that only successful attempts to get the location permission will progress through the Observable chain.

4. Finally, you're using the map operator to convert the Observable back into an Observable<Unit>, which is the initial type returned by the clicks method.

You're probably noticing the error on the flatMap block. Recall that in the **RxPreferences** chapter you had to use the **rxjava-bridge** library to adapt RxJava2 Observables to their RxJava3 counterpart. Just like the **RxPreferences** library, the library you're using to handle permission updates in this chapter hasn't updated to use the RxJava3 library yet. To get this block compiling, replace the body of the flatMap call with the following:

```
RxJavaBridge.toV3Observable(permissions
    .request(Manifest.permission.ACCESS_FINE_LOCATION))
```

You're using the toV3Observable method exposed by the **rxjava-bridge** library to transform the RxJava2 Observable returned by the request method to an RxJava3 Observable.

Take an extra moment to appreciate what's happening, here in this rx chain: Instead of going through all of the cruft and hassle of requesting permissions and overriding on the onRequestPermissionsCallback method, **RxPermissions** gives you a clean, simple interface to request a permission and listen to the results via an Observable.

Since it's hooked into the RxJava world, you can easily combine it with the result of location.clicks to request a permission anytime a user clicks the Location button. Isn't that magical?

Now that you don't need to reference the view model anywhere outside `onCreate`, delete the `lateinit var` from the top of `WeatherActivity`. After you do so, add `val` in front of `model` in the `onCreate` to make that a local constant again.

You can also delete the `locationRequestCode` at the top of `WeatherActivity`, since that's now handled under the hood by `RxPermissions`.

Finally, make sure to actually subscribe to the `locationObservable` and forward its results through to your view model. Add the following below the `locationObservable` declaration:

```
locationObservable.subscribe {
    model.locationClicked()
}.addTo(disposables)
```

The `locationClicked` method simply pipes a value through to a subject that's exposed in your `WeatherViewModel`. Follow the stream and open up **WeatherViewModel.kt** again.

Now that you've got your `locationClicks` receiving values, delete the `updateWeatherFromLocation` method you added earlier and un-comment the Rx blocks declaring `locationObservable` and using it in the `Observable.merge` call. Last but not least, delete the Rx block subscribing to `textObservable` below the call to `Observable.merge`.

Uninstall the app to reset your location permissions, and then run the project. You should see the app request location permissions and progress through to showing you your areas weather just like before.

Requesting another permission

You've got the basics of requesting permissions with **RxPermissions** down, good job! It's time to implement the save and restore features mentioned earlier in the chapter.

First, add two new Observables listening for clicks on the `save` and `load` views in `WeatherActivity` below the existing `locationObservable` Rx block:

```
val saveObservable = save.clicks()
val readObservable = load.clicks()
```

Now, add code requesting the permissions to write on the external storage to both `saveObservable` and `readObservable`:

```
.flatMap {
  RxJavaBridge.toV3Observable(
    permissions.request(Manifest
      .permission.WRITE_EXTERNAL_STORAGE)
  )
}
.filter { it }
.map { Unit }
```

Just like before, you're using the `request` method to request a permission. And just like before you're using the **rxjava-bridge** library to bridge between versions of RxJava. This time, you're requesting the WRITE_EXTERNAL_STORAGE permission so that you can access external storage.

> **Note**: The WRITE_EXTERNAL_STORAGE permission also implicitly gives your app access to **read** from external storage. However, if you do need to request multiple permissions at once time, you can use the `requestEach` method exposed by the **RxPermissions** library.

Now subscribe to your new Observables and pipe the values through to your view model. Add the following below the call subscribing to the `locationobservable`:

```
saveObservable.subscribe { model.saveClicked() }
  .addTo(disposables)
readObservable.subscribe { model.readSaveClicked() }
  .addTo(disposables)
```

Just like before, the save and read save clicked methods on your view model simply trigger existing `PublishSubjects` defined at the top of the `WeatherViewModel` class. You'll use those subjects next.

Reading from external storage

Now that you're calling both the `saveClicked` and `readSaveClicked` methods, it's time to update the `WeatherViewModel` to execute the read and save logic.

Add the following to the top of the `WeatherViewModel` init block:

```
val readObservable = readSavedClicks
  .subscribeOn(AndroidSchedulers.mainThread())
  .flatMapMaybe { readLastWeather(filesDir) }
  .doOnNext { cityLiveData.postValue(it.cityName) }
  .map { WeatherApi.NetworkResult.Success(it) }
```

The above code uses the `readSavedClicks` Observable as a trigger to read the last saved weather object from the external file directory using the helper function `readLastWeather`, which is a top-level function in the **X.kt** file. `readLastWeather` returns a `Maybe<Weather>`, so if there is no saved weather the maybe will complete without any elements.

It then uses the `map` operator to convert the `Weather` object into a `WeatherApi.NetworkResult` so that it's compatible with the rest of the `WeatherViewModel`s code.

Next up, you need to display that saved weather to the user.

At the bottom of the `init` method, add in the `readObservable` into the call to `Observable.merge` as follows:

```
Observable
  .merge(locationObservable, textObservable, readObservable)
```

And that's it! You're now merging three different sources of weather:

1. The weather that's produced when the user clicks the Location button.

2. The weather that's produced when the user enters some text into the edit text.

3. The weather that's produced when the user restores the last saved weather.

You're now reading a weather object from the external storage, but it'd be nice to write one as well!

Writing the weather to external storage

Saving the weather will be just as easy as reading the weather out of external storage. Add the following block to the bottom of the `init` method:

```
saveClicks
  // 1
  .filter { weatherLiveData.value != null }
  .map { weatherLiveData.value!! }
  // 2
  .flatMapCompletable {
    // 3
    it.save(filesDir)
      .doOnComplete {
        snackbarLiveData.postValue(
          "${weatherLiveData.value!!.cityName} weather saved"
        )
      }
  }
  .subscribe()
  .addTo(disposables)
```

Here's a breakdown of the above:

1. Use the `filter` operator to make sure there's a value currently being displayed by inspecting the `weatherLiveData`, and then use the `map` operator to convert the Observable into one emitting the current `Weather`.

2. Use the `flatMapCompletable` operator to `flatMap` from this Observable into a `Completable`.

3. Call the `save` extension method on the `Weather` object emitted by the Observable. `save` returns a `Completable` representing the completed save operation. Once it completes, post a new value to the snackbar indicating that the weather was saved.

> **Note**: You may be wondering why `doOnComplete` is called inside the `flatMapCompletable` block instead of being called before `subscribe()`. When using `flatMapCompletable`, the `Completable` returned by `flatMapCompletable` will only call `onComplete` when the source `Observable` itself completes.
>
> That means that, if `doOnComplete` was added before `subscribe`, it would only be called once the `saveClicks` Observable completed. Since `saveClicks` is driven by a user interaction, it will never complete! You can get around this trickiness by using the do operators inside the `flatMapCompletable` block.

Easy! Run the app and fetch the weather, either by using the Location button or by search via city name. Tap the Save icon next to the Location icon at the bottom of the screen. You should see a message confirming that the location was saved.

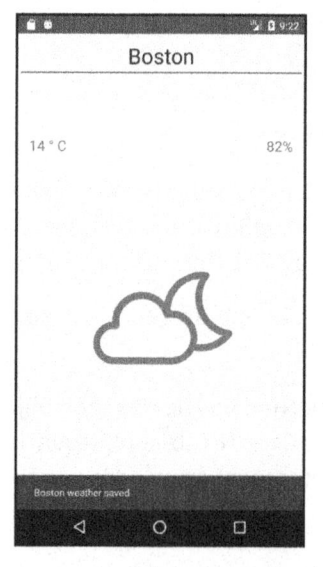

Now, search for a different city or restart the app and tap the Load button to the right of the Save button. You should see the weather details and name of the city that you just saved.

Reacting to orientation changes

RxPermissions is a great library, but there's one big pain point to watch out for.

Imagine a scenario wherein your user clicked a button and that triggered a permission request, just like in **Wundercast**.

Then, before the user clicks Accept or Deny, they rotate their phone. As we all know, configuration changes like this result in the operating system destroying your activity and instantiating a new one. The system will re-create the permissions prompt. Then the user clicks Accept or Deny.

We now have a problem. The old activity or fragment, i.e., the one that existed before the user rotated the phone, was observing the permissions Observable returned by the **RxPermissions** library.

However, the *new* activity or fragment is not observing for those changes unless you called the `request` method directly in `onCreate` or `onStart` or one of the other initialization Android life cycle methods. It would only start observing permission changes after the user clicked the button that triggered the permission in the first place.

Now, if you're just calling the `request` method in `onCreate` or one of the other initialization life cycle methods, you're fine because the new activity or fragment will immediately resubscribe to the permissions Observable, and you'll be all set.

However, that's not what **Wundercast** and a lot of other apps do. They depend on a user clicking something before the prompt should be shown.

You can test this bug out for yourself. Uninstall the app, then reinstall it. Click the location button and then rotate the phone before accepting the permission prompt. Once the phone is rotated and the activity has been restarted, accept the prompt. The app will fail to fetch the weather for your current location because it didn't receive the message that the permission was accepted.

There's a workaround for this particular issue.

In `WeatherActivity`, replace the line calling `flatMap` on the `location.clicks` method with the following:

```
.compose(permissions.ensure(
  Manifest.permission.ACCESS_FINE_LOCATION))
```

There are two new things going on, here:

1. You're using the compose method instead of flatMap. We touched briefly on how compose works in Chapter 16, "Creating Custom Reactive Extensions." If you'd like a quick recap: The compose method allows you to chain custom Observable operators on your Rx chains. For the most part, Kotlin extension functions are a better answer when you're tempted to use compose, but, in this scenario, the fact that the code passed into compose is executed immediately, allowing the **RxPermissions** library to look up any existing permissions requests and immediately reroute them to your Observable.

2. You're using the ensure method instead of the request method you used earlier. request returns an Observable<Boolean>, whereas ensure returns a ObservableTransformer object. ObservableTransformer is an interface primarily used in the compose method mentioned earlier. Both ensure and request will prompt the user for the permissions you ask for, but ensure is compatible with compose allowing you to recover from orientation changes.

Since the **RxPermissions** library is still using RxJava2, you again need to go through the effort of moving between RxJava2 and RxJava3 types, otherwise you'll see an error. Open the **X.kt** file and add the following method at the bottom of the file:

```
fun <T> Observable<T>.ensure(permission: String, rxPermissions:
RxPermissions): Observable<Boolean> {
  return RxJavaBridge.toV2Observable(this)
    .compose(rxPermissions.ensure(permission))
    .`as`(RxJavaBridge.toV3Observable())
}
```

This new ensure method is an extension method on the Observable type. It converts this Observable into an RxJava2 Observable, then uses the **RxPermissions** libraries compose transformer, and then converts the resulting Observable back into an RxJava3 Observable.Phew, that's a lot of back and forth!

Back in WeatherActivity, replace the compose call you just added with the following:

```
ensure(Manifest.permission.ACCESS_FINE_LOCATION, permissions)
```

Your error should disappear.

Now, uninstall and then run the app again. Tap the Location button and rotate the phone, then accept the permission. You should now see the weather updates you'd expect.

Update the logic in the `saveObservable` and `readObservables` to use `ensure` instead of `flatMap` as well:

```
.ensure(Manifest.permission.WRITE_EXTERNAL_STORAGE, permissions)
```

This `compose` trick only works if you make sure to subscribe to the Observable that will trigger the permission request in `onCreate` or `onStart` depending on if you're in an activity or a fragment. Since those initialization life cycle methods happen once your fragment or activity is re-created, it allows you to immediately resubscribe to permission updates so you don't miss any of the action.

One final note: Make sure you're not running the permission requesting logic directly in `onResume`. If you request the permission in `onResume`, your activity will go into a paused state while the permission is shown. Then if the user denies your permission your activity will be resumed, calling `onResume`. This will then trigger a call to show the permission and so on. Using `onCreate` allows you to show the prompt immediately or after some event is triggered without being re-run whenever the activity is resumed.

In general, if you're triggering a permission based off some event, you should be using the `ensure` method. If you're just triggering the permission as soon as the activity or fragment is created, feel free to use the `request` method.

Key points

- The **RxPermissions** library provides an easy mechanism through which to request permissions.
- You can chain Observables you get back from the library with other Observables just like normal.
- Keep in mind that the code requesting permissions has to be made in an initialization method (like `onCreate` or `onStart`).
- Use `ensure` if you're triggering the permission request off some other event.
- Use `request` if you're triggering the permission request as soon as the page loads.

Where to go from here?

RxPermissions is another great example of the Android community embracing the Rx paradigm. In the next chapter, you'll dive into yet another library that equally embraces Rx, however, what makes the library interesting is the fact that Google developed the library. Google's decision to support RxJava through the JetPack components should be a compelling argument in favor of the library. When you're ready, continue onwards!

Section V: Putting It All Together

The "easy" part of the book is over. If you made it this far and are looking to learn even more in order to start creating production apps with RxJava, this section is for you.

The two chapters in this section are going to help you learn how to build real-life applications with RxJava.

The first chapter will cover integrating RxJava with the components of Android Jetpack, in particular, the Room database library and the Paging library. The chapter will build off of knowledge you've gained earlier in the book working with the ViewModel and LiveData components of Jetpack.

The second chapter, and the last one in this book, is going to show you how to setup a reactive application architecture and how to convert callbacks to Rx Observables.

Once you finish working through this section, you will be one of the top RxJava developers out there. There is, of course, more to know about Rx but at this point you will be able to figure out things further on your own.

Also, don't forget to give back to the community! It would not have been possible for us to put this book together without all the amazing Rx folks sharing their knowledge, code, and good vibes.

Chapter 21: RxJava & Jetpack

By Alex Sullivan

Android Jetpack is a suite of libraries provided by the Android team to make developing Android apps a breeze (well, maybe not quite a breeze…). You've already been working with two of the libraries provided as part of Jetpack throughout the book: **LiveData** and **ViewModel**. In this chapter, you're going to explore two more libraries that every Android developer should know about, and how they interact with RxJava.

The first library you're going to utilize is the **Room** database library. Interacting with a database has typically been a painful process when writing an Android app. In the beginning, a developer would usually use a custom instance of the `SQLiteOpenHelper` class to manually create tables and run updates using `SQL`.

This approach worked, but came with a lot of downsides. It was cumbersome to keep all of the `SQL` statements you were writing in code and it was very easy to have the objects you were trying to store in the database and the tables representing those objects get out of sync. To top it all off, you needed a lot of boilerplate to turn those objects into `ContentValues` to then be inserted into the database. Luckily, Room provides an easy to use abstraction on top of `SQLiteOpenHlper` that makes storing data a much simpler task.

The second library you're going to explore is the **Paging** library. Another common task for app developers is to implement a kind of infinitely scrollable list, like **Instagram** or **Facebook** has. The Paging library provides simple hooks for you to use to load new data as a user scrolls down in a list. It even ties together with **Room** to give you an easy way to pipe data from your database into your app.

Best of all, both **Room** and the **Paging** library come with first-class RxJava integrations!

In this chapter, you'll explore both libraries by creating a *Lord of the Rings*-based book collector app, which allows a user to fetch a list of books from the Open Library API, scroll through the books, favorite some of them and mark others as read.

Getting started

Open the starter project in **Android Studio** and run the app. You should see the following screen:

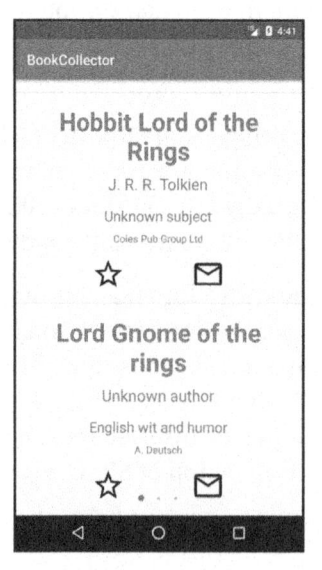

The **BookCollector** app displays a list of books fetched from the Open Library API. A user can then either favorite the book by clicking the **star** icon, or mark it as a book they've already read by clicking the **envelope** icon.

There are three pages in the app. The first page is the screen you see in the screenshot above and the starting screen for the app, which displays the entire list of books. The second page is a favorites page, which displays the books the user has favorited. The third page displays all of the books the user has marked as read.

Each page is controlled by a different `Fragment` in a `ViewPager`. Each fragment is backed by the same view model, which is called `MainViewModel`. Open the `MainViewModel` class now and take a look around.

The first thing you'll notice is that this view model follows a familiar pattern: There are three `LiveData` objects that govern what's shown on an individual page. Then, in the `init` block, the view model queries the Open Library API and uses the `cache` operator to cache the result. Then, the view model subscribes to the resulting Observable three times, once for each live data object, filtering and mapping the results according to what that live data should emit.

There are also two stubbed out methods:

```
fun favoriteClicked(book: Book) {
  TODO()
}

fun readClicked(book: Book) {
  TODO()
}
```

You'll update these two methods governing what happens when a user clicks the **favorite** icon and the **read** icon later on in the chapter. Before you go any further, it's a good idea to get a quick refresher on how Room works.

There are three core components to Room:

1. The `Entity`: An `Entity` is a model object annotated with the `@Entity` annotation, and represents the data that will reside in the database. Room will typically create a table under the hood for each class marked with the `@Entity` annotation.

2. The `Dao`: A `Dao` is an `interface` marked with the `@Dao` annotation. This interface typically exposes high-level methods to insert and query items from the database. You can think of the `Dao` as being akin to a `Retrofit` interface.

3. The `Database`: The `Database` class is a class that you create that extends the `RoomDatabase` object, and it is annotated with an `@Database` annotation, wherein you list all of your `Entities` and expose the version of the database.

Open **Book.kt** to see an example of an `Entity`:

```
@Entity
data class Book(@PrimaryKey val title: String,
                val authorName: String,
                val publisher: String,
                val subject: String,
                val isFavorited: Boolean = false,
                val isAlreadyRead: Boolean = false)
```

The Book class is marked with the `@Entity` annotation to signify that it can be inserted and retrieved from a Room database.

Each `Entity` needs an instance variable marked with the `@PrimaryKey` annotation. The `@PrimaryKey` annotation signifies to Room that this instance variable can determine uniqueness for an object. That means that, in the example above, you could never have two `Book`s with the same title in a Room database, since that would violate a primary key constraint on uniqueness.

Now, open **BookDao.kt** to see an example of a `Dao`:

```
@Dao
interface BookDao
```

As you can see, the BookDao class is empty. For now. :]

Last but not least, open **BookDatabase.kt** to see an example `Database`:

```
@Database(entities = [Book::class], version = 1)
abstract class BookDatabase : RoomDatabase() {
    abstract fun bookDao(): BookDao
}
```

It outlines the entities that will live in the database and the version of the database. For this app, you'll only have one object residing in the database: the Book class. Your only exposed dao will be the BookDao.

RxJava and Room

Now that you're familiar with **Room**, it's time to sprinkle some Rx goodness on top of it.

The team behind Room has exposed a very helpful extension that allows you to utilize RxJava reactive types in a similar manner to the **Retrofit** library.

Add the following dependency to your `build.gradle` file:

```
implementation "androidx.room:room-rxjava2:$room_version"
```

Adding this extension will allow you to return any reactive type you want in your `Dao` object. Unfortunately the **Room** library has yet to update to using RxJava3, so you'll have to use the bridge library you learned about in previous chapters to transition between the types returned by the RxJava2 and 3 libraries.

Database philosophy

Before you start getting your hands dirty, take a minute to discuss what the strategy is going to be moving forward for dealing with the network and the database.

Sometimes, utilizing both a network and a database as a source of information can be a frustrating experience. If one gets out of sync with the other, it can be confusing trying to reconcile which you should believe.

To attempt to mitigate the above issue, you're going to be using the database as the primary source of truth in the app. The goal for the **BookCollector** app is going to be to pull data from the network when the app is started and then immediately insert it into the database. Once the database has been updated with new content you'll use it to populate the information that the user sees.

By utilizing this database first philosophy, you'll be able to sidestep the chaos of choosing who to believe and you'll be able to implement a more reactive pattern of interacting with your data layer.

Now that you've got the philosophy down, it's time to get this project started!

Open **BookDao.kt** and add the following method to the interface importing the `io.reactivex.*` version of `Completable`:

```
@Insert(onConflict = OnConflictStrategy.IGNORE)
fun insertBooks(books: List<Book>): Completable
```

The `insertBooks` method will insert a `List<Book>` into the database. It will ignore any conflicts when the books are inserted. Since all you care about is a confirmation that the items were added into the database, it makes sense to use `Completable` as the return type of `insertBooks`.

If you were instead interested in a list of IDs for the newly inserted books you could've specified a return type of Single<List<Long>> instead of Completable. Just like the **Retrofit** library, Room will look at the return type you provide and adjust the behavior of the library accordingly. You'll see several examples, later on, utilizing the different return types in the BookDao.

What good is inserting items into a database if you can't retrieve them? Add the following method below insertBooks importing the rxjava2 version of Observable:

```
@Query("SELECT * from book ORDER BY title")
fun bookStream(): Observable<List<Book>>
```

The bookStream method will pull all of the books out of the database and return them as an Observable<List<Book>>. Hold onto your seat, because this is where things start to get interesting.

If you specify a return type of Observable or Flowable for your Room queries, the Observable or Flowable you get back will emit a new list of books every time you insert or update a book. That means that, by subscribing to your Observable, you'll get constant updates as the database changes. That allows you to keep your UI perfectly up-to-date and enables that reactive flow you saw outlined earlier.

The reactive return type you specify in your DAO methods have different meanings depending on what type of operation you're executing. Here's a quick breakdown of what the different types mean if you're inserting an item, updating or deleting an item, or retrieving an item from the database.

Inserting an item

If you're inserting an item into the database, you can use the following return types:

1. **Completable**: If your database insertion was successful, your completable will complete as expected. If it wasn't successful, an error will be emitted that will filter into your onError block of your subscription.

2. **Single** or **Maybe**: Single and Maybe work the same when inserting with Room. If the insertion was successful, onSuccess will be emitted with a Long value representing the ID of the newly inserted object. If you're inserting a list or array of items, you can instead specify the return type as Single<List<Long>>, in which each Long in the list represents the id of the correspondingly inserted item in the list.

That's it — you can't declare a return type of Observable or Flowable, since an insertion into a database will only ever return up to one value – the ID of the object that was inserted. Specifying a return type of Observable would be confusing in this scenario since you could use Single or Maybe, which better describe the situation.

Updating and deleting an item

If you're updating or deleting an item in the database, you can use the same return types as inserting but with a slightly different meaning:

1. **Completable**: Just like before, you can use a Completable if all you care about is that the update or delete finished or failed.

2. **Single** or **Maybe**: Similarly to inserting an object, you can return a Single or Maybe when updating or deleting an object in the database. However, instead of returning Single<Long> or Maybe<Long>, you need to return a Single<Int> or Maybe<Int>. The Int value represents the number of rows affected by this update, so even if you update a list of objects you'll still use Single<Int> or Maybe<Int>.

Querying

Querying is where all the magic happens, and you can use the full suite of reactive types, other than Completable, which doesn't make much sense in a querying context:

1. **Single**: If you declare a query's return type as Single, it will return a single instance of whatever object you're querying. If, however, the database doesn't contain the object your querying for, your single will emit an error, since a Single needs to emit exactly one value.

2. **Maybe**: Similarly to Single, a query returning a Maybe will return a single object if it exists in the database. However, if it doesn't exist, the Maybe will complete normally.

3. **Observable/Flowable**: If you specify your return type as Observable or Flowable, you'll receive the items that correspond to that query in the Observable or Flowable. Whenever the underlying data in the database changes, the Observable or Flowable will emit again.

> **Note**: When using a query of type `Observable` or `Flowable`, **Room** will make sure that your query runs off the `main` thread without you needing to use the `subscribeOn` operator.

Reacting to database changes

Now that you've exposed methods to insert and retrieve books from the database, it's time to update the app to utilize those methods.

Open the `MainViewModel` class and replace the `observable` declaration at the top of the `init` block with the following:

```
// 1
val observable = OpenLibraryApi.searchBooks("Lord of the Rings")
  .subscribeOn(Schedulers.io())
  // 2
  .flatMapCompletable {
    database.bookDao().insertBooks(it).toV3Completable()
  }
  // 3
  .andThen(database.bookDao().bookStream().toV3Observable())
  .share()
```

Here's a breakdown of the changes:

1. Just like before, you're using the `OpenLibraryApi` class to search for books.

2. This time, instead of just returning those books, you're inserting all of them into the database using the `insertBooks` method you wrote earlier. Since **Room** is still using the RxJava2 library, you're using the `toV3Completable` extension method to convert an RxJava2 `Completable` to an RxJava3 `Completable`. Don't forget that after this operator the chain will now be an instance of `Completable`.

3. Once you've inserted the books you're using, the andThen operator on `Completable` to transition to the `Observable<List<Book>>` returned by the `bookStream` method. Just like before you're using the `toV3Observable` method to transition from an RxJava2 `Observable` to an RxJava3 `Observable`.

You're now fetching books from the server and saving them to the database. You're then querying and observing the database for books, and powering the views based off that Observable.

Since the type of observable switched from Single to Observable, you'll need to update all of the subscribeBy calls in the class to use the onNext parameter instead of onSuccess, since onSuccess is specific to Single.

Here's an example of the updated Rx chain that pushes new values to the allBooksLiveData object:

```
observable
  .subscribeBy(
    onNext = { item -> allBooksLiveData.postValue(item) },
    onError = { print("Error: $it") }
  )
  .addTo(disposables)
```

Once you've made those changes, run the app. Everything should work the same and you should see the full list of *Lord of the Rings* books on the initial page.

Updating individual items

The next thing you need to do to get the **BookCollector** app up and running is to fill out the details of the favoriteClicked and readClicked methods in the MainViewModel. However, before you do that, you'll need a way to insert a single updated book into the database.

Head back to the BookDao class and add the following method to the interface:

```
@Update(onConflict = OnConflictStrategy.REPLACE)
fun updateBook(book: Book): Single<Int>
```

updateBook takes a book and inserts it into the database, replacing any existing value that's already there. It returns a Single<Int>, where the Int value represents the number of rows updated.

Now that you've got a way to update an individual book, it's time to fill out the favoriteClicked and readClicked methods to utilize that new method.

Back in `MainViewModel` replace the `favoriteClicked` method with the following:

```kotlin
fun favoriteClicked(book: Book) {
  database.bookDao()
    .updateBook(book.copy(isFavorited = !book.isFavorited))
    .toV3Single()
    .subscribeOn(Schedulers.io())
    .subscribe()
    .addTo(disposables)
}
```

You're using the new `updateBook` method and passing through a new instance of Book with the `isFavorited` flag toggled. Note that you're not actually doing anything with the return value. Instead, the app relies on the `bookStream` Observable to emit a new list of items since the data has been updated.

Run the app and click the **star** icon on one of the books. You'll notice the outlined star icon fills in. Swipe to the right to get to the list of favorites for the book, and you'll notice the items you starred show up. You can even "unstar" one of the books from this list and it will disappear. All of this behavior is being driven by the `bookStream` observable, which is emitting a new list of books every time you favorite or unfavorite a book!

Now, replace the `readClicked` method with a similar body:

```kotlin
fun readClicked(book: Book) {
  database.bookDao()
    .updateBook(book.copy(isAlreadyRead = !book.isAlreadyRead))
    .toV3Single()
    .subscribeOn(Schedulers.io())
    .subscribe()
    .addTo(disposables)
}
```

Just like before, you're using the `updateBook` method and sending through a Book with the `isAlreadyRead` flag toggled.

Run the app again. Click the **envelope** icon on a few books and then swipe to the third page. You should see all of the books you marked as read, and just like on the favorites page you can click the **read** icon here and see them disappear!

By utilizing **Room**'s reactive types, you've created a fully reactive app that observes a database and listens for new values, which are emitted every time the saved list of books is updated. Pretty magical, right?

Starting the app with cached data

The app is working great, but it's not fully utilizing the fact that it's using a database. Specifically, when the app starts, it's immediately making a network request and not showing any information until that request finishes. That's a bummer since you've got the data at your fingertips!

Luckily, you can make short work of that issue by using the `startWith` operator. In `MainViewModel`, replace the existing `observable` declaration at the top of `init` with the following:

```
val observable = OpenLibraryApi.searchBooks("Lord of the Rings")
  // 1
  .retryWhen { it.delay(5, TimeUnit.SECONDS) }
  .subscribeOn(Schedulers.io())
  .flatMapCompletable {
      database.bookDao().insertBooks(it).toV3Completable()
  }
  .andThen(database.bookDao().bookStream().toV3Observable())
  // 2
  .startWith(database.bookDao().bookStream().toV3Observable()
    .take(1))
  .share()
```

There're two new operators at play, here:

1. You're using the `retryWhen` operator to retry a failed network request after five seconds. For more information on how `retryWhen` works, check out Chapter 12, "Error Handling in Practice."

2. You're using the `startWith` operator to kick off the Observable with the books already in the database. You're using the `take` operator to take the first `List<Book>` from the database since you only care about what's initially in the database.

Put the phone in Airplane mode and run the app. You should immediately see books from the database populate the app. Once you turn off Airplane mode and wait a few seconds, the app will be populated with the latest and greatest from the network.

Paging data in

Now that you've explored the Room libraries Rx integration, it's time to implement infinite paging using the paging library.

Open **OpenLibraryService.kt** and update the `searchBooks` method to take in a page number:

```
@GET("search.json")
fun searchBooks(
  @Query("q") searchTerm: String,
  @Query("page") page: Int
): Single<OpenLibraryResponse>
```

Now, open **OpenLibraryApi.kt** and update the `searchBooks` method to take in a page number:

```
fun searchBooks(searchTerm: String, page: Int = 1):
Single<List<Book>> {
  return service.searchBooks(searchTerm, page)
  ...
}
```

By default, you'll start at the first page, so you can use a default parameter there.

The paging library utilizes a different type of adapter to handle the special type of lists it works with. Open **BookAdapter.kt** and update the type of adapter BookAdapter to extending the following:

```
PagedListAdapter<Book, BookViewHolder>(getDiffUtil())
```

Getting an item from the underlying list in a `PagedListAdapter` can return a `null` item, so replace the book declaration in `onBindViewHolder` with the following:

```
val book = getItem(position) ?: return
```

Now that your API is ready to go and your adapter is all set up, it's time to hook into the Paging library and start paging some content in!

Just like before, the strategy is going to be to load directly from the database and populate it with more data as the user scrolls in the RecyclerView. To do that, you'll need a `DataSource`. A `DataSource` is a class specific to the Paging library that aids in loading data from some source. Apt name, right?

Now normally you'd have to create a new class that extends `DataSource`. But, since you're using Room, you can do something that kind of feels like cheating in the programming world.

Open **BookDao.kt** and replace the existing `bookStream` method with the following:

```
@Query("SELECT * from book ORDER BY title")
fun bookStream(): DataSource.Factory<Int, Book>
```

Room can actually generate `DataSource.Factory` objects for you just by changing the return type of your query! This factory class will create a `DataSource`, so you don't have to create your own custom data source. The `Factory` in this case is of type `Factory<Int, Book>`, since the object type you're operating on is a `Book` and the page type is an `Int`.

The next step in the Paging library journey is to create a `PagedListBuilder`. A `PagedListBuilder` is a class in charge of creating new instances of `PagedList`, which is that special type of list you updated the `BookAdapter` to handle.

Now, normally, you'd use the `LivePagedListBuilder` class to get a `LiveData<PagedList<Book>>`, but luckily the wonderful team in charge of building the Paging library has created Rx bindings for the library, just like they did for Room!

Add the following to your `build.gradle` file:

```
implementation "androidx.paging:paging-rxjava2-ktx:
$paging_version"
```

Now, open `MainViewModel` and delete everything in the `init` block. That's right everything. The Paging library handles so much behind the scenes that you won't need the code to manually hit the API anymore.

At the top of the now empty `init` block, add the following:

```
val config = PagedList.Config.Builder()
    .setEnablePlaceholders(false)
    .setPageSize(20)
    .build()
```

A `PagedList.Config` is a configuration object that tells the Paging library how you want to page data in.

In this config, you're setting the following configs:

1. You're setting enablePlaceholders to false. If you know the size of your dataset before you start paging data in, you can set placeholder values so the user has an accurate scroll bar on their RecyclerView. Since you're querying an API, you don't have this information so you can just set it to false.

2. You're setting the page size to 20. That means the paged list will load in 20 objects at a time from the database, which will take up several scrollable pages in the RecyclerView.

Below the config declaration, use the RxPagedListBuilder class to create an Observable<PagedList<Book>>:

```
RxPagedListBuilder<Int, Book>(
    database.bookDao().bookStream(), config)
  .buildObservable()
  .toV3Observable()
  .subscribe(allBooksLiveData::postValue)
  .addTo(disposables)
```

RxPagedListBuilder is one of the classes exposed by RxJava paging integration. It allows you build an Observable<PagedList<Book>>, which you can then utilize however you want. In the above example you're passing in the DataSource.Factory returned from the BookDao.bookStream method and the config you just created.

Before you can run the app, you'll need to update the LiveData objects at the top of the class to be of type MutableLiveData<PagedList<Book>>:

```
val allBooksLiveData = MutableLiveData<PagedList<Book>>()
val favoriteBooksLiveData = MutableLiveData<PagedList<Book>>()
val alreadyReadBooksLiveData =
  MutableLiveData<PagedList<Book>>()
```

Now, all the components of your app are speaking the same language.

Run the app. Assuming you haven't uninstalled the app since the last time you ran it as part of this chapter, you should see content paging in from the database on the main page. If you scroll to the other two pages, they'll be empty. Time to fix that.

Open **BookDao.kt** again and add the following two methods below `bookStream`:

```
@Query("SELECT * from book WHERE isFavorited = 1 ORDER BY
title")
fun favoritesStream(): DataSource.Factory<Int, Book>

@Query("SELECT * from book WHERE isAlreadyRead = 1 ORDER BY
title")
fun alreadyReadStream(): DataSource.Factory<Int, Book>
```

Remember how you used to use `filter` and `map` operators to pull out the favorited and already-read books? You're moving that logic into the database and exposing two new queries: one for favorited books and one for books that have already been read. Just like in the `bookStream` method, you're returning a `DataSource.Factory<Int, Book>` to be used with the Paging library.

Open **MainViewModel.kt** again and add matching `RxPagedListBuilder` statements for your new queries:

```
RxPagedListBuilder<Int, Book>(
    database.bookDao().favoritesStream(), config)
  .buildObservable()
  .toV3Observable()
  .subscribe(favoriteBooksLiveData::postValue)
  .addTo(disposables)

RxPagedListBuilder<Int, Book>(
    database.bookDao().alreadyReadStream(), config)
  .buildObservable()
  .toV3Observable()
  .subscribe(alreadyReadBooksLiveData::postValue)
  .addTo(disposables)
```

Now, run the app again. If you scroll to the right, you'll see the favorited and already-read book lists being populated as expected. Toggle the favorited status of a book to confirm that everything works.

Paging in from the network

This app is looking beautiful, but there's one problem: it's not pulling anything from the server! Right now the app is only serving up cached data from the database; it's never actually fetching anything new. If you were to uninstall and reinstall the app, you wouldn't see any content because nothing would actually be downloaded.

Here's a diagram of what's happening right now:

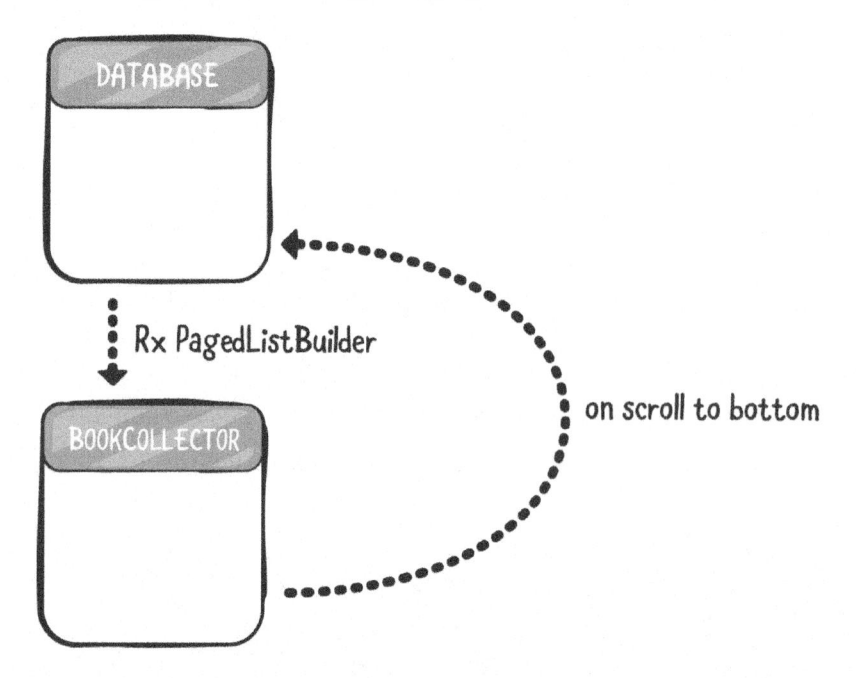

And here's the end goal for the app:

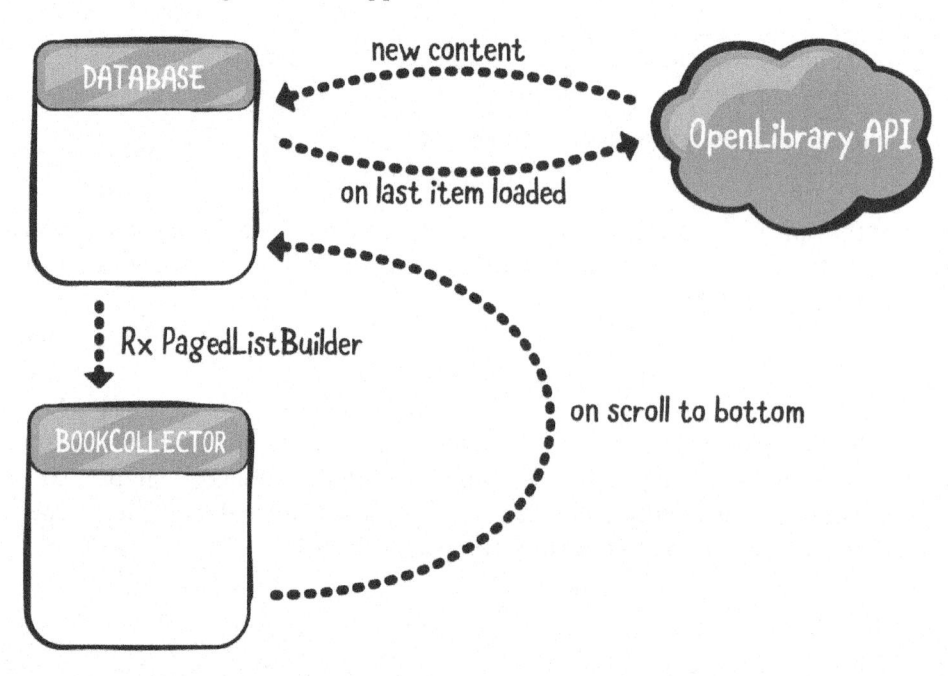

To achieve the desired flow of the app pulling down new books from the server when it runs out of content, you'll need to use another utility that the Paging library provides: a BoundaryCallback.

A BoundaryCallback is a handy utility that you can use to execute some action whenever you've run out of cached content to display. It's use case is specifically oriented towards apps that want to load data into a database and then fetch new data from a server once the app has displayed all of the data already loaded in the database.

Open the **BookBoundaryCallback.kt** class. It has two unimplemented methods that you'll fill out: onZeroItemsLoaded and onItemAtEndLoaded.

onZeroItemsLoaded is called when there's no items yet loaded into the database. That would usually be the scenario after the first time the app runs. You'll use this callback to load the first page of data from the network.

onItemAtEndLoaded is called when the last item is loaded from the database. You'll use this callback to load the latest page of data from the network.

Both methods will have very similar implementations, so you're going to create a helper function. Add the following method at the bottom of the class:

```
private fun loadItems(requestType:
PagingRequestHelper.RequestType) {
  // 1
  helper.runIfNotRunning(requestType) { callback ->
    // 2
    OpenLibraryApi.searchBooks(searchTerm, currentPage)
      // 3
      .flatMapCompletable {
        db.bookDao().insertBooks(it).toV3Completable()
      }
      .subscribeOn(Schedulers.io())
      // 4
      .subscribe {
        currentPage++
        callback.recordSuccess()
      }
  }
}
```

Here's a breakdown of the `loadItems` method:

1. Sometimes `onZeroItemsLoaded` or `onItemAtEndLoaded` can be called multiple times. That can be a bit of a problem because you don't want to kick off multiple network requests to load a single page of data. The paging team has provided a handy `PagingRequestHelper` class to help coordinate running these asynchronous tasks. Here, you're using the `runIfNotRunning` method to run a block of code depending on if the passed in `RequestType` has been started or not.

2. You're using the `searchBooks` method to search for a list of books, passing through the current page, which starts at one.

3. You're then inserting the books you get back from the server into the database.

4. Finally, you're incrementing the page count so the next time you make a network request you fetch the next page. You're also letting the `PagingRequestHelper` know that the initial fetch was finished by calling the `recordSuccess` method on the callback object `runIfNotRunning` provides.

Now, replace the `onZeroItemsLoaded` and `onItemAtEndLoaded` methods with the following:

```
override fun onZeroItemsLoaded() {
  loadItems(PagingRequestHelper.RequestType.INITIAL)
}

override fun onItemAtEndLoaded(itemAtEnd: Book) {
  loadItems(PagingRequestHelper.RequestType.AFTER)
}
```

You're passing a `RequestType` of `INITIAL` for the first download and `AFTER` for subsequent downloads.

Now that you've got a `BoundaryCallback` ready to go, you can set it on the `RxPagedListBuilder` objects you set up earlier.

Back in `MainViewModel`, add the following line after each `RxPagedListBuilder` declaration:

```
.setBoundaryCallback(
    BookBoundaryCallback("The lord of the rings", database))
```

Run the app again. You should be able to scroll to your heart's content. If by some magic you manage to get to the end of the (astoundingly large) list of *Lord of the Rings* books, congratulations! You've officially learned everything there is to know about how many cool *Lord of the Rings* books there are!

Key points

- **Room** allows you to specify reactive types in your Dao objects.
- You can use `Completable` or `Single` or `Maybe` when inserting, updating or deleting items from the database.
- You can use `Observable` or `Flowable` when querying items from the database.
- Your query Observable will keep emitting as data changes in the database!
- The Paging library comes with an RxJava extension that allows you to stream `PagedList` objects.
- Room and the Paging library make for a fantastic reactive combination!

Where to go from here?

The Room and Paging libraries are great examples of how a library can effectively integrate Rx into its API. Given these libraries are written by Google, its nice to know that you're getting first party support for Rx from these libraries.

If you're interested in learning more about either libraries and the extend of their Rx support, you can checkout the documentation (medium.com/androiddevelopers/room-rxjava-acb0cd4f3757)(developer.android.com/topic/libraries/architecture/paging#ex-observe-rxjava2) for a deeper look at the integration.

Chapter 22: Building a Complete RxJava App

By Alex Sullivan

Throughout this book, you've learned about the many facets of RxJava. Reactive programming is a deep subject; its adoption often leads to architectures very different from the ones you've grown used to. The way you model events and data flow in RxJava is crucial for proper behavior in your apps, as well as protecting against issues in future iterations of the product.

To conclude this book, you'll architect and code a small RxJava application. The goal is not to use Rx "at all costs," but rather to make design decisions that lead to a clean architecture with stable, predictable and modular behavior. The application is simple by design, to clearly present ideas you can use to architect your own applications.

This chapter is as much about RxJava as it is about the importance of a well-chosen architecture that suits your needs. RxJava is a great tool that helps your application run like a well-tuned engine, but it doesn't spare you from thinking about and designing your application architecture.

Introducing QuickTodo

Serving as the modern equivalent of the "Hello, world" program, a "To-Do" application is an ideal candidate to expose the inner structure of an Rx application.

In the previous chapters, you've used `ViewModel`, `LiveData`, and `Room` from the Jetpack suite of libraries to build your apps.

In this chapter, you'll wrap them all together and create a modularized architecture that allows you to separate your data layer from your presentation layer.

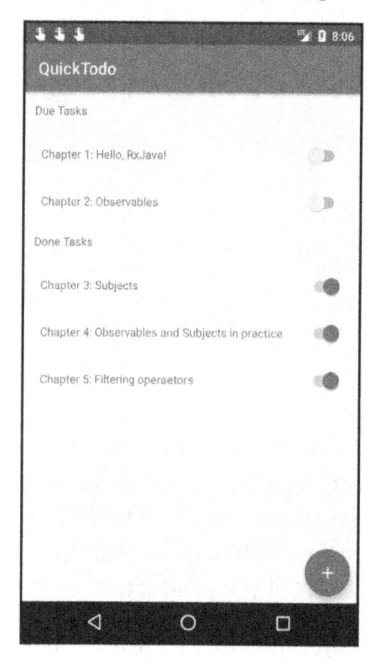

Architecting the application

One particularly important goal of your app is to achieve a clean separation between the user interface, the business logic of your application and the services the app contains to help the business logic run. To that end, you really need a clean model where each component is clearly identified.

First, some terminology for the architecture you are going to implement:

- **View model**: Defines the business logic and data used by the view to show a particular view.

- **Repository**: A provider of content from some store. A repository could fetch objects from a database or from a network. Either way, it's abstracted from the view model so that it can concentrate on view logic.

- **Model**: The most basic data store in the application. View models and repositories both manipulate and exchange models.

You've used view models throughout the book. Repositories are a new concept and another good fit for reactive programming. Their purpose is to expose data and functionality using `Observable` and the other reactive types as much as possible, so as to create a global model in which components connect together as reactively as possible.

For your QuickTodo application, the requirements are relatively modest. You'll architect it correctly nonetheless, so you have a solid foundation for future growth. It's also an architecture you'll be able to reuse in other applications.

The basic items you need are:

- A `TaskItem` **model** that describes an individual task.

- A `TaskRepository` **repository** that provides task creation, update, deletion, storage and search.

- A **storage medium**; you'll use a Room database here and, of course, its Rx adapters.

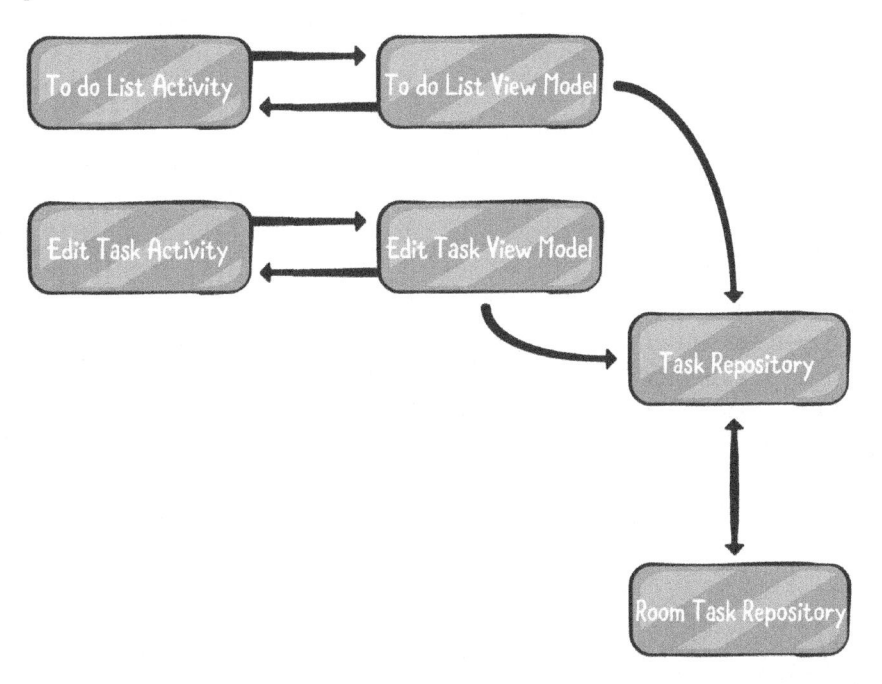

As you've seen in the previous chapters, the view model exposes the business logic and the model data to the activity. Just like in previous chapters you'll use `LiveData` objects to emit updates to the activity. Doing this ensures that the activity is kept up to date even after a configuration change.

LiveData vs. Observables

You may be wondering why you've been using `LiveData` instead of just exposing `Observables` from your view model. There are a few reasons to use both utilities:

1. `LiveData` has the benefit of being directly tied to Android lifecycle events. That makes it a fantastic candidate for use inside an `Activity` or `Fragment`, because it means you don't need to worry about disposing of any subscriptions as lifecycle events fire.

2. You don't need to worry about **when** you're subscribing or observing your lifecycles. If you were to use `Observables` instead of `LiveData` objects, you'd have to make sure that your activity or fragment is only subscribing after the UI is setup, since otherwise you may run into an exception when you try to reference a non-existent UI component. That's not a large problem for Activities, but it can be painful in Fragments where the lifecycle is more complex.

3. `LiveData`, while powerful and helpful, has nowhere near the power of an RxJava `Observable`. The power of RxJava should be clear at this point. While both `Observable` and `LiveData` implement the observer pattern, `Observables` have a huge array of operators and utilities that they can use to create complex streams. `LiveData` is a much simpler construct.

Task model

Now that you've got the basic theory down, it's time to put these concepts into practice. Open the starter project in Android Studio. Note that the project won't build at first; this chapter's starter project is less fleshed out than previous chapters to give you an opportunity to go through all different sections of a reactive application.

Without further ado, you'll start by adding in the task model. Populate **TaskItem.kt** as follows:

```
@Entity
data class TaskItem(
  @PrimaryKey(autoGenerate = true) val id: Int?,
  val text: String,
  val addedDate: Date,
  val isDone: Boolean
)
```

Your task model is simple and is marked as a Room entity. A task is defined as having text (the task contents), a creation date and a checked flag. You'll use the creation date to sort tasks in the tasks list.

Task data access object

Now that you have a `TaskItem` that is a Room entity, you'll need a DAO or data access object to store and fetch `TaskItem` model objects from the database.

Open **TaskDao.kt**. You'll notice that it's already marked as a @Dao interface, but, other than that, it's completely empty.

For this project, your DAO will need four methods:

1. A method to insert a single `TaskItem` for when the user creates a new task and saves it.

2. A method to insert a list of `TaskItems` to allow the app to pre-populate the database with several default `TaskItems`.

3. A method to fetch an individual `TaskItem` from the database by a given `id`.

4. And finally a method to observe all of the `TaskItems` currently in the database.

Add the following to the body of the `TaskDao` interface, importing the `io.reactivex.*` reactive classes (not the `io.reactivex.java3.*`), and AndroidX database annotations. At the time of this writing, Room does not work with RxJava3:

```
// 1
@Insert(onConflict = OnConflictStrategy.REPLACE)
fun insertTask(taskItem: TaskItem): Single<Long>

// 2
@Insert
fun insertTasks(tasks: List<TaskItem>): Completable

// 3
@Query("SELECT * FROM TaskItem WHERE id = :id")
fun fetchTask(id: Int): Maybe<TaskItem>

// 4
@Query("SELECT * FROM TaskItem ORDER BY addedDate")
fun taskStream(): Observable<List<TaskItem>>
```

Here's a breakdown of the above DAO implementation:

1. When inserting a single task, you're specifying a return type of `Single<Long>`, where the `Long` represents the number of updated rows, which we'd expect to always be one.

2. When inserting multiple tasks, you're setting the return type to be `Completable`. This method is used to add default tasks to the database, so you're less concerned with the number of updated rows.

3. When fetching an individual `TaskItem` from the database, you're setting the return type to be `Maybe<TaskItem>`. Since there's no guarantee that a task exists for any given `id`, a `Maybe` makes the most sense here. See Chapter 21, "RxJava & Jetpack," to learn how `Maybe`s work with Room.

4. Finally, the return type for `taskStream()` is naturally `Observable<List<TaskItem>>`. Every time a new `TaskItem` is inserted or updated `taskStream()` should emit a new `List<TaskItem>` representing all of the task items in the database.

Next, you'll seed the database with some sample todo items. Open **TaskRoomDatabase.kt** and replace the existing TODO with the following:

```
val taskDatabase = database ?: return
taskDatabase.taskDao().insertTasks(
  listOf(
    TaskItem(null, "Chapter 1: Hello, RxJava!", Date(), false),
    TaskItem(null, "Chapter 2: Observables", Date(), false),
    TaskItem(null, "Chapter 3: Subjects", Date(), false),
    TaskItem(null,
      "Chapter 4: Observables and Subjects in practice", Date(),
      false),
    TaskItem(null, "Chapter 5: Filtering operators", Date(),
    false)
  )
)
.toV3Completable()
.subscribeOn(Schedulers.io())
.subscribe()
```

The above uses the `taskDao` interface on an existing Room database to insert five sample todo `TaskItems`.

Since these todos haven't been added to the database yet, you're passing `null` in for the ID field. Passing in `null` works for now, but when the rest of your app is creating `TaskItems` and inserting them into the database you'll want a more elegant form of ID to pass around.

Since the **Room** library is still using Rxjava2, you're using the `toV3Completable` extension method to transition from a v2 RxJava `Completable` to a v3 version. You'll use v3 for the rest of the app, so keep that in mind when adding your imports.

You should now be able to build and run the application. You'll be greeted with a truly unique and novel screen:

Beautiful! A true work of art. The brush strokes in particular are truly riveting.

As gorgeous as it is, it doesn't do a whole lot right now. It's time to build a repository to actually store your data.

Task repository

The task repository is responsible for creating, updating and fetching task items from the store. Since you're a responsible developer, you'll create a `TaskRepository` interface to hide the specifics of how tasks are accessed.

For this app, you'll only add a single `RoomTaskRepository`. By hiding the specifics behind an interface you could add a `NetworkTaskRepository` in the future if the app starts communicating with an API.

First, create the interface. This is what you'll expose to the users of the repository. Open **TaskRepository.kt** and add the interface definition:

```
interface TaskRepository {
  fun insertTask(taskItem: TaskItem): Single<Long>
  fun getTask(id: Int): Maybe<TaskItem>
  fun taskStream(): Observable<List<TaskItem>>
}
```

Make sure you're importing the RxJava3 versions of `Observable`, `Maybe`, and `Single`. This is a basic interface providing the fundamental services to create, update and read query tasks. Nothing fancy here. The most important detail is that the repository exposes all data operations as reactive elements. Even the functions which create, delete and update tasks return a `Single` or a `Maybe`.

Now open **RoomTaskRepository.kt** and see that the `RoomTaskRepository` class implements the `TaskRepository` interface.

For now `RoomTaskRepository` is going to delegate most of its methods to the `TaskDatabase` object passed into it. Add the following to the `RoomTaskRepository` to make it properly implement `TaskRepository`:

```
// 1
companion object {
  const val INVALID_ID = -1
}

override fun insertTask(taskItem: TaskItem): Single<Long> {
  TODO()
}
// 2
override fun getTask(id: Int): Maybe<TaskItem> {
  return database.taskDao().fetchTask(id).toV3Maybe()
}

override fun taskStream(): Observable<List<TaskItem>> {
  // 3
  return database.taskDao().taskStream().toV3Observable()
}
```

There are three things to note about this implementation:

1. You've introduced a new INVALID_ID constant to avoid having other classes pass in null for the TaskItems ID. You want to avoid null values as much as possible, since they're laborious to work around and error-prone.

2. You're delegating getTask() and taskStream() to the TaskDatabase object passed into RoomTaskRepository

3. You're again using the toV3X() methods to transition from RxJava2 to RxJava3 types. One of the benefits of having this repository layer is that you can hide the fact that **Room** uses an old version of RxJava from the rest of your application.

All that's left is to fill out insertTask().

insertTask() is a bit unique because it will have two distinct use cases:

1. A user could use it to create a new TaskItem in the database.

2. A user could use it to update an existing TaskItem.

Add the following to replace the body of insertTask():

```
val validIdTask =
  if (taskItem.id == RoomTaskRepository.INVALID_ID) {
    taskItem.copy(id = null)
  } else {
    taskItem
  }
return database.taskDao().insertTask(validIdTask).toV3Single()
```

The above code checks to see if the task items id is equal to the INVALID_ID constant you defined earlier. If it is, it creates a new copy of the task item with a null id. Otherwise, it uses the passed through ID.

If you didn't do this check then whenever a user attempted to insert a new task item into the database you would instead overwrite whatever task was added with an id of INVALID_ID.

Todo list view

Your repository is up and running now, this means you can start working through listing all of the todos. The list of todos is going to be segmented into two sections. First, you'll have the todos that still need to be done. Below that, you'll have the todos that are already finished. There will be a header list item before the unfinished todos and another header list item before the finished todos to visually separate out the lists.

If you've worked with `RecyclerView` enough, you'll know that creating lists that have different types of data can be challenging. You're often forced to have two separate lists of items and to do frustrating math to figure out which item you should be displaying at a given time. To avoid this headache, it's often advantageous to make a new data type specifically to work with your adapter.

Open **TodoListItem.kt**. Replace the existing `TodoListItem` class with the following:

```
sealed class TodoListItem(val viewType: Int) {
  object DueTasks : TodoListItem(0)
  object DoneTasks : TodoListItem(1)
  data class TaskListItem(val task: TaskItem) : TodoListItem(2)
}
```

`TodoListItem` takes in a `viewType` which you'll use in a moment in an adapter.

You've created three different types of `TodoListItems`:

1. A `DueTasks` object which represents the first header grouping together the tasks that are yet to be done.
2. A `DoneTasks` object which represents the second header grouping together the tasks that have been finished.
3. And a `TaskListItem` data class that represents one of the tasks in either the done or due sections of the list.

By creating a common data type abstraction on top of all the different visual treatments, you'll want, in the list you're allowing, the adapter to still only operate on one list of items. Instead of operating on a `List<TaskItem>` it'll instead work on a `List<TodoListItem>`.

Using a ListAdapter

Open **TodoAdapter.kt** and look at the class header:

```
class TodoAdapter : ListAdapter<TodoListItem,
  RecyclerView.ViewHolder>(TodoDiffUtil())
```

There are two interesting pieces, here:

1. `TodoAdapter` extends `ListAdapter` rather than `RecyclerView.Adapter`. `ListAdapter` is an extremely handy class in the `RecyclerView` library that will compute a diff between the current list and a new list you provide. It will then dispatch `Adapter.notifyItem` calls depending on the differences between the two lists. Using this smart diffing tool allows you to focus on submitting new lists rather than considering which specific items have changed.

2. You're supplying a `TodoDiffUtil` object to the `ListAdapter` superclass. `ListAdapter` isn't magical. It still needs a way to tell that two list items aren't the same item. It uses the `DiffUtil.ItemCallback` class to differentiate between the two lists.

You'll need to update the `TodoDiffUtil` class to properly dispatch updates to the adapter.

Open **TodoDiffUtil.kt**. There are two methods that you'll need to implement to get proper diffing:

1. `areItemsTheSame()`, which checks to see if two items represent the same item.

2. `areContentsTheSame()`, which checks to see if two items have the same contents.

The distinction may seem strange, but it makes sense after some thought. You can have an item in two lists that represent the same item but have different contents. One could have been before a user marked the task as done and one could have been after. The items still represent the same item but their contents are different, because the user took some action on the item.

Add the following to replace the body of `areItemsTheSame()`:

```
return when (oldItem) {
  // 1
  TodoListItem.DueTasks -> newItem is TodoListItem.DueTasks
  TodoListItem.DoneTasks -> newItem is TodoListItem.DoneTasks
  // 2
  is TodoListItem.TaskListItem -> {
    if (newItem !is TodoListItem.TaskListItem) return false
    oldItem.task.id == newItem.task.id
  }
}
```

Here's a breakdown of the above:

1. Two `DueTasks` items are always equal since they're represented as `objects`. The same is true for two `DoneTasks` objects.

2. Two `TaskListItems` are the same if they have the same id. Even if they have different contents they represent the same item.

The `areContentsTheSame` method is much simpler. Add the following to replace the body of `areContentsTheSame()`:

```
return oldItem == newItem
```

Two items have the same contents if they're equal to each other. Data classes keeps this short.

Navigate back to `TodoAdapter`. Now that the `TodoDiffUtil` has been fleshed out you can finish the rest of the adapter.

First, replace the body of `getItemViewType()` with the following:

```
return getItem(position).viewType
```

`ListAdapter` exposes `getItem()` to fetch an item from its list of items. When using `ListAdapter` you don't manage the list of items yourself, which is why `getItem()` is necessary.

Since `TodoListItem` has a `viewType` field, getting the `viewType` for a given position is trivial.

Now, add the following to the body of `onBindViewHolder()`:

```
val item = getItem(position)
val resources = holder.itemView.context.resources
when (item) {
  TodoListItem.DueTasks -> {
    holder.itemView.section_title.text =
        resources.getString(R.string.due_tasks)
  }
  TodoListItem.DoneTasks -> {
    holder.itemView.section_title.text =
        resources.getString(R.string.done_tasks)
  }
  is TodoListItem.TaskListItem -> {
    holder.itemView.task_title.text = item.task.text
    holder.itemView.task_done.isChecked = item.task.isDone
  }
}
```

The above code uses the Kotlin Android Extensions to reference views on the `TodoSectionViewHolder` and sets them according to what type of item `getItem()` returned.

Note again that by using a `sealed class` to represent the items in the list applying different visual treatments to different items is trivial. No messy logic indexing into multiple lists!

Reactive programming is made much easier by having components and widgets that are receptive to having their state reset at any time. If `ListAdapter` didn't exist then you would instead be forced to carry around **state** in your **ViewModel** to differentiate between the two lists. It would also require an expanded API contract between your **View** and **ViewModel**, since the **ViewModel** would need to convey a lot more information about which list items should be created, updated, moved, or deleted.

Setting up the list view model

You've got your repository ready to go. You've got an adapter up and running. It's time to build out the list view model to start seeing some todos.

Open **TodoListActivity.kt**. At the bottom of `onCreate()` you'll notice the following block of code:

```
val viewModel = buildViewModel {
  TodoListViewModel()
}
```

`buildViewModel()` is a convenience function to abstract away the boilerplate of instantiating a `ViewModel`.

`TodoListViewModel` will be in charge of querying for todos so it will require a few dependencies. Replace the body of the lambda provided to `buildViewModel()` with the following, knowing that you'll have a compiler error until you get to work on `TodoListViewModel`:

```
val repository =
    RoomTaskRepository(TaskRoomDatabase.fetchDatabase(this))
TodoListViewModel(repository, Schedulers.io())
```

`TodoListViewModel` will take in two dependencies: a `TaskRepository` and a background scheduler. You're passing in the background scheduler so that you can control what scheduler your Rx operators run on, which will make unit testing the view model much easier.

Open **TodoListViewModel.kt** and update the class header to accept the new dependencies:

```
class TodoListViewModel(
  repository: TaskRepository,
  backgroundScheduler: Scheduler
) : ViewModel()
```

As mentioned earlier, you'll expose `LiveData` objects for the activity to consume. Add the following instance variable to `TodoListViewModel`:

```
val listItemsLiveData = MutableLiveData<List<TodoListItem>>()
```

Now that everything's in place, you can finally query your `TaskRepository` for some `TaskItems`!

Create an `init` block in `TodoListViewModel` and add the following to it:

```
repository
  // 1
  .taskStream()
  // 2
  .map { tasks -> tasks.map { TodoListItem.TaskListItem(it) } }
  // 3
  .map { listItems ->
    val finishedTasks = listItems.filter { it.task.isDone }
    val todoTasks = listItems - finishedTasks
    listOf(
      TodoListItem.DueTasks,
      *todoTasks.toTypedArray(),
      TodoListItem.DoneTasks,
      *finishedTasks.toTypedArray()
    )
  }
  // 4
  .subscribeOn(backgroundScheduler)
  .subscribe(listItemsLiveData::postValue)
  .addTo(disposables)
```

That's a beefy chunk of code, so here's a breakdown:

1. You're calling `taskStream()` on `TaskRepository`. `taskStream()` should return an `Observable<List<TaskItem>>` that emits a new `List<TaskItem>` every time the database is updated.

2. You're then using `map()` to transform that `List<TaskItem>` into a `List<TodoListItem>`. Don't be confused by the `map()` within a `map()` here - the second `map()` is being called on the `List<TaskItem>` and is a method exposed on `List`s by the Kotlin standard library.

3. You're then taking the `List<TodoListItem>` returned by the previous `map()` and adding in the two section header list items. Before you do that you need to separate out the tasks that have been finished and the tasks that haven't. To that end you're using `filter()`, again in the Kotlin standard library.

4. Finally, you're subscribing on a background scheduler and forwarding the results onto the `listItemsLiveData` object. You're using a method reference to avoid some boilerplate.

The last step before you can run the app and see some progress is to observe the `listItemsLiveData` in the `TodoListActivity`. Add the following below the `viewModel` declaration in **TodoListActivity.kt**:

```
viewModel.listItemsLiveData
  .observe(this, Observer(adapter::submitList))
```

> **Note**: Make sure to import `androidx.lifecycle.Observer` and not its Rx equivalent when adding this line!

Again, you're using a method reference to avoid some boilerplate. You're using `submitList()` to update the list of items in your adapter. `submitList()` is a method exposed by `ListAdapter` that takes care of doing all of the diffing logic between the old list and the new one.

Run the app. You should see a screen that looks like this:

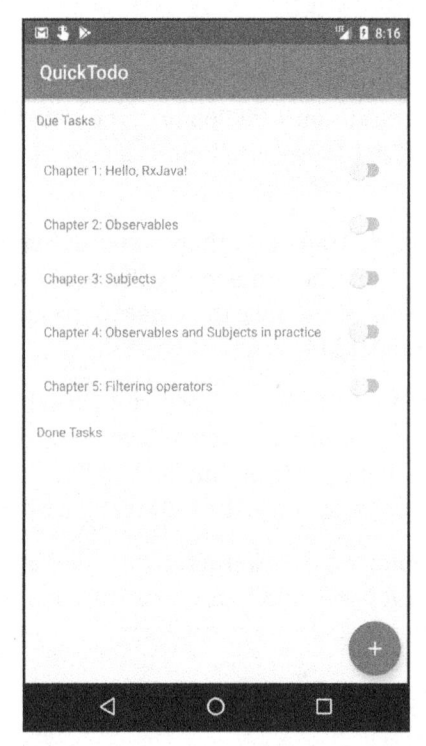

However, toggling the individual tasks does nothing. You'll change that next.

Replacing callbacks with observables

Since the individual list items each have a switch on them, you'll need to communicate with the `TodoAdapter` whenever the user toggles a switch. Typically, you'd do that using a callback. However, you can always rework a callback into an Observable to preserve the reactive chain.

Open **TodoAdapter.kt** and add the following instance variables to the top of the class:

```
private val taskClickSubject = PublishSubject.create<TaskItem>()
private val taskToggledSubject =
  PublishSubject.create<Pair<TaskItem, Boolean>>()
val taskClickStream = taskClickSubject.hide()
val taskToggledStream = taskToggledSubject.hide()
```

The user is going to be able to take two separate actions on a list item:

1. They can toggle an individual task to mark it as completed.

2. They can click a task and edit some of the details.

To capture those two different actions, you've created two private `PublishSubjects` which you'll use shortly. You're also exposing corresponding Observables. It's important to hide the details of your subjects from outside consumers so they don't have the opportunity to push unexpected objects into your stream.

Scroll down to the bottom of `onBindViewHolder()` and add the following in the `TodoListItem.TaskListItem` block of the when statement:

```
holder.itemView.task_done.setOnClickListener {
  taskToggledSubject.onNext(
      item.task to holder.itemView.task_done.isChecked)
}
holder.itemView.setOnClickListener {
  taskClickSubject.onNext(item.task)
}
```

Whenever someone clicks the `task_done` Switch you're calling `onNext()` on the `taskToggleSubject` with a pair of objects. The first object is the `TaskItem` the user took an action on. The second object is a `Boolean` indicating that the task has been marked as finished or not.

Additionally, whenever a user clicks on anything in the adapter row you're calling `onNext()` on the `taskClickSubject`, passing through the `TaskItem` that was selected.

Utilizing Subjects and Observables is a common approach to reworking a callback based API into a reactive one. Don't be afraid to use this strategy liberally.

Updating the TodoListViewModel

Now you need to notify your view model when the above Observables fire. Ideally you'd be able to pass the newly created Observables into your `TodoListViewModel`. Unfortunately, if you were to do that, when the user rotated the screen your view model would stop receiving callbacks, since the adapter would create new `PublishSubjects` which your view model would not know about.

Instead, you're going to subscribe to the Observables in your `TodoListActivity` and forward the information through to the `TodoListViewModel`, just like you did in previous chapters.

Start off by adding two new `PublishSubject` values to `TodoListViewModel`:

```
private val taskClicks = PublishSubject.create<TaskItem>()
private val taskDoneToggles =
  PublishSubject.create<Pair<TaskItem, Boolean>>()
```

`taskClicks` represents a user clicking on a task in the list, while `taskDoneToggles` represents toggling a task on and off.

Next up add two methods to forward events into your two new `PublishSubjects`:

```
fun taskClicked(taskItem: TaskItem) =
  taskClicks.onNext(taskItem)

fun taskDoneToggled(taskItem: TaskItem, on: Boolean) =
  taskDoneToggles.onNext(Pair(taskItem, on))
```

These use `onNext()` to notify each `PublishSubject` of the event.

Next, add a `CompositeDisposable` to the top of `TodoListActivity`:

```
private val disposables = CompositeDisposable()
```

This will allow you to responsibly dispose of your observable chains.

Last but not least, add the following below the call building the view model:

```
adapter.taskClickStream.subscribe {
  viewModel.taskClicked(it)
}.addTo(disposables)

adapter.taskToggledStream.subscribe {
  viewModel.taskDoneToggled(it.first, it.second)
}.addTo(disposables)
```

You're subscribing to both the `taskClickStream` and `taskToggledStream` Observables you defined in your adapter and forwarding the result into the `TodoListViewModel`.

When the user toggles a task as done, you want to call into the `TaskRepository` to update the state of the task item that was toggled. That will then trigger the `taskStream` that you subscribed to at the top of the `init` block, which will keep your UI up to date.

Add the following to the bottom of the `TodoListViewModel`'s' `init` block:

```
// 1
taskDoneToggles
  // 2
  .flatMapSingle { newItemPair ->
    // 3
    repository
      .insertTask(
          newItemPair.first.copy(isDone = newItemPair.second))
      .subscribeOn(backgroundScheduler)
  }
  .subscribe()
  .addTo(disposables)
```

Here's a section by section break down of the above:

1. You're using the `taskDoneToggles` Observable you added into the view model earlier to listen for a user tapping the switch one any of the task items.

2. You're then using `flatMapSingle()` to transform this stream from an `Observable<Pair<TaskItem, Boolean>>` into a `Single<Long>`. You need to use `flatMapSingle()` because `flatMap()` expects the lambda you pass it to produce an `Observable`, but `TaskRepository.insertTask()` produces a `Single`.

3. You're using the aforementioned `insertTask()` to save the updated version of the `TaskItem` the user toggled. The emitted `Pair` contains both the `TaskItem` to update and whether that item has been marked as completed or not, which you're using to create a new `TaskItem` to save off in the database.

Run the app and toggle a few tasks back and forth. You should see them move fluently between the done and due sections.

Editing tasks

When a user clicks on one of the task items the app should take them to another screen where they can edit the details of that task.

Open **TodoListViewModel.kt** and add another `LiveData` object:

```
val showEditTaskLiveData = MutableLiveData<Int>()
```

The activity will observe `showEditTaskLiveData` to be informed when it should open an activity to edit a task. The `Int` passed into the activity will represent the id of the task item to be edited.

> **Note**: You could make your `TaskItem` implement `Parcelable` and then pass it as an extra in an `Intent`. However, it's generally considered best practice to pass around the smallest piece of data you can between activities so you don't end up exceeding the maximum amount of information an `Intent` can carry. In this scenario, you can easily fetch a `TaskItem` from its id.

Add the following to the bottom of the `init` block:

```
// 1
taskClicks
  // 2
  .throttleFirst(1, TimeUnit.SECONDS)
  // 3
  .subscribe {
    val id = it.id ?: RoomTaskRepository.INVALID_ID
    showEditTaskLiveData.postValue(id)
  }
  .addTo(disposables)
```

From top to bottom, the above code:

1. Subscribes to the `taskClicks` Observable you passed in earlier. Remember that `taskClicks` emits every time a user taps one of the rows in the list of tasks.

2. Uses `throttleFirst()` to ensure that only one tap goes through. `throttleFirst()` is a new operator that works similarly to `debounce()`. Instead of delaying the mission of the Observable until the time unit has passed, `throttleFirst()` immediately emits an item and then skips any new items that come within the designated time period. By using `throttleFirst`, you can ensure that multiple activities aren't started by quickly tapping the task.

3. Fetches the `id` from the task, defaulting to the `INVALID_ID` if the `id` on the task item is null. Finally, you're posting the `id` to `showEditTaskLiveData`, indicating that the activity should launch the edit task activity.

The above flow looks beautiful, but if you were to add unit tests for it you'd run into an ugly surprise: you have to wait a full second every time you want to emulate a task being clicked!

To control that timing information, it's best practice to pass in a dedicated `Scheduler` to use for timing tasks, that way you can advance time manually using a `TestScheduler` in your unit tests.

Update the `TodoListViewModel` class header to accept another `Scheduler` as a parameter:

```
class TodoListViewModel(
  repository: TaskRepository,
  backgroundScheduler: Scheduler,
  computationScheduler: Scheduler
) : ViewModel()
```

And update `TodoListActivity` to pass a `Scheduler` in:

```
TodoListViewModel(
  repository,
  Schedulers.io(),
  Schedulers.computation()
)
```

Back in `TodoListViewModel`, update the call to `throttleFirst()`:

```
throttleFirst(1, TimeUnit.SECONDS, computationScheduler)
```

Now you can easily control time in your unit tests. Far out, man.

Head back to **TodoListActivity.kt** and add code to observe the `showEditTaskLiveData` at the bottom of `onCreate()`:

```
viewModel.showEditTaskLiveData.observe(this, Observer {
  EditTaskActivity.launch(this, it)
})
```

Now, run the app and tap one of the tasks. You should be presented with a blank edit screen that looks like this:

Saving an edited task

On this edit page you'll want to achieve several tasks:

1. You want to pre-populate the `EditText` at the top of the screen with the title of the `TaskItem` being edited. If there is no `TaskItem` being edited, then you'll leave it blank.

2. You then want to listen for taps on the done FAB in the bottom right, and save an updated `TaskItem` that contains the new title.

3. Finally, you want to finish this new activity and return to the task list after the user taps the done button.

Open **EditTaskActivity.kt** and replace the existing `EditTaskViewModel` being build in `onCreate()` with the following. Again, it won't compile until you edit the view model too:

```
val repository =
  RoomTaskRepository(TaskRoomDatabase.fetchDatabase(this))
val taskIdKey =
  intent.getIntExtra(TASK_ID_KEY, RoomTaskRepository.INVALID_ID)
EditTaskViewModel(
  // 1
  repository,
  // 2
  Schedulers.io(),
  // 3
  taskIdKey
)
```

You're supplying three dependencies to the **ViewModel** for the `EditTask` **View**:

1. A `TaskRepository` instance, which you'll use to fetch and save `TaskItems`.

2. A background `Scheduler`.

3. The id of the `TaskItem` you're editing, which was fetched out of the `Intent`.

Open **EditTaskViewModel.kt** and change the class header to accept the new dependencies:

```
class EditTaskViewModel(
  taskRepository: TaskRepository,
  backgroundScheduler: Scheduler,
  taskId: Int
) : ViewModel()
```

There's two different pieces of user input you'll need to react to:

1. A user clicking the done floating action button.
2. A user inputting the name of a task.

Just like before, you'll need to expose methods and subjects in your view model to handle those actions. Add the following to the top of `EditTaskViewModel`:

```kotlin
private val finishedClicks = PublishSubject.create<Unit>()
private val taskTitleTextChanges =
  BehaviorSubject.create<CharSequence>()
```

Then, add two new methods to pipe values into the two subjects:

```kotlin
fun onFinishClicked() = finishedClicks.onNext(Unit)

fun onTextChanged(text: CharSequence) =
  taskTitleTextChanges.onNext(text)
```

Your view model is now ready to accept user input.

Next up, navigate to `EditTaskActivity` and add the following to the top of the class:

```kotlin
private val disposables = CompositeDisposable()
```

Last but not least, add the following below the `viewModel` declaration:

```kotlin
done.clicks()
  .subscribe { viewModel.onFinishClicked() }
  .addTo(disposables)
title_input.textChanges()
  .subscribe { viewModel.onTextChanged(it) }
  .addTo(disposables)
```

You're using the **RxBindings** `clicks()` and `textChanges()` methods to listen for user input events and forwarding them to your view model. You're now all setup to start reacting to user input.

There are two dynamic pieces to the edit task UI:

1. Displaying the title of the `TaskItem` being edited in the `EditText` at the top of the page.
2. Finishing the activity after the user taps on the done FAB.

Therefore you'll need two `LiveData` objects exposed in the `EditTaskViewModel`. Add the following instance variables in `EditTaskViewModel` below the `disposables` variable:

```
val finishLiveData = MutableLiveData<Unit>()
val textLiveData = MutableLiveData<String>()
```

You can think of `LiveData` objects as having a one-to-one relationship with any dynamic pieces of your UI. Any static component, like a `TextView` with text that doesn't change, doesn't need a corresponding `LiveData`.

Interacting with the TaskRepository

The first thing you'll need to do in the `EditTaskViewModel` is retrieve whatever `TaskItem` is being edited, if there is one.]

Add an `init` block to `EditTaskViewModel` below the variable declarations:

```
init {
    val existingTask = taskRepository.getTask(taskId).cache()
}
```

You're using `getTask()` on `taskRepository` along with the `taskId` passed into the view model to get a `Maybe<TaskItem>` representing whatever `TaskItem` is being edited. If there is no `TaskItem` that corresponds to the passed in id, the `Maybe` will emit nothing and complete.

You're also using `cache()` so you can utilize `existingTask` in multiple places without remaking the call every time, since that could be expensive.

Now add the following Rx block after `existingTasks` declaration:

```
existingTask
    .subscribeOn(backgroundScheduler)
    .subscribe { textLiveData.postValue(it.text) }
    .addTo(disposables)
```

You're subscribing to the `existingTask` Maybe you fetched earlier on the `backgroundScheduler` and then posting the resulting `TaskItems` text in the `textLiveData`.

Open **EditTaskActivity.kt** again, and subscribe to the `textLiveData` in the bottom of `onCreate()` (again making sure to import `androidx.lifecycle.Observer` and not its Rx equivalent):

```
viewModel.textLiveData
    .observe(this, Observer(title_input::append))
```

Run the app again and tap on a task. You should see the title of that task pre-populated in the `EditText`:

Saving an updated task

The next feature for the Edit Task screen is to save the updated task when the user taps the done button.

You have access to two crucial Observables in the EditTaskViewModel that will help you implement this feature: If you combine the finishedClicks Observable with the taskTitleTextChanges Observable, you'll have the latest text whenever the done button is tapped.

Open **EditTaskViewModel.kt** and start off another Rx chain at the bottom of the init block:

```
Observables.combineLatest(finishedClicks, taskTitleTextChanges)
  .map { it.second }
```

combineLatest() will combine whatever the latest element is in the finishedClicks and taskTitleTextChanges Observables into a Pair<Unit, CharSequence>. The Unit portion of that Pair is the data type passed in from the finishedClicks Observable. All you care about is that that Observable triggers the combined Observable, so you can use map() to transform the resulting Observable from a Observable<Pair<Unit, CharSequence>> into an Observable<CharSequence>.

Now append the following to the bottom of the Rx chain:

```
// 1
.flatMapSingle { title ->
  existingTask
    // 2
    .defaultIfEmpty(
        TaskItem(null, title.toString(), Date(), false))
    // 3
    .flatMap {
      val taskItem =
          TaskItem(it.id, title.toString(), Date(), it.isDone)
      taskRepository.insertTask(taskItem)
    }
    // 4
    .subscribeOn(backgroundScheduler)
}
```

Here's a breakdown of that short but dense block of code:

1. You're using `flatMapSingle()` to convert this `Observable` into a `Single`. You'll find that whenever you're executing a network or database call that returns a `Single` after some user interaction, you'll want to use `flatMapSingle()`. Converting from an `Observable` to a `Single` can make the intent of your Rx chain clear to other developers.

2. `flatMapSingle()` expects the lambda passed into it to return (shocker!) a `Single`. However, the `existingTask` variable you declared earlier is a `Maybe`. If there's no `TaskItem` associated with the `taskId` passed into this view model, you want to save a new `TaskItem` instead of modifying an existing one. Enter `defaultIfEmpty()`. `defaultIfEmpty()` takes a `Maybe` and converts it into a `Single` by supplying a default item that the `Maybe` will use if it's empty.

   That way you can always guarantee that your `Maybe` will return an item, and it now satisfies the requirements of being a `Single`.

3. You're then using the `flatMap()` operator to take the `TaskItem` and save it in the database using `insertTask()`, which returns a `Single<Long>`.

4. You're doing all of the above work on the `backgroundScheduler` because you're a good Android citizen, and you don't want to freeze the UI!

That was a powerful batch of code. Congratulations for working your way through it! Finish off the new Rx chain by subscribing to it and making sure it's properly disposed of. Make sure this goes outside of the `flatMapSingle()`:

```
.subscribe { finishLiveData.postValue(Unit) }
.addTo(disposables)
```

Once you're done saving off the `TaskItem` you can signal to the activity to call `finish` via the `finishLiveData` variable.

To finish off your editing feature, open **EditTaskActivity.kt** and add code to observe the `finishLiveData` at the bottom of `onCreate()`:

```
viewModel.finishLiveData.observe(this, Observer { finish() })
```

Now run the app and tap one of the tasks. Edit the title for the task, then tap the done FAB. You'll see that the updated task appears in the list, and it moves to the bottom of whatever section that task is in since you updated the date for that task.

Creating a new task

There's only one thing missing from your app: The user has no way to create a new task. Luckily, you can lean on the work you finished in the edit section to complete this.

First, open **TodoListViewModel.kt** and add one last PublishSubject at the top of the class:

```
private val addClicks = PublishSubject.create<Unit>()
```

Next up, add a corresponding method to push events through your new subject:

```
fun addClicked() = addClicks.onNext(Unit)
```

Then add another Rx chain to the bottom of the init block:

```
addClicks
  .throttleFirst(1, TimeUnit.SECONDS, computationScheduler)
  .subscribe {
    showEditTaskLiveData
      .postValue(RoomTaskRepository.INVALID_ID)
  }
  .addTo(disposables)
```

The addClicks stream represents taps on the add FAB. You're using throttleFirst() again to make sure only the first tap is acted upon. When the user does tap, you're reusing the showEditTaskLiveData, but this time purposefully passing an INVALID_ID so a new TaskItem is created and saved into the database.

Last but not least, open **TodoListActivity.kt** and pipe add click events through to your view model by adding this to onCreate():

```
add_button.clicks()
  .subscribe { viewModel.addClicked() }
  .addTo(disposables)
```

Now the run the app and add a new task item. You should see the new task inserted at the end of the due tasks list!

Challenges

Challenge 1: Support item deletion

You've probably noticed that it isn't possible to delete items. You'll need to make changes to both `TodoListActivity` and `TodoListViewModel` to add this functionality. Once you complete the challenge, the users will be able to swipe away a task to delete it.

The project includes a helper file named **SwipeToRemoveHelper.kt**, which facilitates the swipe to remove process. Start off by uncommenting the code in `onSwiped()` and `getMovementFlags()`. You'll also need to add a new method to the **TodoAdapter.kt** file to allow your `SwipeToRemoveHelper` class to access files:

```
fun getListItem(position: Int): TodoListItem {
  return getItem(position)
}
```

You can add the following code in `TodoListActivity`'s `onCreate()` to hook it up to your `RecyclerView`:

```
val swipeHelper = SwipeToRemoveHelper(adapter)
ItemTouchHelper(swipeHelper).attachToRecyclerView(todo_list)
```

Now you can get to the core of the challenge: handling the actual deletion. The solution to this challenge involves:

- Creating `deleteTask()` on the `TaskRepository`, `RoomTaskRepository` and `TaskDao` classes. For the `TaskDao` method, you can use the `@Delete` annotation to instruct Room that you're deleting an item.

- Using `swipeStream` variable exposed by `SwipeToRemoveHelper` with your `TodoListViewModel` to listen for remove events.

- Subscribing to the `swipeStream` and calling `repository.deleteTask()` with the swiped away task.

Challenge 2: Add live statistics

To make the UI more interesting, you want to display the number of **due** and **done** items in your list. A text view is reserved for this purpose at the bottom of the TodoListActivity view; it's called statistics. For this challenge, start from either your solution to the previous challenge, or from the chapter's final project.

First off, set the statistics view to be visible in onCreate of TodoListActivity:

```
statistics.visibility = View.VISIBLE
```

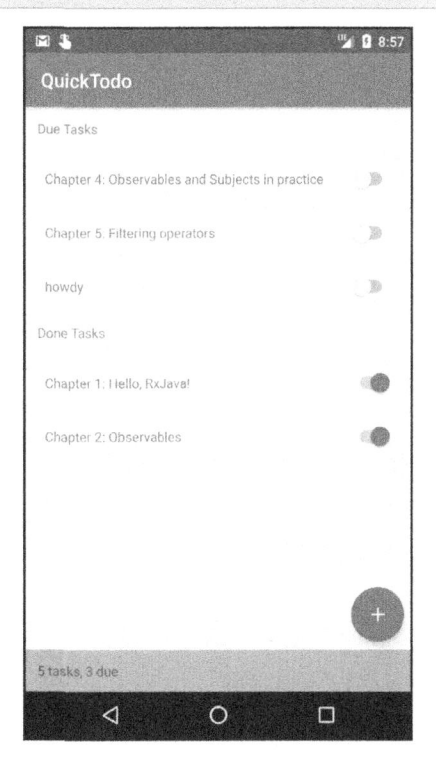

Next up you'll need to create a new LiveData object to carry the statistics information from the TodoListViewModel to the activity.

You'll then need to subscribe to that LiveData in the TodoListActivity and update the statistics text view.

To get the actual statistics, you'll want to work off of the taskStream exposed by the repository. You're already subscribing to the taskStream Observable, so consider using cache() to do multiple subscribes!

Where to go from here?

This concludes the final chapter of this book! We hope you loved it as much as we did. You now have a solid foundation of programming with RxJava, RxKotlin, and RxAndroid to build on as you continue your learning. Good luck!

Chapter 23: Conclusion

If you have any questions or comments as you work through this book, please stop by our forums at http://forums.raywenderlich.com and look for the particular forum category for this book.

Thank you again for purchasing this book. Your continued support is what makes the books, tutorials, videos and other things we do at raywenderlich.com possible. We truly appreciate it!

– The *Reactive Programming with Kotlin* team

Made in United States
Orlando, FL
18 June 2023